RELIGION, POLITICS, AND GLOBALIZATION

(1955–2008)

Frontispiece. Galina Lindquist, In Memoriam.

To the back of beyond, where the buses don't go.

Courtesy of Anton Gourman.

RELIGION, POLITICS, AND GLOBALIZATION

Anthropological Approaches

Edited by
Galina Lindquist and Don Handelman

Berghahn Books
NEW YORK • OXFORD

First published in 2011 by

Berghahn Books

www.berghahnbooks.com

©2011, 2013 Galina Lindquist and Don Handelman
First paperback edition published in 2013

Library of Congress Cataloging-in-Publication Data

A C.I.P. catalog for this book is available at the Library of Congress.

British Library Cataloguing in Publication Data

A catalogue record for this book is available from the British Library

Printed in the United States on acid-free paper.

ISBN: 978-0-85745-904-6 (paperback) ISBN: 978-0-85745-925-1 (retail ebook)

For

Anton Gourman and Max Lindquist

Galina's Beloved Sons

CONTENTS

III. The Tight Embrace of Religion and Politics

IV. Opening New Space for Religion

FIGURES

PREFACE

Don Handelman

In 1998 I was invited by Stockholm University to be the examiner—the *Opponent,* in Swedish—of Galina Lindquist's PhD thesis in social anthropology.[1] As was customary, the thesis defense took place in a large auditorium, Galina and I seated on the podium at separate tables angled toward one another in front of a large audience that included colleagues, family, and friends. Reading Galina's thesis in Jerusalem, reading her discussions of rituals, realities, and the play of living, I knew, intuitively but knowingly, that this work was written by a woman blessed with unusual sensibilities and capabilities for feeling (knowingly) the worlds of others through those others. This is what fascinated her, personally, humanistically, intellectually. This is what she sought through anthropology. Her text was suffused with intense curiosity about worlds seen and unseen, pervaded by a sense of quest that I felt could never be stopped, never satiated, never brought to a close. Indeed, closure was anathema to Galina's perception of persons and their doings; in her view we are in continuing emergence, remaking being, always becoming. As she was. Perhaps integral to this was her inborn playfulness, her impishness, the imp who quietly upset comfortable consensus, even one she had belonged to a moment before—not because she especially enjoyed doing so but because it was the natural thing to do, to perceive phenomena from multiple perspectives, to sense and comprehend in this way. Perusing Galina's thesis, I felt her potential to develop as researcher and scholar. Developing, she would unfold her wings and fly, fly in so many different directions. And fly she did.

As we relaxed into our joint performance on the podium in Stockholm, we discussed the problematics and fascinations of studying ritual, play, and each within and through the other, as well as quite a few other subjects. The under-

lying ethos in these thesis examinations in Sweden is that examiner and candidate engage one another in intelligent, penetrating discourse that is no less
intellectually entertaining to the audience. So it was on that occasion, the first
of many interchanges with one another, the beginning of a fruitful and mutually
illuminating collaboration, one especially precious to me.[2]

Writing this preface to a volume Galina planned yet was unable to complete
is deeply saddening. In that thesis examination I midwifed her official birth
into the vocation and profession of anthropology and now, at her request, I
am closing the book of her active life in anthropology—born in 1998, died
in 2008, aged fifty-two. A brief career of many sweet and bittersweet fruits,
of fieldwork that she loved, on neoshamanism, agency, and ritual innovation
in Sweden and elsewhere in Europe; on hope, healing, and magic in post-
Soviet Moscow (Lindquist 2006); and on shamanism and Lamaism in southern
Siberia, of which her chapter in this volume is one of numerous exemplars (a
subject on which Galina leaves behind an unfinished book). A lot of research
and writing in a career that spanned less than a decade of good health. Galina
always was short of time, always scrambling, always juggling—raising her two
beloved sons, Anton and Max; flying around Europe to earn money as a simultaneous translator; doing her research; teaching; giving conference papers.
When I would ask her how she could manage all this and more, she would look
sweetly, responding solemnly, "Russian women work hard." Indeed, during her
years in Sweden she never had any job security … until a short period before
her premature death.

A lover of language, of writing as craft and art, Galina wrote deftly, expres-
sively, always listening, always questioning, always learning, always growing in
soul, spirit, and knowledge, evolving into a fine scholar of the human condition
in its manifold aspects. And no less, sensuous, restless, endearingly eager to
enter into the next adventure, into the next journey into unknown space and
experience. And she did. The neoshamans with whom she apprenticed initiated her as one of their number during the traditional party for fellow scholars,
family, and friends thrown by the candidate on the evening of the successful thesis examination; in Tyva, powerful shamans recognized her shamanic
sensitivities—some taking umbrage at her qualities, others asking her to heal
them.

This volume's emergence has followed a halting, winding path. In the autumn of 2005, Galina organized a postgraduate course on Politics, Religion,
and Globalization at Stockholm University and was able to invite a number
of friends and colleagues to give lectures within this framework. The lectures
were substantial, and she decided they would form the basis of a book of valuable case-studies. In the summer of 2006, Galina went to Tyva to continue her
fieldwork. She felt unwell on and off, though the research went well. Returning
to Stockholm at summer's end, she was diagnosed with advanced ovarian can-

cer. Galina wrote a draft of the introduction to the book bit by bit in between surgery and harsh bouts of a lengthy chemotherapy regimen. The following summer Galina seemed in remission and traveled to a notable healer in Brazil, examined a PhD thesis at Cambridge, and returned to the book. Yet the respite was heartbreakingly brief, a meager few months, the cancer especially aggressive, and by autumn Galina was driven back to surgery, back to chemotherapy until late spring of the following year.

Galina had applied for a permanent position at Stockholm University before her illness. In late 2007 the department told her that the appointment was virtually assured since the evaluators of her candidacy (who came from other universities) had ranked her so highly. Indeed, these external evaluators wrote that Galina had published more than enough work of quality to be deserving of a professorship. Galina was so proud. When she received the appointment in 2008, Galina was dying. Her only comment to me then, said wistfully, quietly, was, "How ironic." Galina approached her impending death by emptying herself of angers and grudges, by clearing out envies, expelling jealousies. She engaged intensively with self-healing, with healing her self, telling me that heaviness had fled from within her as she filled with light, filled with brightness, even as she suffered the tortures of advancing metastasis. In the early morning of May 26, 2008, Galina passed on.

A month before her death, Galina asked me to shepherd the book through to publication. Marion Berghahn of Berghahn Books had given Galina a contract for the book and waited patiently for the manuscript. The readers of the manuscript for Berghahn Books, Bruce Kapferer and Martin Mills, gave useful comments. As this preface indicates, I made the book into a small yet heartfelt commemoration of Galina. Michael Jackson agreed to contribute a memoir of her. During his years in Copenhagen, Michael, through his experimenting with forms of joining subjectivity and objectivity in research and writing, became a beacon to Galina's finding her way as scholar and writer. They were good friends. As was Robert Innis, philosopher and semiotician, who encouraged Galina's interest in Peirce, in understanding dynamics between healer and client that became central to her *Conjuring Hope*. Robert agreed to contribute the afterword. Other of the contributors were Galina's close friends, collaborators, colleagues.[3] I told them that a few words of their own for Galina were welcome, and these are interspersed throughout the volume, at the close of individual chapters. For my own part, I decided to expand the introduction substantively and substantially, to offer a perspective on the relationship between religion and holism—one I feel Galina would have largely agreed with, and one which might be of general use to readers, including students. All of the above took time; but now the volume reaches fruition.

Spirited, gentle, determined, Galina was the most spontaneous person I have ever known, her expressions ever changing, ever transforming, living in the now, as she put it, living the contours and textures of her own life in relation to those of others. Galina walked in beauty. An ethnographer of valor, Galina always wanted to go to the back of beyond, where the buses don't go. I hope you're there now, Galina, where the buses don't go, somehow, somewhere, walking in beauty, continuing to be so. Bless you, Galina, for gracing us with your clarity of perception, with your wonderful sense of quest.

NOTES

1. The thesis is entitled "Shamanic Performances on the Urban Scene: Neo-Shamanism in Contemporary Sweden" (1997). My own appreciation of this work is given in Handelman 1999.
2. We coedited two volumes on play and ritual: Lindquist and Handelman 2001; Handelman and Lindquist 2005.
3. For example, see Lindquist and Coleman 2008.

REFERENCES

Handelman, Don. 1999. 'The Playful Seductions of Neo-Shamanic Ritual,' *History of Religions* 39: 65–72.

Handelman, Don, and Galina Lindquist, ed. 2005. *Ritual in its Own Right: Exploring the Dynamics of Transformation.* New York: Berghahn Books.

Lindquist, Galina. 1997. *Shamanic Performances on the Urban Scene: Neo-Shamanism in Contemporary Sweden.* Stockholm: Department of Social Anthropology, Stockholm University (Stockholm Studies in Social Anthropology, no. 39).

Lindquist, Galina. 2006. *Conjuring Hope: Healing and Magic in Contemporary Russia.* New York: Berghahn Books.

Lindquist, Galina, and Simon Coleman, ed. 2008. *Beyond Belief?* Special issue, *Social Analysis* 52, no. 1.

Lindquist, Galina, and Don Handelman, ed. 2001. *Playful Power and Ludic Spaces: Studies in Games of Life.* Special Issue, *Focaal: European Journal of Anthropology*, no. 39.

AFTER UNDERSTANDING

A Memoir of Galina Lindquist

Michael Jackson

In 1999, Galina Lindquist returned to Moscow after ten years away. She walked around the city as a revenant, finding it familiar yet utterly strange. This was not only because she had changed; Russia itself was no longer the country she had known during the years of perestroika. The late 1980s were a time of jubilant expectation; the despised Soviet *sistema* had collapsed, you could buy books in subway kiosks that only recently you could have been sent to the gulag for possessing, and you were ostensibly free. Ten years later, this mood of abundant possibility had gone, replaced by a sense of anarchic limitlessness (*bespredel*) that called to mind the savage ruthlessness of the jungle. "Faith in the new institutions of the market and banking were crushed; people lost the money they had been saving for decades, the numerous businesses that had sprung up in the preceding years went to the wall, and the tokens of plenty that started to appear on the store shelves after the emptiness of the early 1990s became unaffordable for most of the people" (Lindquist 2006: xiv). The prevailing mood of disillusionment and despair deepened as evidence emerged with every passing day of corruption at all levels of government, criminality in business, growing unemployment, and the atrophy of state welfare for the old, the sick, and the disabled. In this desperate situation, Galina became fascinated by the strategies people adopted to cope with the dire predicament in which they found themselves. She observed, both in her old friends and in herself, a longing for a lost time, a kind of aphasia in which one lacked a language to articulate this sense of a vanishing life, and with it the eclipse of one's own sense of self. At the same time, Galina noticed how this space of dissolution and absence was being filled with pornography, pulp fiction, escapist videos, and cheap magazines, as well as

New Age paraphernalia that offered magical, paranormal, and occult possibilities of healing and renewal. Working closely with an occult practitioner (magus) and one of her clients, Galina began to see that magic was a way in which people sought to regain a sense of control over their own lives in circumstances where normal socioeconomic avenues had been blocked.

In her first account of her fieldwork in Moscow (Lindquist 2000), Galina emphasizes the complementarity of markets and magic. When the market (or banking system) becomes a place of danger that one can longer trust, "business magic" becomes an alternative strategy for making money, obtaining a loan, succeeding in business or keeping a job. This switch from the material to the ethereal—from market to magic—is predicated upon a Western New Age cosmology that imagines the physical body to be surrounded by a "biofield" that holds information about a person's past, present, and future life and connects a human being to higher realms of astral power and divine influence (Lindquist 2000: 324). When one's physical or financial situation seems hopeless, channeling this mysterious biofield may bring a windfall or begin a flow of regenerative power.

Six years later, in her monograph *Conjuring Hope,* Galina's emphasis is less on business magic per se than the occult search for the "lost sense of tomorrow," and for increased hope (2006: 199). Objective transformations are less significant than subjective transformations, in which a person's confidence is bolstered, despair is assuaged, hope restored, and, rather than being stuck, a person is able to feel that he or she is getting somewhere. This emphasis on magical action as a transformation in the way the world *appears* to a person echoes Sartre's famous essay on the emotions (1976), and is evidence of Galina's attempt to reconcile her early attachment to Peirce's semiology with a growing interest in phenomenology. At the same time, she seems to be seeking a mode of analysis that can encompass both the macropolitics of the state and the micropolitics of individual lifeworlds at the margins of state power. This search for a rapprochement between models of secular and sacred power—politics and religion, market and magic—preoccupied Galina as well as me, and in the course of numerous conversations in Stockholm and Copenhagen between 2000 and 2005, Galina pressed me to explain how phenomenology could possibly speak to issues of political economy. Galina found some answers to this quandary in Bourdieu's later work, where he argues that forms of symbolic capital—wellbeing, hope, and recognition—though unequally distributed in any social system, never derive entirely from external sources but reflect inner resources that are difficult to pin down and cannot be explained sociologically. Galina's determination to do justice to the mysteries of subjectivity and intersubjectivity helps us understand why, in *Conjuring Hope,* she often suspends the question of diagnostic or analytical meaning in order to explore an "indexical mode of transformation" in which a person is changed, or healed, through direct sensory experience rather than objective knowledge, and through ritual rather than political action (2006: 80). In such instances, the charismatic power and caring presence of a healer may count for more than his or her medical qualifications, just as a client's faith in a healer's power counts for more than his or her understanding of how a séance or healing session actually works. What is at stake is not so much a cure—for we cannot be cured of being-in-the-world—but an uplifting of the spirit, a replenishment of the will, a resuscitation of hope. "For the people I talked to, hope was an existential doorway out of the deadliest of deadlocks, the light at the end of the longest of tunnels; a tool for expanding the horizons of the life-world, for intentionality to unfold, for will to return: the will to life, no matter what" (2006: 229).

A few months before *Conjuring Hope* was published in 2006, I attended a conference in Oxford on "The Anthropology and Psychology of Fieldwork Experience." Galina was also there, and we spent time together, over lunch and in breaks between sessions, catching up on news. But Galina was under a cloud, waiting for the results of medical tests and fearing the worst. Although she had little appetite for food, she talked passionately about her recent stint of fieldwork in Tyva, southern Siberia, where she had been working closely with Tyvan healers since 2001, studying the shifting balance of religious power between Tibetan Buddhism and traditional shamanism. In the course of her fieldwork in Moscow, Galina had become very close to her key informants. This involvement seemed to me even more intense with her Tyvan collaborators. Drawn deeply into their religious life, she had become unsettled, like many ethnographers before her, by the impossibility of drawing a line between participation and observation. But Galina's ability to dwell in the ambiguity of the ethnographic method reflected a personal disposition as well as an intellectual commitment to joining "objective analysis to lived experience." Indeed, she shared Merleau-Ponty's view that this process was "the most proper task of anthropology, the one which distinguishes it from other social sciences" (1964: 119). It was her refusal to assimilate instant experience to extant knowledge that made her skeptical of institutional religion, biomedicine, and academic fashions. Perhaps this was why, when she first fell ill, she relied on homeopathy and acupuncture, and traveled to Tyva in the summer of 2006 not only for further fieldwork but for healing.

Back in Sweden, she submitted to chemotherapy, and for a while it appeared to be working. Then the blow fell. "I am ill again," she wrote in November 2007. "It all came very quickly and in a month developed into an inoperable tumor. They are now giving me more chemotherapy, hoping it will shrink, but i can neither eat nor move, almost. I'm not sure what will happen to me; the optimistic prognosis is that i'll remain chronically ill, for whatever length of time, living on chemos. Whatever else it means, one thing is that i can no longer make any plans and can't have people depending on me. My teaching this and next semester was cancelled, a conference on 'institutional transformations of suffering' that i have been working on organizing for three years is now going on without me."

Galina had roped me into organizing a workshop at the European Association of Social Anthropologists' conference at Ljubliana, scheduled for the summer of 2008. It was a way of addressing some of the personal issues of fieldwork that we had discussed at length during our occasional meetings. One of our concerns was to broach the question of putting other people's epistemologies on a par with our own, of breaking the historical habit of privileging European worldviews. In our draft proposal we wrote:

> Despite the fact that ethnographers often spend many years in societies other than their own, acquiring conversancy in local languages, becoming familiar with very different ways of understanding the world, sometimes advocating politically on behalf of their host society and espousing respect and affection for individual collaborators, it is rare that an anthropologist adopts a non-western epistemology in his or her work or even places such an epistemology on the same footing as theories derived from his or her own intellectual traditions. Invidious distinctions between "scientific" and "folk" models or reason and faith continue to hold sway over our thinking, so that while we may venture to speak, say, of African 'philosophy' or 'religion,' these Eurocentric and logocentric rubrics determine which phenomenon we will include under or exclude from such headings and how we will approach the subject we define in these ways. Assumptions drawn from classical Greek thought, or Judeo-Christian teleology and soteriology, or from Euro-American preoccupations with politico-economic power and instrumental rationality continue to constitute the dominant paradigms whereby we decide meaning, assign cause, and explain human behavior. But if we are going to critique the power inequalities between West and East, North and South, we must also critique the discursive inequalities associated with these geopolitical divisions, and this means taking other worldviews seriously, and seeing our own epistemologies from the vantage point of the other. This does not mean, however, that we cease to be skeptical of the epistemological claims and pretensions of the views of the world that various people espouse. It simply means abandoning the notion that the veracity of any worldview lies in its correspondence to objective reality or its logical coherence, and exploring, instead, the real entailments of any worldview for human lives. A corollary of this pragmatist turn is that we see beliefs and worldviews not as scripts that actors faithfully follow or principles that guide their actions, but as ways that people give legitimacy to their actions or rationalize, after the event, the often unforeseen and unintended consequences of what they have done. *Moreover, in a reflexive vein, we want to explore our own familiar experience of physical and social reality from the standpoint of unfamiliar philosophies, to see what aspects of our social existence they might illuminate, and what alternative solutions to our existential quandaries and political dilemmas they might offer.*

In italicizing the last sentence, I remind myself how deeply Galina's experiences in Siberia, and her own consultations with shamans, influenced her attitude to her cancer, delaying her reliance on orthodox medical treatment. And in retaining her quirky use of the lowercase 'i' in her email, I remind myself of how her personal world shrank as her tumor grew, and how the hope she ascribes to her Swedish doctors was something she could not share.

Three months passed before I found the time and means to travel to Sweden, and as I waited at our agreed rendezvous in the concourse of Arlanda-Stockholm airport, I felt nervous and fearful, expecting to face a diminished and unrecognizable version of my friend. But Galina looked her old self, and confident enough to drive to a nearby lake where we strolled for an hour before finding a lakeside restaurant for lunch. It was like old times, though we now talked of mortality rather than anthropology. I remember Galina commenting on the unseasonal thaw, the unpredictability of our times, and her own experience of reaching a point where there is no future. "One lives from day to day, not knowing whether there will be two more weeks, two more months, two more years," she said. "But I no longer cling to life, and therefore I do not suffer. Suffering is resistance, not wanting to die, not wanting the pain. But I have let go, and in this yielding I have found peace."

Paradoxically, it is more often the living than the dying who cannot bear the thought of death. And I had to tread carefully, as I pressed Galina for details of her treatment, lest I appear unsympathetic to the course of action she had decided upon. There was an alternative therapy, Galina said, but as a result of the lack of communication between hospitals and laboratories, she had had to do all the hard work liaising with the lab and working with the doctors who could administer the experimental drugs. It was too much to ask of a patient, and she had reached the point where the effort was costing her what little energy she had. Besides, she was feeling better than she had in many months, miraculously so.

I confessed surprise at how well she looked. But Galina set no store by appearances. Nor did she hold out any hope of a medical breakthrough or divine intervention. "Unfortunately, none of my family or friends can accept this," she said. "Nobility lies in fighting the cancer, not giving in to it. My mother tells me not to be selfish. My friends urge me to seek treatment abroad. My ex-husband, who is devoutly Russian Orthodox, implores me to embrace the faith. But God is indifferent to me, and I will live without God, though still believing God exists, His ways beyond our understanding."

In Galina's "reckoning with life," I was reminded of Gillian Rose's memoir, written during her dying days[1]—the co-presence of a profound vulnerability and an extraordinary strength. "I am dying," Galina said. Her voice quavered for a second, and then she recovered. And I saw that she had attained a state of grace where death and life cancelled each other out, and the ego has been transcended.

I went to Uppsala for a few days, then returned to Stockholm to see Galina one last time. There were no good-byes, though we both knew we would not see each other again.

Having recently taken up a position at the Harvard Divinity School, I was pondering, for the first time in my life, whether something we might call "religious experience" could be identified in all cultures and all people (including skeptics like myself), and what meaning could be ascribed the term *religion* when the people with whom I had sojourned as an ethnographer in West Africa and Aboriginal Australia had no equivalent concept in their languages. Mindful of Talal Asad's argument that Euro-American notions of religion tend to be uncritically grounded in post-Enlightenment, Judeo-Christian thought, and that "religious experience" can never be reduced to institutionalized "religious belief" (1993: ch.1),[2] I decided to turn my attention to those critical situations in life where we come up against the limits of language, the limits of our strength, the limits of our knowledge, yet are sometimes thrown open to new ways of understanding our being-in-the-world, new ways of connecting with others (Jackson 2009). Whether such border situations[3] are quintessentially "religious," "secular," "spiritual," "historical," "social," or "biographical" may be beside the point, for though such terms help us describe the conditions of the possibility of our experience or help us retrospectively explain our experience to ourselves and to others, the meaning of all human experience remains ambiguous, containing within it both the seeds of its own comprehensibility *and* nuances and shadings that go beyond what can be comprehensively thought or said. At the same time, I was convinced that the conceptual and ritual ways that human beings address the macrocosm from their specific vantage points in space and time are remarkably similar. Whether our analysis is focused on the political sphere, the divine sphere, or the cosmos, human relations with the powers-that-be tend to be informed by the same anxieties and mediated by the same techniques of communication and control. This implies that attempts to demarcate politics and religion as separate spheres may ignore the existential and experiential questions that make them coterminous (Jackson 2007).

Galina would have been the perfect interlocutor for me, because her thinking had taken her beyond questions of belief to a pragmatist perspective that sought to explicate the repercussions of our actions, both outwardly in the social field in which we move physically, and in the intrapsychic field where we are moved emotionally. But while Galina continued to set great store by Charles Sanders Peirce's pragmatism, I found in William James a more accessible and homely approach to the same philosophical assumptions: that truth is a matter of what an idea or action accomplishes for us, and that the existential contexts to which our words and deeds refer are always beyond our complete comprehension and control. "Reality, life, experience, concreteness, immediacy, use what word you will, exceeds our logic, overflows and surrounds it,"

James declared in a lecture given in Oxford in the spring of 1908, adding that by *reality* he meant "where things happen" (1977: 96–97).

One can, I think, readily understand why James's notion of radical empiricism, with its emphasis on relations as well as relata—flights and perchings, rivers and embankments, verbs and substantives, conjunctions and disjunctions—proved so difficult to spell out and so irksome to many of his readers, for who in his right mind would identify reality with things that cannot be readily grasped or systematically named, with phenomena outside the reach of reason? Yet James insisted: "Our fields of experience have no more definite boundaries than have our fields of view. Both are fringed forever by a *more* that continuously develops, and that continuously supercedes them as life proceeds. The relations, generally speaking, are as real here as the terms are" (1976: 35).[4] Nor is it the world that lies about us that is refractory to comprehension and control; it is also the world within. "Whatever it may be on the *farther* side, the 'more' with which in religious experience we feel ourselves connected is on the *hither* side the subconscious continuation of our conscious life (1958: 386)."[5]

There is probably no human being who has not been intrigued and troubled by the mysterious relationship between his or her own immediate world—a world of direct experience—and all that lies beyond it. It is never simply a matter of acknowledging or naming this extramundane dimension of our existence; it is most vitally a question of our relationship with it—how we reckon with it, draw on it, and control it. Of this liminal[6] zone, John Dewey observed:

> The visible is set in the invisible; and in the end what is unseen decides what happens in the seen; the tangible rests precariously upon the untouched and ungrasped. The contrast and the potential maladjustment of the immediate, the conspicuous and focal phase of things, with those indirect and hidden factors which determine the origin and career of what is present, are indestructible features of any and every experience. (1958: 43–44)

Although we often assume that reason enables us to grasp the unseen intellectually, if not actually, Dewey declares that this invocation of scientific rationality is as much a "magical safeguard against the uncertain character of the world" as the so-called mumbo-jumbo and superstition we attribute to premodern peoples.

Dewey's remarks echo certain passages in William James's *The Varieties of Religious Experience*, where he too speaks of the ways in which our private and mundane lives are embedded in wider fields of being from which we draw inspiration and vitality. Though there are countless ways in which any one of us construes and interacts with this nonimmediate realm, James prefers to speak of it in fairly neutral terms as "a wider self," or "the more" or simply "life" rather than as *God* or the *Global*. As such, it bears a family resemblance to what Freud called the *over-I*, Jaspers called the *encompassing*, Heidegger called *Dasein*, and Durkheim conceptualized as the *social*. As a pragmatist, James is less concerned

with whether our language actually captures the essence of the elusive world
that lies about us, since what is most crucial are the *entailments* of what we say
and do for our own wellbeing and the wellbeing of others. "Does God really exist? How does he exist? What is He? are so many irrelevant questions," James
writes. "Not God, but life, more life, a larger, richer, more satisfying life is, in the
last analysis, the end of religion" (1958: 382).

Basic to all these reflections is the view that one's wellbeing depends on one's
relationships or connectedness to an "elsewhere" or "otherness" that lies beyond
the horizons of one's own immediate lifeworld. This "other" world is sometimes
identified with the dead, and ritual labor enables the living to fuse their being
with ancestral being in a life-giving union.[7] Sometimes, as in traditional Christianity, it is a realm of divine power and presence, associated with the empyrean.[8]
Sometimes it is identical to the natural environment of forest, bush, and stream.[9]
Sometimes it is conceptualized as the sociopolitical or globalized world.

Although, as Alfred Schutz observes, most philosophy and religion attempt
to reduce the extramundane "to a concept, to make it graspable and accessible
to accustomed experience, to tame it" (1989: 101), it remains at the limits of
what can be thought or said, encompassing our relationships with ancestors,
nature, God, foreigners, and even the unborn (194–95).

In Gillian Rose's last book, *Love's Work*, I glimpse a vision that Galina might
well have developed had she lived. Rather than focus on *revealed religion*, Rose
explores what she calls *unrevealed religion*, "which has hold of us without any
evidences, natural or supernatural, without any credos or dogmas, liturgies or
services." It is, she goes on to say, "the very religion that makes us protest, 'But
I have no religion,' the very Protestantism against modernity that fuels our
inner self-relation" (1995: 135–36). Gillian Rose claims that "this very protest founded modernity, an ethic without ethics, a religion without salvation"
and that enlightenment rationality is "the dependant, the cousin-german" of
this unrevealed religion (136), as is "reason's offspring, postmodern relativism"
(139). I take these remarks as ironic commentaries on the impossibility of ever
attaining a comprehensive and authoritative knowledge of the world, or of our
ever being completely in control of it. In all experience—personal, social, scientific, or religious—there is a tension between two conceptions of control.
The first implies management and mastery, in which the world bends to our
will, and our knowledge promises to light up the darkness, offering us greater
certainty in our relationships with objects and others. The second is dramatically different. In this more elusive vein, Gillian Rose writes "of a sense which,
nevertheless, saves my life and which, once achieved, may induce the relin-
quishing of 'control' in the first sense—'control' means that when something
untoward happens, some trauma or damage, whether inflicted by the com-
missions or omissions of others, or some cosmic force, one makes the initially
unwelcome event one's own inner occupation. You work to adopt the most

loveless, forlorn, aggressive child as your own, and do not leave her to develop into an even more vengeful monster, who constantly wishes you ill. *In ill-health as in unhappy love, this is the hardest work: it requires taking in before letting be*" (98, emphasis added).

In Galina's last writings on the politics of religion, there is, curiously, no hint of this second notion of control as acceptance and yielding. Yet, even as she reprised Peter Berger's image of the sacred canopy, she was, as those closest to her knew, embracing a view of power born of the experience of powerlessness, a technique of the self that, as Foucault noted toward the end of his life, implied a shift away from the study of competing ideologies or identity politics to the study of how people could "effect a certain number of operations on their own bodies, on their souls, on their own thoughts," modifying themselves or acting "in a certain state of perfection, of happiness, of purity, of supernatural power" (1980, cited in Miller 1993: 321–22). Perhaps we can understand the gradual shift from the more reflexive tone of *Conjuring Hope* to the more convention-ally academic style of Galina's final essays as a gesture toward a profession that demanded masks and jargons as the price of initiation. Perhaps it was a bid for greater presence at a time when her world was falling away, and even the project of understanding appeared irrelevant. This may also be the case for those who survive bereavement, for in the face of the overwhelming love that, paradoxically, wells up in us when we are thrown open to the ultimate, we pass beyond understanding, with our work of words, having reached the limit of what can be said, redeemed by our silence.

NOTES

1. Gillian Rose was an eminent British philosopher and critical theorist. She con-tracted ovarian cancer in her early forties.
2. Jacques Derrida also cautions against a "globalatinized," Greco-Roman bias in our thinking about religion (1998: 4, 30). It should also be noted that current notions of religion and of religions as domains of intelligible truth(s), rather than faith and passion, are largely products of seventeenth-century enlightenment rationality (Cantwell Smith 1978: 37–50).
3. The term is from Karl Jaspers (2000: 97). Though Adorno (1978: 152) treats the term *frontier-situations* as part of a jargon of authenticity—on a par with *being-in-the-world, individual existence,* and *heroic endurance*—a way of "usurping reli-gious-authoritarian pathos without the least religious content," I see it as a way of escaping from the two dominant discourses of our time, the first that reduces all meaning to political economy, the second to religious belief or doctrine. In my

view, it is precisely this tendency to politicize or intellectualize religious experience that the existential concept of situation helps us to overcome.

4. I have discussed at length elsewhere the ways in which James's relational view of reality anticipates D. W. Winnicott's work on "transitional phenomena" (1974), replacing notions of ontologically discrete domains like self and other, object and subject, inner and outer, with the image of "transitional" or "potential" space as an indeterminate zone where various ways of behaving, thinking, speaking, and feeling are called forth from a common pool, combining and permuting in ever-changing ways, depending on who is interacting and what is at stake (See Jackson 2005).

5. There are, of course, profound similarities between James's notion of "the more" and Jaspers's notion of "The Encompassing" (*das Umgreifende*) (Jaspers 1997).

6. My project may be seen as a phenomenology of what Victor Turner called "liminality," for my emphasis is on the various ways in which temporal, spatial, personal, and cultural in-betweenness is experienced in human life, both through conventional conceptual or ritual manifestations and inchoate, oneiric, poetic, and imaginary expressions. Yet I eschew a phenomenology that defines religion in terms of an allegedly sui generis modality of experience or existence, since what is important, in my view, is the unstable relationship—the écart, the cusp, the broken middle—between our experience of immediate and nonimmediate fields of experience—a mutually-constituting and fluid relationship that lacks any essence that can be tagged with one particular label. Hence my dissatisfaction with the psychoanalytic notion that religious experience is grounded in a yearning for the sublime, pre-Oedipal phase of fusion or union with the mother, with Otto's notion of "the wholly other" and "the numinous" (1958), with Eliade's notion of an "abyss" that divides "two modalities of experience—sacred and profane" (1959), and with Csordas's thesis that religious experience springs from a "primordial sense of 'otherness' or alterity" (2004: 164).

7. Among the Yolngu of northeast Arnhem Land, for example, *maarr* is the invisible and ancestral power "necessary for the health and fertility of the Yolngu world, including the environment in which people live." Through ritual labor, members of Yolngu clans cooperate in drawing this power out from the totemic sites where it resides, so that it "can be spread wide and be beneficial and bring a sense of well-being to all who participate with a good heart. (Morphy 1991: 103). For the people of the Daly River region of northern Australia, ceremony and *wangga* songs "provide the primary locus of human engagement with the ancestral dead," and this ceremony and song is associated "with liminal states of being—dream states, and the states of being in the twilight zone between life and death, or between childhood and adulthood" (Marrett 2005: 3, 5).

8. Note that the Indo-European word for a deity is *deiwos*, from the root *diw/dyu* (the bright sky or daylight) and designating a sky god.

9. In the Upper Amazon, the forest stands in the same relationship to people as the moiety from which they receive wives. While the forest provides food, allies provide women, which helps explain why the forest is said to smell like women, and entering the forest is compared to sexual intercourse. Rules governing the exploitation of forest resources—game, medicines, fruit, and narcotics—are also

analogous to rules governing correct sexual conduct (Reichel-Dolmatoff 1996, ch. 6).

References

Adorno, Theodor. 1978. *Minima Moralia: Reflections from Damaged Life*. Trans. E. F. N. Jephcott. London: Verso.

Asad, Talal. 1993. *Genealogies of Religion: Discipline and Reasons of Power in Christianity and Islam*. Baltimore: Johns Hopkins University Press.

Cantwell Smith, Wilfred. 1978. *The Meaning and End of Religion*. New York: Harper and Row.

Csordas, Thomas. 2004. "Asymptote of the Ineffable: Embodiment, Alterity, and the Theory of Religion." *Current Anthropology* 45 (2): 163–85.

Derrida, Jacques. 1998. "Faith and Knowledge: The Two Sources of 'Religion' at the Limits of Reason Alone." In *Religion*, ed. Jacques Derrida and Gianni Vattimo, 6–31. Stanford, CA: Stanford University Press.

Dewey, John. 1958. *Experience and Nature*. New York: Dover.

Eliade, Mircea. 1959. *The Sacred and the Profane: The Nature of Religion*. Trans. Willard R. Trask. New York: Harper and Row.

Jackson, Michael. 2005. *Existential Anthropology: Events, Exigencies and Effects*. Oxford: Berghahn.

———. 2007. "Imagining the Powers that Be: Society versus the State." In *Excursions*, 40–60. Durham, NC: Duke University Press.

———. 2009. *The Palm at the End of the Mind: Relatedness, Religiosity and the Real*. Durham, NC: Duke University Press.

James, William. 1958. *The Varieties of Religious Experience: A Study in Human Nature*. New York: Signet.

———. 1976. *Essays in Radical Empiricism*. Cambridge, MA: Harvard University Press.

———. 1977. *A Pluralistic Universe*. Cambridge, MA: Harvard University Press.

Jaspers, Karl. 1997. *Reason and Existenz*. Trans. William Earle. Milwaukee: Marquette University Press.

———. 2000. *Karl Jaspers: Basic Philosophical Writings*. Ed., trans., and with introductions by Edith Ehrlich, Leonard H. Ehrlich, and George B. Pepper. New York: Humanity Books.

Lindquist, Galina. 2000. "In Search of the Magical Flow: Magic and Market in Contemporary Russia." *Urban Anthropology* 29 (4): 315–57.

———. 2006. *Conjuring Hope: Healing and Magic in Contemporary Russia*. New York: Berghahn.

Marrett, Allan. 2005. *Songs, Dreamings, and Ghosts: The Wangga of North Australia*. Middletown, CT: Wesleyan University Press.

Merleau-Ponty, Maurice. 1964. "From Mauss to Lévi-Strauss." In *Signs*, trans. R. C. McLeary, 114–25. Evanston, IL: Northwestern University Press.

Miller, James. 1993. *The Passion of Michel Foucault.* New York: Simon and Schuster.

Morphy, Howard. 1991. *Ancestral Connections: Art and an Aboriginal System of Knowledge.* Chicago: Chicago University Press.

Otto, Rudolph. 1958. *The Idea of the Holy: An Inquiry into the Non-Rational Factor in the Idea of the Divine in Its Relation to the Rational.* Trans. John W. Harvey. London: Oxford University Press .

Reichel-Dolmatoff, Gerardo. 1996. *The Forest Within: The World-View of the Tukano Amazonian Indians.* Dartington, UK: Themis Books.

Rose, Gillian, 1995. *Love's Work: A Reckoning with Life.* New York: Schocken.

Schutz, Alfred, and Thomas Luckmann. 1989. *The Structures of the Lifeworld,* vol. 2. Trans Richard M. Zaner and David J. Parent. Evanston, IL: Northwestern University Press.

Winnicott, D.W. 1974. *Playing and Reality.* Harmondsworth, UK: Penguin.

RELIGION, POLITICS, AND GLOBALIZATION

The Long Past Foregrounding the Short Present—
Prologue and Introduction

Don Handelman and Galina Lindquist

This book offers a range of case-studies from around the globe—India, Indonesia, the Middle East, North Africa, Spain, the United States—that take up the tangled relationships between religion and politics in the presentness of this globalizing age. Mostly by anthropologists, the chapters exemplify how a relevant anthropology concentrates especially on the ethnographic and the factual. The case-studies illuminate the finer details of conflicts in the entanglement and the difficulties of resolving these. They add to the current understanding in the social sciences of just how mistaken were the claims of a generation and more ago that with modernization, religion withered away while much of the world's people secularized, thereby becoming heirs of the Western Enlightenment. Such claims maintained that as heirs of the Enlightenment, people should have a greater appreciation of the very metaphysics of science-based knowledge, and not only of the uses of technology. This appreciation should inspire confidence in rational decision making whose premises and outcomes are transparent and explicitly accountable for in terms of linear cause-and-effect relationships, without any irrational, mystifying mumbo-jumbo.[1] Nonetheless, states that can best be called "theocratic"—religious-political systems that modernity sought to relegate to history—proliferate all over the globe and claim their say in international affairs. In avowedly secular states including those that

Notes for this chapter begin on page 55.

(like the United States) formally separate church and state, religious institutions actively and influentially take part in the life of political and civil society, and groups and individuals inspired by "religious" values change cultures and societies in ways that few could have predicted. To be legitimate in the modern Western world, groups active in civil society, in social movements, and in political parties are expected to posit and position themselves based on secular rationality. Yet evidence from different parts of the globe show that these secular projects increasingly turn to whatever version of "religion" is at hand.

Our Prologue and Introduction foregrounds the chapters in this volume in broader perspective by arguing that at the roots of what we call "religion" are values of holism. The chapters illuminate numerous aspects of the conflicts and convergences between religion, politics, peoplehood, and nationhood, in which people hold together against others on the basis of often tacit feeling, but, too, the knowing of values that we are calling holistic. Moreover, we contend that such values were never extinguished during very lengthy periods in ancient and traditional worlds in which holism related first and foremost to cosmos—indeed to cosmos, as we discuss further on, that in our terms holds itself together from within itself. This kind of cosmos was shattered by the historical emergence of the monotheisms that shaped cosmoses that were "encompassed" and held together from outside themselves. These developments are associated with a lengthy period that historian Karl Jaspers and others have called the *Axial Age*. In this Prologue and Introduction, we call this shattering of cosmos the *first great rupture*, which occurred in parts of the ancient world. Nonetheless, values of holism continued through modern Western worlds, as these values became lodged in what came to be called "religion," and still later in peoplehood, nationhood, statism, ethnicity, and not least in the individual (perhaps culminating in Foucault's idea of the care of the self).

In our broad historical tracing of "religion" further on, cosmos (and its relation to holism) will take precedence over "religion" (and its relation to holism), since the emergence of "religion" as a distinct domain in its own right occurred relatively late in human history, especially in Western Europe through the Reformation (and Enlightenment). We call this the *second great rupture* of cosmos, and discuss this further on. During that period, the "political" also emerged as a distinct domain in its own right (Dumont 1977). Therefore in this trace we also give priority to "religion" over "politics," since the political as a distinct sphere emerged in counterpoint to that of religion. Yet, even as religion and politics moved into the modern age, often in competition with one another, this conflict may well point to how in today's world both religion and politics often are imbued with values of holism.[2] We underscore that in doing this trace, our concern is not with causal relations through time, with any historical causality, but rather with the order of developments, with what came after what, and the significance of this for our arguments.

Values of holism in varieties of scale, density, and intensity are integral to human conditions of being, indeed, perhaps to being human. Values of holism may be thought of as cultural seed pods from which, when social conditions are ripe, holism germinates, ripens, and flourishes anew in varieties of form and context. We suggest that it is the value of holism in human ordering that often acts (both as sensibility and as intellect) in human life-worlds, in human cosmoses, to keep them together metaphysically.[3] In order to state this claim, we must consider broadly the fates of values of holism during lengthy durations, even though this means that our trace must indeed remain superficial. Nonetheless, in this Prologue and Introduction, we make a start toward laying out such a trace. And, on the basis of this trace, we contend that in today's world *where values of holism are present*—often in the secular lineaments of nationalism, statism, ethnic peoplehood, and so forth—*religion is close by*. Arguing in this way, we are cutting against the grain of most contemporary studies of religion and politics that argue that in postmodernity, ties loosen and structures fall apart. In fact, this does not contradict our contention that even as things fall apart, values of holism re-form on different scales, in different patterns, and that as this occurs, religion is close by.

The chapters of this book were not written with the problematic of holism in today's globalizing world in mind—as Handelman outlined in the Preface, this volume has had a complex development. Yet we have no doubt that if one reads these works with this problematic in mind, it will become evident in a number of the chapters that when religions are present, *values of holism are close by*. In other words, we question whether modern (and postmodern) social orders in their manifold dimensions, whether secular or religious, can survive during lengthy periods without the "religiosity" that is embedded in values of holism, despite the claims of modernization and secularism to do away with religion, especially on rational grounds that are perceived to be embedded in science, progress, and secular ideological revolution (see especially Ezrahi 1990 on the role of science in democracy). Our contention is, of course, tautological if one thinks in terms of linear, cause-and-effect explanation: thus the tautology in arguing that values of holism index religion while in turn religion indexes values of holism. Nonetheless this is the logic of cosmos that is nonlinear in its (even partial) self-relating, self-integrating, and this too in the current era of globalization no less. Since the excision of tautology from linear, causal explaining is central to social-science thinking, we will return briefly to the issue of tautology in the section "Holism, Cosmos, Religion." The linear claims of modernization-as-progress are especially poignant in this age of intensified globalization and migration, as the entanglements of religion and politics also close in on themselves as they intensify; witness the following two examples.

In the beginning of February 2007, newspapers reported that Abdel Karim Nabil Suleiman, a twenty-two-year-old Egyptian, faced a court trial. His crime was writing a blog, and he was charged with "disturbing the public order, spreading malevolent rumors and instigating hatred against Islam." Blogs are private journals, a form of self-expression known as long as literacy has existed. The difference is that today's journals are laid out on the internet, to be read and commented on by any number of people unknown to the author. Private journals become a public resource; private worlds are unfolded in public space. Personal voices bypass censorship, reaching unexpected audiences, creating contacts and communities, spreading ideas and cultural forms beyond confines of national borders and political regimes.

Due to the World Wide Web, blogging today is far from a purely Western phenomenon.[4] From Saudi Arabia to Morocco there are perhaps three to four thousand blogs, with fifty to one hundred popping up every day, where young people express their views. Egyptian authorities have long been trying to create a precedence by indicting a blogger; now Abdel Karim Nabil Suleiman (or Karim Amer, his internet name) was picked, and this choice prevented any protest in his support from whatever internal oppositional forces there are in Egypt. Whatever the different ideological and political opinions in this Muslim country, no one would defend a person who in his blog pronounced Islam "the root of all evil" (as the Swedish newspaper, *Svenska Dagbladet*, reported).[5] His private statements, made public by the new practices of global cyberspace, demonstratively showed an attitude to religion as fervent as that of any religious devotee, albeit with the opposite sign. For his blog entries, Amer was sentenced to several years in prison.

This case illustrates what we know well: complex webs of power known as "politics" and actions fueled by sentiments connected to what we classify as "religion" cannot be understood separately from each other. Yet much more than this, this instance implies the following: Suleiman's blogging critique of Islam depends on the clear-cut separation of state and religion, such that religion is treated as a separate category, a distinct sphere of living, which is detachable, disposable, and can be disregarded in keeping with the thesis that modernization and secularization advance together. Perhaps from its beginnings (though perhaps some centuries later), Islam implicated a cosmos governed by the tenets of Islam that would encompass the political sphere of activity; a cosmos that was a religious polity, as it is sometimes called. For devout Muslims, Suleiman had attacked the existential legitimacy of the integral Muslim cosmos which encompasses the entirety of the world of existence, however this is understood. This instance demonstrates in a (cosmic) nutshell the perhaps endemic conflicted relationship since the onset of the European Enlightenment between "religion" and "politics." This instance entangles national politics, religious interests, and the globalizing internet as a powerful venue of the values of individualism and freedom of expression espoused by liberal democracies, but very much in question in so many other states.

The uproar over the Mohammed cartoons that erupted a few years ago was another indication of the entanglement between spheres that—historically, socially, culturally—came to be separated during a lengthy period into the rubrics of religion and politics. World publics watched with amazement and anxiety how fervent emotions characteristic of religious faith erupted to cause tensions in international relations; and how consequences of what seemed at first an imprudent joke spread with the speed and intensity of a forest blaze all over the globe, provoking riots in distant places. The case of the Mohammed cartoons demonstrated once again the overflowing (and ever-flowing) global character of today's world, its unexpected connectivities, the permeability of national borders, and the relativity of ideologies and values considered fundamental for Western democracies, such as "freedom of speech." Especially in the instance of the Mohammed cartoons, religious attitudes generated an internal political issue that quickly became a matter of international concern; neither religious values and ideologies nor national judicial norms and regulations could for long be contained and managed within national borders.[6] Beyond telling us that increasingly all over the globe, politics and religion cannot be understood separately and that globalization is a key process in this entanglement, these two examples urge us to question once again our ideas of private and public, of national and global spheres of secular politics and religious faith.

Indeed, the last two decades have seen a spate of research on the entwinements of politics and religion. These have focused on the involvement of churches and religious movements in the politics of states and civil societies (e.g., Haynes 1998, 2006; Casanova 1994; Bruce 2003), on the role of religion in nation building and in the constitution of national and ethnic identity (Van der Meer and Lehman 1999; Halliday 2000; Hastings 1997; Goldschmidt and McAlister 2004), and on antisecularist or "fundamentalist" movements (an early example is Westerlund 1996). Attention too has been given to the role of globalization in changing the world's religious landscapes (e.g., Beyer 1994; Vasquez and Marquardt 2003). The individual chapters of this book broaden this focus, problematizing the tenuous equation between secularism and modernity. For that matter, the chapters suggest that we might well question any clear-cut distinction between the categories of "politics" and "religion" as applicable in today's world. The chapters bring globalization into this picture as vast interacting flows of ideas, plans, and practices that alter the constitution of the processes these categories attempt to chart.

In the 1960s it was commonplace in the social sciences and religious studies to assert that the world was "secularizing": that in modern social orders, religion had lost its role, lost its way, becoming increasingly marginalized and relegated to the private, inner sphere. The modernization-secularization thesis (with its implicit evolutionist morality) was close to the hearts (and not only the minds) of many social scientists. Prominent was that which Geertz (2005: 10) calls "the reductive version of the so-called 'secularization thesis'—that the rationalization of modern life was pushing religion out of the public square, shrinking it to the dimensions of the private, the inward, the personal, and the hidden." Three decades later, many of the proponents of the secularization paradigm admitted that it was wrong. In 1999, Peter Berger (1991), a prominent sociologist of religion and one of the foremost theorists of secularization, declared that secularization theory was essentially mistaken. "The world of today," he said, "is as furiously religious as it ever was, and in some places more than ever." Asked to reconsider his recantation, Berger (2001: 194) responded that, "if modernization and secularization are intrinsically linked, one would have to argue that the United States is less modern than, say, the United Kingdom." Another prominent sociologist of religion, Grace Davie (2007: 64), wrote recently that given the decline of the modernization-secularization thesis, "the task of the sociologist shifts accordingly: for he or she is required to explain the absence rather than the presence of religion in the modern world. This amounts to nothing less than a paradigm shift in the sociology of religion."

Social scientists have not had a fruitful record in studying present-day religions from within themselves, through their cosmoses, their metaphysics. At the core of social-science research ideologies is the premise that scientific progress is attained through fact-based and transparent research results that are replicable. Mainstream models of social-science research are by-and-large deeply influenced by the natural and experimental sciences (though this is much less so for sociocultural anthropology and its qualitative research approaches). In these terms this means that religion can be well studied for its sociological parameters, and this is the direction that most social-science researchers take.

Yet, as phenomenon, as practice, as belief, we researchers generally position religion closer (perhaps very close to) the pole of the irrational on a continuum that runs from the irrational to the rational (where we position our disciplines and ourselves, at least our public and professional selves). Representative of this view is the recent writing of the anthropologist, F. G. Bailey (2008: 21): "Revealed Truth (God's Truth) is asserted without evidence, and to that extent, it is unauthentic; it has nothing to do with knowledge, it evades criticism, and it answers only to the emotional discomfort that accompanies feelings of uncertainty." On the other hand, the task of the rational, of reason, "is to inquire and to demand evidence, which is, ipso facto, to put faith [i.e., religion] into question" (2008: 23). Yet should we, as social scientists, accept the common-sense logic of this continuum? Should religion at all be positioned on this continuum that is the intellectual product of the European Enlightenment and later of European modernization? By putting religion on this continuum it is, indeed ipso facto, forced to reflect the premises of the rational and the secular; and, as such, religion can only be understood as irrational. Since the politics of religion commonly reflect conflicts between secular and religious institutions, religion as cosmology (which is also a way of saying religion in its own right) can neither escape nor evade its positioning on the continuum.

Elementary premises of cosmos, of religion-as-cosmos, can run extraordinarily deep, and this must not be elided in the scramble of scholarship to attribute the resurgence of religion (and, in the recent past, the decline of religion) almost wholly to current social, political, and economic conditions in movement globally. Throughout this Introduction we are arguing, more loudly, more quietly, that the human propensity toward holistic organization, in multiple domains, on multiple levels, is profound and cannot be reduced simplistically to historical processes, nor to particular social formations. Consider, for example, one aspect of cosmic organization that the anthropologist working in a traditional social order would study as a matter of course—the dynamics of time. How time is conceived and practiced is essential to the rhythms of living, as these rhythms are essential to the existence of a world, perhaps every world. People who are synchronized through temporal rhythms share together what Ernst Cassirer (1953: 40) called "the 'concrete form' of the 'inner sense.'" Being in time together is being connected interiorly in ways that seem so exterior and concrete. The rhythmicity of these connections enable what Alfred Schutz called, "making music together." Thus in his wonderful study of the counting system of the Iqwaye people of New Guinea, Jadran Mimica (1988: 136) writes: "An intrinsic rhythmicity which temporalises the entire structure of numeration … is the source of its dynamics." Time—often a cosmic dynamic—has propensities to organize values of holism. The consequences of this for politics must not be discounted.

After the founding of Israel in 1948, the state adopted the Hebrew calendar, which was also the Judaic cosmic calendar. Embedded in the calendar are the requisite dates (and observances) of the sabbaths and holidays. These organize holistic temporal rhythms and their values throughout the year (and, no less, longer blocks of years, moving toward the eschatological End of Time). The adoption of this calendar was done in the name of tradition by a nominally secular, nominally socialist (and hence "progressive") government that emphasized its building of a new society and a new person. Yet living these rhythms and impulsions of cosmic (religious) time as the taken-for-granted experiencing of existence have helped to prepare many secular Israeli Jews for their turn to serious religious observance, with profound consequences for the growth of Israeli ultranationalism and Israeli colonization of the occupied Palestinian territories. And, no less, for perceiving time as progressing with messianic impulsion (Handelman 1998: 223–33). Intervening in, meddling with elementary premises of cosmos (whatever they are) is never a light matter, and this is no less so when done in the name of rational, scientific, constructivist thought. The deep dynamics of cosmic holism are powerfully resistant to elementary change.

This became especially clear when, in the name of rationality, science, and secularism, revolutionary European states decided to change radically the Western Christian Gregorian calendar, thereby making the new periodicities independent of religious rhythms. In the aftermaths of both the French and Russian revolutions, the Republicans and the Bolsheviks planned to utterly remake temporal order and reckoning. Here we mention the French case: "The French Republican calendrical reform is undoubtedly the most radical attempt in modern history to have challenged the calendrical system that prevails in the world to this day. It is hard to overemphasize the extent to which the reformers obliterated the existing system of units of time as well as the existing time-reckoning and dating frameworks" (Zerubavel 1981: 83). This took place, of course, in an age that "advocated the total obliteration of the existing order in the name of progress and modernity. … the calendrical reform … was supposed to mark the total [cosmic] discontinuity between past and present" (Zerubavel 1981: 83).

The Republicans advocated de-Christianizing the calendar, creating a new annual cycle based on nonreligious principles. Thus New Year's Day was to be 22 September 1792, the beginning of the Republican Era, replacing the Christian one. The revolutionaries planned to organize units of time and the passage of time to inculcate rationalism through the experiencing of precision, promptness, simplicity, facility, clarity, and enlightenment (Zerubavel 1981: 88). Using the decimal as the cornerstone, the principles of reason and science were to prevail. And, through all of this and more, the Revolutionary calendar was intended to be particularly French, imbued with the values and vigor of a rejuvenated French nationalism. This project of the revolution failed utterly and, by 1802, Napoleon reinstated the Gregorian calendar. Over a century later, the Bolshevik revamping of Orthodox Christian temporal rhythms and pulsations also ended in failure (as did with time their attempts to banish the life-crisis religious rites).[7]

The question stays: should the irrational-rational continuum continue to dominate so many of our attempts to understand religion? Bruce Kapferer (2001: 342) argues, "Anthropology is secularism's doubt," that is, anthropology is the cutting edge of rationalism's doubt especially when it is "radical doubt" joined to the phenomenological "suspension of disbelief." Yet just how suspended is disbelief, buttressed intellectually by a phenomenology that must be called rational despite its claims to begin from within the perceptions of the feeling subject as observer? Disbelief radically simplifies the task of the anthropologist, leaving him or her entirely ensconced on the continuum we are discussing without any attempt to actually critique this, for example, by asking whether it is "belief" that is relevant to radical doubt. Perhaps intuition is a wiser guide than is reason, detached as the latter is from the human feel for holism? Perhaps, as Robert Innis writes in the Afterword (paraphrasing Charles Sanders Peirce) "We must not … pretend to doubt with our minds what we do not really doubt with our hearts." Perhaps the sense of cosmos from which religion eventually emerged in the distant past makes intuitive sense as *a-rational* dynamics, dynamics that are neither rational nor irrational? One can argue (though we will only touch on this in the section after the next) that for the kind of holism characterizing ancient cosmoses (and, too, of many tribal peoples, including those abutting the present) current Western ideas of the rational and the irrational are flatly irrelevant. Ironically, the comprehension of ancient and tribal cosmoses of holism just might be more accessible through (non-linear) thinking which argues for wholes that are "open" yet whose logic of composition is that of a whole that constitutes its parts from its very holism (rather than a whole that emerges from its parts, such that the addition of parts to one another produces the whole).[8]

The irrational-rational axis not infrequently (though tacitly) becomes evolutionist as "primitive" replaces "irrational" and "modern" replaces "rational." There are two evolutionist premises embedded sotto voce in much of Western social science that are worth highlighting here if we are to understand the trajectory of scholarship on religion and politics. The premises are the following: First, of all religions, it is Judeo-Christian monotheism that has evolved in linear fashion from the primitive into the highest order of morality; and second, that especially since the Enlightenment, the world has evolved linearly from primitive to modern, from irrational to rational, from slavery to tradition to the freedom of individualism. This evolutionary vision (often with its more or less unilineal connotations) is treated as predictive but no less as normative: the finest, indeed the highest expression of this evolution is taken to be the democratic liberal polity, rationally joining individual agency to the freedom of public will. Religion as wholly embracing, smothering the individual's existence, driving the human being to be dominated by the transcendent, chaining her to the inexplicable, is seen as a force encroaching on agency, rationality, freedom, a power that has to be kept at bay. Thus religion in the public, national, and transnational spheres tended to be seen as a throwback to the primitive, to the hindrance of the irrational, stultifying progress to a better life (indeed, a throwback that returns periodically, atavistically, modernity as "a binding collage of the archaic and the new" (Seitler 2008: 234).

The realization that religion was not dead and gone or at least safely secluded away in the private sphere, together with the realization of just how silly was the intellectual claim for the death of God (a claim peremptorily Christian, correlating with the retreat of European colonialism [Hardt and Negri 2000: 375]) forced social scientists to recognize that religion was upfront, visible, and powerful. This presented not only new vistas for scholarship, but signified shattered illusions and new threats for many. A paradigm shift in religious studies has never occurred (or, perhaps has failed to materialize, see Brewer 2007); and students of religion and politics grapple with the present situation, one thoroughly unlike that which the founding fathers of sociology and anthropology envisaged. Even so, social scientists do their grappling on an ad hoc basis, fine-tuning analytical tools that sometimes seem blunt, crude, and obsolete for making sense of present-day entanglements.

The Chapters

This volume is divided into four sections, with an Afterword by the philosopher and semiotician Robert Innis. Section I is entitled *Shaping Religion Through Politics*. Its chapters address attempts in Tyva (Southern Siberia) to shape religion as a national force through politics and in India to subsume religion within the politics of national culture and nationhood. The chapters of Section II, *Open Conflicts Between Religion and Politics*, take up two such confrontations, in the small, new state of East Timor and in Spain. In Section III, *The Tight Embrace of Religion and Politics*, case studies of the United States and Iran discuss how religion and politics are joined together and synthesized to varying degrees, more tacitly, more officially. The chapters of Section IV, *Opening New Space for Religion*, consider the grounds for two sorts of penetration, that of evangelical Christian proselytizing in Amazigh (Berber) North Africa and that of Islamist terrorism. The religions that appear in this book are predominantly monotheistic—Islam and Christianity—in interaction with different polities, democratic, theologic. The adherents of Islam and Christianity consider them "universal religions," that is, religions applicable to and open to all peoples, indeed, religions intended to convert the world; and Islam and Christianity arguably are the most active of religions in the world today in seeking converts. Neither (like the third surviving monotheism, Judaism) officially permits concurrent membership in another religion, this in itself is something of an exception in the overall history of religions.

In Section I, Galina Lindquist's contribution explores the vying of Tibetan Buddhism and shamanism in post-Soviet Tyva (Russian, *Tuva*) in the making of a traditional religion that represents the population of this small republic. Buddhism and shamanism in Tyva differ in their capacities to define the limits of the socially significant global world (that Ulf Hannerz [1996] called the "ecumene"). Even as religion comes increasingly to be used in identity politics all over the world, particularly in postcolonial contexts, some religions are better suited for this than are others. As the Russian Empire loosened its grip on its subjects, newly emerging polities were faced with the task of forming national identities. In such historical postcolonial moments, the idea of "traditional religion" often comes to the fore. When there are several ethnic categories with different religious traditions, or when there are several religions that an ethnic category may consider as traditional, religious competition may well appear

(Balzer 2005). Outcomes are decided by local power games, social configurations, and transnational and global environments, yet the internal properties, the internal logics of the religions in question, are certainly crucial.

Both Tibetan Buddhism and shamanism exist within holistic cosmoses that somewhat overlap with one another. The Buddhist cosmos is overwhelmingly vertical and hierarchical in its logic of organization, canonic in its self-knowledge, everything in its rightful place, fully continuous within itself, carefully controlling every being within itself, through itself. This cosmos is held together from within itself, not through being encompassed by God (like the monotheistic ones)—remember that the Buddha was fully a human being, not a transcendent deity. The shamanic cosmos, on the other hand, could be called more lateral in its topology and more slanted in its verticality. The shamanic cosmos spreads laterally across the vast Tyvan landscape, following the shape of rivers, streams, steppe, taiga, mountains, with concentrations of varieties of beings here and there, like swirls in the horizontal landscape. Knowledge of the shamanic cosmos is decidedly noncanonic. Tyvan shamans are experiential beings, much of whose knowledge of cosmos is self-learned through their experiences in traveling, healing, doing ritual, dreaming. Though the reservoirs of knowledge certainly overlap among shamans, there are substantial variations in shamans' conceptions of cosmos. Shamanic cosmos is continuous, its exterior boundaries (if there are such) fuzzy and porous. This cosmos in all its variations is held together first and foremost by its interactivity, or, more accurately, by its intra-activity within and through its self-continuity (see Lindquist 2008; Handelman 2008: 188–89).

In Tyva it has proven decidedly difficult to shape shamanism into the state religion. Even though Tyvan shamanism has an international cachet especially in Europe and North America as the (perhaps original) heartland of shamanism, within Tyva itself the social breadth of shamanic ritual can do little more than map extended families onto the landscape. Buddhism is much more conducive to becoming the state religion of Tyva (as it once was, in the early twentieth century). Tibetan Buddhism, argues Lindquist, maps the Tyvan nation onto its land and is formative for the national identity of Tyvans. Indeed, the entire topology of Tyva is present symbolically in the construction and composition of a single Buddhist stupa (which is sometimes a reliquary, and other times a receptacle for offerings and sacred objects). Lindquist shows us that politics is not reducible to power games, to individual and clique interests, to struggles over economic resources and so forth (as many Western political scientists would have it). Though we do not minimize these and other factors, cultural forms and their potentialities must be factored into understanding how polity responds to religious influences.

The problems of unifying a vast state with great regional differences, language differences, local caste systems, many religions, large minorities, all characterize India. The scale of India, with over 1 billion inhabitants, utterly dwarfs that of Tyva, yet as Henrik Berglund, a political scientist, argues through historical, political, and social complexities, the fate of a major rightist, nationalist, political party, the BJP, has depended in large measure on re-creating the many forms of Hinduism into a national culture for political and economic purposes. In the recent past this has been a major departure from the ideology of secularized, democratic, centralized statism of the Congress Party that controlled national-level politics since independence in 1949. Through the efforts of the BJP, this shift is reaching also into the globalized Hindu diaspora, which is used by BJP politicians as a resource for mustering economic means and broad popular support, and to help present Hindu nationalist ideology as a source of cohesion and loyalty to the state, cutting across lines of caste, class, gender, and ethnicity. A significant fundament for the re-forming of Hinduism is the ideology of *Hindutva*, Hindu-ness, which turns the "Hindu nation" and "Hindu culture" into an integral and integrated unit defined as an organism, rejecting modern ruptures along the lines of class and ethnicity within this organism, and perhaps encompassing minorities (like that of the large Muslim population) as kinds of Hindus (Gellner 2001: 338). However Islam-as-monotheism is exclusivist in terms of its Muslim membership and cannot be encompassed by Hindu-ness (which includes Hindu religion), and thus Islam in India opposes cultural and national Hinduism, which becomes anti-Muslim.

Hinduism as the commonly shared, supposedly standardized religion of most of India has colonial origins. As the indologist Wendy Doniger (2009) argues, early British scholars of India contributed greatly to creating perceptions in the West of a unified Hinduism with a canon of ancient, originary, philosophical texts in a near-sacred language, Sanskrit. One model for this regimenting of India's numerous polysemic polytheisms was, argues Doniger, Protestant monotheism. In the well-known terms of Eric Hobsbawm and Terence Ranger, the cultural Hinduism of the BJP is an "invented tradition." The efforts of colonial scholarship to reorganize Hinduism into a "proper religion," Western-style, one that was necessarily transcendental in monotheistic terms rather than fluid and self-organizing in the great variations of its practices, was abetted by nineteenth-century Indian reform movements dedicated to returning Hinduism to its ancient, essential foundations, revived and purified of its numerous corrupting "pagan" and "superstitious" accretions. (During this period the same process also instigated by Europeans was at work further south in the Theravada Buddhism of Sri Lanka).

The BJP's re-forming of Hinduism as a national political vehicle of culture took the invented tradition one large step forward, giving to it in theory qualities of encompassment, of a totality of value for all of India. Berglund shows how this nationalist re-forming also has enabled the global export of Hindu nationalism for purposes of shaping Hindu diaspora identity and energizing

Hindu self-reliance through economic development and economic export. In nationalist ideology, this totalism is intended to globalize India by providing a strong national, economic identity that also will strengthen nationalist political ideology at home and abroad.

Section II, on open conflicts between religion and politics, contains chapters by anthropologists David Hicks and Eva Evers Rosander. Echoing Berglund's study, both of these chapters underscore secularization as a matter of degree rather than one of absolute difference from religion. Hicks takes up the emerging confrontation between the Catholic Church and the secular government of Timor-Leste (East Timor), a tiny state with very substantial oil and gas resources in the Timor Sea that are of great interest to powers in the area and beyond. Timor-Leste had been a Portuguese colony from the sixteenth century. Following the fall of Portugal's Salazar regime in 1974, East Timor was invaded by Indonesia in 1975 and occupied until 1999, when a referendum under UN sponsorship overwhelmingly rejected Indonesian rule. In 2002 the new nation attained independence as a democratic and secular state. East Timor was the first nation-state to become a member of the UN in the twenty-first century. As a result of the Indonesian occupation, though estimates vary, some 180,000 East Timorese died, out of a population of some 600,000 persons.

Nominally the church is separated from the state in East Timor. Hicks describes how little these labels may tell us about the relations between religion and politics in different contexts. The grounds for conflict between church and state are clear. The universal theology of the church transcends and encompasses Christian cosmos. The very separation and formal dominance of the secular state challenges this. In 2005 the church, popular and respected in East Timor, for the first time openly challenged the government's political authority, and this contributed to the resignation of the prime minister a year later. The openness of the church's challenge emerged after the secular authorities announced that Catholic doctrine would no longer be a compulsory subject in the state primary schools, thereby threatening the assurance of Catholic socialization for children. The church responded to the government's decision with measures quite outside the conventional range associated with "democratic society," not stopping short of instigated insurgence that came dangerously close to erupting into violence (the resonances to aspects of Rosander's study of Spain are deep). The church called for its adherents to come to the capital in large numbers from all over the country, which they did in mass protest at the government's decision. The causus belli of education was hardly mentioned, if at all, in this protest and it deliberately was turned into one antigovernment and antisecular, lasting seventeen days and ending with a negotiated compromise that shaped the church into a more powerful, local, political force. Two points should be emphasized: The political system of East Timor almost automatically opens space for political contestation; and the global breadth and reach of the church ensures that even a miniscule branch will have the attention of the international media and powerful organizations when the church deems this so.

After the Spanish Civil War between Republicans and Nationalists, the relationship between the dictatorial, conservative, Nationalist Franco regime (1936–1975) and the Catholic Church had something of the texture, aura, and feeling tones (not the social structures, of course) of the relationship between pre-Reformation European kingship and the church. The church holistically encompassed the Christian cosmos, protected in the main by kingship (Generalissimo Franco indeed had become the de facto regent of a revived Spanish kingship). Catholicism was made the official religion of the Spanish state, women were expected to stay home and to be the mainstays of their family, and "tradition" (as Berglund's study of the BJP underscores) was elevated as an essence of Spanish-ness. The church was a powerful and influential institution during the Franco era. The post-Franco period has brought back democratic liberal governance, secularization, and the opening up of social and moral order, and, too, an influx of immigrants, especially from Muslim North Africa, arriving with their own versions of a monotheism that no less holistically encompasses social order. Eva Evers Rosander's study focuses her fine-grained and detailed analysis on one signal case—that of the imam of Fuengirola—in which liberal democracy was contested by values of a maximalist version of Islam, but also indirectly by the position of the church. Multiculturalism ushered in by globalization forces a Western democratic state to confront religion that transgresses the parameters set by secularization in the name of religious freedom.

In 2000 the imam of Fuengirola published a book (in a small edition) interpreting the Koran as a guiding principle for Muslim daily living. One small part upheld the right of a husband to beat his wife for disobedience. A public furor ensued. Subsequently the imam was sentenced to a prison term, though released after a brief stay. Locking horns here were gender discrimination as enunciated by Spanish law in a democratic society and the freedom of persons to practice their religion, even though the practice of this religion required (according to the imam's interpretation) infringing on the gender rights of another human being. The position of the imam and his supporters implied that a religious individual can impose on others (beginning with his wife) a logic of religious law (like that of the other surviving monotheisms) that demands (in the most favorable of circumstances) its imposition on the entirety of social order encompassed by that religion. In this there was a direct challenge to the authority of the secular state. One could say that this is especially embedded in the so-called universal monotheisms, Christianity and Islam.

Extending her analysis beyond the case of the imam, Evers Rosander points out that the reaction of the Spanish church to a new law requiring compulsory education in civics in Spanish schools (while "religion" has become an optional subject) echoes that of many Muslims to the affair of the imam. *Civics* here refers to teaching human values and human rights, which subordinates church doctrine (and Christianity's encompassment) to the state (echoing the struggle in East Timor).[9] More generally, the church is striving to reassert the presence of its own encompassment of cosmos—witness the contentious lecture of Pope Benedict XVI at the University of Regensburg in 2006. Benedict argued that Christianity is "rational" (a religion for all ages of history), while Islam (its major global competitor) is "irrational" (implying, as we argued earlier, primitivism). Christianity, he contended, synthesizes faith (utter obedience to God, with its Judaic roots) and reason (as this emerged within ancient "Greek" philosophy). Therefore Christianity transcends (and encompasses) the opposition between faith and reason. Islam, by contrast (and the distinction in Benedict's speech is absolute) embraces only the pole of faith, of total obedience to God. Islam in Benedict's terms is "a fanatical rather than a rational religion" (Nirenberg 2008: 7–8). In global terms (extrapolating broadly from the two chapters in this section), the two huge monotheisms (with all their local, contextual variations, of which there are indeed a great many) struggle for the hegemony of their own encompassment of cosmos, just as both struggle against any inroads of secularism.

Section III, *The Tight Embrace of Religion and Politics*, has chapters by Simon Coleman, an anthropologist, on Protestantism in the United States and David Thurfjell, a historian of religion, on Iran and takes us into a sphere in which religion and politics tightly embrace, the two synthesized to the extent that, at the present time at least, their joining is inseparable. The American Constitution formally separates state and religion, yet America probably has the most religious of populations among all of the Western democracies. Quite simply, this means that religion and politics find one another and intertwine in a myriad of ways. It is this problematic that led American social scientists in the 1970s to conceptualize the idea of "civil religion" (which we discuss in the final section of this Introduction). Iran on the other hand is an Islamic republic, but one modeled in part on Western design, as Thurfjell explains. This influence gives to Iran a particular confluence of fundamentalist rigidity in matters of religion (for example, in severely persecuting the members of the Baha'i faith, who are officially classified as heretics of Islam) and degrees of openness in other matters (at least until the 2009 presidential election there); in, for example, the professional occupations women have been able to pursue and in the works of noted Iranian film directors who have attained international repute.

Coleman's chapter concerns the expanding role of the Protestant Right in American politics and, by extension, the spectacular global success of the Evangelical movement, touched on again in Amiras's chapter on the Tamazigh of North Africa and Protestant Evangelical proselytizing via the internet.

The success of political Evangelicals in the United States lies in their being a "counter-counter-culture," built on rhetoric of universal (Christian) moral values and on the dynamics of continuous personal revival (which is no less the continuous revival of those universal moral values). This ongoing revivalism creates a logical link to American conservative politics, which is so concerned with the rejuvenation of values understood as truly, essentially American and upon which the fate of America of the Founding Fathers is said to depend. Thus devout Protestants coexist well with secular conservatives through the strategic use of rhetorical language by the former that can be understood on two levels: in the discernible reality of the secular and in the spiritual reality available only to believers. In this way, Evangelical discourse can appeal both to secular audiences and to the devout.

Salvationist religion in the United States effectively functions as an operational civil religion, and millennial assumptions and expectations are readily remapped onto the broader ideals and aspirations of American political piety. Indeed, it is again on both levels of the mundane and the sacred that the "war on [religious] evil" is waged, primarily against a universal Islam, as it had been previously waged on "godless communism" (and socialism). Thus divine significance is given to mundane resources, justifying violence as redemptive force (which is no less so for the forces of religious terrorism, as Handelman argues in his chapter). The intimations of the power of these simultaneous levels were already present in the anthropologist W. Lloyd Warner's (1961) classic 1930s study of Christian life in America and its relationship to the war dead, and again in the anthropologist Carol Greenhouse's (1989) study of the effects of the Vietnam War on a small American city. Greenhouse found that many Christian fundamentalists fought because of belief in a higher good, and so there is no moral contradiction between peace and war because both are supported by a transcending belief in order, discipline, and faith. We wonder if this is also so for the many Evangelical missionaries who spread the gospel throughout the globalized world. As Coleman argues, the evangelical is made for traveling.

In his chapter, David Thurfjell, a historian of religion, discusses the current contradiction in Iran of how a country of encompassing monotheism is understood by so many of its people as thoroughly modern. Exploring the history of the Islamization of Iranian society, he argues that Islamism developed in reaction to a deep contradiction that marred the European Enlightenment project: the combination of lofty ideals of freedom, equality, and brotherhood on the one hand, and, on the other, the systematic atrocities, exploitation, and oppression done through colonialism. Iranian Islamism in its early form joined forces with European ideals of secular democracy, yet the latter were later discredited globally by oppression in the name of those selfsame ideals.

Iranian Islamism discarded some of these ideas but reshaped and retained others in developing its own version of modernity, in which religion was always

a key element of political and social life. The Ayatollah Khomeyni and his revolutionary movement were explicitly not opposed to modernization. Thurfjell
demonstrates how throughout the Iranian history of colonial times, its leaders found various ways to use traditional religious institutions to pursue the
ends of the modernized political struggle. He presents a succession of historical
episodes that constituted the process through which the *'ulamā*, the Islamic
clergy, turned from passive critics of the regime to becoming political activists
with a clear vision of an alternative society, one of religious encompassment, in
our terms. Nonetheless, argues Thurfjell, the constitutional foundation of the
Islamic Republic, the fruit of the revolution, brought together and perhaps synthesized to a degree traditional Islamic law and a European form of government.
The French constitution was the prototype of the latter, thereby Islamizing the
premises of the revolutionary statement of *The Declaration of the Rights of Man
and of the Citizen* of 1789. Iranian Islam thereby transcended and encompassed
the revolutionary thrust of combining secularism, individualism, and liberalism
that France most of all had brought to Western polities. In Iranian understanding, secularism is not oppressed by this transcendent encompassment, so long
as it knows its place. The struggle over this "place" became such a prominent
feature of the aftermath of the 2009 presidential election. Despite what we
are calling in Iran the synthesis of religion and politics through encompassment, by placing themselves between religious tradition and the secular ideals
of Western modernity, the Islamist leaders created tensions strongly felt in Iranian society.

Section 4, *Opening New Space for Religion*, relates to the opening of new
spaces for religion in postmodern globalism through chapters by Mira Amiras and Don Handelman. Amiras's chapter explores how the rejuvenation of
ethnic identity and language among the Amazigh (Berber) people of North
Africa opens potential space for evangelical proselytizing in this almost entirely
Muslim area. Drawing on the classic anthropological idea of nativism and nativistic movement, she shows how the Amazigh try to preserve (or recreate) an
Amazigh identity in the face of domination by Arabized regimes. Amazigh patriots urge legal recognition of indigenous language and culture, while regimes
in North Africa embrace Arabism, a growing ideology in the Maghreb since the
late 1940s. Arabic is the language of political society and religious revelation,
as well as that of the public sphere and mass culture. Islam and Arabism strive
for the formation of hegemonic scriptural states. Those North Africans who argue against indigenous separatist movements claim that Islam transcends (and
encompasses) both differences of ethnicity and national borders. To reject Arabic, the sacred language of revelation, is to reject Islam, the *'ummah*, and one's
place in the Hereafter. From the perspective of Amazigh activists, however,
there can be no excuse for the blatant Arab suppression of indigenous identity.
It is the language, the Tamazight, that has become the foremost marker of iden-

tity, "the purest thing a culture holds." Language is becoming the touchstone of Tamazight striving for nativistic holism, and it is the language that is suppressed most brutally by the North African regimes.

The attitude of the Amazigh activists to religion comes to hinge on religion's attitude to language, another factor that plays a role in religious competition (if it is possible to use this term in these overwhelmingly Muslim North African contexts). Evangelical proselytizing draws on the importance of indigenous language and culture (thus, the Gospels translated into Tamazight), making intense use of modern electronic media. So too do the activists of postmodern nativistic movements. Both political and religious activists, ruthlessly suppressed on the ground, thrive on the internet, in the anonymity of the online persona (though "virtual" agitation can be dangerous as well, witness the example of Karim Amer). The question is whether these "postmodern" identities, shifting, situational, individually chosen, can have any potential for insurgency comparable to that of nativistic movements of the past.

Religious terrorism in the present-day often blasts open space for religion. To explore aspects of terrorist phenomena, Handelman proposes taking on the idea of the "rhizome," developed by Deleuze and Guattari, and earlier applied to a variety of postmodern phenomena. The rhizome is a tuberous plant that has minimal roots, no clear boundaries, growing unpredictably and sporadically in all directions, yet with uncontrollable speed. Any point connects to any other, and the making of connections never ceases. Thus it is difficult to speak of "structure" in the usual sense in relation to the rhizome. So, too, it is difficult to speak of "network," which implies stable points of rest that do not exist in the rhizome. Rather, the rhizome is constituted by dynamics that are continuously self-transforming. Rhizomic dynamics characterize periods in the history of Al-Qaida, today the best documented (though murky) of global terrorist "organizations"—loosely put together, decentralized, flexible, spawning in all directions. Weak coupling between cells allows for (and encourages) greater agency and better adaptation to different environments; tight bonding within cells provides the sense of fictive kinship and loyalty. The rhizomic dynamic is antithetical to the bureaucratic organization of the modern state, its military, its police, with their hierarchical institutions, chains of command, and strict divisions of labor. Yet just as Islamism is related to European modernity, so terrorism as well has deep resonances in the atrocities of the modern, when it became so common for states to kill their own and others' subjects in organized military and paramilitary violence.

In line with earlier theorists who pointed to the deeply ritual character of religious violence, Handelman analyzes acts of terror as "self-exploding" self-sacrifice, a holistic ritual shaping of self and cosmos. Following recent research, he suggests that motivations for these acts are indeed "religious," lying beyond social and economic reasons, even beyond the pragmatism of political life. The religiosity underlying these acts is in a way postmodern. Islamic history and authority become disaggregated, no longer clustered within distinct lineages of doctrine or ideology, related more tenuously to traditional models of community solidarity. Traditional forms of grouping and identification are fragmented, scattered elements recycled for temporary constructions.

In his Afterword, Robert Innis takes a philosophic, semiotic perspective on the contributions, commenting that the basic source of strife that has been described is "epistemological," based in the right to manage material and symbolic resources, and arising from, as he writes, the "quest for power based upon certainty—or, to put it paradoxically, out of the felt, and needed, certainty of being certain." In struggling over certainty there is a "great refusal," that of refusing fallibility or others' refusal of infallibility. In order to explore this perspective, Innis refers to the semiotics of Charles Sanders Peirce, the great American polymath. Bringing in Peirce to think on the study of conflict, particularly through his "pragmatic maxim," is an unusual step and a fruitful one.

The rest of this Introduction is given over to foregrounding the chapters we have just discussed. We do this by first discussing the profound connections between values of holism, cosmos, and religion, and then by following a historical trace that offers one interpretation of how (not why) the West (particularly Western Europe) formed the kinds of relationships of religion and politics that the chapters come to address in the present day. We follow this by relating to the relationships of religion and politics in the present day through discussions of secularization, the New Paradigm in understanding religion, civil religion, and totalitarianism.

Holism, Cosmos, Religion

In foregrounding the studies of this volume, we must attend to the present-day neglect in research of religion as the prime conveyor of values of holism (of whatever scale) in a world continuously fragmented and reworked through politics. In using the term *holism* (referred to briefly earlier on), we modify the formulations of the anthropologists Louis Dumont (1977, 1986) and Bruce Kapferer (1988). Both Dumont (who developed his ideas of hierarchical holism through his monumental study of the structure of Hindu caste [1981]) and Kapferer (who contrasted the hierarchical holism of the Sri Lankan Buddhist state and the egalitarian individualism of Australia) understand holism (and individualism) as a value through which the social is organized.[10] Dumont (1986: 279) gives the following succinct definition of holism: "We call holist [holistic] an ideology [which he understands as "value"] that valorizes the social whole and neglects or subordinates [the value of] the human individual."

We modify this conception, especially in relation to religion, as follows: Holism entails the *integrity* of the *entirety*, where the entirety may be any kind of human unit—cosmos, group, and even the individual in certain instances—of differing scales, complexities, and consequences, and where these units are not necessarily bounded clearly (in the sense of being contained from their boundaries inward). In many instances the boundaries of entireties may be quite fuzzy or virtually nonexistent. We return to this problem further on in discussing cosmic holism and religion in archaic and traditional social orders. In our usage, the emphasis within an entirety is on *integrity*, of which there are (likely many) different ways of accomplishing. We use *integrity* here in the sense of entireness, completeness, soundness. Integrity is related to integration. But while *integration* refers more to parts added together to constitute a whole—so that in the first instance the connection between parts is additive—our intention for integrity refers more to the synergetic relationships within and among the parts of a whole—that is, the connections between parts must be *relational*.[11] In suggesting this perspective, we are disinterested in a definition of religion (of which there is more than a profusion). Instead we propose to refer to what can be called the *propensity* to holism with its intimations of religion in its many forms. Put otherwise, our concern, roughly speaking, is with how ontological worlds are holding together (rather than being held together) through the metaphysics of the human, through the imaginaries of the human, where "world" may vary from the cosmic to the individual, even as, for example, religion becomes civil, political, national, secular, individualized, as domains and niches of religion are forming and re-forming around the globe, carrying their seeds of holism.[12]

Our sense of *cosmos* refers to the epistemological entirety of the phenomenal lived-space of all entities, however the people in question understand this (without any necessary agreement amongst them on just what all of these entities are, as in the case of shamanic cosmos in Tyva). Thus, *cosmos* refers to the entirety of a life-world of all dimensions of existence (again, however this is understood by those who live in and through a particular cosmos). The idea of *cosmology* refers to the logic or logics of "order," as the ancient Greeks would have it. More precisely, the idea of cosmology refers here to the logic or logics of organization (for example, the kinds of connectedness and separation) through which a cosmos is put together. We return to logics of organization in the following section. With regard to cosmology, cosmos is an entirety, even as cosmoses may well overlap with one another (or contain great variation within themselves), and even as cosmoses vary substantially in their degrees of interior integrity. So, too, in the tiniest of human units, the individual: the interiority of the individual may constitute a whole or a search for personal holism—consider the sixteenth-century miller, the records of whose inquisition were studied by the historian Carlo Ginsburg (1981). One also may argue that the interiority of individual selfness is indeed social, constituted by a polyphony (indeed a dissonance) of interacting voices (Handelman 2002: 236–40) even as selfness is necessarily constituted no less through interaction among persons.

By enabling holism to take shape and to be lodged in vastly different scales of human existence, we give to the value of holism a very broad cachet in the organization of human units. This perhaps dulls its value in comparative analysis, which both Dumont and Kapferer powerfully and fruitfully engage with. Nevertheless, we proffer recognition to a value or complex of values that we think are essential to the existence of human being. Giving this cachet to holism enables us to think with it through lengthy durations with their potential continuities (perhaps we can say, their radical continuities), no less than relating to their radical transformations. So, too, this usage enables us to attribute the search for holism, the power of holism, to a variety of phenomena, especially the political in a variety of forms (civil, totalitarian) that have been termed "religions" while these attributes hardly recognize perhaps the most powerful quality of all—holism—that these phenomena share with religion. In this formulation we may well be accused once more of thinking tautologically, in circular fashion, in that there is no clear distinction between cause and effect in the relationship between our attribution of holism to a broad variety of phenomena and our discovery of holism in a broad variety of phenomena.

This concern should be lessened if we try to think less with linear cause-and-effect relationships and more with nonlinearity. In our view, (cosmic) worlds are organized primarily through nonlinearity. To put this otherwise: in different domains, on different levels, there is a *propensity*, a strong tendency, an ongoing dynamic toward holism.[13] The dynamic can be described as one of *folding*, of a concentration, intensification, densification of the relational, a folding that becomes an *enfolding*.[14] The distinctions between one enfolding and another (without relating to scale and complexity) are in the qualities mentioned in the previous sentence, while these may well be fuzzy and indistinctive, enabling overlapping, interpenetration, and the like.

When applied to the idea of cosmos, the idea of folding~enfolding enables the thinking of cosmos as holistic, to whatever degree. This leads to an elementary question, yet one rarely asked, in the postmodern age: *How is a cosmos held together?* Our preliminary response, however crude yet useful, has been that cosmos is held together either from its inside or from its outside, but it is held together. Now, one way of thinking on "religion" is that *it takes everything into itself*, without needing to specify what "everything" might be. Potentially, "religion" is just that, everything. As such, cosmos and "religion" in the ancient sense are isomorphic to a high degree, with cosmos taking in "religion." This enables us to use Dumont's idea of holism to relate to ancient cosmoses and to traditional and tribal ones. It also enables us to argue, again following Dumont, that (cosmic) holism was deeply fragmented with the Protestant Reformation, with the Enlightenment and the rise of individualism in European social orders.

We differ with Dumont, however, in arguing that holism never disappeared (in Protestant Europe as well), whether in terms of religion, in terms of social organization or, for that matter, in terms of the individual. This holistic folding continues without surcease.

Our point here is that holism revives relatively easily in relation to various local and global conditions (including those of secularism), whether through nationalisms, civil religions, new religions, translocal migration, foreign workers, and so on; and, wherever (and on whatever scale) holism resurges, it will have the qualities of holism we discussed. This is so regardless of what the surge or resurge is called, whether in academic disciplines or through popular propensities. One can think historically on the chapters by Lindquist, Hicks, Rosander, Coleman, and Amiras in this way. Historically, too, "politics" as a separate category (as with "religion") depended from the breakup of the holism of cosmos in much of Central and Western Europe. The prime reason that we began our discussion of religion and politics with "religion" is precisely because of the very long-term and continuing relationship between religion and holism.

Talal Asad (1993, 2003), among others, has argued that defining religion is a political exercise. Quite so, especially if one does only social history and/or the sociological study of society.[15] Yet if one tries to comprehend phenomena of religion from within themselves and/or to explain the continuities through time of religions of practice (which we think religions must be), then case-by-case deconstructionist approaches that explain how religions are put together—historically, socially, which is what Asad does—are of much less value. Religion as holism can hardly be deconstructed from within itself, since one of the qualities of holism is that quite often it submerges and conceals its origins as human creation.[16]

We use "politics" in a more commonsensical way than we do "religion." _Politics_ in the broadest sense refers to mundane games of power, struggles for access to and the right to manage material and symbolic resources that give prestige and satisfaction, including those of safe belonging and a secure identity in a mobile and fragmented world. Political ideologies resonate with religions in that they may offer full designs of social order; yet, unlike religion, political ideology is often openly a human creation insisting on its human origins, open to questioning, critique, negotiation, and revision. Yet even as the Western mindfulness of linear logic, schooled in the scientistic ethos of rational democracy, seeks to keep politics and religion apart, over and again to the chagrin of heirs of the Enlightenment, political communities that themselves are submerged and steeped in ideologies of peoplehood and nationhood take on attributes of holism (and correspondingly become difficult to deconstruct).

If we understand the profound affinity between holism and "religion," and to a degree between holism and modern nationalism, then the entanglement of religion and politics comes into clearer focus. The states that arose in the latter duration of the modern era also commonly insisted that their nationalisms— often keyed to peoplehood and nation—were holistic; thereby ensuring the ongoing entwinements between holisms of politics of nationhood and religion, clashing and converging. Thus for religion and nationalism to be strongly related, it is not necessary to argue that nationalism is the religion of the modern state (see Hayes 1968), nor to suggest (as Asad puts this, commenting critically on the jurist and philosopher, Carl Schmitt [1985: 36], whom we discuss in the last section of this Introduction) that "if we accept that religious ideas can be 'secularized,' that secularized concepts retain a *religious essence,* we might be induced to accept that nationalism has a religious origin" (Asad 1993: 189). We contend that what religion and modern nationalism have in common are *values of holism,* though the scale and organization of holisms differ. Whether a "religion" is or is not an "invented tradition" (Hobsbawm and Ranger 1983), a newly created phenomenon and, so, with little or no historical depth, is irrelevant to our argument. Relevant are values of holism, their embedment, organization, practice.

Moreover, of the surviving world religions, it is the monotheisms that generally have given special importance to their own historical depths as validating their significance in the world. Monotheistic holisms insist that (historical) time (both past and future) is integral to their own organization, thereby encompassing both "history" and its end, the End Time of linear time. The connection between monotheism and modern nationalism is clear. Modern secular nationalisms grew from the monotheistic premise of the significance of historical depth together with the monotheistic stress on absolute difference as a criterion of membership, which the modern nationalisms made their own. As Gray (2007: 191) argues, "Secular thinking is a legacy of Christianity and has no meaning except in a context of monotheism."

We emphasize again that holism is not an "essence"—rather, holism indexes how people and things (indeed, cosmos) are, are not, or are partially put together. Clearly, we agree that what constitutes holism varies historically, contextually. Yet we also think that the propensities toward holism in the human condition were and are widely spread, and that in general the human quest for the dynamic of holism is quite continuous, even if this is sought within and among fragments (including that of the individual) of what historically were different unities of cosmic organization. However, the issue of secularization (addressed further on), of persons becoming less religious in terms of formal observance or their leaving formal religion entirely has somewhat beclouded the problematics of holism; values of holism that in our view are very much present and influential.

Beginnings: Holistic Cosmos Held Together From Within Itself

Historically and ethnographically, cosmoses may be distinguished very broadly if crudely in terms of their logics of organization, between those held together largely from within themselves and those held together largely from their boundaries, from outside themselves. The former distinction applies to a wide variety of archaic, traditional, and tribal cosmoses; the latter distinction is relevant particularly to the surviving monotheisms (especially because of their effects around the globe). Cosmoses held together from within themselves are likely to be open ended. In such instances, cosmos goes on and on without meeting its own boundedness, its own limits, since it is not held together from outside itself, for example, by the impassability of the monotheistic Gods. In the most general of ways, what should this sort of cosmos be called? Perhaps *organic* (harking back to the overly maligned *Golden Bough* of Sir James Frazer)? Especially interesting at this point is that in the English language there is no word we can find to describe how something is integrated from within itself (perhaps the neologism, *intragrated,* would do?) rather than from outside itself, from its boundaries, a perfect monotheistic understanding of integration. In English (translated from the French) the word made prominent by the anthropologist Louis Dumont (1981) to describe how something is held together from outside itself is "encompassment." Our dictionary defines "encompass" as "to surround, to encircle, to include, to contain, to get in one's power."[17] And it is this kind of being held together that is crucial to monotheistic cosmos, to which we will turn to shortly.

Consider the following imaged dynamics of an ancient, holistic cosmos of Mahayana Buddhism, one that holds together from within itself, that of the cosmos of the Chinese Hua-yen school of Buddhism from the seventh century CE (Cook 1972: 2):

> Far away in the heavenly abode of the great god Indra, there is a wonderful net which has been hung by some cunning artificer in such a manner that it stretches out infinitely in all directions. In accordance with the extravagant tastes of deities, the artificer has hung a single glittering jewel in each "eye" of the net, and since the net itself is infinite in dimensions, the jewels are infinite in number. There hang the jewels glittering like stars of the first magnitude, a wonderful sight to behold. If we now arbitrarily select one of these jewels for inspection and look closely at it, we will discover that in its polished surface there are reflected *all* the other jewels in the net, infinite in number. Not only that, but each of the jewels reflected in this one jewel is also reflecting all the other jewels, so that there is an infinite reflecting process occurring. ... This is a cosmos in which there is an infinitely repeated interrelationship among all the members of the cosmos.

"This relationship is said to be one of simultaneous ... mutual inter-causality [which we can read as, of the mutually relational]." *Every* jewel would be said to be the sole cause for the infinity of jewels, but simultaneously the infinite whole of jewels is the cause for every single jewel. In terms of persons, "each ... is at once the cause for the whole and is caused by the whole, and what is called existence is a vast body made up of an infinity of [persons] all sustaining each other and defining each other. The cosmos is, in short, a self-creating, self-maintaining, and self-defining organism. ... what affects one item in the vast inventory of the cosmos affects every other individual therein" (Cook 1972: 3–4). The Hua-yen cosmos has no center, or, if there is a center, "it is everywhere. Man certainly is not the center, nor is some god" (Cook 1972: 4).[18] To these qualities we can add that the Hua-yen cosmos, as noted, has no external boundaries, unlike the absolute, impassable boundary between God and human being to which the surviving monotheisms have accustomed us to as natural and commonsensical. The cosmos is not enclosed from outside itself, in contrast to our understanding of the kind of holism suggested by Dumont's idea of "encompassment."

The absence of boundaries in the Hua-yen cosmos is attested to by the emphasis on the *infinity* of interrelationships that in a very strong sense *are* this cosmos. This cosmos holds together from within itself, through its intrarelationalities, the very compactness of these connections creating a dense mesh of intensities of mutual being. This is the kind of cosmos sometimes called "organic" in which cosmos lives wholly through itself, and within which human beings and most other entities are thought to be alive and interactive, if to differing degrees. This, for example, is how the historian of religion Diana Eck (1981: 161) writes of Hindu cosmos:

> The ontology of the Hindu tradition, insofar as it is a worldly tradition, is organic. ... By an "organic ontology" I mean that being is, by its very nature, living, growing, and divine. Creation ... is not an act of fashioning by a creator, but literally a "pouring forth" from the creator, as a spider emits a web from the stuff of its own body, or as a plant emerges from the contents of the seed, or as a whole person is shaped from the very cells of the embryo. ... This world is not a created order, but an ongoing process, a flow, a growth.

The Hua-yen and Hindu cosmoses are *continuous within themselves*—the continuousness is graduated, of gradations between levels without any abrupt shifts or ruptures between human beings and deities throughout itself—hierarchical yet flowing, with an abhorrence of stasis, identified with chaos. We contend that a continuousness of cosmos is generally immanent, not transcendent, since continuousness is primarily self-referential, referring to nothing outside itself since it has no exterior even as it is open-ended. This is a profound quality of the logic of organization of such cosmologies, for example, that of ancient Mesopotamia. Mesopotamian cosmos was more one of continuousness, of gradation, between deities and human beings, the deities integral to the ongoing existence of cosmos that was organic, alive, integrated from within itself, through itself (Jacobsen 1963: 142–46).

Consider the comment of an anthropologist of native South American peoples, asking: "Why cling to the modern obsession for separating humans and non-humans that is so foreign to the cosmologies of most peoples and—as the debates on the nature of the Indians in the sixteenth century suggest—is at the root of the division between "them" and "us"? (Velho 2004: 181). Consider too an instance from a Native American people, the Winnebago of the Great Lakes region. The story tells of a meeting of the most feared deity, Disease-Giver, and a Winnebago man. The man doubted the powers of Disease-Giver, mocked the deity, saying that were he to meet him he would " kick him off the earth" (Radin 1927: 375). Some time later he met Disease-Giver who asked him whether he still thought he could carry out his threat; to which the man replied that he did. "Thereupon Disease-Giver pointed his deadly finger at him, straight at his heart. The man did not budge. ... The deity pleads with the man to die, at least for a short time, so that people might not say that he, Disease-Giver, had failed in his mission!" (Radin 1927: 376). Though the man is later punished for his defiance, this does not detract from the continuousness between man and deity, without rupture, blockage, or hard-and-fast boundary making.

Analogous descriptions of organic cosmos with the qualities we ascribe to this abound for a host of tribal cosmologies.[19] Without being romantic about this, tribal cosmologies had integrity: These were cosmoses that were true to themselves within themselves, held together from within themselves through the density, the fullness of interacting connectivities with deep resonances between deities, human beings, other beings, and the continuousness of their shared cosmos (see Fishbane 1981: 30; Berger 1981: 15; Bellah 2005: 70; Jacobsen 1963: 143–48). It is worth quoting here the historian of religion, Michael Fishbane (1981: 29–31), writing of cosmos in ancient Near Eastern social orders: "I have in mind a cosmos perceived as a plenum [a condition of fullness], interlocking and interconnected in substance. This substance is a unity—insofar as nature is perceived as an unbroken continuum pulsating with divine life. ... It is the very power and vitality of the gods which constitutes this chain of natural being. The world is not merely the garment of the gods, it is also their very body and substance. ... The gods are immanent and near, and there is a deep harmony linking man and god and world. This harmony is truly ontological. And how could it be otherwise? Do not man, god, and world share the same substance. ... The same energies flow throughout all being. ... The 'sympathies' and homologies between gods-men-nature/world are most fully present in the rhythms of life itself." In our terms, in such cosmologies holism only sometimes depended on cosmic closure. Indeed, much of the historical and ethnographic evidence points to the contrary direction of *open, holistic cosmologies*. The qualities of "organic" cosmos that we discussed are crucial to our thinking that there indeed are alternative, holistic modes of holding cosmos together from within itself, in contrast to Dumontian encompassment, and that this is so especially in archaic, traditional, and tribal social orders.

In relation to the eventual emergence of Western cosmology, two great ruptures of holistic cosmoses developed historically. The first emerged during what is often called the Axial Age, roughly between the eighth and the third centuries BCE; and the second, the separation of politics from religion, sometimes referred to as the Great Separation (Lilla 2007), the deep rupture in Western European Christiandom provoked in particular by the Protestant Reformation, beginning in the sixteenth century. During this latter period, the Western Christian cosmos, shaped holistically during a thousand years of domination by the Roman Catholic Church, shattered, fragmented, and from these shards emerged the categories we came to call "religion" and "politics" (which, as Dumont [1977] argues so cogently, had not existed beforehand as distinct and distinctive domains). But it is the first great rupture of holistic cosmoses in antiquity that produced a monotheistic cosmos that contained the beginnings of a foundational break within itself, though the implications of this rupture took some hundreds of years to develop more explicitly.

Nonetheless, the relationship between cosmos and holism never disappeared, even through the Reformation and the social-historical emergence of the value of individualism that came to dominate much of the Western world through the present time, and, even as "religion" as a separate category was declared to be disappearing, with secularism in the ascendancy. Though we are underlining here the resonances between holism and "religion" through a broad, schematic, historical trace, we nevertheless emphasize that holism through its different scales and textures is nonetheless a still broader cosmic and social inclusion than is "religion," and so it has been through the ages. We say this with the understanding that values of holism in the emergent West came to be lodged in what are thought of as largely secular formations (the nation-state, civil religion, a large variety of communes, and indeed the individual himself and herself as a social unit with self-integrity).[20] The outcomes of social formations with powerful propensities toward holism were of course often so different from one another, and holisms themselves certainly differed (as yet a largely unexplored area); yet holism and the human are powerfully related. Values of holism, of differing holisms, inform and help to shape a very wide variety of social formations through time.

Returning to our immediate concern here with "religion," we suggest a general rule of thumb, one that borders on a proposition, to wit that *holism is a hallmark of what came to be called "religion,"* including religion that emphasizes the value of individualism, and, that understanding this even in rough-and-ready terms is crucial to appreciating most of the chapters of this book. Though we are not Durkheimians, we do think that when Durkheim (1995 [1912]: 429) wrote that "there is something eternal in religion that is destined to outlive the succession of particular symbols in which religious thought has clothed itself," he was implicating values of holism that we think resonate so powerfully with religion. We reiterate (though we can only intimate this in what follows) that values of holism never fully disappeared, neither in antiquity nor during the makings of modernity together with the rise of values of individualism, nation-alism, secularism. The so-called return of (the holism of) religion during the age of secularism is nothing of the kind, since values of holism had never been extinguished.

The First Great Rupture: The Axial Age

During the lengthy period between the eighth and the third centuries BCE, a variety of civilizations are said to have experienced what in our terms can be called ruptures of cosmic holism. The continuous, graduated cosmos held to-gether from within itself, which we outlined above, shattered. The rupture was ideational and social, though we concentrate on the former. The cultural loci for these radical ruptures in cosmic organization are usually given as Greece (of the philosophers), Palestine (of the Hebrew prophets), Iran (of Zoroaster), China (of Lao-tse), and India (of the Buddha). The rupture of cosmic holism severed the graduated continuousness of cosmos, such that deities were made separate from human beings. We surmise that this separation enabled what scholars call "transcendence" to emerge within cosmos. On the other side of the rupture, Deity became unknowable to human being, positioned way be-yond the capability, capacity, and knowability of the latter. How were human beings able now to relate to the now transcendent divine?

In a continuous cosmos, divine kings wove together human beings, nature, and gods. With the discontinuity of rupture, kings depended on gods yet were no longer divine beings themselves, no longer continuous with the divine. With the rupture, time left the cyclical, the circular, which usually had no be-ginning and no ending, except for a new beginning continuous with those that had occurred many times before. Instead, time became progressive, advancing, linear, seemingly historical, beginning with creation, its ending projected into the future when a soteriological (salvational) eschatology promised the healing of the cosmic rupture and the redemption of the human being in a perfected existence. The rupture created the otherworldly transcendence of the gods. God and gods were no longer of this world, even of this cosmos, no longer of the same substance as human beings and nature. God and gods become the absolute creators of cosmos rather than living within and integral to it, no longer sharing with human beings the substances from which cosmos was con-stituted.[21] Given the emergence of these qualities of cosmos, this is where the idea of encompassment enters our historical trace. S. N. Eisenstadt (1986: 1) in particular stresses the "basic tension between the transcendental and mun-dane orders" that encouraged the growth of reflexive rethinking on axioms of cosmos. Others have called this "critical thinking" and (borrowing from cyber-netic systemics) "second-order thinking."

Our Axial Age concern here is with what the historian of religion Jan Assman (2008: 75) calls the "revolutionary monotheism" of ancient Israel, and
how this indelibly changed the logics through which cosmos was held together.
The emergence of monotheism, regardless of how slowly this crystallized
(Wright 2000), ruptured the "concordance of all-in-all" (Fishbane 1981: 32)
and eventually came to posit the absolute separation of God the transcendent
Creator and humankind. God crossed this chasm at will; but human beings,
only through prayer and sacrifice. That which survived in the Hebrew Bible
(after all the ancient quarrels, exclusions, and redactions) was a cosmos constituted through the uncompromising difference between transcendent God and
mundane human being. Fishbane (1981: 34) comments, "No power could be
more embracing, no god more omnipotent, than the nameless, imageless God
of Israel." The Frankforts (1963: 241–44) argue that, "The God of the Hebrews
is pure being, unqualified, ineffable. He is *holy*. That means he is *sui generis*. ...
It means that all values are ultimately attributes of God alone. ... Only a God
who transcends every phenomenon ... can be the one and only ground of all
existence." This cannot be put too strongly in drawing the contrast between a
cosmos that holds together from within itself through itself, an organic cosmos,
in a sense a cosmos *without any outside yet also without hard-and-fast boundaries*,
and the emerging monotheistic cosmos of the Hebrew God who is boundless,
infinite, unnameable, unfathomable, who creates His finite cosmos as one ruptured from Himself.[22]

The rupturing of cosmos was emphasized in ancient Hebrew myth through
the Fall from Eden, the tearing apart of the continuousness between God and
humankind, which formed the boundary between God and the human, a
boundary unalterably and uncompromisingly moral (Evens 1995: 133). Harmony, *eudaimonia*, disappeared, given God's requirement that human beings
morally perfect themselves—unending efforts doomed to fail over and again
(Frankfort and Frankfort 1963: 244–45). Given the rupture and absolute
boundary between God and the human, the ancient Hebrew cosmos was held
together from its outside, its exterior, by the transcendent God whose eternal
existence did not depend on that of his finite cosmos. The integration of this
cosmos depended on its being *encompassed* by God, by his moral injunctions. As
noted, it is through the cosmic rupture that the transcendent comes into existence, that cosmos acquires exteriority, and so the capacity to be encompassed
from outside itself by transcendent deity. One consequence of this encompassment is as follows, "If the God of Israel is an All-Powerful God ... his 'all'-
powerfulness signifies that it is at his sole disposal, to be used as he sees fit,
that he may withdraw it just as he may withdraw himself from it, and that he
is above all alone in his power to make a covenant with man" (Nancy 2003:
42).[23] This aloneness of transcendence, we may say, the very separation, even
absence of the ancient deity from the cosmos he encompasses might also have

shaped him as so jealous and wrathful no less than loving. And, wrathful, un-able on occasion to control his fury, he might destroy his creation had he not put into place reminders of self-control, self-reminders of what he could find himself doing to human beings (Lorberbaum 2009: 539–40).

Nonetheless, the value of holism continued to exist powerfully, though as noted previously this value was turned into duration, into the passage of time, turned into mythistory (McNeil 1986) and stretched ontologically into the future, to the End of Days when the moral boundary between God and the human would dissipate.[24] The rupture of the monotheistic cosmos turned the perfection of the human being into the divine purpose of the universe and set before human beings the goal of organizing the world into one that was truly human and truly humane (Weil 1975) to be realized perhaps only in the distant future. The standards set before monotheistic humankind in a broken cosmos, before *every* monotheistic human being, came to be high and demanding, in practice, not to be met (as they never have been). Such a cosmos, organized around its ontological rupture, had contradiction and conflict rooted in its very epistemology of living (Dumont 1975). A bounded cosmos, and one whose in-ternal contradictions generated dynamics of difference (Dumont 1975: 156).[25] This cosmos differed, perhaps profoundly, from the kind of cosmos that held itself together within itself, through itself, without radical ruptures within itself, and so, relatively harmonious in its dynamics, yet unbounded. And if not har-monious, then so densely and intensely intrarelated that conflict and disrup-tion were worked through in the course of practices of existence.

In his classic study of the Hindu caste system, *Homo Hierarchicus*, Louis Dumont (1970) applied the idea of encompassment to interpret the workings of Hindu caste structure. Yet if we translate encompassment into cosmological terms, this Dumontian concept works best with a monotheistic cosmos (He-brew, Christian, Islamic) held together from outside itself by a transcendent be-ing. The concept of encompassment works far less well, if at all, with an organic cosmos holding itself together within and through its interiority of dense intra-connections. We surmise that Dumont's conception of encompassment that exfoliated in the most continuous and long lasting of ways in the monotheisms, was influenced by Durkheim (Dumont seems to give little direct attention to Durkheim, yet the affinities are difficult to evade).[26] We surmise further that Durkheim's conception of *totality* was influenced by the cosmic logic of mono-theism (though he likely would have denied this). In his great, late work, *The Elementary Forms of Religious Life*, Durkheim identified the "whole" with "the category of totality" (Nielsen 1999: 181, 186). Totality is the most inclusive of all social (one could say, cosmic) categories (Nielsen 1999: 202). Nielsen (1999: 229) continues: "Durkheim is keenly interested in the whole, or the notion of totality. This is the prime unifying category, the one enveloping [i.e., encompassing] all other categories. He equates this notion with both divinity and society. Divinity, or, more generally, religion, is, in turn, seen as a product of society. ... [Religion] is also an expression of society's essential nature, and, in fact, symbolically captures that nature better than any other form of representation." Put into our terms, this may be phrased as follows: monotheistic society encompassed itself and unified itself through cosmos, from which, later on, the category, religion, was generated. It was through cosmos (and later, through the category of religion) that society gestated. This may be why, as we contend, when the value of holism is around, "religion" (and/or its analogues) are close by.

We are arguing that the cosmic holism of ancient Hebrew monotheism, emerging during a lengthy period (see Serandour 2005: 44), and then the emergence of the other surviving monotheisms and their cosmic holisms, were strongly associated with a cosmic logic of encompassment. A holistic, cosmic logic of encompassment is profoundly, if crudely, distinct from a holistic, cosmic logic of a universe that holds itself together from within and through itself (for which we suggested the neologism *intragration*). This distinction enables us to argue that holism continued to be crucial in the historical emergence of monotheistic cosmoses even as, over a millennium later, the Western Christian cosmos was torn asunder into "religion" and "politics."[27] In other words, values of holism hardly disappeared when "religion" and "politics" emerged as relatively autonomous domains, and, this is so even when the idea of cosmic entirety slowly fades in significance in postmodern times.

Jan Assman (2008: 84) sees in ancient monotheism that which he calls the "mosaic distinction." This is the distinction between absolute truth and falsehood, such that religion became the province of truth. In our terms, absolute truth was integral to cosmic encompassment and to the rupture between God and human being. Absolute truth belonged to the transcendent realm of God and His revelation, while falsehood, its duplicity and fuzziness, was located in mundane living. In making these absolutist distinctions in its ruptured cosmos, ancient Hebrew monotheism showed itself as exclusive (Assman 2008: 110), and from this exclusivity according to Assman (2008: 144) was born *religious* violence, "violence with reference to the will of God," violence that took its force from the very will and Being of God, a phenomenon that later became (through the present) self-evident in the struggle between European religions and between religion and secularity. In these terms the self-exploders of Handelman's chapter are doing religious violence. Are the Americans fighting the "war against evil," foregrounded by Coleman's chapter, also doing so? The absolutist distinction between truth and falsehood enabled the absolutist distinction between friend and foe, pure and impure (pagans, unbelievers, heretics, the enemies of God). Cosmic holism in the ruptured cosmos could perhaps only exist through being encompassed by God~religion.

The Second Great Rupture:
Encompassment, Protestantism, Individualism

The first great cosmic rupture eventually shaped ancient Hebrew monothe-ism as cosmos encompassed by deity. One more thought before departing this thread, but one that continues something of the interior holism of the organic cosmos. The psychologist and Judaic scholar, Mordechai Rottenberg, argued some decades ago that Judaism values the social relationship and its survival above that of human being as an autonomous, agentic individual. Without pursuing this here, something of the holism of organic cosmos continued in ancient Judaism. However, as Louis Dumont argues, the early Christianity of late antiquity—within the Hellenistic world with its powerful thrusts toward individualism—already carried the seeds of the value of individualism into monotheism and, we add, in this broke with ancient Judaism.[28] That ancient value of the Christian individual was not similar to that of our era: The ancient Christian individual was an individual-in-relation-to-God, thus an out-worldly individual (one could say, an otherworldly individual), as against our individ-ual-in-the-world, our in-worldly individual (Dumont 1986: 26–51). Nonethe-less, the ancient Christian individual undoubtedly was encompassed by deity and by the church as an institution.

Scholars generally agree that early Christianity emerged from, and to vari-ous degrees in relation to, ancient Judaism. Like Judaism (and later, Islam), Christianity claimed a monopoly of the truth, and so was hardly open to syn-cretism with other religions of the Roman Empire. Moreover, Christians formed themselves not as the cult of a particular people or nation within the empire, but "claimed that they had replaced the Jews as the chosen people on earth, yet they also claimed that their kingdom was in heaven; and as the supranational agents of an œcumenical message they naturally aspired to convert the entire world, let alone the empire" (Athanassiadi and Frede 1999: 10). Despite the mediation of the God-man, Jesus (the logic of such mediation and modifica-tion of the cosmic rupture was absent from Judaism), the Kingdom of Heaven encompassed that on earth. Whatever else it was, this truth was the mono-theistic encompassment of cosmos, and this was integral to Christian self-understanding as a universal religion. With the conversion to Christianity of the Emperor Constantine at the beginning of the fourth century, and Christi-anity becoming the state religion of empire, the issue of church-state relations became preeminent. As Dumont (1986: 44) put this, "What was to be a Chris-tian State?" What was to be superior, state or church? In other words, what was to encompass what? Here our concern is with the Western, Latin church, leading directly into Europe and beyond (on developments in the Eastern Or-thodox church, see Al-Azmeh 2004).

Values of holism, as they continued to be carried, were embedded deeply in the ongoing struggle between the church and political authority. Around 500 CE, Pope Gelasius stated that though in mundane matters priests were to obey imperial law, ultimate authority, the opening to salvation, lay with the priests. Said Gelasius, "Priests are superior, for they are inferior only on an inferior level" (Dumont 1986: 46). Dumont (1986: 48) understands Gelasius's texts as saying that, "if the Church is *in* the Empire with respect to worldly matters, the Empire is *in* the Church regarding things divine" (italics in the original). In terms of cosmos, church encompassed empire; but, no less, became increasingly political during the coming centuries. In becoming political, the church spiritualized the state. The distinction between church and state became less one of a division of labors between priest and king, and more one of differences of degree. Church and state were of the same divine nature, of which the church had more, the state less. The difference became that of the "spiritual" and the "temporal," with "the spiritual ... conceived as superior to the temporal on the temporal level itself, as if it were a superior degree of the temporal, or, so to speak, the temporal raised to a superior power." Dumont continues, "later on, the Pope will be conceived as "delegating" the temporal power to the Emperor as his 'deputy'" (Dumont 1986: 50).

Yet, in becoming spiritualized, the political realm was made to participate in the absolute, universal values of the church. The state, argues Dumont (1986: 51), was "consecrated in quite a new manner." A unified political configuration, call it the state, emerged with the potential to carry absolute values—realized much later in the *modern state* that, says Dumont (1986: 51), is a "*transformed Church*" (our emphasis). In our terms, the modern state has profound propensities toward holism even as so many of its political lineaments are powerfully secular; and, through these propensities, conceptions like nationalism-as-religion, civil religion, secular religion, and so forth, arise and abound.

During late antiquity and the Middle Ages, Western monotheistic kingship became one sort of inflection of sacral kingship. Just as encompassing divinity was irreducible and indivisible, so, too, was royal power. Values of cosmic holism were continuous with values of the holism of royalty and kingdom; and God and king both partook of qualities of limitless energy, boundless majesty, and absolute virtue (Al-Azmeh 2004: 110). From Clovis (the first Catholic king of the Franks) onward, French kings received their royal, ritual anointing (a reprise on baptismal anointing) with chrism (myrrh) said to have been brought from heaven by a dove (Nelson 1987: 163), and later on the Virgin herself brought holy oil to Thomas à Becket for the anointing of English kings (Al-Azmeh 2004: 21). The anointing, intended to make the king immune to physical attack, singled him out and set him apart from other nobility (Saberwal 1991: 118). According to historian Janet Nelson (1987: 155–69, 250–55), this ritual implied that the church could make a king, yet, too, it could unmake the king. On Christmas Day, 800, Charlemagne was made emperor in the name of the Christian empire by the pope in Rome.[29] Just as God, encompassing his cosmos, was absolutist, so, too, ideally was the sacral monarch who made and guarded order holistically. Values of encompassing cosmic holism permeated everyday popular culture of the European Middle Ages. Furthermore, medieval historian Aron Gurevich (1985, 1990) argues powerfully that such popular culture was characterized by the realism of the existential continuity of deity and human (for one of many instances, see Nagy 2004). In sum, the church, the triumph of holism through encompassment (and the most direct instantiation of cosmic encompassment), constituted "an organisational model of continental scale and extraordinary durability" (Saberwal 1991: 120). Glossing, we can say that this configuration generally held together more or less until the Protestant Reformation.

For our purposes, the Reformation put to the test our argument that the values of holism continue on in Europe, through the rise of the value of the individual and the onset of European secularization. The Reformation upended and took apart the holistic encompassment of cosmos that the church embodied. This dismemberment and leveling of the hierarchy of cosmic embodiment generated the individual as a being in its own right, a being independent in its agency, an essentially nonsocial moral being (Dumont 1977: 8), and, as such, a being in direct relationship with all-powerful God. God, we can say, came to encompass each individual within a multitude of individuals (thereby also encompassing the multitude), each of whom became responsible to a high degree for his and her own fate in the totality of divine cosmos. The church turned into an "association made up of individuals" (1986: 58). As such, from the ruins of the encompassing cosmos, "religion" came into existence as a distinct category. Without the encompassing hierarchy of the cosmic church, egalitarian values of social order came to the fore, and the "political individual" emerged as an active agent in its own right and so, too, the category or domain of the "political."

With Calvinism, "the Church encompassing the State ... dissolved as a holistic institution" (Dumont 1986: 59). And with the ethos of Calvinist predestination, individualist values ruled. The hierarchical Christian state "was atomized at two levels: it was replaced by a number of individual States, themselves made up of individual men" (Dumont 1986: 73). Did this mean that within the Protestant states the propensities toward encompassing holism disappeared? Dumont (1986: 74) certainly does not argue this with respect to the state in relation to itself, as a hierarchically coherent entity based on the union of men. Indeed he (1977: 15) says that "the State inherited its essential features from the Church, which it superseded as the global society." Yet implicit in the state as an association of individuals is a powerful thrust of coercion in the image of the Leviathan of Hobbes. A multitude of hierarchical, sovereign states—ruled top-down—rose into prominence.

Not to be overlooked is, as Dumont implies above, that the category of the political acquired qualities of the values of holism even as values of individualism began to flourish. In at least one major example in Central Europe, that of the German-speaking lands, the propensity to values of holism, now within the form of the sovereign state, was very powerful. This propensity endeavored to institute a kind of state holism through what was called "the science of police," and to do this in encompassing fashion, from the top down, so that this holism would flourish from the bottom up. The intention was to bring encompassing order—individual, social—to most domains of life. The science of police shifted encompassing holism from religion and lodged this in the political while not denying the value of the individual within the social, within the group, through which the individual took in the very sense of "value" itself. Within this too were the first stirrings of secularism in Central Europe, though this term had yet to come into existence. We discuss aspects of secularism and individualism in the section after the coming one.

The Rational Holism of the Well-Ordered Police State in Central Europe

The onset of the great rupture of the Protestant Reformation in the early sixteenth century marked the beginning of the end of the dominance of the cosmic encompassment of the church and of its theological, political acolyte, the Holy Roman Empire. In Foucault's (2007: 348) terms, that which came into being was "a new rationality by … carving out the domain of the state in the great cosmo-theological world of medieval and Renaissance thought." The empire was characterized by a multitude of smaller and larger states and principalities that were wracked by the wars of religion between Catholics and Protestants. The primarily religious conflict of the Thirty Years' War (1618–1648) was ended by the peace of Westphalia (1648), which recognized Calvinism as the third legal religion of the empire along with Catholicism and Lutheranism, and legitimated the existence of the nation-state. The peace of Westphalia emerged from "the strong conviction at the time in the virtues of a centralized and unified political authority as a guarantor of virtuous governance" (Harding and Harding 2006: 411). Westphalia formally recognized the territorial integrity of the multitude of German-speaking principalities (which for a century many had been exercising in practice). The empire lost its holy status but continued to survive as a state of sorts. Foucault (2007: 317) comments on these principalities, "We can think of these German states, which were constituted, reorganized, and sometimes even fabricated at the time of the treaty of Westphalia ... as veritable small, micro-state laboratories that could serve both as models and sites of experiment."

During the seventeenth and eighteenth centuries, the principalities practiced ways of ordering the state through what has been called "police," "the well-ordered police state," or "the science of police" (Raeff 1983; see also Oestrich 1982: 155–65). The science of police emerged fully from the domain of the political in the German microstates. These states, coming out of the feudal structure of the occidental Christian Empire, had no tradition of specialized administrative personnel, though administrative specialization began to be developed and taught in the German universities. Foucault (2007: 318) calls this specialization "something with practically no equivalent in Europe ... which from the middle or end of the seventeenth century to the end of the eighteenth century is an absolutely German speciality that spreads throughout Europe and exerts a crucial influence." With the shattering of the occidental Christian cosmos and Christian Empire and the rejection of ecclesiastical institutions, it was the secular authorities, the secular political domain, that stepped in with ordinances of the science of police (Raeff 1983: 56). The science of police was neither the police nor police state in today's sense of these terms. The practices called the science of police deliberately planned and administered the shape and substance of community (*gemeinschaft*), such that people would behave as they should for the common good (*res publica*), the good that encompassed them all and that in this case specifically included the "set of means that serve the splendor of the entire state and the happiness of all its citizens" (Foucault 2007: 313–14), the desirability of their living happy, fruitful, productive lives. This was to be accomplished by "establishing a closer connection between the moral realm and the life-style of the population ... [the] acceptance of the duties of earthly existence for its own sake. It was imperative that the *same* norms and values inform every activity of the individual and group" (Raeff 1983: 88, italics added). In this, the beliefs and teachings of the churches had a vital role; yet the churches were under the protection of the state, and in the Protestant states the ordinances of police regulated the proper performance of all aspects of church life, and first and foremost, ritual (Raeff 1983: 59).

To practice, and so to create the good of all—the state and its citizens—required the deliberate, one could say rational, standardization and exactness in specifying similarity and difference in order to shape uniform classifications, thereby to compare and to control persons in the most specific of ways (Kharkhordin 2001: 227). Thus statistical information was collected on the resources and capacities of populations and their territories (rates of birth and death appeared; covert denunciation of neighbors was commended). New classifications based on age, sex, occupation, and health were invented, intended to increase wealth and population, but also to enable intervention in and to alleviate a wide variety of social problems. People would be enabled to live happier lives, as individuals, as groups, within the nexus of concerned regulation. Through correct practices, people were *naturalized,* one could say, into perceiving these ways of living *as best for the well-being of one and all.* These practices of togetherness affected the group-centered character of social order, the sense that good ways of living were integral to good social relationships. Though the beginnings of the science of police had powerful qualities of imposition and coercion, with time these ways of living, and living together, came to be felt as naturally right for the interiority of collectivity, perhaps even of sprouting from values of community (*gemeinschaft*) and undergirded we think, by values of holism. Nonetheless, the culture of these states was occidental Christian, and the values of holism were those of encompassment. These states were, as Dumont contended, a transformed church.

The science of police was practiced by promulgating and applying standardized administrative ordinances and rules for behavior within very broad domains of intervention, yet in highly specific detail. So, in various places the science of police set rules for the use of the personal pronoun between parents and children, enumerating what should be drunk and consumed during wedding feasts, the number of people permitted to attend a christening, and so forth and so on.[30] A rational science of endless, detailed listings of classification in the interests of the "good order of public matters" (Pasquino 1991: 111), in the interests of forming and shaping of collectivity as a community of disciplined, hardworking, industrious people, for the good of the state (Raeff 1983: 87–88). Police regulations tried to organize everything that went unregulated, that lacked clear form in a society of the three estates. This was "a great effort of formation of the social body, one that demanded degrees of order that reached beyond law and encroached on domains new to becoming occupied by public ordering (Pasquino 1991: 111).[31] The science of police established a "gridwork of order" (Gordon 1991: 20) that paid close, regulating attention to the itemization, movement, and flow of persons and goods. Above all, this grid of order and its classifications were totalizing in their control of difference, variance, variation, idiosyncrasy.

The science of police totalized the control of sameness and difference through taking responsibility for society and sociality (Foucault 2007: 326). Central to the ethos of living that was to be more than just living was the linking of state's strength and the felicity of the individual, such that men's happiness was turned into the utility of the state, indeed the very strength of the state (Foucault 2007: 327). The same kind of link held for communities. Through compartmentalization (like the number of people permitted to attend a christening) the family was made more private, separated more from extended kin and social networks. The person was individualized (and expected to become a more productive and efficient worker) and individuated (and accentuated as a unit of counting and governance). But together with this the community became *solidary* through its self-managing and self-policing, all for the common good; and persons felt the significance of the organizing community in their lives, as individuals and as group members. Thus the public sphere penetrated deeply within the private, so that the emergence of the private sphere (the family, the individual) incorporated powerful visions of the public good as a collective endeavor, one that made the private domain reliant on that of the public and its governance. Governance had opened points of entry into the private sphere, and the private sphere was imbued with values of the public.

The powerful sense of solidary, organic groupness and gemeinschaft that came into existence in the German principalities emerged together with the power of this groupness to shape and discipline the person as an individual, yet as the exercise of power integral to the happiness of both community and individual. In Foucault's terms, the pastoral care of the state was joined to the care of selfhood. Articulated together were the welfare of the group and the well-being of the individual who was managed in the first instance from outside himself, leading him to value his membership in and feelings for groupness and community, and his creative independence within groupness. Most intriguing, the enabling of both division (through classification) and unification eventually came to grow from the deeply organic sense of groupness, bottom-up, as it were—out of the well-being and happiness of community and not simply from the coercion of authority. The German sociologist Ferdinand Toennies called this adhesion to the holism of gemeinschaft, the "spontaneous will" (*naturwille*), in our terms the utter naturalization of the individual into the encompassment of the social whole. Therefore this enablement did not alienate levels of social order from one another, for culturally they came to grow out of one another—their relationship was continuous with one another, with individual and individualism not alienated from the totality of the social, but rather firmly embedded within and integral to community. This continuousness of state, nation, community, and the individual were (and are) profoundly related to the socialization of the child, the cultural project of upbringing and education (*erziehung*), such that "the smallest unit [the individual] carries the burden of the largest [the community], both bound within one order" (Norman 1991: 18).

By the beginning of the nineteenth century, the German philosopher Johann Gottlieb Fichte could say that the goal of social order was "the complete unity and unanimity of all its members" (quoted in Hartman 1997: 123). In Europe there were powerful accelerations into individualism, especially in the aftermath of the Declaration of the Rights of Man and the Citizen of 1789 (given pride of place both by Dumont and Foucault). Yet in the German-speaking lands in the aftermath of the science of police, despite the drive to individualism, there also were strong propensities that had shifted religious encompassment toward secular holism that merged together what we are calling cosmos held together from within itself and the encompassing cosmos that took the values of the modern state. In the Prussian state, which unified Germany politically in the nineteenth century, the top-down formation of the absolutist statehood met the more bottom-up values of holistic community, the long-term effects of the science of police.

Some Directions of Secularization

As we noted the political philosopher, John Gray (2007: 190) points out that "secular thinking is a legacy of Christianity and has no meaning except in a context of monotheism." Indeed, "secularization" was a process rather peculiar to Western Europe. Certain of the intellectual grounds for the idea of secularization—most radically, atheism, a cosmos without God—were formed in France by Jean Bodin's *Heptiplomeres* (1596), a critique of fundamental doctrines of Christianity that circulated widely in manuscript but was not actually published until the nineteenth century; in England by Thomas Hobbes's seventeenth-century theory of the state in his *Leviathan,* in which the church's monopoly on decision was challenged and broken; and in Germany by Gotthold Lessing's play, *Nathan the Wise* (1779).[32] In Lessing's drama, Christianity is shown as only one of the monotheisms, such that the religion of Christ the Savior was turned into that of a deistic belief in a general, abstract deity (see Ulmen 1985: 38–40). Yet one should note that until today, rarely (and with mixed success) are absolute distinctions made between religion and secularity, such that secularity would be equated with atheism. In this regard, secularization has only rarely developed into a-theism, but more into agnosticism. In terms of the scholarly forming of the secularization concept, the first usage seems to date from 1908, in a lecture on "The Secularization of History" (Ulmen 1985: 15), though the most significant application was that of Weber in his *Protestant Ethic and the Spirit of Capitalism* (1958), in which he related secularization to modernization. Weber often linked the "disenchantment of the world," the loss of magic in the cosmos, to its "rationalization," while insisting that rationalization itself was the product of Occidental culture. Analytically, the cognitive mode of the rational was linked to the secularization of society and the individual, and rationality and secularization were linked to the emergence of capitalism and modernization. Within this configuration of processes, the autonomous economic sphere emerged from that of the political.

This configuration worked best in Protestant Europe, where the individual-as-value flourished within Pietism, which located religion in a personal, inner realm of freedom, and which gave the state greater leeway in forming the political around the individual. Thus on the one hand, civil rights began not as freedom from religion, but as freedom for religion, represented by radical Protestant sects (Casanova 1994: 56), while on the other, the multiple principalities

that emerged from the Peace of Westphalia developed national churches that
were dependent on these states. As we intimated in the previous section, the
new, autonomous, secularizing state encompassed the means of social control
and violence within its territory, took over from the church the tending to the
welfare of its citizens, and regulated, organized, and mobilized a spectrum of
social domains in its service and legitimation. The church became one of these
domains under the protection of the state and was called upon to buttress the
authority and power of the latter. Capitalism introduced new relations between
individual and state, new norms and values that were at odds with those of
the Catholic Church, such as attitudes toward poverty, charity and usury. Yet
as the economy emerged as an autonomous sphere of activity, it became less
amenable to moral regulation by religion, and money became an impersonal
and generalizable medium of social interaction and relationship. Not only was
capitalism not in need of the moral and ideological support of religion, but
capitalist relations also began to penetrate and colonize the religious sphere
itself, subordinating this to the logic of commodification through which relations between people and things came to take precedence over relations among
people (Casanova 1994: 25; Dumont 1977: 15).

We underscore once more the significance of the forming of the value of the
individual as an autonomous moral being, one wholly in the world (Dumont
1977: 8), in counterpoint to the continuing intimations of holism in community but also in the diverse fragments of Protestantism. The significance of the
individual-as-value for the positioning of Western religion in the emergence
of modernity cannot be overemphasized. Here we point especially to the great
advantage that the individual-as-value gave to the very religion that fragmentation, secularization, and Economic Man were thought to be destroying.
The individual became the (creator of and) carrier of new religions, whatever
names were given to them. Thus religions came into existence through small,
even tiny social units; these had the advantage of malleability, of growing in
the interstices between institutions and organizations, and of flexibility, of the
individual carrier able to slip into social cracks that institutions could not …
and so it continues through the globalizing present.

Perhaps to a greater extent than previously, historical individuals became
freer to invent and shape religions (and their cosmoses) regardless of the scale
of these religions in practice. And, if as we contend, the presence of holism intimates religion, however tiny or seemingly insignificant the cosmos concerned,
then (*pace* Asad) there is a profound dynamic shared in practice by a great
variety of "religions," both those called religious and those labeled secular. The
Catholic Inquisition did its determined best (especially before the Reformation,
but later as well) to suppress and destroy the creative Christian religious imagination and the invention of religions (which spanned a very broad spectrum
of potentialities) (see, for example, Le Roy Ladurie 1978; Ginzburg 1980), as

it did to the creative science of Galileo and others. By contrast, Protestantism generated (and continues to do so) a profusion of sects, churches, persuasions, and cults. Moreover, in varieties of Protestantism, like Pietism (with its emphasis on personal holiness), much of the locus of being religious in spirit became focused in the laity, within the deep, emotional interior of the individual who prized this inwardness of devotion as against the formalism of worship in the major churches of the seventeenth and eighteenth centuries (e.g., Fogleman 2003).

In very broad terms, the implications of religious individualism for globalization have been and continue to be profound in the present day (witness the international shamans of Lindquist's chapter and the Imam of Fuengirola of Evers Rosander's). Csordas (2009) refers to the degrees of "portable practice" of religious rites; thus the ease with which rituals can be learned, and whether religions are necessarily tied to particular cultural contexts, among other factors in their globalization. Clifford Geertz (2005: 11), with his inimitable turn of phrase, referred to what we can call the traveling religious individual, the traveling carrier, as "a portable persona, a movable subject position." "Globalizing smallness" likely has had a tremendous impact on the potential permutations of religious groups, hybridic or not. But "smallness" may also refer to simple technological devices that enable religious groups and congregations separated by vast distances to participate together. For example, transnational Haitian religious communities—Vodouist and Catholic—are widely dispersed. Yet the use of audio- and videocassettes sent back and forth between Haiti and its diaspora create vast performative spaces through which coreligionists do their rites together (Richman and Rey 2009). Another instance was that of the late Lubavitcher (Chabad) rebbe whose actual presence was valued immensely by his disciples. But his headquarters were in New York City and many of his disciples were in Israel. To address his followers in Israel by cassette necessarily involved a time lag, which destroyed the value of the immediacy of presence. So he would call them in their religious boarding schools via satellite transmission, often tumbling them out of bed (given the time difference), but giving them the precious immediacy of his presence.

The holistic intimations of religion also had a profound effect on the shaping of the liberal, secular individual. The watershed of secular individualism undoubtedly was the great egalitarian Declaration of the Rights of Man and the Citizen of the French Revolution. Yet, as Dumont (1986: 97) notes, Tocqueville understood that "the French Revolution had been at bottom a religious phenomenon in the sense of a movement which had willed itself absolute and wanted to recast the whole of human existence, in contradistinction to the American Revolution where democratic political theory remained confined to its proper domain [that of politics] and was complemented and supported by a strict Christian faith."

For many of its contemporary advocates, secularism became, as Gray (2007: 190) argues, "not so much a view of the world as a political doctrine. In this sense a secular state is one that banishes religion from public life while leaving people free to believe what they like." Gray regards this "rationalist" position as utterly unreal, its adherents not only ignoring history but also forgetting that "secular creeds are formed from religious concepts, and suppressing religion does not mean it ceases to control thinking and behaviour. Like repressed sexual desire, faith returns, often in grotesque forms, to govern the lives of those who deny it" (2007: 190). Rather than refer to "faith" as such, we prefer to argue that the propensities for varieties of holism reassert their intimations and implications. Perhaps the most extreme case of the twentieth century was that of the Soviet Union, in which "scientific materialism" and Marxist-Leninist philosophy came to underlie and inform an all-embracing totalization of social order, giving legitimacy to all spheres of life, regulating the methods and contents of science, providing an evolutionist theory of history (historical materialism), and buttressing political absolutism. Atheism (Bercken 1989: 121–28) undertook the war against the "opium of the people," as Marx called religion, killing clergy by the thousands and destroying churches or turning them into museums of atheism, events so relevant to Lindquist's discussion of the revival of religion in post-Soviet Tyva. Soviet atheism was no less preoccupied with the evolution of the correct, world-saving, egalitarian holism to be produced through time by dialectical materialism. Despite atheism's extreme hostility to religion, its absolutism nonetheless contained propensities toward holism. Again, despite the destruction of religion, these propensities intimated varieties of religion, even if this one was called "scientific atheism."

Religious Pluralism, the New Paradigm, Globalization

In late modernity the pluralization of religious options became a focus of theorizing, and the New Paradigm was developed to fine-tune ideas of secularization. The argument is that the disestablishment of the official churches engenders the pluralistic setting in which religions of all kinds thrive, as world-views and practices, in public spheres and in popular imagination. Cultural pluralism is said to inspire religious creativity, and religion, in its turn, becomes the main carrier of cultural pluralism (Warner 1993; Smith 1998). Many of these religions are "small, portable, accessible" (Smith 1998: 106). Myth, magic, and mystery return in individual religiosities created through the "mixing of codes" (Voye 1995), through blending the esoteric and the popular, scientific, and religious discourses, ideas, and practices from various parts of the world. In many new religions (and New Age phenomena), knowledge and knowledge-gathering emphasize lateral movement across conventional boundaries to gather elements in putting together hybrid practices and beliefs. As Swatos and Christiano (2002: 221) argue, a "religious ferment of contesting epistemologies" is at work in the world. Religious pluralism creates the grounds for religious competition, a marketplace where buyers are free to pick and choose from the menu of "religion a la carte" (e.g., Luckman 1967). Certainly one question is why certain religions win this competition in particular circumstances. In his book on the Evangelical movement, Coleman (2000) demonstrated how Evangelicism has spread over the globe owing to its message of economic prosperity and indeed, not least, to its very image of being global. Lindquist's chapter in this volume shows how Northern Buddhism and shamanism in Tyva provide different versions of being global, and how an advantage in religious competition depends on particular historical circumstances, yet no less on the internal logics of these religions.

In such pluralistic conditions, religion becomes the most vital and visible means for expressing group identities, and thus a primary tool of identity politics. Despite the degrees to which religion turns individualistic, it remains no less holistic, valorizing wholes regardless of their scale.[33] This may be why religious identities are so deeply ingrained and so passionately adhered to: to live by as well as to die for. There are many claims that the nation-state is losing its foothold in the globalizing world, and so is turning to religion to boost its authority, as transpires from the case studies in this volume, especially those set in the postcolonial world. Bauman (1997) suggests that the allure of fundamentalism lies exactly in its power to offer strong identities, "emancipating the converted from the agonies of choice," lifting the responsibility of putting together postmodern identities that ensure material success and experiential satisfaction.

Early on in discussions of globalization, religion was pointed to as one of its oldest and most important channels, or, as Hannerz (1996: 48) puts it, frames that organize flows of meaning and cultural diversity across the globe. There is little doubt that at the very least since the Axial Age, there were great movements of ideas and materials between the Mediterranean and East Asia. When Buddhism spread in India under Emperor Ashoka (273–232 BCE), and when Yellow Emperor Taoism and Confucianism spread in China during the Han Dynasty (206 BCE–220 CE), it was the movement of people, texts, practices, that was accepted in places far from those of their origin and that changed cultural landscapes in the process, connecting peoples over space and through cultural differences. What, then, is new?

Trying to grasp the emergent features of the world brought about by globalization, analysts talk about the new web of connectivities, the intensity, extensivity, and velocity of connections between people and places that restructures life for many populations most everywhere, redefining time, space, identity, and agency at the most local levels. As Peter Beyer (1994) notes, perhaps not all local cultures have been changed, but what has definitely changed is the world in which these cultures exist. Csordas (1997) suggests that globalized religious movements are shaped by the "post-modern condition of culture," in which symbolic forms are dissociated from their referents, and when there no longer is any shared reality behind their signs. Authority over meaning and discourse is decentered, and politics becomes a struggle over signification—over defining master signifiers such as "Islam," "Christianity," or "Human Rights." When religious forms are entwined with other frameworks of globalization—notably those of trade, popular culture, and communication technologies—genres and cultural forms mix and merge, attenuating the differences between high and low culture; between economics, religion, and art; between real and imagined. Symbols and practices, disengaged from their referents and circulating around the globe, provide raw materials for creating identities, supporting local and regional voices earlier quelled by grand narratives. Patterns of migration are changing: the image of an impoverished and uprooted migrant, leaving his country behind for good and trying to assimilate in the melting pot of a Western country, is only part of the picture. Connected through myriads of embodied and disembodied networks, migrants maintain close contacts with their home-lands, constructing hybrid, fluid, multiple identities.

Nation-states no longer represent social space for primary identification—the world is becoming deterritorialized. Concurrently, through the process of reterritorialization, people bring their "cultures" to new localities. Religious forms and meanings, flowing along the trajectories of globalization, offer new resources for migrants with which to remap their territories and to reconnect with old homelands (Vasquez and Marquardt 2003). Do these arguments affect our contentions regarding propensities to holism? We think not. These propensities are integral to the social (including the hidden social within the individual [Handelman 2002]). The interesting queries become those questioning how propensities to holism re-form in conditions in which cosmoses (of whatever scale) themselves become reterritorialized, and perhaps strangely begin to approximate cosmoses that hold themselves together from within. However, little research that we know of has been done on problems of this kind. (Mormonism may be such an instance. See Cannell 2005).

The terms of postmodern globalized culture resonate with S. Sayyid's explanation of the development of world Islam (2003 [1997]). Sayyid sees Islam as a "master signifier," to which various Muslim communities over the world attach themselves on their own conditions. In Sayyid's reading, Islam (as well as "Christianity," "the West," and other such labels) is a shorthand summation for complex, mobile, amorphous transnational formations, whose boundaries are sites of constant political struggle. This kind of Islamic resurgence is enabled by globalization, making it a universalizing religion not specific to location or ethnicity, nor reducible to cultural and national practices, and thus able to embrace the entire 'ummah. The Arabizing of Islam in North Africa, discussed by Amiras, also derives tangentially from this resurgence. Islamic resurgence is also enabled by a Muslim diaspora in the West where Muslims, unified by the experience of alienation, are brought into contact with each other as Muslims rather than as members of ethnic and national communities. This is underpinned by a Muslim structuring of a kind of "civil society"—of advocacy organizations competent in dealing with corresponding structures of the West, as well as media outlets, radio and television channels, and intense internet traffic. The mosque becomes a major local center for the spread of ideas and the organization of political activities, on the home turf as well as in the diaspora, outside the control of the dominant polity, a hub where theology and everyday life meet and interact. All of this enables the development of transnational or global Muslim subjectivity and identity that helps to form interpretations of Islam, not only as a framework for the relationship between the human and the transcendent divine, but no less as personal and political agendas. Handelman's chapter on transnational terrorism largely agrees with this perspective. Much of the incitement for revolution and the overthrow of the shah, central to Thurfjell's chapter, was done from the diaspora by supporters of Khomeyni (much of it via audiocassettes). In somewhat analogous ways, the Hindu diaspora contributes to redefining Hinduism as a "culture," helping to develop versions of Hindu nationalism more suitable for political mobilization within India practiced as a nation-state (see Berglund's chapter). Amiras's discussion of the impact of diaspora Amazigh intellectuals on the formation of national Tamazigh culture is a further example of the critical interactions and interventions between peoplehood and diaspora.

Two Extremes of Polity and Religion in the Twentieth Century: Civil Religion and Totalitarianism

The French Revolution shaped the first great assault of a major polity (then in the making) on religion in general and religion-as-transcendence in particular, intending to replace religion with extreme secularism, focusing these (only partially successful) attempts through the value of the individual and the dominance of the secular state—the attempt to recast the whole of human existence, as Dumont put it. Moreover, in an interesting way, the emerging, revolutionary French cosmos denied the monotheistic cosmos held together (by God) from outside itself and moved toward a cosmos held together from within itself, through itself, a cosmos that was entirely human, human-made, and in the best of instances, humanistic. Cosmos contained through itself, yet open ended, thereby enabling movement within itself from any point to any other, and therefore utterly egalitarian and democratic within the open-ended totality of itself.[34] In this regard, the revolutionary French cosmos was the most radical departure from all of the relationships between polity and religion that dominated both Europe and its colonizing projects and enterprises. By the nineteenth and twentieth centuries there were two other significant departures in the relationship of polity and religion whose forms came to be globalized with great impact—the "civil religion" that developed especially in the United States and the totalitarianism that developed in Europe, especially in the So- viet Union and in Nazi Germany. Unlike the postrevolutionary French cosmos, both civil religion and totalitarianism resacralized the polity, though through entirely different routes, and both are discussed here briefly.

Civil Religion

The concept of "civil religion" (first introduced by sociologist Robert Bellah in the 1960s) is tailored foremost for the analysis of politics and religion in the United States and travels elsewhere less well, though Bellah and Hammond (1980: ix) argued that any coherent and viable society rests on a common set of moral understandings about good and bad, right and wrong, in the realm of the individual and social action, and therefore that the idea of civil religion should have a broad cachet. In our terms, Bellah is implying that common moral understandings must depend from cosmological premises that provide the grounds and depths through which these understandings make sense in practice. These grounds and their symbols are related to the nation-state, and resonate pervasively through the entirety of social life, giving an overarching sense of (holistic) unity. In Sweden, for example, these symbols include sea- sonal celebrations such as Christmas and Midsummer, but no less, the very idea of "Swedish nature" as essential to Swedishness, to what it is to be a true Swede (see Dahl 1998). These symbols are sacred, closed to questioning and criticism, providing a sense of awe across social boundaries.

The Constitution of the American nation-state formally separates state and church (the usual sequencing of these two terms in American talk, where what comes first is indeed first, and so is "church and state," which implicitly em- phasizes the transcendence of religion in relation to state and politics, and, so, the great difficulty of formally diminishing religion in the American state). For- mally, America is a model secular regime, yet the entanglement of polity and religion is profound (Gray 2007: 190). The secular state formally rules the Amer- ican Republic without the interference of, or consultation with, "religion." Indeed, "the secular state is one that banishes religion from public life while leaving people free to believe what they like" (Gray 2007: 190). Yet the republic is cultural order within which is the profound presence of religious values. Gray (2007: 119) writes of America's "unrivaled religiosity. The US is a secular re- gime, but unlike nearly every other long-established democracy America lacks a secular political tradition. Though the separation of church and state is a pillar of the Constitution, this has not prevented religion from exercising enormous power in American political life." This thread runs throughout Coleman's chapter. For that matter, one can argue that it was precisely the constitutional separation of state and church that set both of them onto the ongoing agenda of their relation within their nonrelationship, as Coleman's chapter emphasizes. Thus civil religion comes into existence in America when politics is joined to religion while the state/church constitutional separation continues. In which case the sacred holism of religious values is free to engage with the values of the polity to shape beliefs "about our national purpose and about the destiny of our national enterprise. Vague and visceral it may be, but there is an American creed, and to be an American is to believe the creed. America is, in this sense, a religious venture" (Rouner 1999: 3; quoted in Angrosino 2002: 245–46).

Anthropologist Michael Angrosino defined civil religion as "an institutionalized set of beliefs about the nation, including a faith in a transcendental deity who will protect and guide [the country] as long as its people and government abide by its laws."[35] The pillars of this civil religion are the virtues of liberty, justice, charity, and personal integrity (Angrosino 2002: 241). This civil religion is not bound to particular organizational forms nor to the theological or philosophical premises of any organized religious body. According to Angrosino, civil religion functions primarily through mundane secular institutions such as administrative agencies, patriotic organizations, and outlets of popular culture like pop music and movies. Made pervasive through a broad range of secular institutions, civil religion in its American variant lodges in the independent individual, its most profound carrier and agent, thereby reproducing American ethos in the smallest unit of being. This argument supports that of French scholar Alexis de Tocqueville, who in the nineteenth century commented at length on the significance in America of the egalitarian individual. Yet the German sociologist Max Weber, after his extensive travels in America at the beginning of the twentieth century, contended that historically there were powerful Protestant underpinnings of collective (indeed, holistic) values that came to support the development of "a thick civic sphere." This was introduced "in the American colonies by ascetic Protestant sects and churches in the seventeenth and eighteenth centuries. ... its [the civic sphere's] singular political-ethical action injected a decisive 'community-building energy' into American society," which fostered the growth of innumerable civic associations concerned with the alteration of society as a whole and focused through the individual infused with an ethos of initiative-taking and entrepreneurship, yet no less one of involvement in their communities and in social reform (Kalberg 2009: 118, 121, 123). One implication of Weber's analysis is that politics was made a religious obligation and so, later on, nationalism was no less religious. Though Weber's analysis of the American civic sphere both overlapped with and opposed that of Tocqueville (who emphasized more free institutions, public spirit, and economic interests per se), we see that both together—religious and secular—became foundational to what Bellah called American civil religion.[36]

The degrees of symbolic interpenetration of polity and religion in America can be shown very concisely through the oath of office taken by the newly elected president. The oath may be administered by anyone legally authorized to do so, and has been done mostly by the chief justice of the Supreme Court, the highest office of the (secular) judiciary. Article 2 of the Constitution states that the oath or "affirmation" of office must be taken before the president enters office, and this particular oath is the only one specified by the Constitution. The wording as given in Article 2, Section 1, Clause 8, is: "I do solemnly swear (or affirm) that I will faithfully execute the Office of President of the United States, and will to the best of my ability, preserve, protect and defend the Constitution of the United States." The wording of the oath is secular, though there might be the intimation of religion in the phrase "to swear." During the last century, most incoming presidents have sworn with right hand raised and the left placed on a Bible while taking the oath (though one of the early presidents, John Quincy Adams, swore on a book of law). So, too, most have appended the phrase, "So help me God," to the end of the oath (and most of the recent ones have also kissed the Bible). Though none of these acts are required by law, they have become customary (one could say, normative) for incoming presidents.

The Constitution is the highest and most authoritative separation of state and church in America, and leaves religion out of the oath taken by the highest democratically elected official of the state who is also the commander-in-chief of the armed forces. We can say on the whole that it is the presidents themselves who feel the absence of (Christian) religion and its values in the oath and so add the presence of the supreme deity. This joining of secular and religious is one of American cultural common-sense. The secular Constitution meets Christianity in the person of the president, even as the former are formally distinguished and separated from one another. This joining through cultural common sense takes place on the border of or within American civil religion.[37]

When the power of religion legitimates and enhances the state so that the state itself is defined by its transcendent holistic power, civil religion is transformed into religious nationalism or nationalism-as-religion. Indeed, civil religion becomes transcendent religion when the nation's history provides the context for the relationship between God and World, when the nation's history takes on the character of sacred myth, expressed through religious values and sanctified ideals. Michael Walzer (1985) insightfully shows how the Exodus myth of the Hebrew Bible helped shaped Western political culture. Religious nationalism is always a potential of civil religion, with its propensities to values of holism.[38] Angrosino (2002) discusses how themes of religious nationalism play out in American political culture, but other Western democracies have not been radically different. In today's Europe as well, democratic principles, institutions, and the voice of the people are implicitly presented as "sacred" (though much more in discourse than in practice). Margaret Jacobs's (1992) studies of Freemasonry show how a new pattern of sentiments, beliefs, and ceremonial activities—a "new religiosity"—contributed to the emergence of liberal democracy, sacralizing reason and civil society in Western Europe.

However it is in American democracy that these themes are incorporated pervasively as part of the overarching, properly religious faith, presupposing a transcendent, benevolent deity that gives to America the sense of higher purpose and unique destiny, integral to the American creed (and brought out brilliantly for 1930s New England by the anthropologist W. Lloyd Warner [1961] and continued incisively by Marvin and Ingle [1999] in their study of sacrifice and the regeneration of the American nation-state). Thus the cultural common sense of American presidents adds the transcendent Christian deity to the final act of secular democratic elections, implicitly orienting civil religion toward the potentialities of religious nationalism. Unlike Europe, the abundance of religious symbols in American politics gives it an aura of religious zeal that seems awkward for many secularized Western Europeans. As Coleman shows in his chapter, the Protestant Right has no difficulty finding its place in the political establishment exactly because its ideas and political technologies are of a piece with American civil religion. Even so, in Europe as the European Union megabureaucratic state comes into existence (Walby 1999), regional and local responses begin to exhibit strong values of holism (and, so, in our expectations, intimations of religion).

Holistic Encompassment in Modernity: Theorizing the Totalitarian State

We argued earlier that values of encompassing holism, emerging from the monotheisms, never disappeared from European cosmoses, even as Europe secularized and the value of individualism rose into great prominence.[39] We stated at the outset that values of holism intimate the potential for the implicit presence and emergence of religion—whether as revival, renewal, or creation—even when phenomena that appear are formally unlike the numerous definitions of religion whose roots are in monotheistic tradition (and this covers the bulk of the multitude of definitions). We implied no less that with the Axial Age shattering of holistic cosmos, utter metaphysical transcendence came into existence, among the ancient Greeks through Aristotelian logic and among the ancient Hebrews through God the Creator and the One who came to be located outside the cosmos of his creation, holding cosmos together from its outside, and that these metaphysics continue especially through the mono-theisms. The ancient Greeks and Hebrews, we noted, were the most potent examples of what is called the Axial Age breakthrough. Utter monotheistic transcendence is just that because it is virtually unreachable by living mortals who exist on the inside of cosmos. Thus utter monotheistic transcendence is immeasurable just as the inside of cosmos is interminably measurable by com-mandment, classification, law, edict, and on.

Hardt and Negri (2000: 355) argue that today, "when political transcen-dence is still claimed, it descends immediately into tyranny and barbarism." In our terms, in such instances cosmos is contained by transcendence, with pro-pensities to holism held together from its exterior. In twentieth-century Europe these attempts at holism become totalitarian, with intimations of nationalism-as-religion. No less than civil religion, European totalitarianism is an offshoot of the attempts to banish metaphysics of religion from all remnants of its en-compassment of polity, and indeed to banish it from polity altogether. Forgotten in the mazes of ideology is that, to do so, values of monotheistic holism must be banished as well. Otherwise some form of transcendence returns. In twentieth-century Europe, the propensities of encompassing holism (with its intimations of monotheistic premises) to shape secular politics have been profound. We note here very briefly three theorists of secular totalitarian statehood; all three acknowledge in their own ways that the totalitarian state depends on transcen-dence and encompassment. Louis Dumont insists that the holism of totalitarian encompassment must be merely *pseudoholism*. Political theorist Claude Lefort also intimates this. The third, the German juridical theorist Carl Schmitt, is the most open in acknowledging in Europe the ongoing dependence of political authoritarianism on transcendent monotheistic premises.

Dumont (1977: 12) considers totalitarianism a form of pseudoholism: given that "it is quite different from the traditional naïve conception of the society as a whole ... totalitarianism results from the attempt, in a society in which in-dividualism is deeply rooted and predominant, to subordinate [individualism] to the primacy of the society as a whole." Totalitarianism subsumes values that are in severe contradiction and conflict—on the one hand, the autonomy and freedom of choice of individuals and, on the other, the sovereign drive to force everyone, every individual agency, into the same mold of values, goals, and po-litical organization. Thus violence is substituted for holistic value in the attempt to *force* acceptance of a societal, indeed a cosmic vision of how social order should be put together. The totalitarian effort (Nazism, Sovietism) is based on turning aggregates of individuals into collective being (of nation, of socioeco-nomic class), into collectivity that has a destiny (Dumont 1986: 156). Should this be called pseudoholism, a veneer of traditional holism, or is it another kind of holism that, whether forced (Sovietism) or naturalized (Nazism) into col-lective being, operates through encompassing social order, and that through its encompassing qualities resonates with monotheism (rather than with cosmos that holds itself together from within itself)?

Dumont's understanding joins remarkably well with that of Lefort, who asks how it is that totalitarianism is such a major event in our time. Lefort (1986: 297) writes (referring primarily to the Soviet state) that "at the foundation of totalitarianism lies the representation of the People-as-One"—society homogenized yet without the transcendental guarantee of encompassing order. The People-as-One who are being made, one could say, into the sameness of oneness (whether the oneness is that of race, nation, ethnicity, social class), such that social division is intended to be banished from society, apart from that between the people and its enemies: "a division between inside and outside, no internal division" (1986: 297). The People-as-One homogenized, becoming the people in its essence led by a Power-as-One, power ultimately concentrated in an individual who embodies the oneness of the people.

Lefort (1986: 288) argues moreover that the social order led by a Power-as-One becomes transcendent by hiding how it is held together: "The 'whole' must remain outside its articulations and [is] therefore a secret ... the centre of omniscient power hidden" (1986: 289). Therefore radical uncertainty dominates each and every individual, whatever his rank, whatever his status, with regard to the reasons for decisions taken at the top and as to the limits of his own authority. The Great Terror that Stalin unleashed in the 1930s and that continued in myriad ways until his death is an exemplar of such radical uncertainty (see the detailed accounts in Rogovin 2009; Shentalinsky 1995). The secret is that the Power-of-One is *inside* society even as he acts as if moral and social order are encompassed wholly from the *outside*, in the name of value and ideology. Thus it is the "secret" itself of "as if" encompassment that is transcendent, the (Godly) Power-of-One mysterious in his omnipotent, omniscient ways, sacrificing himself for society, holding cosmos together (so long as it holds) from outside itself. Not for nothing did Trotsky (quoted in Lefort 1986: 275) write: "Louis XIV identified himself only with the State. The totalitarian state goes far beyond ... for it has encompassed the entire economy of the country as well. Stalin can justly say, unlike the Sun King, "La Societé, c'est moi [I am society]."

The thinking of Carl Schmitt during and after the Weimar Republic is a useful, contrasting case. Sociologist Zygmunt Bauman (2009: 76) has called him "arguably the most clear-headed, illusion-free anatomist of the modern state and its in-built totalitarian inclination." Schmitt's concern lay with the stability of the sovereignty of the German state, which for him was the repository of the values of being German, of Germanness. By contrast he gave little importance to the German conception of nation (*volk*), rejecting it as romantic organicism lacking the capacity to make fateful decisions and to take action that would save the sovereignty of the state in crisis (Schmitt 2005: 49). Nonetheless he embraced the idea that true Germans share essential qualities of race-as-being. A student of Weber, he accepted that secularization entailed the disenchantment of the world, but understood this as emptying the human cosmos of value. He maintained that "the idea of the modern constitutional [democratic] state triumphed together with deism [belief in an abstract, remote deity], a theology and metaphysics that banished the miracle"—the miracle transgressed the laws of nature and intervened directly in the world through the exception, through the miraculous.

Schmitt's concern was to reject the rational theology of deism and "to try to restore to the concepts of sovereignty and political authority in a secular age the [divine, majestic] qualities that they had earlier" (Strong 2005: xxv). This entailed restoring political transcendence in a secular age of the Rousseauian "general will" of democracy. To do this, the general will of the people had to be differentiated into the friend, into those who truly shared in this general will, and into the enemy, those who were different and therefore divisive and threatening to the essence shared by friends. Friends were those who shared, homogeneously, qualities of upbringing (*erziehung*), of character building (*bildung*), of values and perceptions. In other words, by contrast the universal, general will was deceitful, duplicitous worthless, and enemies had to be destroyed in order that sovereignty true to itself would emerge. This confrontation of friend and enemy had to "take place at the metaphysical level—that of one faith against another. For this reason the confrontation is one of 'political theology'" (Strong 2005: xxviii). The echoes of monotheistic Christian kingship in all of this are loud and clear.

Schmitt's solution could be called that of the State of Encompassing Transcendence, that would "interpret the present in light of a Christian conception of history"—theistic, salvational, holding off the coming of the Antichrist (Koskenniemi 2004: 501).[40] After the Nazi takeover, Schmitt strongly supported the ethnic cleansing of Jewish jurists from the German courts, given that, as he put it, "it is an epistemological verity that only those are capable of seeing the facts [of a legal case] the right way, listening to statements rightly, understanding words correctly and evaluating impressions of persons and events rightly, if they are participants in a racially determined type [*artbestimmsten Weise*] of legal community to which they existentially belong" (quoted in Scheuerman 2001).

According to Schmitt, the stability of the state depended on the sovereign use of the exception.[41] The sovereign state could not rely on the maxim of rational democratic jurisprudence, to wit that just as nature was universally lawful (in keeping with the thinking of democratic science) so, too, the law applied universally without exception (Schmitt 1985: 48). When extreme circumstances demonstrated the ineffectiveness, the indeterminate capacity, of legal norms to maintain the sovereignty of the state, only the exception could destroy these norms, enabling the reemergence of order (1985: 12). He continued, "The exception in jurisprudence is analogous to the miracle in theology" (1985: 36). The rule is destroyed within the exception (1985: 12) and order is made in the space of the exception where order made is saved from chaos (i.e., from Judaism and Jews, and from all other essentialist differences) through the exception, and therefore chaos is ordered only because there is the exception. He who decides on the exception, writes Schmitt, is sovereign (1985: 5). In other words, the sovereign is he who takes transcendence upon himself and in the process becomes encompassing. One could say this about Stalin as the Power-of-One, and the Soviet Union of the time as a state of permanent exception (of which Agamben writes). Yet note that in a strong sense it is no less the condition or space of exception that itself is transcendent—for Schmitt (1985: 13) argues that "The *exception is that which cannot be subsumed*; it defies general codification [and is] the [juridical] decision in absolute purity" (our emphases). If the exception cannot be subsumed, then *the exception itself is encompassing.* And, so it is the exception in the person of the sovereign that encompasses the entirety of the state. This is the exception as miracle, the sovereign as pure miracle. (Yet one must consider that the state of exception potentially can become self-generating, self-organizing, becoming its own existential decision-making grounds). This view of political sovereignty powerfully resonates with Christianity, since the sovereign not only occupies the place of God but is no less the miracle of Christ, the God-man who is indeed the exception who orders cosmic chaos and promises salvation. One important aspect for us of Schmitt's conception of the exception, then, is that cosmos is encompassed, held together from outside itself.

We think that both Lefort and Schmitt, despite Dumont's argument for the link between individualism and pseudoholism, do show us how encompassing holism remains a propensity of the modern European period; and that, given what has occurred after the fall of the Soviet Empire and elsewhere, intimations of religion continue to be close by. This is discussed in Lindquist's chapter. One significant lesson is that the distinction between values of holism and values of individualism is hardly a hard-and-fast difference. The mixes, their interweaving, are complex. The Nazi state not only forced together like and like and began the extermination of the unlike, but values of encompassing holism with organic inlays were deeply embedded in basic premises and practices of German culture. (Though distant, the holistic resonances of Police resound). This enabled the potential to transform the friend/enemy distinction through the sovereign exception into the existence of the infinite existential enemy. The destruction of the infinite enemy would have continued on and on, one population after another turned into targets of destruction, a logic of ruination analyzed brilliantly by the philosopher Edith Wyschogrod (1985); the destruction of the infinite existential enemy that reaches its apex in the secular state (yet that has its roots and continuities in Christianity).

Perhaps the great tragedy of modernity (and, no less, its greatest irony) is that any attempt to put things together, to keep things together in holistic ways (as we have used the term here) will have intimations of religion, and of encompassment, and so, the likely inevitable, destructive, ongoing face-off between the "irrational" and the "rational" (so long as this continuum dominates intellectual pursuits in the West and its spinoffs throughout the world). Is this changing in postmodernity, through the increasing value of individual agency, the fragmentation of long-accepted social units and ideologies, the reforming of fluid identities? Our guess is that though there is indeed change, the pursuit of holism continues, from that of the "whole" individual as such (which is beyond our purview in this book), to the "sudden emergence in all Western monotheistic religions of new forms of religiosity, all of them communitarian (but of a purely religious community), exclusive (a clear dividing line separates the saved from the damned), and inclusive (all aspects of life must be placed by the believer under the aegis of religion)" (Roy 2007: 6), and perhaps no less, to the holism of secular communitarianism.

Yet just as the prominence (and perhaps existence) of the modern nation-state is being questioned severely (we dislike the popularity in academia of the postmodern term, *interrogated*, for obvious reasons) in globalizing postmodernity, the state is privatizing, withdrawing its services, reorganizing into what Kapferer (2005: 294) calls the oligarchic "corporate state," which often is no less a gated security state (both Israel and the United States are prime examples of obviously differing scales, but also of procedures). The corporate state retreats from the mass of its citizenry, "enclaving and guarding against the dangers of the mass at large … [and is] oriented to the creation of micro social orders of total control highly adapted to a social world premised on movement and displacement in which the social is always in the process of being reconstituted." Does this mean that holism is dead within these dynamics? Or, that there is one manner of holism for economic-political elites and another (perhaps rhizomic?) for the mass that must choose (individually) between being excluded or being controlled?

How has our contention—that when values of holism are present, religion is nearby—fared through this entire discursus? As a mixed bag, we think. We also think that enough has been said to make the problematic of the presence of ongoing values of holism and the emergence of religion well worth pursuing. Perhaps this would reveal ways to short-circuit the continuum between the irrational and the rational. This is our expectation. … With this thought we move to the chapters.

Notes

1. Yaron Ezrahi (1990), philosopher and political scientist, argues brilliantly that rather than Enlightenment science rationalizing politics (only to be eventually overpowered by the forces of unreason), science took on political functions, becoming in our time the handmaiden of the state.

2. The values of holism that we refer to are not those of perfect moral and social order that so many functionalist utopian visions (ancient and Enlightenment) desire and depend on. Gray (2007: 56–57) comments on holism, "No society has ever been a harmonious whole ... with its suspicion of conflict and diversity" as the European Romantics of the eighteenth and nineteenth centuries desired. This view of holism was bolstered by organicist social theorists who conceived of "society" (itself a new concept) physiologically, as a living being, and who also influenced Durkheim's thinking on the social conception of "society" (Barberis 2003: 66f). In anthropology perhaps the best example of organicist holistic thinking was A. R. Radcliffe-Brown's *A Natural Science of Society*. However, our use of cosmic holism as taking in everything there is in relation to a moral/social order and asking how such a cosmos holds together to greater or lesser degrees through practices of living operates to a great extent through actions of every kind in real time and hardly gives undue influence to visions of social order perfected, visions largely inspired by the surviving monotheisms.

3. In our thinking, values of holism (indeed, as value) are basic to cosmology in its perhaps infinite human varieties. The value of holism is ineluctably related to the being of human and therefore to human being and to human beings in concert. In certain respects this position resembles that of cosmologists like Titus Burckhardt (1987). We agree in large measure with Burckhardt (1987: 19) as cosmologist as he writes, "It is thus perfectly possible for traditional cosmology to possess, as it does, a knowledge that is real—and incomparably more vast and profound than that offered by the modern empirical sciences—while retaining childlike (or, more precisely, 'human') opinions about realities of the physical order."

4. Despite attempts by many regimes to control access to the World Wide Web, persons find ways to disseminate information through the Web, as in the recent crisis in Iran following the reelection of Ahmedinajad. See the *New York Times,* 23 June 2009.

5. Egypt has operated under Emergency Regulations since 1981 (following the assassination of President Anwar Sadat by Muslim fundamentalists associated with the Muslim Brotherhood). Under the regulations the state can arrest and detain any citizen without warrant or charge for an indefinite period. Bloggers who criticize the regime are seen as subversive, and may be treated as such. See, Rannie Amiri, "Journalists in danger: The perils of blogging in Egypt," *The Electronic Intifada,* 23 February 2009, http://electronicintifada.net/v2/printer10333.shtml, accessed 24 February 2009.

6. This controversy continues to resonate. Recently the prestigious academic publisher Yale University Press decided not to republish the twelve cartoons in a book on the affair, saying that whoever was interested could find them on the internet. (*International Herald Tribune,* 14 August 2009).

7. Especially interesting in this regard were the techniques used in Ceausescu's Romania to disrupt the rhythm of rituals and holy days during various time cycles of the Church, in order to facilitate the creation of the new socialist person. To mention just a couple, fixed holy days were not to be observed, while days of leisure were distributed at random across the week; and, from one year to the next, the specific purposes of secular holidays of commemoration were altered—last year one hero, this year, another. Verdery (1996: 54) argues that the purpose of the state was to control time by introducing arrhythmia into the religious temporal cycles.

8. In scholarly thinking, arationality is commonly understood as irrationality that is close to (religious) faith. See, for example, the biophysicist Nicholas Rashevsky (1968). This of course is not our intention. The arational draws attention to other potentialities (in a Deleuzian sense) of how worlds may be constituted, by breaking with the rational-irrational continuum. Thus in current Western intellectual thinking on how wholes are constituted, the (constructivist) addition of parts to form a whole would be considered rational, while the dynamic of a whole constituting its parts would likely be considered irrational, because the prior existence of a social whole would be understood as an irrational act of faith. We, on the other hand, think that the dynamic of wholes constituting their parts is arational. On wholes that constitute their parts, see Rosen (1994) and Bohm (1995).

9. The church does not easily accept any diminishing of its propensity to encompassment. In neighboring post-Salazar Portugal, the state has subsidized private universities only on condition that these institutions of higher learning be controlled by the Vatican (Pina-Cabral 2001: 332).

10. Hierarchical holism and egalitarian individualism are (especially in Kapferer) logics of cosmic organization as value/values of the social that permeate how cosmic order is put together.

11. Perhaps we could call this *intragration*, though this neologism is awkward.

12. We agree generally with the anthropologist Thomas Csordas (2004) that "religion" is a primordial sensibility that is ever present. Csordas emphasizes the primordial intersubjectivity of self and other (ultimately, the transcendent Other) as the phenomenological "kernel" of the origin and continuation of "religion." We do not take issue with this as a principled position, but are concerned with the "how" of religion, with its epistemologies, rather than with its "why," its ontologies. We would argue further that by attending to the potential opening to holism in the primordial self-other relationship, one would also open toward the development of religions "in their own right," as Csordas (2004: 164) puts it (see Handelman and Lindquist 2005 on "ritual in its own right").

13. For us, the idea of "propensity" comes from the sinologist, Francois Jullien (1995: 78). Phenomena with propensity need to be understood as having within them a dynamic of continuing process.

14. We take the idea of folding from Deleuze (1993), and use it in the introduction to Handelman and Lindquist (2005).

15. The conception of "society" as real is itself a late nineteenth-century European construction of the Organicists, see Barberis (1993).

16. The holism of "intentional communities" is usually consciously formed.

17. *The Concise English Dictionary* (London: Omega Books, 1982).
18. For a postmodernist understanding of Zen Buddhism through Indra's Net, see Loy (1993).
19. For a few examples, the Pueblo Tewa (Ortiz 1969), the Mescalero Apache (Farrer 1991), the Navaho (Farella 1984), the Iatmul (Bateson 1958) and Yagwoia (Mimica 1988) of Papua New Guinea, and so many others.
20. Our emphasis on (cosmic) holism as historically taking precedence over the idea of religion points to the continuing precedence of holism in whatever form. The religious studies scholar Timothy Fitzgerald (2009: 195) asks, "How can you have a non-religious religion?" The answer, we already have suggested, is quite simple: "Religion" emerges from values of holism, as do numerous other cultural and social formations. Given values of holism, "religion" and other formations have powerful resonances with one another. Elsewhere, Fitzgerald (2000: 240) quite misunderstands the significance of holism, as does Gray (2007), which we noted earlier. Fitzgerald (2009) is arguing against Benson Saler's conception of religion, developed through Wittgenstein's idea of "family resemblance" (see also Vygotsky's [1962] idea of "chain complexes"). Through family resemblance, Saler (2000: 218) argues that "there is no hard and fast line" that separates religion and nonreligion. Fitzgerald contends that using "family resemblance" "is an excuse for lazy thinking," one that produces "useless or contradictory concepts" (2009: 195). Fitzgerald seems to think that the only useful concepts are ones that make hard-and-fast absolutist distinctions. This kind of thinking accords with "bureaucratic logic" (Handelman 2004: 19–42). Scholars should know when clear-edged distinctions are called for or when fuzziness is more called for. For ethnographers this is even more crucial.
21. The construct of a widespread Axial Age that generated the transcendental in ancient civilizations is becoming quite problematic. Ancient China seems emphatically this-worldly. Buddhism, though often discussed in terms of the highest transcendence to enlightenment and nothingness, can also be understood as the deepest of personal and cosmic implosions into nothingness. Would the latter be considered transcending or, perhaps, the clumsy neologism, "intrascending"? The cases of axiality most often invoked come down to ancient Greece and ancient Israel, the latter especially of profound significance to the emergence of the three surviving monotheistic traditions and to the emergence of the West. This raises the suspicion that it is these cases that are treated as paradigmatic, and that the others are formed as modifications of these cases—perhaps another instance of the West serving (in the eyes of its scholars) as a model for the rest.
22. The argument for an organic cosmos without any outside has been developed by Handelman and Shulman (2004) for the South Indian Saiva cosmos.
23. The monotheistic rupture of continuous cosmos encourages Nancy (2003: 42) to argue that *within* Christian cosmos there is no god; Christian cosmos is a-theistic, indeed atheistic: "monotheism is in truth atheism."
24. In this discussion we have omitted a crucial precursor that influenced the formation of "revolutionary monotheism," Zoroastrianism. Sometime between 1500–1200 BCE, the Iranian prophet Zoroaster imagined a dynamic cosmos imbued with

a divine plan for the ultimate perfection of cosmos forever and ever (Cohn 1993: 77, 82, 89, 95, 227). The forces of order and the forces of chaos would struggle through lengthy durations, with human beings in their daily practices of living having a crucial role in this battle. Gradually and then eventually the forces of order would triumph, removing every form of disorder from the cosmos (Cohn 1993: 114), perfecting the goodness of the cosmos and its inhabitants. These themes reappear in their own ways in the postexilic Hebrew text of Second Isaiah, who may have been the first of the Hebrew revolutionary monotheists, and perhaps the first of the monotheists altogether (Cohn 1993: 152). Cohn (1993: 222) argues that the similarity between the apocalyptics of Zoroastrianism and Judaism were not likely coincidental. And he makes the important link between Zoroastrianism and the Jesus sect, and so with Christian apocalyptic thinking that resonates so powerfully through the present.

25. In this, Dumont finds seeds of contradiction and dialectic that are familiar to Western models of conflict.

26. Francois Dosse (1997: 13) referring to the influence of Durkheim on French intellectual thought prior to World War II, quotes Raymond Boudon as saying that "anthropologists took in a bit of holism along with their mother's milk." Dumont likely would be affected by this penumbra. For example, he (1986: 74) embraces the Durkheimian position that "society ... is sociologically prior to its individual members."

27. A partially dissenting note is sounded by Jan Assman. Assman (2008: 84–86) argues that ancient Hebrew monotheism transformed the unity of religion and divine kingship into the separation of religion and politics. The king, no longer divine, was entirely and utterly human, while the priesthood tended to matters of religion. Assman does not use the idea of encompassment, yet his argument for the autonomy of religion is no less one for the superior authority and normativity of religion, verging on religion as encompassing other domains of social life, including the political. He argues further that the armature of terms that we know from modern times—religion, politics, church, state, and so forth—was made possible by the rise of monotheism, though these distinctions were not systematic in those times.

28. Within the many cosmic currents of Late Antiquity, one should not overlook the numerous thrusts toward monotheism in the thinking of pagan philosophies (Athanassiadi and Frede 1999).

29. The analogy to a new Christian holy birth cannot be overlooked.

30. The philosopher Montesquieu, in distinguishing between civil law and police, commented, "Matters of police are things of every instant, which usually amount to but little; scarcely any formalities are needed. The actions of police are quick and the police is exerted over things that recur every day; therefore major punishments are not proper to it. It is perpetually busy with details; therefore great examples do not fit it" (cited in Foucault 2007: 360).

31. Foucault (2007: 338) likens police to a "permanent *coup d'Etat*," one that "is exercised and functions in the name of and in terms of the principles of its own rationality, without having to mold or model itself on the otherwise given rules of

justice." In this formulation, Foucault comes close to those of Schmitt, and then Agamben in "the state of exception." Yet in certain ways, Foucault's formulation is the more profound because he is referring to a state of *permanent* exception concerned with endless regulation and continuously renewing itself.

32. Keane (1998) argues that the strains of secularism are older.

33. An issue into which we will not enter here is the propensity to holism of the self of the individual, and whether other forms of holism apart from the religious have become prominent in this. The sociologist Philip Rieff argued in *The Triumph of the Therapeutic* (1965) that a therapeutic ethos has come to dominate how the Western (middle-class) individual has made his or her own well-being the center of better living. Psychological Man and his therapies replace the (religious) commitments of faith, virtue, social responsibility, and enduring truth. Psychiatry and psychology replace religion in making the individual whole and, beyond this and unlike religion, make the individual the epicenter of his or her own cosmos.

34. Until World War II, French ideology and, to varying degrees, French colonial ideology held that any person who fully took on French culture became French and would be treated as French. This was, in part, the impact of the revolutionary, secular French cosmos, self-contained yet open ended. This was not so in the British Empire, where if one took on British culture one became second-class British, able to function within British bureaucratic structures. Nor in Germany where one's Germanness was incomplete unless one had German blood.

35. The emphasis on "transcendental deity" here (see also Lincoln 2003) is interesting, since in our view it clearly delineates and marks civil religion as an offspring of monotheism, which is not quite what Bellah intended.

36. It may well be relevant that Tocqueville, heir to the Declaration of the Rights of Man, witnessed the individualism of America, while Weber, heir to the science of police, witnessed the significance of moral collectivism.

37. Interestingly, many other federal oaths do formally include the phrase "So help me God." The authority and values of God are perhaps taken for granted and unquestioned. However, entanglements within civil religion are also contested continually in terms of the relative balance of secular and religious values, though we will not enter into this here except to mention changes in American currency (also a prime symbol of American collective might and individualistic entrepreneurship) and national mottos. By an Act of Congress in 1864, the phrase IN GOD WE TRUST first was inscribed on an American coin. Since 1938 all United States coins bear this inscription, and since the 1960s, all currency notes do too. In 1956, Congress passed (with presidential approval) a resolution making IN GOD WE TRUST a national motto. It joined the other national (secular) motto, E PLURIBUS UNUM.

38. Asad (2003: 194–95) eschews the existence of holism and therefore denies that religion forms nationalism. Thus, nationalism is essentially secular, rooted, as he says, in human history and society. Concurrently, nationalism is neither religion nor shaped by religion. Similarly, Lilla (2007: 254) is bemused by how "mystical and messianic impulses cultivated by the biblical tradition survived the Great Separation" that detached "Western political thought from all theological and cosmologi-

cal speculation." Thus the Great Separation was to do away with values of holism which, in our view, have never disappeared.

39. Dumont seems to accept historian Otto Gierke's argument quoted in Dumont (1986: 74) that following the fragmentation of the church, "the idea of the State as an *organic whole* which had been bequeathed by classical and medieval thought, was never completely extinguished" (emphasis in original).

40. Schmitt did not advocate an overtly religious cosmos; a Roman Catholic, he perceived the sixteenth-century as the last flourishing of Christian cosmos.

41. Schmitt's thinking on the exception is foundational for Giorgio Agamben's influential "state of exception."

REFERENCES

Al-Azmeh, Aziz. 2004. "Monotheistic Kingship." In *Monotheistic Kingship: The Medieval Variants*, ed. Aziz Al-Azmeh and Janos M. Bak, 9–29. Budapest: Central European University Press.

Angrosino. Michael. 2002. "Civil Religion Redux." *Anthropological Quarterly* 72 (2): 239–67.

Asad, Talal. 1993. *Genealogies of Religion*. Baltimore: Johns Hopkins University Press.

———. 1999. "Religion, Nation-State, Secularism." In *Nation and Religion: Perspectives on Europe and Asia*, ed. Peter van der Veer and Hartmut Lehman, 178–98. Princeton, NJ: Princeton University Press.

———. 2003. *Formations of the Secular: Christianity, Islam, Modernity*. Stanford, CA: Stanford University Press.

Assman, Jan. 2008. *Gods and Men: Egypt, Israel, and the Rise of Monotheism*. Madison: University of Wisconsin Press.

Athanassiadi, Polymnia, and Michael Frede, ed. 1999. *Pagan Monotheism in Late Antiquity*. Oxford: Clarendon Press.

Bailey, F. G. 2008. *God-Botherers and Other True Believers: Gandhi, Hitler, and the Religious Right*. Oxford: Berghahn Books.

Balzer, Marjorie Mandelstam. 2005. "Whose Steeple is Higher? Religious Competition in Siberia." *Religion, State and Society* 33 (1): 58–69.

Barberis, Daniela. 2003. "In Search of an Object: Organicist Sociology and the Reality of Society in *Fin-de-siecle* France." *History of the Human Sciences* 16 (3): 51–71.

Bateson, Gregory. 1958. *Naven*. Stanford, CA: Stanford University Press.

Bauman, Zygmunt. 1997. *Postmodernity and its Discontents*. New York: New York University Press.

———. 2009. "Seeking in Modern Athens an Answer to the Ancient Jerusalem Question." *Theory, Culture & Society* 26 (1): 71–91.

Bellah, Robert N. 2005. "What is Axial About the Axial Age?" *European Journal of Sociology* 46: 69–87.

Bellah, Robert N., and Phillip E. Hammond. 1980. *Varieties of Civil Religion*. New York: Harper & Row.

Bercken, William van den. 1989. *Ideology and Atheism in the Soviet Union*. Berlin: Mouton de Gruyter.

Berger, Peter L. 1981. "The Other Side of God—Problem and Agenda." In *The Other Side of God: A Polarity in World Religions*, ed. Peter L. Berger, 3–27. New York: Anchor Press/Doubleday.

———. ed. 1991. *The Desecularization of the World: Resurgent Religion and World Politics*. Grand Rapids, MI: Eerdmans.

———. 2001. "Postscript." In *Peter Berger and the Study of Religion*, ed. Linda Woodhead with Paul Heelas and David Martin, 189–98. London: Routledge.

Beyer, Peter. 1994. *Religion and Globalization*. London: Sage.

Bohm, David. 1995. *Wholeness and the Implicate Order*. London: Routledge.

Brewer, John D. 2007. "Theology and Sociology Reconsidered: Religious Sociology and the Sociology of Religion in Britain." *History of the Human Sciences* 20 (2): 7–28.

Bruce, Steve. 2003. *Politics and Religion*. Cambridge: Polity Press.

Burckhardt, Titus. 1987. *Mirror of the Intellect: Essays on Traditional Science and Sacred Art*. Albany: SUNY Press.

Cannell, Fenella. 2005. "The Christianity of Anthropology." *Journal of the Royal Anthropological Institute* (N.S.) 11: 335–56.

Casanova, Jose. 1994. *Public Religions in the Modern World*. Chicago: University of Chicago Press.

Cassirer, Ernst. 1953. *An Essay on Man: An Introduction to a Philosophy of Human Culture*. New Haven, CT: Yale University Press.

Cohn, Norman. 1993. *Cosmos, Chaos and the World to Come: The Ancient Roots of Apocalyptic Faith*. New Haven, CT: Yale University Press.

Coleman, Simon. 2000. *The Globalisation of Charismatic Christianity: Spreading the Gospel of Prosperity*. Cambridge: Cambridge University Press.

Cook, Francis H. 1972. *Hua-yen Buddhism: The Jewel Net of Indra*. University Park: Pennsylvania State University Press.

Csordas, Thomas J. 1997. *Language, Charisma and Creativity: The Ritual Life of a Religious Movement*. Berkeley: University of California Press.

———. 2004. "Asymptote of the Ineffable: Embodiment, Alterity, and the Theory of Religion." *Current Anthropology* 45 (2): 163–85.

———. 2009. "Introduction: Modalities of Transnational Transcendence." In *Transnational Transcendence: Essays on Religion and Globalization*, ed. Thomas J. Csordas, 1–29. Berkeley: University of California Press.

Dahl, Gudrun. 1998. "Wildflowers, Nationalism and the Swedish Law of Commons." *Worldviews: Environment, Culture, Religion* 2: 281–302.

Davie, Grace. 2007. *The Sociology of Religion*. London: Sage.

Deleuze, Gilles. 1993. *The Fold: Leibniz and the Baroque*. London: Athlone Press.

Doniger, Wendy. 2009. *The Hindus: An Alternative History*. London: Penguin Press.

Dosse, Francois. 1997. *History of Structuralism*, vol. 1: *The Rising Sign, 1945–1966*. Minneapolis: University of Minnesota Press.

Dumont, Louis. 1975. "Understanding Non-Modern Civilization." *Daedalus* 102 (2): 153–72.

————. 1977. *From Mandeville to Marx: The Genesis and Triumph of Economic Ideology.* Chicago: University of Chicago Press.

————. 1981. *Homo Hierarchicus.* Rev. ed. Chicago: University of Chicago Press.

————. 1986. *Essays on Individualism: Modern Ideology in Anthropological Perspective.* Chicago: University of Chicago Press.

Durkheim, Emile. 1995 [1912]. *The Elementary Forms of Religious Life.* New York: Free Press.

Eck, Diana. 1981. "The Dynamics of Indian Symbolism." In *The Other Side of God: A Polarity in World Religions,* ed. Peter L. Berger, 157–81. New York: Anchor Press/Doubleday.

Eisenstadt, S. N. 1986. "The Axial Age Breakthroughs—Their Characteristics and Origins." In *The Origins and Diversity of Axial Age Civilizations,* ed. S. N. Eisenstadt, 1–28. Albany: SUNY Press.

Evens, T. M. S. 1995. *Two Kinds of Rationality: Kibbutz Democracy and Generational Conflict.* Minneapolis: University of Minnesota Press.

Ezrahi, Yaron. 1990. *The Descent of Icarus: Science and the Transformation of Contemporary Democracy.* Cambridge, MA: Harvard University Press.

Farella, John R. 1984. *The Main Stalk: A Synthesis of Navajo Philosophy.* Tucson: University of Arizona Press.

Farrer, Claire R. 1991. *Living Life's Circle: Mescalero Apache Cosmovision.* Albuquerque: University of New Mexico Press.

Fishbane, Michael. 1981. "Israel and the "Mothers." In *The Other Side of God: A Polarity in World Religions,* ed. Peter L. Berger, 28–47. New York: Anchor Press/Doubleday.

Fitzgerald, Timothy. 2000. *The Ideology of Religious Studies.* New York: Oxford University Press.

————. 2009. "Benson Saler: 'Conceptualizing Religion: Some Recent Reflections': A Response." *Religion* 39: 194–97.

Fogleman, Aaron Spencer. 2003. "Jesus is Female: The Moravian Challenge in the German Communities of British North America." *William and Mary Quarterly* 60 (2): 295–332.

Foucault, Michel. 2007. *Security, Territory, Population: Lectures at the College de France, 1977–1978.* New York: Palgrave/Macmillan.

Frankfort, Henri, and H. A. Frankfort. 1963. "The Emancipation of Thought From Myth." In *Before Philosophy: An Essay on Speculative Thought in the Ancient Near East,* by Henry Frankfort, H. A. Frankfort, John A. Wilson, and Thorkild Jacobsen, 237–63. Harmondsworth, UK: Penguin Books.

Geertz, Clifford. 2005. "Shifting Aims, Moving Targets: On the Anthropology of Religion." *Journal of the Royal Anthropological Institute* 11 (N.S.): 1–15.

Gellner, David N. 2001. "Studying Secularism, Practising Secularism. Anthropological Imperatives." *Social Anthropology* 9 (3): 337–40.

Ginzburg, Carlo. 1981. *The Cheese and the Worms: The Cosmos of a Sixteenth-Century Miller.* London: Routledge & Kegan Paul.

Goldschmidt, Henry, and Elizabeth McAlister, ed. 2004. *Race, Nation and Religion in the Americas.* New York: Oxford University Press.

Gordon, Colin. 1991. "Governmental Rationality: An Introduction." In *The Foucault Effect: Studies in Governmentality,* ed. G. Burchell, C. Gordon, and P. Miller, 1–51. London: Harvester Wheatsheaf.

Gray, John. 2007. *Black Mass: Apocalyptic Religion and the Death of Utopia*. London: Allen Lane.

Greenhouse, Carol. 1989. "Fighting for Peace," In *Peace and War: Cross-Cultural Perspectives*, ed. Mary LeCron Foster and Richard A. Rubenstein, 49–60. New Brunswick, NJ: Transaction Books.

Gurevich, A. J. 1985. *Categories of Medieval Culture*. London: Routledge & Kegan Paul.

Gurevich, Aron. 1990. *Medieval Popular Culture: Problems of Belief and Perception*. Cambridge: Cambridge University Press.

Halliday, Fred. 2000. *Nation and Religion in the Middle East*. London: Saqi Books.

Handelman, Don. 1998. *Models and Mirrors: Towards an Anthropology of Public Events*, 2nd ed. New York: Berghahn Books.

———. 2002. "Postlude: The Interior Sociality of Self-Transformation." In *Self and Self-Transformation in the History of Religions*, ed. David Shulman and Guy. G. Stroumsa, 236–53. New York: Oxford University Press.

———. 2004. *Nationalism and the Israeli State: Bureaucratic Logic in Public Events*. Oxford: Berg.

———. 2008. "Afterword: Returning to Cosmology—Thoughts on the Positioning of Belief." *Social Analysis* 52 (1): 181–95. Special issue, *Against Belief?* ed. Galina Lindquist and Simon Coleman).

Handelman, Don, and Galina Lindquist, eds. 2005. *Ritual in its Own Right: Exploring the Dynamics of Transformation*. New York: Berghahn Books.

Handelman, Don, and David Shulman. 2004. *Siva in the Forest of Pines: An Essay on Sorcery and Self-Knowledge*. Delhi: Oxford University Press.

Hannerz, Ulf. 1996. *Transnational Connections*. London: Routledge.

Harding, Christopher, and Nicola Harding. 2006. "Who Designed the Westphalian System?" *Law, Culture and the Humanities* 2: 399–419.

Hardt, Michael, and Antonio Negri. 2000. *Empire*. Cambridge, MA: Harvard University Press.

Hartman, Geoffrey H. 1997. *The Fateful Question of Culture*. New York: Columbia University Press.

Hastings, Adrian. 1997. *The Construction of Nationhood: Ethnicity, Religion and Nationalism*. Cambridge: Cambridge University Press.

Hayes, Carleton. 1968. *The Historical Evolution of Modern Nationalism*. New York: Russell and Russell.

Haynes, Jeffrey. 1998. *Religion in Global Politics*. London: Longmans.

———. 2006. *The Politics of Religion: A Survey*. London: Routledge.

Hobsbawm, Eric, and Terence Ranger, ed. 1983. *The Invention of Tradition*. Cambridge: Cambridge University Press.

Jacobs, Margaret. 1992. *Living the Enlightenment: Freemasonry and Politics in Eighteenth-Century Europe*. New York: Oxford University Press.

Jacobsen, Thorkild. 1963. "Mesopotamia." In *Before Philosophy: An Essay on Speculative Thought in the Ancient Near East*, by Henri Frankfort, H. A. Frankfort, John A. Wilson, and Thorkild Jacobsen, 137–234. Harmondsworth, UK: Penguin.

Jullien, Francois. 1995. *The Propensity of Things: Toward a History of Efficacy in China*. New York: Zone Books.

Kalberg, Stephen. 2009. "Max Weber's Analysis of the Unique American Civic Sphere." *Journal of Classical Sociology* 9 (1): 117–41.

Kapferer. Bruce. 1988. *Legends of People, Myths of State.* Washington, DC: Smithsonian Institution Press.

———. 2001. "Anthropology. The Paradox of the Secular." *Social Anthropology* 9 (3): 341–44.

———. 2005. "New Formations of Power, The Oligarchic-Corporate State, and Anthropological Ideological Discourse." *Anthropological Theory* 5 (3): 285–99.

Keane, John. 1998. "The Limits of Secularism." *Times Literary Supplement,* January 9, 1998. http://tls.timesonline. Accessed 9 August 2009.

Kharkhordin, Oleg. 2001. "What is the State? The Russian Concept of *Gosudarstvo* in the European Context." *History and Theory* 40: 206–40.

Koskenniemi, Martti. 2004. "International Law as Political Theology: How to Read *Nomos der Erde?*" *Constellations* 11 (4): 493–511.

Lefort, Claude. 1986. *The Political Forms of Modern Society: Bureaucracy, Democracy, Totalitarianism.* Cambridge, MA: MIT Press.

Le Roy Ladurie, Emmanuel. 1978. *Montaillou: The Promised Land of Error.* New York: George Braziller.

Lilla, Mark. 2007. *The Stillborn God: Religion, Politics, and the Modern West.* New York: Knopf.

Lincoln, Bruce. 2003. *Holy Terrors: Thinking About Religion After September 11.* Chicago: University of Chicago Press.

Lindquist, Galina. 2008. "Loyalty and Command: Shamans, Lamas, and Spirits in a Siberian Ritual." *Social Analysis* 52 (1): 111–26.

Lorberbaum, Yair. 2009. "The Rainbow in the Cloud: An Anger-Management Device." *Journal of Religion* 89: 498–540.

Loy, David. 1993. "Indra's Postmodern Net." *Philosophy East and West* 43 (3): 481–510.

Luckmann, Thomas. 1967. *The Invisible Religion: The Problem of Religion in Modern Society.* New York: Macmillan.

Marvin, Carolyn, and David W. Ingle. 1999. *Blood Sacrifice and the Nation: Totem Rituals and the American Flag.* Cambridge: Cambridge University Press.

McNeil, William. 1986. *Mythistory and Other Essays.* Chicago: University of Chicago Press.

Mimica, Jadran. 1988. *Intimations of Infinity: The Cultural Meanings of the Iqwaye Number and Counting Systems.* Oxford: Berg.

Nagy, Piroska. 2005. "Religious Weeping as Ritual in the Medieval West." In *Ritual in Its Own Right: Exploring the Dynamics of Transformation,* ed. Don Handelman and Galina Lindquist, 119–37. New York: Berghahn Books.

Nancy, Jean-Luc. 2003. "Deconstruction of Monotheism." *Postcolonial Studies* 6 (1): 37–46.

Nelson, Janet L. 1987. "The Lord's Anointed and the People's Choice: Carolingian Royal Ritual." In *Rituals of Royalty: Power and Ceremonial in Traditional Societies,* ed. David Cannadine and Simon Price, 137–80. Cambridge: Cambridge University Press.

Nielsen, Donald A. 1999. *Three Faces of God: Society, Religion, and the Categories of Totality in the Philosophy of Emile Durkheim.* Albany: SUNY Press.

Nirenberg, David. 2008. "Islam and the West: Two Dialectical Fantasies." *Journal of Religion in Europe* 1: 3–33.

Norman, Karin. 1991. *A Sound Family Makes a Sound State: Ideology and Upbringing in a German Village*. Stockholm: Department of Social Anthropology, University of Stockholm (Stockholm Studies in Social Anthropology, no. 24).

Oestrich, Gerhard. 1982. *Neostoicism and the Early Modern State*. Cambridge: Cambridge University Press.

Ortiz, Alfonso. 1969. *The Tewa World: Space, Time, Being and Becoming in a Pueblo Society*. Chicago: University of Chicago Press.

Pasquino, Pasqualle. 1991. "Theatrum Politicum: The Genealogy of Capital—Police and the State of Prosperity." In *The Foucault Effect: Studies in Governmentality*, ed. G. Burchell, C. Gordon, and P. Miller, 105–18. Hemel Hempstead, UK: Harvester Wheatsheaf.

Pina-Cabral, Joao de. 2001. "Three Points on Secularism and Anthropology." *Social Anthropology* 9 (3): 329–33.

Radin, Paul. 1927. *Primitive Man as a Philosopher*. New York: D. Appleton and Company.

Raeff, Marc. 1983. *The Well-Ordered Police State: Social and Institutional Change Through Law in the Germanies and Russia, 1600–1800*. New Haven, CT: Yale University Press.

Rashevsky, Nicholas. 1968. "On the Possible Reversible Changes Between Arational and Rational Behavior of Society." *Bulletin of Mathematical Biophysics* 30: 519–25.

Richman, Karen, and Terry Rey. 2009. "Congregating by Cassette: Recording and Participating in Transnational Haitian Religious Rituals. *International Journal of Cultural Studies* 12 (2): 149–66.

Rieff, Philip. 1965. *The Triumph of the Therapeutic: Uses of Faith After Freud*. New York: Harper and Row.

Rogovin, Vadim Z. 2009. *Political Genocide in the USSR: Stalin's Terror of 1937–1938*. Oak Park, MI: Mehring Books.

Rosen, Steven M. 1994. *Science, Paradox, and the Moebius Principle: The Evolution of a "Transcultural" Approach to Wholeness*. Albany: SUNY Press.

Roy, Olivier. 2007. *Secularism Confronts Islam*. New York: Columbia University Press.

Saberwal, Satish. 1991. "On the Rise of Institutions, Or, the Church and Kingship in Medieval Europe." *Studies in History* 7 (1): 107–34.

Saler, Benson. 2000. *Conceptualizing Religion: Immanent Anthropologists, Transcendent Natives, and Unbounded Categories*. New York: Berghahn Books.

———. 2008. "Conceptualizing Religion: Some Recent Reflections." *Religion* 38: 219–25.

Sayyid, S. 2003 [1997]. *A Fundamental Fear: Eurocentrism and the Emergence of Islam*. London: Zed Books.

Scheuerman, William E. 2001. "Down on Law: The Complicated Legacy of the Authoritarian Jurist Carl Schmitt." *Boston Review*. http://boston review.net/BR26.2/scheuerman.html. Accessed 16 February 2009.

Schmitt, Carl. 1985. *Political Theology: Four Chapters on the Concept of Sovereignty*. Cambridge, MA: MIT Press.

Seitler, Dana. 2008. *Atavistic Tendencies: The Culture of Science in American Modernity*. Minneapolis: University of Minnesota Press.

Serandour, Arnaud. 2005. "On the Appearance of a Monotheism in the Religion of Israel (3rd Century BC or Later?)." *Diogenes* 205: 33–45.

Shentalinsky, Vitaly. 1995. *The KGB's Literary Archive.* London: Harvill Press.

Smith, Christian. 1998. *American Evangelism: Embattled and Thriving.* Chicago: University of Chicago Press.

Strong, Tracy B. 2005. "Foreword" In *Political Theology*, by Carl Schmitt, vii–xxxiii. Chicago: University of Chicago Press.

Swatos, William H. Jr., and Kevin Christiano. 2002. "Secularization Theory: The Course of a Concept." *Sociology of Religion* 60 (3): 209–28.

Ulmen, G. L. 1985. "The Sociology of the State: Carl Schmitt and Max Weber." *State, Culture and Society* 1: 3–57.

Vasquez, Manuel A., and Marie Friedman Marquardt. 2003. *Globalizing the Sacred: Religions Across the Americas.* New Brunswick, NJ: Rutgers University Press.

Velho, Otavio. 2004. "Comment" on Thomas J. Csordas, "Asymptote of the Ineffable." *Current Anthropology* 45 (2): 180–81.

Verdery, Katherine. 1996. *What Was Socialism, and What Comes Next?* Princeton, NJ: Princeton University Press.

Voyé, Liliane. 1995. "From Institutional Catholicism to 'Christian Inspiration.' Another Look at Belgium." In *The Post-War Generation and Establishment Religion*, ed. W. C. Roof, 191–206. Bloomington: Indiana University Press.

Vygotsky, Lev S. 1962. *Thought and Language.* Cambridge, MA: MIT Press.

Walby, Sylvia. 1999. "The New Regulatory State: The Social Powers of the European Union." *British Journal of Sociology* 50: 118–40.

Walzer, Michael. 1985. *Exodus and Revolution.* New York: Basic Books.

Warner, W. Lloyd. 1961. *The Family of God: A Symbolic Study of Christian Life in America.* New Haven, CT: Yale University Press.

Warner, R. Stephen. 1993. "Work in Progress Toward a New Paradigm for the Sociological Study of Religion in the United States." *American Journal of Sociology* 98: 1044–93.

Weber, Max. 1958. *The Protestant Ethic and the Spirit of Capitalism.* New York: Scribners.

Weil, Eric. 1975. "What is a Breakthrough in History?" *Daedalus* 104 (2): 21–36.

Westerlund, David, ed. 1996. *Questioning the Secular State: The Worldwide Resurgence of Religion in Politics.* London: Hurst.

Wright, J. Edward. 2000. *The Early History of Heaven.* Oxford: Oxford University Press.

Wyschogrod, Edith. 1985. *Spirit in Ashes: Hegel, Heidegger, and Man-Made Mass Death.* New Haven, CT: Yale University Press.

Zerubavel, Eviatar. 1981. *Hidden Rhythms: Schedules and Calendars in Social Life.* Chicago: University of Chicago Press.

❧ I ❧

SHAPING RELIGION
THROUGH POLITICS

1

ETHNIC IDENTITY AND RELIGIOUS COMPETITION

Buddhism and Shamanism in Southern Siberia

Galina Lindquist

Introduction: Religion and Ethnonationalism

When modernity arrived and the "sacred canopy" above Western Europe disintegrated, the allegiance to the nation-state was assumed to become one of the primary political and personal identifications of groups and individuals. Allegiance to the nation-state was expected to overshadow, if not completely replace, loyalties to ethnic and religious communities, supposedly more primordial, but rendered obsolete by modernity. This was one among many premises of theories of modernity that had to be modified in postmodern times. In the second half of the twentieth century, empires disintegrated and nation-states became less significant as identity markers and as symbolic entities of emotional attachment and loyalty for their citizens. In these conditions, people once again resort to ethnicity and religion as cementing forces of their diverse collectivities. Religion becomes, increasingly, the ground for redefining newly emerging polities, nation-states as well as ethnic groups in postcolonial and post-Soviet political formations. Local political and intellectual elites seek to shape distinct group identities, constructed differently than those that dominated them before. In these projects, they often turn to what they perceive as "traditional religions," reconstructed in response to expectations and pressures of metropolitan and global powers. Everywhere, "traditional" or "indigenous" religions are rediscovered by new political and intellectual elites, in order to bear symbols of new nationalisms (Lorentzen 2001).

Notes for this chapter begin on page 87.

As discussed in the Introduction to this book, the nation-state generally has been considered a prominent marker of a secularized world. After the Enlightenment, the nation-state was supposed to take over most of the political and social functions of religion in the West. Recently, however, the role of religion in the architecture of nation-states has been reconsidered. The historian Adrian Hastings (1997) demonstrated the centrality of religion in shaping certain European nationalisms: Anglicanism in England, Calvinist Protestantism in the Netherlands. The core identity of the nation, he argued, has often been exercised through discourse and ritual grounded in religion. Religious nationalism, in his view, is a logical development, an "overspill," of religion's contribution to the construction of nationhood. This contribution consists of, among other ways, sanctifying the starting point of the nation, mythologizing threats to national identity, providing religious models for nations, and discovering unique national destinies (1997: 187). These features are used, for example, in the rhetorics of Hindu nationalism, as described by Berglund in this volume.

In cases when ethnicity serves as a foundation for the nation-state, the importance of religion is paramount. The relationship between language and ethnicity is well known; indeed, shared language is one of the basic defining features of ethnicity. Hastings (1997) shows that in the processes of merging disparate kin or tribal groups into ethnic collectivities, the roles of religion and language are interrelated and pivotal. Religion, organized into hierarchical institutions and fixed in written canon, was central in turning regional oral vernaculars into written languages that define ethnicity. Amiras (this volume) shows how ethnic self-consciousness emerges out of the protest against eradicating the group's language, and how the attitudes to different religions are formed in response to whether and, if so, how, these religions accept the ethnic language.

The destiny of ethnic groups, or of ethnically based nations within colonial empires, is borne by religion; the examples of nations that empires failed to "digest" are Catholic Poland surviving in the face of the Stalinist empire and Catholic Ireland holding up against that of the British (Hastings 1997: 185). During more than half a century of its existence, the Soviet empire did succeed in "digesting" many ethnic groups, or, as they were called in the Soviet parlance, "nations and nationalities," within its confines. The system did this by destroying these groups through forcible relocation; by disrupting their modes of sustenance; by imposing industrialization that entailed the mass immigrations of other ethnic groups, such as Russians and Ukrainians settling in Siberia; by remodeling their traditional ways of subsistence in the patterns of Soviet ideology (as described by Vitebsky [2005] for the Northern Siberian reindeer herders); by coercive sedentarization of nomadic pastoralists and the subsequent establishment of *kolkhoses*, as in Tyva, the locale of this chapter. Most importantly, the cultures of these small nations were made weak and vapid by forbidding or delegitimizing their core traits, their rituals and institutions that were classified as "religious." Religious experts and spiritual leaders were executed, imprisoned, or exiled; monasteries and churches were pulled down or turned into storage houses; rituals were forbidden; world views that accommodated the sacred, the local cultures' soul and spirit, were ridiculed as backward superstitions. Despite this devastation, some ethnic groups within the Soviet empire did survive as distinct cultural entities, plunging, after perestroika, into vigorous projects of ethnic revival, developing different versions of "ethnonationalisms." To what extent their survival had to do with their success in retaining their religions in the face of Soviet persecution and beneath the surface of Soviet modernization efforts is an open question. In all these efforts of revival, conditioned by various degrees of political, economic, and cultural autonomy, religion came to play the central role.

In Soviet times ethnicity was neatly and strictly trimmed to fit the ideological formula of "national in form, Soviet in content"; but even in such conditions, ethnicity in the Soviet empire had a different role in nation building than in most Western nation-states. While in the West ethnic loyalties were somehow expected to give way in the face of sentiments toward the nation-state, east of Western Europe ethnicity tended to remain the core of the "nation." Here, however, terms such as *nation* and *ethnicity* had different meanings. Pål Kolstoe, a political scientist, offers a political definition of nation accepted in the West and enshrined, e.g., in the name of "United Nations": "the sum of all citizens, kept together by common territory, government authority, and political history" (2000: 2). He compares this definition with the understanding of a more "cultural" brand, common in Russia and Eastern Europe, where multinational empires survived much longer. In this context, "nation" was "a cultural entity, held together by common language, traditions, folklore, mores and religion"—more familiar in the West as a definition of ethnic group. In the common parlance of the 1960s and 1970s in the Soviet Union, "nation" and "nationality" were used interchangeably, the former more in the popular speech, the latter as an official term denoting "ethnicity." The Soviet Union was a political unity, where the fifteen "union republics" as well as many more "autonomous republics" and still more "autonomous oblasts" were based on titular ethnic groups. To these, no political and economic independence was allowed, whereas some measure of cultural identity was tolerated (as long as active practices of "religion" were not involved). When, at the turn of the 1990s, the Soviet giant loosened its grip, the fifteen "republics" became independent "nation-states," and declared political independence. Their tight economic connections with Russia are still painfully felt, e.g., when the burly neighbor threatens to cut energy supplies and ban the imports of goods. After the collapse of the Soviet Union, the republics designated "autonomous" remained economically integrated within the Russian Federation, while politically they were allowed some independence, modeling their governance structures and constitutions on the Western models of liberal democracy. They were allowed to use their own languages in governance to a much greater degree than had been possible before. Cultural autonomy implied the freedom to pursue local ethnic identities by varying means. Among these means, religion became paramount. After the demise of communist ideology, different religions came out from under the surface, where they had survived Soviet oppression, to be reconstructed and reinvented, and to assume the role of moral and spiritual guidance, ecological compass, and sometimes public national ideology in various designs of ethnonationalism.

Ethnonationalism is a term taken on by political scientists (e.g., Kolstoe 2000; Balzer 1999) for strategies of nation building based on ethnic belonging. The "architects" seek to create the best correspondence between the ethnic and the political "nation," by turning the ethnic culture into an ideological tool and by celebrating this "culture" as shared identity. This is when religion comes to the fore in public life. It is here that conflicts arise between the titular ethnic group and others, that thus become "minorities" and are forced to assimilate or to migrate, to continue a marginal existence, or, if sufficiently strong, to compete for their place in the new polity. This is when "religious competition" (Balzer 2005) may become salient. These are political processes that can turn into bitter struggle, reflecting power games and constellations of forces on larger regional and global political fields.

Politics of Religion in Tyva

Tyva (Tuva in Russian), an autonomous republic within the Russian Federation, is separated by the Sayan mountains from neighboring Khakassia and Krasnoyarskii krai, and borders Altai and Mongolia. The ethnic group known as Tyvans was formed from several Turkic groups, as well as from Turkified Mongols, Samoyeds, and Ket speakers. Scholars claim that as early as the tenth century, "Tuva" was used as an ethnonym (a self-identification name) to define nomadic pastoralist groups dispersed in mountain valleys separated by the Tannu-Ola and Sayan mountains, but united by the language that was part of Old-Uigur (an Ural-Altaic language family) (Balzer 1999). Tyvan territories were controlled by Mongols from the thirteenth to the eighteenth century, and between 1757 and 1911 it was part of the Chinese (Qing dynasty) empire. Russians began settling in Tyva from the nineteenth century, and in 1914 it became a Russian protectorate, placed under Russian commission. In 1921 independence was declared and Tyva became the "Tyvan People's Republic," a Bolshevik state within the Soviet sphere of influence. It was important for the Soviet Union at that point to demonstrate the principle of sovereignty of the young "people's republics," the principle of "self-determination up to secession," as the rhetoric of Lenin's time put it.

In practice the Tyvan state elite had been schooled in Stalin's University of the Peoples of the Orient in Moscow, which provided the cadres for the most fierce Bolshevik regimes in Asia and the Far East. Most Tyvans now agree that the worst repressions in Tyva were executed by Tyvans themselves, even though the young state's domestic politics were always closely controlled by the Stalinist Soviet Union. In 1944 Tyva was incorporated in the Soviet Union and became an "autonomous oblast" and later an autonomous republic. In 1990, when perestroika began and a measure of freedom became possible for the local political subjects, Tyva declared unilaterally the political status of the Tyvan Republic, which gave it greater economic control over resources and industries, with consequences for local ecology and taxation structure (Balzer 1999). But, the disintegration of Soviet economic and industrial structures was as devastating for Tyva as it was for the rest of the country: the few existing factories closed and heavy unemployment ensued. In the early 1990s the situation was exacerbated by ethnic violence against Russians (who constituted a third of the Tuvan population of about 150,000) that led to emigration of thousands.

The Mongolian version of Tibetan Buddhism became dominant in Tyva by the eighteenth century, and before the formation of the people's republic there were twenty-two monasteries (*khurees*) in Tyva. Tibetan, Mongolian, and local Tyvan lamas numbering over three thousand ran the monasteries, performing daily rituals and annual festivals. By the early twentieth century, the lamas were among the very few educated people in the country, and it was no coincidence that the new people's republic relied heavily on them, despite the separation between state and church stipulated in its first Soviet-modeled constitution. Until 1929 the institutional structure of Buddhism in Tyva was still intact, lamas enjoying a number of privileges such as the right to private land and cattle holdings and certain tax exemptions. The Soviet Decree "on religious associations" and the constitutions of 1936 and 1977 declared "freedom of conscience," the right to belong to religious confessions and to adhere to religious beliefs and practices. According to the same law, however, religious education and other forms of what was called "religious propaganda" (which could include any form of religion's appearance in the public arena) were forbidden and could be classified as criminal offence. Extrajudicial pressures on religious communities meant that any representative of clergy, any religious practitioner or religious community, could be dispersed and imprisoned. This is what happened to thousands of priests, monks, and nuns in Russia, as well as to almost all Buddhist lamas and many shamans in Tyva (Balzer 1999; Mongush 2001).

During World War II and the postwar period, the attitude of the regime toward religion became slightly milder. Stalin needed to boost people's patriotism, and the Russian church had historically fulfilled this function well. Another reason was the adoption in the international arena of a new Declaration on Human Rights in 1948. In Buryatia, the center of Buddhism in Russian southern Siberia, a handful of Buddhist monasteries opened to serve as a show-case for religious freedom in Rossiya. Two Buryat monasteries, Ivolginskii and Aginskii, were allowed to pursue educational activities. The former became the seat of Pandito-Kambo-Lama, the official head of the Buddhist *sangha* in the USSR. These monasteries, which retained their ritual and educational traditions, had an enormous importance for the preservation of Buddhism in the Russian Federation, and especially for the Buddhist renewal in Tyva after perestroika (Zhukovskaya 1997).

In Tyva, the hardest repressions against religion were carried out at the end of the 1920s. The Buddhist community of practicing lamas, the sangha of the early twentieth century, played a central role in the establishment of the independent state. In the first decade of its Soviet existence, its monks cooperated with the Bolshevik authorities. A Buddhist renewal movement was instituted in Tyva (as well as in Buryatia, another traditionally Buddhist republic inside the Russian Federation) in the early 1920s. Its aim was to "cleanse Buddhism from folk superstitions" (which referred to popular rituals for solving everyday problems). In practice, these internal reforms aimed at reaching a compromise with the regime, turning Buddhism into philosophy and ethics that would not contradict the communist ideology. But this did not help: at the end of the 1920s, Buddhist clergy in Tyva was marginalized and stripped of all its privileges. In 1930 the Great Khural (the local analogue of the Supreme Soviet) passed a law denying lamas, shamans, and representatives of other religions (denoted in Soviet parlance by the derogatory label of the "cult officials" [*slu-zhiteli kul"ta*]) the right to vote. The monasteries were divested of the status of a juridical entity, their property was confiscated, prayers and religious festivals were forbidden. Starting from 1930, monasteries were closed, and later all of the twenty-two monasteries that had existed in Tyva were destroyed. Lamas were imprisoned and killed, including those who had taken an active part in state building. Some managed to leave Tyva, others retreated to their villages and herder stations and in secret continued to perform rituals of blessing and healing among their closest family. By the beginning of post-Soviet reforms, there were a handful of old lamas living in remote corners of Tyva who had been young novices in the period of independence.

The spirit of perestroika, and Gorbachov's attempts to liberalize home policy, were reflected in the Law on Religion of 1990, the most liberal in the history of the Soviet Union. It recognized religion as a citizen's "inalienable right" (Article 4) and had no provisions limiting religious expression in the public sphere. The Law of 1990 enabled missionary activities of citizens from outside the Soviet Union; it stipulated the right of religious organizations to register as they wished. Registration of a group as a "religious organization" gave it the status of a juridical entity, which granted tax exemption, the right to organize public events and educational projects, the right to invite foreign citizens, and more.

It was stipulated that religion was separated from the state.[1] The collapse of the system that left Rossiya in a condition of ideological chaos, coupled with a strong spiritual thirst after half a century of religious persecution, prepared the terrain for an unprecedented spate of old and new, home and foreign religious confessions and movements that proliferated in Rossiya from the early 1990s.

A couple of years later, however, some quarters within the Russian Orthodox Church that during the first years of perestroika wielded a considerable influence started to voice the need to limit this "wild" religious pluralism. Although all religions were declared equal in the Law of 1990, the so-called historical confessions (those that were seen as "historically" belonging to various cultural segments of Rossiya) claimed a special role for particular "national" or ethnic groups. The concept of "ethnoreligious balance" was formulated on the assumption that religion formed "national" (read "ethnic") mentality. Thus, certain religions claimed the exclusive right of presence in certain ethnic communities. (Shterin 2000). In Rossiya this right was given to the Russian Orthodox Church, although "great world religions" such as Islam, Buddhism, and Judaism were accepted as "traditional religions" for certain groups of its population.

This is how the idea of "traditional" or "historical" religions took root in popular understanding and in the public sphere of Rossiya. Sociological surveys made in early 1990s among ethnic Russians showed that the number of those who considered themselves "believers" or "practicing religious" remained unchanged compared to a decade earlier, while 94 percent of the respondents considered themselves "Russian Orthodox." This pointed to a change in identification rather than to one in "religiosity," understood as adherence to religious practices and ideas. This also reflected a growth in credibility that the Russian Orthodox Church enjoyed in the early 1990s (which deteriorated somewhat by the end of the millennium and in the subsequent decade), while religious tolerance toward other religions diminished. Sociologists of religion defined this tendency as the "Orthodox consensus" (Shterin 2000). This development is perhaps better understood if we remember, as Kolstoe (2000) points out, that in Eastern Europe especially, religion has always been a much more important marker of national/ethnic consciousness than it has been in the West.

Somewhat later, autonomous polities of the Russian Federation passed their own laws in a similar vein. In Tyva such a law was adopted in 1995. The "traditional confessions" listed in it were shamanism, Buddhism, and the Russian Orthodox Church. The sociological statuses of these religions, however, were not quite the same. While Russian Orthodoxy was an obvious identification of ethnic Russians, for Buddhism and shamanism the balance was more intricate. Statistical surveys run in Tyva at the time showed that about a half of the respondents (43 percent) considered themselves Buddhists, while only a fraction identified as "shamanists" (about 3 percent) (Pimenova 2007).[2]

In the late 1990s, so-called centers of shamanism appeared in Tyva. These centers were organized as quasi-clinics where shamans received their clients (for more details on this, see Lindquist 2005). It is not clear what came first, the "juridical confessionalization" of shamanism (Kharitonova 2006) or this specific organizational form of shamanism. Perhaps the view on shamanism as religion, "the most ancient religion of humankind," was impressed on the minds of the bureaucrats by the efforts of local and metropolitan intelligentsia, especially scholars in ethnology and history of religion. Shamanism as an ur-religion is an idea well established in Western academia, starting from the work of Mircea Eliade and finding its way into anthropology. It has been much criticized lately (e.g., Kehoe 2000), but is by no means discarded. It is significant that the man who made the great efforts to have shamanism established as one of the officially recognized (or "traditional") religions in Tyva was himself an ethnologist and a researcher of shamanic tradition.

Mongush Barakhovich Kenin-Lopsan, now in his late eighties, is a Tyvan poet and playwright renowned from Soviet times. He also holds a prestigious academic degree, the Doctor of History (*Doktor istoricheskikh nauk*), from a university in St. Petersburg. While the contents of his literary work have been totally in line with Soviet ideology, the subject of his scientific research was at the time more contentious. He studied Tyvan shamanic practices when shamanism was derided and ridiculed, and could only be presented as folklore, the remnants of old beliefs and practices that survived in the memories of the elders. The corpus of Kenin-Lopsan's ethnographic work is impressive, and to this day he remains the most important, perhaps the only solid and coherent, written source of shamanic knowledge in Tyva. It is this work that in the early 1990s drew the attention of the Western anthropologist and founding father of Western "urban shamanism," Michael Harner.

Harner was a head of the Center for Shamanic Studies in Mill Valley in California, and in 1993 he and his associates, jointly with Kenin-Lopsan and other Tyvan shamans, organized the First International Conference on Shamanism in Tuva.[3] During a couple of weeks, Harner and his friends, some of them anthropologists, others psychotherapists, all practicing shamanists in their home countries of the United States, Austria, Germany, and Switzerland, worked together with Tyvan shamans. In spectacular rituals, Tyvan shamans, donning their garments complete with feathers and claws, drummed, chanted, and performed group rituals of healing (for an eyewitness description, see Peters 1993). This conference effectively established Tyva as a shamanist mecca on the international map. Articles appeared, accounts circulated, and interest in Tyva grew among Western researchers and spiritual seekers. Kenin-Lopsan was awarded a title of "living treasure of shamanism," which he bears proudly to this day, and a small lifetime fellowship that was quite important for the aging scholar in a country with a disintegrating economy.

Kenin-Lopsan's work did much to textualize shamanic knowledge and to bring it closest to what can be seen as a "canon": a coherent authoritative corpus, in line with conventional Western (and Russian) understanding of "religion." It was this type of "shamanic knowledge" that, in the understanding of Russian scholars, was to be transmitted from teacher to student as oral tradition, through personal instruction and initiation. During Soviet times, many shamans were killed or exiled to gulags, and many more had their drums and shamanic garments confiscated. But, as both scholars and lay Tyvans agree, some shamans managed to escape to distant *aals* (herder stations) where they survived the Soviet persecution. After perestroika, when shamanism came out of the shadows, both as a "traditional religion" in the public sphere, and as an everyday means of problem solving, some of these elderly shamans came back to Kyzyl, the Tyvan capital, to take their place in the new "centers" and in public ceremonies.

The shamans of the new generation, who felt the calling and experienced the abilities, and who perhaps went through shamanic illness,[4] started to practice, both in the centers and on their own. In the eyes of Russian scholars and local bureaucracy, their legitimacy as "real shamans" was based, significantly, on the ability to show that they had shamans among their grandparents with whom they grew up, and so could (in theory if not in fact) undergo some kind of personal instruction. While most of the Tyvan shamans can claim such ancestors, the actual instruction that defines for researchers the shamans' authenticity remained a contested issue, making individual practitioners always vulnerable to accusations of being impostors. The ability to present a plausible "origin story," as well as the shamans' ritual performance, determined a shaman's standing vis-à-vis the audience of metropolitan researchers and foreign spirituality and image seekers. These ethnographic details were to match the researchers' knowledge of "traditional shamanism," based on the work of Kenin-Lopsan and other Russian and foreign ethnographers.

For the new shamans, who started to test their strength with Tyvan clients and foreign visitors, the books of Kenin-Lopsan were, to a certain degree, a source of "shamanic knowledge." Textualized, this knowledge takes on a deceptive aura of coherence, which belies the nature of shamanic practices in Tyva. Once a person starts to practice with local clients, it is not the spectacularity of performance that matters, but, rather, the efficacy of healing and the clarity of vision. The clients do not care about the shaman's credentials in terms of origin stories and accounts of shamanic illness. Each shaman's knowledge, her or his cosmology and ritual design, are given to them by their spirits (or, as rational outsiders would say, are creatively imagined by each individual). These individual universes intersect, forming a core of what can be called "cultural knowledge," but this can differ in considerable detail.

Thus, the very nature of shamanic knowledge makes it problematic for the practitioners to work together. The indigenous explanation is that the shamans' spirits have difficulty agreeing with each other. There are stories of shamans' life-and-death combats, with protagonists sitting on mountain tops hundred of kilometers apart. People say that today's shamans are not "real shamans" exactly because they perform in groups. Despite this understanding, it was exactly the public events focused on shamans that from the start, in the early nineties, defined shamanism-as-religion.

To begin with, "shamanism" seemed to vie with Buddhism for the right to represent the nation in the public sphere, to serve as a marker of collective identity. The venues of these public performances were, first and foremost, scientific conferences, such as the one of 1993 mentioned above, and one of 2001, in which I was lucky enough to participate (Lindquist 2006). There the shamans of rival centers, rival groups, had to perform together. These performances were always willingly attended by the local people, who used these occasions as opportunities to be exposed to the shamans' powers in hope of bettering their lives.

The main prerequisite of these public events was for the shamans to be organized in the associations ("centers") that bureaucrats could consider as "religious communities" ("*religioznye obshchestva*"). To start a center, a person had to possess a degree of "urban literacy," social competence in dealing with authorities: thus the chief ideologue of Tyvan "shamanism-as-religion" was Mongush Barakhovich Kenin-Lopsan, who had spent many years in Russian academia as writer and scholar. Kenin-Lopsan declared himself "the doctor of shamanism" and "the chairman of the Tyvan shamans," bringing together in his own gestalt the practitioners and those who study them. Along with many others, in the early 1990s Kenin-Lopsan openly identified as a shaman and came up with a story of a grandmother, a strong shamaness who predicted a bright future for him.

Most of his closest associates were members of the local intelligentsia, artists, actors, and educators. After perestroika these people discovered shamanic abilities in themselves and went to various healing courses in big cities in Russia. At home in Tyva, many of these same people (though not Kenin-Lopsan himself) took part in Buddhist lay societies that started to appear even before the shamanic centers became a reality. In the Buddhist societies, people gathered to gain the lost knowledge of Buddhist philosophy and rituals. Some of the best-known shamans in Kyzyl started as apprentices to old lamas, then getting healers' diplomas, before bureaucratic expediency urged them to come together in shamanic centers. These centers, loci of shamanism's visibility in the public arena, were necessary for the shamans not only to be able to perform for visiting scholars. Being registered as a "religious association" meant having better access to clients. Several practitioners who started their careers in clinics later split off, to work on their own and then to start their own establishments. In addition, shamans working in clinics did not need to get licenses, required by the state if anyone advertises as a "healer" and entailing a long and arduous bureaucratic procedure (this procedure parallels the distinction between healers and magi in Russia, Lindquist 2005b).

Kenin-Lopsan was one of the very few I met in Tyva who was fond of declaring that "shamanism is the ancient religion of the Tyvans." On many occasions, he ardently voiced the opinion that shamanism was also the *only* "true" or "authentic" religion of Tyvans, meaning that Buddhism was as foreign and imported as Russian Orthodoxy. As should be clear from the above, Kenin-Lopsan was one of those who had everything to gain from the status of shamanism as a religion. The rest of the shamans I worked with, however, had great respect for Buddhism or even considered themselves Buddhists. Buddhism and shamanism in Tyva are closely intertwined, and many everyday problems are solved, many key rituals performed, either by lamas or by shamans. Still, as the survey quoted above indicates, most Tyvans identify themselves as Buddhists, rather than shamanists.

When I started my fieldwork in Tyva in 2001, I had an impression that shamanism and Buddhism had equal or at least comparable presence in the Tyvan public arena as "traditional religions." Perhaps this was because I first came to Tyva as a conference participant: research and media are two segments of global networks that meet shamanism (rather than Buddhism) as the Tyvan public face. It is fair to say that "shamanism-as-religion" provided Tyva with a certain way of being global, gave it a place in certain types of "global assemblages"[5]: those involved in Western and Russian networks of tourism, media, and science. To nuance the analysis of globalization, Ulf Hannerz (1996: 7), after Kroeber, once proposed to talk about "ecumenes," locally imagined limits of the inhabited world. In these terms, shamanism-as-religion, as a marker of Tyvan identity, opened for Tyva an ecumene delimited in a certain way. (The Tyvan Buddhism ecumene was different, as I will show below). Importantly, global networks that defined this ecumene also played their vital role in defining shamanism as "religion."

Thus, in the beginning of the 1990s shamanism and Buddhism seemed to compete for the status of *the* traditional religion, a visible marker of national identity, providing an example of "religious competition." During the six years of my fieldwork, however, shamanism seemed gradually to retreat from the public sphere. By 2006 the place of Buddhism as *the* Tyvan religion appeared virtually uncontested. A reason that some Tyvans indicate is the government's special support for Buddhism, by personal preference or by considerations of political expedience. Perhaps Tyvan politicians, in their attempts to forge a national religion, also sensed the factors I have already hinted at above: the idiosyncratic character of each shaman's "knowledge," cosmology, and ritual design; the difficulty for shamans in working together in groups; and the reluctance of the local people to perceive such performances as plausible, as traditionally and spiritually authentic. To bring out this configuration, in the remainder of this chapter I compare two specific public formations of shamanism and Buddhism in today's Tyva. One is centered on a shamanic performance, and on its public resonance. The other concerns a well-known form of Buddhist architecture, the stupa, and the symbolic transformations of space and identity these edifices achieve. My purpose is to show how public formations of Buddhism can be socially cohesive and conducive to the formulation of national identity, while collective appearances of shamanism in the public sphere tend to have more divisive consequences. To make this clearer, a brief account of the post-Soviet history of Buddhism in Tyva is necessary.

Buddhism in Tyva after 2000

As indicated above, all forms of institutionalized Buddhism were eradicated during the Soviet period. Buddhism suffered more complete destruction that shamanism did. It is likely that the Soviet regime in Tyva saw the Buddhist sangha as a compact, organized ideological rival, with a reasonable potential to wield political power (despite the early attempts of Tyvan lamas to be ideologically neutral and loyal to the state). In pre-Soviet times, shamans were not organized in any institutions and had less potential to claim a place in politics. Still, thinking about how many shamans did, in fact, suffer repressions (and there is a rich lore to this effect, in Tyva as elsewhere in the indigenous Siberian nations), survival of shamans in Tyva was perhaps a consequence less of politics, but more of natural topology: it was easier for a shaman to disappear into the taiga, out of sight of the authorities, while lamas were concentrated in monasteries, and thus formed an easy target.

The system of knowledge transmission in Tyvan Buddhism was destroyed. Local intelligentsia and scholarly observers agree that the main problem that besets Buddhism in Tyva today is the low educational level of its clergy. Buddhist "knowledge" comprises bookish knowledge of philosophy and history, as well as practical knowledge of ritual performances. The latter also includes the construction of khurees (monasteries), stupas, and mandalas, themselves markers of the formative presence of Buddhism in the public sphere.

After 2000, local lamas mostly performed practical rituals of blessing, healing, and problem solving for individual families, much in the same vein as shamans did. The visit of Dalai Lama XIV to Tyva in 1992 was a milestone in its post-Soviet history, a happy occasion for everybody. There was unanimous agreement about its significance and its overall beneficial influence on the life of Tyva among people of all walks of life. Among other things, the Dalai Lama performed the ritual of blessing of what many Tyvans consider one of their most sacred sites: the mountain of Khairakaan, about a hundred kilometers from

Kyzyl. A small monument of a stupa-like shape was built there to commemo-rate the occasion, with *Om mani padme hum* painted on a banner in front of it.[6] Through the Dalai Lama's blessings, the site became even more powerful. The shamans of the Tos Deer center (the main shamanic center in Tyva) built their own *ovaa* there, a construction of stones and poles, decorated with variegated ribbons, *chalama,* as their own contribution to honoring the Masters of the place. The stupa and the shamanic ovaa stood at the foot of the mountain, in view of the automobile road passing by. People of all persuasions would stop, say a prayer, and leave an offering to the masters of the place.

After his visit, the Dalai Lama sent five Tibetan monks to live in Tyva, with the intention to promote Buddhist education in the country, to the elation of the intelligentsia. The local sangha, however, was less enthusiastic, espe-cially after some rifts in understanding of Buddhist practice became evident. For example, Tibetans were intransigent on the issue of married lamas, while the Tyvans claimed that this was "traditional" for Tyva. Some of the Tibetans showed harsh attitudes to the young novices (*khuurak*) and lack of understand-ing for small transgressions of the local lamas that, the latter considered, should have been kept quiet as internal concerns. Soon Tibetan lamas were isolated, disallowed to lecture and to officiate in local rituals. Some of them married and left the sangha, while others continued as spiritual instructors for the local lay public. During this time Tyvan boys were sent to study in the monasteries of Buryatia, Mongolia, and India. The issue of funding these studies is still central in Tyva: since religion in Rossiya (including Tyva) is separated from the state, the Tyvan Buddhist Administration (Administration of Kambo-Lama) must rely on private sponsors for all its projects. In practice, it is mostly the young men's relatives in the villages that collect the money. The novices often lack both means and strength to engage in the long education that Tibetan mon-asteries are known for. They return home four or five years later, to assume their roles as local lamas. Actively practicing lay Buddhists rely on teachers from Russian metropolises, who come regularly to lecture, to officiate at rituals, and to enable initiations.[7] Local lamas and visiting teachers do not have much interaction, but both categories represent Buddhism in people's eyes and their respective types of activity contribute to a greater visibility of Buddhism in the public sphere.

The Sacred Site Contested: Shamanic Ritual at the Khairakaan Mountain

In 2003 the shamans of Tyva celebrated the tenth anniversary of their first conference on shamanism in 1993, the one so important for putting Tyva on the global map. The aging patriarch of Tyvan shamanism, Mongush Barakhovich Kenin-Lopsan, presided over the occasion. The shamanic centers of Kyzyl were forced to forget their strife and to meet the foreigners as a united re-ligious community. The guests were researchers, urban shamanists, and sha-manic therapists from Northern Europe. Two days of scientific conference were followed by "practical work," when groups of shamans from various centers took the guests to sacred sites, springs and ovaas, to perform shamanic rituals together. When the scientific program was over, a spectacular collective *kam-lanie* (shamanic ritual using the drum) was to be performed at the foot of the Khairakaan mountain, next to the stupa-like construction commemorating the Dalai Lama's visit.

From the start, the plan was steeped in controversy. The grand kamlanie was to be preceded by unveiling a gravestone dedicated to Heimo Lappalainen, a Finnish anthropologist who had worked in Tyva earlier and loved it so much that he requested that his ashes be scattered on the Khairakaan mountain. Heimo Lappalainen had been a personal friend of Kenin Lopsan, who considered it a matter of honor to implement this request. Yet there was strong opposition: people considered the Khairakaan mountain inappropriate for being associated with death and burial. *Sunezin,* the spirit of the dead, is in Tyva considered as an ambivalent, dangerous presence that, some strongly felt, would defile the sacred mountain. Despite these sentiments, a small, private ceremony of em-placing a gravestone did take place. Later, shamans, conference participants, local authorities, and media people gathered on the slope of Khairakaan. It was a matter of prestige to decide who would open the ritual drumming, and in what order the shamans of different centers would join in. The Western guests, brought to the site at the agreed time, were waiting for several hours before the leader, Ai Churek, decided to start the ceremony. Time passed, the chilly night descended. The frozen Westerners started to drum discreetly in a small circle around their bus, to raise the mood, only to face the full strength of Ai Churek's wrath: it was only her, the local, who was to decide when the ceremony was to be started. It was explained that the shamans were waiting for propitious signs, and the unauthorized drumming was not to be taken lightly, because it was bound to anger the masters of the place.

Finally, the moon came out of the clouds, indeed making a majestic view (Ai Churek is an unsurpassed stage director), and the grand kamlanie was per-formed, in its full glory. It started with a shaman splashing alcohol on his naked torso and lighting it up; it continued with Ai Churek performing throat sing-ing, one of her best specialties. Then shamans from other centers joined in, drumming, chanting, seemingly in trance, forming what to an outside observer seemed like a perfect ensemble. The Western shamanists were discreetly tranc-ing on the margins between the Tyvan shamans, the main characters of the play, and the lay spectators. Toward morning, when the fire burned out, Kenin

Lopsan made a speech translated into English by one of the Tos Deer shamans, a Moscow journalist. He was talking about the "ancient mystery-plays [*misterii*] of shamanism, the original religion of humankind retained by Tyvans."

For the fieldworking anthropologist, an outside observer, the spectacle was indeed dazzling, and I assume that the foreign guests thought all the tribulations were worth their while. However, the accounts that I heard from shamans and lay people a year later were less rapturous. Not surprisingly in the light of what I already knew about shamanic rivalries, my shaman friends told me about bitter combats between the spirits, allies of the shamans who were drumming around the fire. They also told me that the spirits of Khairakaan were displeased with the funerary ritual that defiled their territory. The positive, benevolent powers of the place, augmented by the Dalai Lama's blessing, showed their negative sides of enmity and anger. I was told later that during the following year many local people were tortured by bad dreams, so that drunkenness and depression grew in the area. In subsequent years, when I accompanied people in cars passing by the site, many refused to stop, saying that the place was bad now. The shamans' ovaa was abandoned: after that night, nobody came here to perform kamlanie, I was told. Through the ceremony of "shamanism-as-traditional-religion" shaped in response to expectations of global networks of science, media, and neoshamanic spirituality, the sacredness of place defined in local terms was undermined if not downright negated.

It must be noted that interaction between the shaman and the masters of a place (*eeler*) on behalf of clients is one of the most important and often performed rituals in Tyva. Its essence is paying homage to the spirits of the place that a family or a kin group considers as their own. The aim of this ritual is to connect the family and the place, to define the family's identity in terms of this place, and to construct the links between the social unit, its history, and the land. A greater cultural significance of this ritual is to socialize the land, mapping it through a web of families and kin groups embedded in the land in terms of their personal histories. While in Tyva many sacred places have general significance,[8] the family places are somewhat different. They are considered to have a special power for the members of the group: the family is enjoined to make pilgrimage to these places, to feed its masters, and to maintain the ovaa, the sign of respect to the masters. Healing ceremonies performed in these places by the shaman (or lama) are considered most powerful and are resorted to in most serious cases. Thus, a shaman who drums at a certain place (always alone, save occasional apprentices and a field-working anthropologist), underscores its "sacredness" for a social unit. In the case above, as we have seen, the "community" (or, rather, the disunity) of shamans succeeded de facto in desacralizing (even though perhaps only temporarily) the place considered sacred for the whole nation.

Mapping the Nation: Stupas in Tyva

Lamas are asked to bless the family ovaas, as well as other sacred sites referred
to above. Blessing the ovaa by a lama is likewise a family affair, although, with
both shamans and lamas, this ritual can gather up to a hundred people for
especially big *aimaks* (extended kin groups). During recent years another, parallel way of constructing a sacred topology has become widespread in Tyva: the
practice of building stupas, that in Tyva are called *suburgan*. Stupas are ancient
Buddhist monuments, first built as shrines over Buddha's relics, later sometimes used to contain ashes or relics of famous lamas or saints in order to marks
their tombs, and more generally, as receptacles for offerings and sacred objects.
Stupas are venerated around the Buddhist world and assert the consecration
of space into the cultural space of Buddhism (Tucci 1988 [1932]). They have a
canonical and complex symbolism; on the most general level, stupas are said to
represent the five elements—earth, water, fire, air, and space, and the attributes
of the enlightened mind associated with these. In Tyva, stupas are built on
those sites that have a wider significance for a given geographical area—locally
acknowledged sacred places. Furthermore, they may be built on the spots of
prerevolutionary khurees, or else in places pointed out by respected teachers.

The construction of a stupa, as much a spiritual as a technical process, requires a wealth of detailed ritual knowledge. While the place for a stupa is chosen by the sponsors, the secular authorities of the *kozhuun* (the administrative
unit), the time of the laying of the foundation stone and the exact spot are to be
thoroughly verified, astrologically and ritually. The correct proportions of the
constituent parts must be known, but the most important is the stupa's content, what is hidden inside. The following brief sketch does not begin to probe
into this specialized realm belonging to Buddhist studies (see, for example, the
studies in Dallapiccola and Lallemant 1980); rather, it summarizes the knowledge that my friends, Tyvan lamas, chose to share with me. In the fundament
of a stupa, a vessel called a *bumba* is placed, in which lamas put different sacred
or valuable objects. There are local medicinal herbs: to heal the Masters, so
that they will not harm the people. There are precious stones, and wool from
local species of cattle. Pages of Buddhist texts (sutras) are placed above these.
There should be special prayers dedicated to the Sagysyns, Tyvan for Dharma-
pala, the Protectors of the Faith, including the eeler who were once converted
to Buddhism under rituals performed by lamas. On the sutras one can place
a knife with which a man was once killed—it means that the spirit of war is
cemented down in the earth, forever. There is a bag of *dolgan* (fried millet flour,
a staple food of Tyvan herders). There can be clothes and paraphernalia of a
great teacher, e.g., a rimpoche. Dried *artysh* (sage) is poured over everything,
and all is sprinkled with *arzhan* water. Prayer texts are covered with the earth
from sacred places of all kozhuuns of Tyva, so that in one stupa all Tyva is pres-

ent. The axis of the stupa is a dried tree, debarked, with prayers inscribed on it in gold (more generally, see for example, Irwin 1980).

This is traditional knowledge from Tibet and Mongolia, which, even if it ever were a part of Tyvan practice, was lost during Soviet times. Therefore, in the beginning Tyvan lamas had to rely on visiting Tibetan, Mongolian, and Buryatian colleagues. Thus, even as stupas are symbols of Buddhism's revival in Tyva, they are indexes, if not of globalization, then certainly of an ecumene, defined in a certain way. This "imaginable" or culturally significant transnational topos stretches to India (to the monasteries of Gomang and Gjudmed in the south, and Dharamsala in the north), and embraces the neighboring and culturally close countries of Mongolia and Buryatia. Stupas are products of knowledge that defines this ecumene, of human contacts, networks, and travel routes that comprise it. Stupas also stand for Tyva within these networks, as Tyva is iconically represented by every stupa, through the earth of its kozhuuns and the water of its arzhans, incorporated into the context of Buddhism, the great global religion.

Building stupas and venerating gives merits for better reincarnations and is said to be beneficial for the nature and people around. Stories of auspicious signs and miracles around the stupas abound: spectacular rainbows, propitious weather phenomena, unlikely convalescences. People tell about a more peaceful atmosphere, better economy, and commerce in villages in whose vicinity stupas are built. To build a stupa is a feat of ingenuity and endurance: to muster money and resources from the strained local administrations; to organize the transportation of building materials to distant, inaccessible places, to which the roads close when rains make rivers rise. There are Tyvan lamas who specialize in the knowledge of stupas, having learned this while working with guest lamas from Buryatia or Tibet; these lamas are well respected and in high demand. When a newly built stupa is inaugurated, lamas from the central administration arrive in groups to officiate at ceremonies, chanting sutras, clanging cymbals, beating drums. Local lamas as well as guests (who are quite frequent in the Tyvan sangha) are easily incorporated in these ceremonies that gather crowds of local people from far and wide and serve as occasions for amateur theater performances and official speeches.

The question of funding is an interesting one. Since religion in Tyva is constitutionally separated from the state, the state is not supposed to give money for such projects. On the other hand, the state sponsors "projects of national cultural significance," and in each case it is the task of the people who drive the project to bring home its importance to the authorities. It is the job of local administration to find sponsors. Wealthy families of the area sometimes take part in funding the construction of stupas. Then they have a say regarding the site, that can be connected with the history of their own aimak. They also become responsible for the stupa's maintenance, which is tacitly considered their own.

They are considered good Tyvans and good Buddhists. With stupas appearing everywhere in Tyva, it declares itself a Buddhist country, the local sangha becomes visible, and people's local identity is strengthened and metonymically defined within the national Tyvan and larger transnational ecumene. Buddhism is established ever firmer as a national religion.

* * *

Stupas and rituals around them, as well as shamanic rituals of blessing the family ovaa can be seen in a classical functionalist way as promoting group cohesiveness. The groups defined by shamanic rituals in today's Tyva are limited in scale: while shamanic rituals can hold together an aimak (a kin group), they do not seem to be able to define Tyva as a nation. As I have tried to show, shamanism and Buddhism in Tyva, as "national religions," work in a twofold way. First, they represent Tyva as a nation to the outside, in the transnational arena, for global publics; second, they define Tyva as a nation for the inside, on the home turf. Both shamanism and Buddhism have succeeded in the first task, although the ecumenes they define for Tyva, the ways to be global, are outlined by shamanism and Buddhism in different ways. While shamanism, figuring as "an authentic wisdom of the native people, the survived ur-religion of humanity," stages Tyva on the global scene for Western (and Russian) spiritual seekers, tourists, researchers, and media, Buddhism defines Tyva as a Buddhist country within the cultural geography of Tibetan Buddhism, drawing it closer to Tibet, India, Buryatia, and Mongolia.

For the second task, however, that of internal cohesiveness across social and geographic divisions, working to define an ethnic nation as one extended family—one aimak (which is what ethnonationalism is all about)—shamanism-as-religion in Tyva has proved to be less appropriate. The reason, I suggest, lies in the internal logic of shamanism as it is understood and practiced in Tyva today, as compared to that of Buddhism. Buddhist monasteries and the sangha itself are organized on the principles of hierarchical order. Despite inevitable personal frictions and political splits (such as took place in Tyva in the early 1990s), Tibetan Buddhist monasteries endure even transplantation to a different soil.[9] The Buddhist cosmos is hierarchical: Buddhas, bodhisattvas, dharmapalas, local deities and spirits, all have their proper place. Notwithstanding human skirmishes and political disagreements that can disrupt local sanghas, lamas share the same cosmos, which they have studied and learned, into which they socialize through formal education and ritual participation.

Shamans' cosmos, however, comes from his or her own experience (they would say they are shown it by their spirits). Even though these worlds share basic cultural traits, shamans, their creators, do not necessarily want to share these worlds with their fellow practitioners and rivals. True, shamanic clinics in Kyzyl, the organizational form imposed on shamanic practice by bureaucratic (post)modernity, are hierarchical structures, each presided over by a strong sha-man to whom the rest have to submit themselves. But these hierarchies tend to be unstable and splitting, practitioners coming and going, uneasy alliances forming and dissolving, and overt and covert rivalries erupting into accusations in curses and other kinds of shamanic warfare. Politicians are also human, and in Tyva they resort to shamans just like the rest of the population, when the nature of practical problems calls for it.[10] The claims of some shamans to have ensured the election victory for high-up politicians are confirmed by sudden spurts of wealth that these shamans display. All this activity, however, proceeds behind closed doors.

Perhaps learned ideologists of shamanism (such as Kenin Lopsan) will con-tinue to advocate its primacy as *the* "traditional religion" of Tyvans. Despite this, shamanism in Tyva clearly failed to become a "national religion." This does not mean that shamanism under no circumstances can assume the role of national identity marker in the political arena. History knows a number of such examples, not least in the north Asia of which Tyva is a part, as Humphrey and Thomas have persuasively argued (1994). Closer to our times, in the post-So-viet context, the competition between shamanism and other religions on the market can turn out differently than described in this chapter, when the title of the national religion is up for grabs. In Sakha (Yakutia), for example, where Buddhism has never been a strong presence, different versions of "shamanism" are much more visible in the public arena, showing stronger resemblance to an established religion (Balzer 2005). These versions, however, exhibit such a different internal logic that the use of the term, shamanism, even in the plural, becomes obscuring. Yet who said that academics have a monopoly on defining terms? One of the empty signifiers, mentioned by Csordas (1997) as a mark of postmodern religion, "shamanism" joins the range of other contested labels, to contribute to politics of religion as struggle for signification.

NOTES

1. This implied that no particular confession was entitled to the special support of the state, but the state could sponsor or take part in particular public or educational events.
2. The 17% adhering to the Russian Orthodox Church reflected the dwindling Rus-sian population in Tyva and an increasing cultural marginalization of Russians there. In the 1990s, the Russian population was diminished by emigration after

the ethnic strife of the beginning of the 1990s, the shut-down of industries where Russians had predominantly worked, and a sharp decline in living standards. In the first decade of 2000, the Tyvan language became increasingly dominant in government and bureaucracy, and the public domain seemed to be exclusively defined by the Tyvan culture.

3. This conference was the first one in Tyva, but it had precedents in other Siberian nations. Thus, e.g., an international conference on shamanism was organized in 1992 in Yakutsk, the capital of the republic of Sakha (Yakutia), signifying similar processes, though in a somewhat different context (Balzer, personal communication).

4. Shamanic illness is a severe psychophysical affliction, which traditionally has been a part of shamanic initiation. It can have symptoms of acute psychosis or epilepsy, among others. It is incurable by biomedicine and can be lethal, but stops when a novice accepts the vocation. In Soviet times, when shamanic initiation was not a culturally viable option, people thus afflicted often ended their lives in mental asylums.

5. In a recent book, Collier and Ong (2005) propose seeing globalization not as a cluster of processes, but as a set of problem-spaces that frame certain subjects as social fields in interaction and tension with other phenomena. These authors try to convey the logic of structuring these fields by the term *assemblages*: "products of multiple determination, not reducible to a single logic"; emergent, shifting, partial and situated (p.12).

6. *Om mani padme hum* is the most often used mantra in Tibetan Buddhism. Repeating it, or seeing it written, is supposed to attract the beneficial attention of Chenrezig, the Buddha of compassion.

7. In Tantric Buddhism that is practiced in Tibet, Mongolia, Buriatiya, and Tyva, "initiations" are ways for the practitioners to establish direct contact with a given deity. This is done by a teacher who transfers the mantra and certain techniques of visualization and meditation pertaining to this deity.

8. In Tyva, certain lakes, mountains, mountain passes, and water springs (*arzhan*) are generally considered sacred places. There are rules of behavior in these places—for example, it is forbidden to swim and fish in some lakes, to wash the body and clothing in some rivers, and so forth. Some of these places are considered to have healing powers, especially arzhans, popular spas for Tyvans who camp there with family and friends in summer, bathing and drinking water to heal different ailments. Arzhans are also places of choice for healing rituals, conducted by shamans or lamas.

9. This is the case with great Tibetan monasteries in south India, which are today largely the same they have been in Tibet for centuries; see Dreyfus 2002.

10. Even though shamans and lamas largely attend to the same problems, in Tyva it is said that if the problem is one's own fault, one goes to a lama, while if someone else's malice has caused it, the shaman can help better. Also, people turn to shamans to solve problems that have already erupted, while lamas are better in preventing problems. Lamas are better for blessing, while the specialty of shamans is retaliation. These distinctions are tentative, however; people go to both lamas and shamans in parallel or in succession.

REFERENCES

Balzer Mandelstam, Marjorie. 1999. "Dilemmas of Federalism in Siberia." In *Center-Periphery Conflict in Post-Soviet Russia: A Federation Imperiled*, ed. M. A. Alexseev, 131–66. New York: St. Martin's Press.

———. 2005. "Whose Steeple Is Higher? Religious Competition in Siberia." *Religion, State and Society* 33 (1): 58–69.

Collier, J. and A. Ong. 2005. "Global Assemblages, Anthropological Problems." In *Global Assemblages: Technology, Politics, and Ethics as Anthropological Problems*, ed. A. Ong and J. Collier, 3–21. Oxford: Blackwell.

Csordas, Thomas J. 1977. *Language, Charisma and Creativity*. Berkeley: University of California Press.

Dallapiccola, Anna, and Stephanie Zingel-Ave Lallemant, ed. 1980. *The Stupa: Its Religious, Historical and Architectural Significance*. Wiesbaden: Franz Steiner Verlag.

Dreyfus, Georges B. J. 2002. *The Sound of Two Hands Clapping: The Education of a Tibetan Monk*. Berkeley: University of California Press.

Hannerz, Ulf. 1996. *Transnational Connections*. London: Routledge.

Hastings, Adrian. 1997. *The Construction of Nationhood. Ethnicity, Religion and Nationalism*. Cambridge: Cambridge University Press.

Humphrey, Caroline, and Nicholas Thomas, ed. 1994. *Shamanism, History and the State*. Ann Arbor: University of Michigan Press.

Irwin, John. 1980. "The Axial Symbolism of the Early Stupa: An Exegesis." In *The Stupa: Its Religious, Historical and Architectural Significance*, ed. Anna Dallapiccola and Stephanie Zingel-Ave Lallemant, 12–38. Wiesbaden: Franz Steiner Verlag.

Kehoe, Alice. 2000. *Shamans and Religion: An Anthropological Exploration in Critical Thinking*. Prospect Heights, IL: Waveland Press.

Kharitonova, Valentina. 2006. *Phoenix From the Ashes? Siberian Shamanism at the Turn of the Millenium*. Moscow (In Russian).

Kolstoe, Pål. 2000. *Political Construction Sites: Nation-Building in Russia and the Post-Soviet States*. Boulder, CO: Westview Press.

Lindquist, Galina. 2005a. "Healers, Leaders and Entrepreneurs: Shamanic Revival in Southern Siberia." *Culture and Religion* 6 (2): 257–79.

———. 2005b. *Conjuring Hope: Magic and Healing in Contemporary Russia*. Oxford and New York: Berghahn Books.

———. 2006. *The Quest for the Authentic Shaman: Multiple Meanings of Shamanism on a Siberian Journey*. Stockholm: Almqvist & Wiksell.

Lorenzen, Lois Ann. 2001. "Who Is Indian? Religion, Globalization, and Chiapas." In *Religions/Globalizations: Theories and Cases*, ed. D. H. Hopkins, L. A. Lorentzen, E. Mendieta, and D. Batstone. Durham, NC: Duke University Press.

Mongush, Marina. 2001. *The History of Buddhism in Tyva*. Novosibirsk (In Russian).

Moskalenko, Nelli. 2004. *Ethnopolitical History of Tyva*. Moscow (In Russian).

Peters, Larry G. 1993. "In the 'Land of Eagles': Experiencing Shamanism in Tuva." *Shaman's Drum: Journal of Experiential Shamanism* 33: 42–49.

Pimenova, Ksenia. 2007. *Revival and Transformation of Traditional Tuvan Beliefs and Practices in the Post-Soviet Period*. Dissertation for the degree of the Candidate of Sciences, the Miklukho-Maklai Institute of Ethnology and Anthropology, Moscow (in Russian).

Shterin, M. 2000. "Interaction between the Church and the State and Religious Legislation in Russia in the 1990s." In *Old Churches, New Believers,* ed. D. E. Furman, 182–208. Moscow (in Russian).

Tucci, Guiseppe. 1988 [1932] *Stupa: Art, Architectonics and Symbolism.* New Delhi: Aditva Prakashan.

Vitebsky, Piers. 2005. *The Reindeer People: Living With Animals and Spirits in Siberia.* London: HarperCollins.

Zhukovskaya, N. L. 1997. *The Revival of Buddhism in Buryatia: Problems and Perspectives.* Moscow: IEA RAN (in Russian).

2

THE GLOBAL CONSTITUTION OF RELIGIOUS NATIONALISM

Hindutva and Globalization

Henrik Berglund

Born in the shadows of ethnic cleansing, India opted for a secular constitution, committing itself to no special faith. This solution was to some extent a result of the horrors of the partition of British India, which included serious Hindu-Muslim riots, and which left millions dead or homeless. The partition resulted in the formation of Pakistan, which became more or less a Muslim state, while India, although dominated by the Hindu majority, still included a large Muslim minority. Based on the experiences of the partition of British India, the liberal and socialist political forces that dominated Indian politics at the time supported the formation of a secular state. Further support was found among the global community of social scientists and intellectuals, who predicted the demise of religion as a political factor (Lerner 1957; Luckmann 1967; Weber 2002). In the first decades of independence, India seemed to fulfill this prophecy under Prime Minister Jawaharlal Nehru: religion took a backseat and the leadership of the new state was fully focused on economic and social development, building the "Nehruvian state" (Brass 1990; Nayar 2001). In the 1970s this model began to crumble, the dominant Congress Party was for the first time challenged, and new political identities emerged, based not on ideology, but on features such as religion and ethnicity (Jaffrelot 1996; Madan 1997; Gupta 1985; Kohli 1992) These identities were mobilized by various forces, resulting in political unrest and separatist claims in several states, but also in a further reorientation of national politics in which political parties drew increasingly on religion, especially the Hindu nationalist Bharatiya Janata Party

(BJP) (Malik and Singh 1995; Ghosh 1999). The solution to the problem of reconciling religion and democracy has generally been some kind of secularism, in which the state is either essentially nonreligious or uncommitted to any particular faith. In India there has been long-standing and broad-based support for the latter approach, but this consensus has in the last decades been seriously challenged by the BJP. Since the early 1980s, the party has continuously gained in influence and was the leading force in the coalition government that ruled 1999–2004. While being based on a Hindu nationalist ideology, the party has also welcomed further liberalization and globalization of the Indian economy.

This chapter will address the uneasy link between politics and religion, and discuss the implications of the Hindu nationalist challenge in relation to the established and largely liberal form of Indian democracy. It will also analyze the possible connection between the current wave of intensification of religious political identities and the ongoing process of globalization. How do the Hindu nationalists view the linkage between politics and religion? What were the factors behind the success of the BJP from the 1980s and onward? What have been the effects of globalization on the Hindu nationalist movement?

The Religious Roots of Hindu Nationalism

The rise of the BJP came as a break with the existing secular tradition of Indian politics, and confirmed the increasing criticism formulated against modernization theory. "Religious nationalism" emerged as a concept, and signified a trend in large parts of the world in which nationalism and religion appeared to be compatible with each other, and also able to develop alongside both modernization and globalization (van der Veer 1994; Huntington 1996).

Modern Hindu nationalism claims to base itself on ancient Hindu culture but has been influenced also by other sources. This culture includes many different traditions, but most would agree that there exists a core, a kind of classical Hinduism that is common for almost all branches and that includes a respect for certain holy texts, the worshipping of certain gods, the importance of pilgrimage, and the usage of a Hindu calendar (Klostermaier 1989; Hellman 1993). The most important texts are the *vedas*, the *upanishads*, and the *agamas*, which all include both philosophical and practical guidance. These are supplemented by texts that are considered to be theologically less important, but that have had a huge popular impact, such as the *Mahabharata* and the *Ramayana*, which present the stories and myths of the Hindu gods. The specific gods that are worshipped may differ from family to family (even from individuals of the same family), but are usually incarnations or descendants of the two main gods Vishnu and Shiva. While the style of worshipping differs depending on caste, sect, and region, both temple and home worshipping are parts of life for most

Hindus. Almost all temples keep a *murti* (a visible deity in form of a sculpture or an image) in their center, and the ritual in the temple is common for most branches of the Hindu faith, with the *puja* (worship of the *murti*) as the core. Also the architecture of the temples is common and follows two basic patterns: one southern and one northern (Shattuck 1999). Home worshipping to deities in the form of sculptures or images often focuses on minor gods, usually with only regional or local recognition, and is for most Hindus as important as temple worship.

Hindus are also united in their belief in pilgrimage, a tradition that is very much alive and that annually attracts millions of devotees. Pilgrimage usually includes a gathering at special geographic locations that are either mentioned in the holy texts, or that have later come to gain prominence because of, for example, association to important persons or events in Hindu history. While pilgrimage is often of local or regional character, events like the religious mass meetings and ritual bathing of the *kumbh mela* draws millions of Hindus from all over India, and the tradition of pilgrimage is alive also in the Hindu communities outside of India. Similarly the Hindus are united by a religious calendar, marking the most important holidays and festivals. Also here, differences between sects, regions and castes can be recorded. One example is the celebrations during *diwali,* which are held all over India but which differ in style and content. In the north of India it is held to commemorate the homecoming of the god Ram after his victory over the demon Ravana. The festival is in the west of India, however, celebrated in honor of the god Lakhsmi, and in the West Bengal and in Orissa in the east it is connected to Kali. This shows both the unity and the discrepancy of the various forms of Hinduism: the same festival is observed but not necessarily at the same date or with the same content.

The Hindu nationalist movement often uses its purported link to classical Hinduism and traditional Hindu culture in its political mobilization and in some cases reinterprets basic religious concepts. One example is the Hindu nationalist definition of *dharma,* a concept that is usually translated as a set of duties, which differs depending on a number of factors, most importantly caste and age. While *dharma* is considered highly important to fulfill, most see it as a personal or philosophical issue. The Hindu nationalists reinterpret the concept and also give it political meaning: it is the duty of every Hindu to work for the supremacy of Hinduism, and some organizations within the movement have also defined the BJP as the political force that works for the fulfillment of dharma (Hellman 1993). References to ancient Hindu culture, and to a glorious Hindu state—the so-called *ram rajya*—are common in the rhetoric of the BJP, and the party often refers to classical Hindu texts and traditions in its political mobilization (Gold 1991; Banerjee 1998). The most obvious example of this is the Ramjanmabhoommi campaign that was launched in the late 1980s with the purported intention of liberating the birth place of the god Ram, the main deity in the classical epos *Ramayana*. The indicated spot was at the time covered by a sixteenth-century mosque, which the campaigners demanded to be shifted or destroyed. Although no historical or archaeological evidence existed for these claims, the Hindu nationalist movement managed to turn the conflict into a national issue that dominated the domestic political scene in the early 1990s. Both the attempts to redefine dharma and its strong engagement in the Ayodhya issue must be interpreted as strategies to link religion to politics, or rather to use religion as a political tool, and as examples showing that the Hindu nationalist movement in general and the BJP in particular, are not primarily interested in the religious aspects of the Hindu faith, but rather in Hinduism as the basis of a cultural and political identity.

The Hindu nationalist movement was inspired by the reformism established within Hinduism from the eighteenth century and onward, a movement that to some extent opened up Hinduism to a global audience and also contributed to the globalization of Indian society (Jaffrelot 1996: 12–19; Embree 1989). Groups such as the Brahmo Samaj and the Ramakrishna Mission took a stand against what they perceived as superstitious and oppressive practices within Hinduism: child marriages, *sati* (the ritual burning of widows), excessive forms of polytheism, and idolatry. They were also critical of the caste system and were partly inspired by other faiths. The Ramakrishna Mission under Swami Vivekananda was very successful in spreading Hinduism abroad and visits to Europe and North America by Vivekananda (especially his presence at the Parliament of Religions in Chicago 1893) was a starting point for an increased interest in Hindu religion and philosophy in the West. The Arya Samaj, on the other hand, suggested a less open and more nationalistic reformism, and in its teachings there is also a tendency toward fundamentalism since the *Veda* books are defined as the fundament of Hinduism (Llewellyn 1993). In rejecting the influences from Christianity and Islam, and by emphasizing the national Hindu heritage, the Arya Samaj contributed to the formation of an early Hindu nationalist movement. Some of its leaders, like Lala Lajpat Rai and Bal Ganghadar Tilak, were active within the Indian National Congress (INC), where they were defined as "radical," as opposed to the liberal mainstream. The radicals took a tougher stand against the British, argued for a more militant approach of the freedom movement, and were critical of the largely nonviolent resistance strategies of the congress.

The first national Hindu nationalist organization, the Hindu Maha Sabha, was formed in 1915, and during its early years many of its members were active also within the INC. The conflict between Hindu nationalists and moderates eventually led to a split and the transformation of the Hindu Maha Sabha into a political party, formally founded in 1937. This party constituted the political wing of the growing Hindu nationalist movement that had found its ideological basis in the writings of V. D. Savarkar. In his treaty *Hindutva*, Savarkar made the first systematic presentation of the Hindu nationalist ideology and presented Hinduism as the foundation of Indian culture, and as a religion threatened by both Muslim and Christian influences. The book was written in a prison cell in the Andaman Islands where Savarkar served a sentence for anti-British activities, and was first published under pseudonym in 1923. Savarkar launched the term *Hindutva* as a definition of a common bond between all Indians, a strong feeling for India as the motherland and for Indian culture. In this book, as in most Hindu nationalist texts, the concepts "Hindu" and "Indian" are interchangeable, implying that the true culture of India is Hindu in its origin (Savarkar 1942). His position toward the religious and ethnic minorities in India is that they can coexist with the Hindu majority, but that they would have to adapt culturally and accept that India is a Hindu nation. Any failure to do so would call into question their allegiance to the Indian nation, which could lead to serious conflicts, even the annihilation of the minorities.

Despite its strong emphasis on domestic culture, the Hindu nationalist movement was influenced also by modern ideas of nationalism, developed primarily in Europe (Bhatt 2001; Nandy et al. 1995). The idea of the nation as the bearer of political and cultural meaning, with the nation-state as its natural extension, was imported through the colonial experience, and spread with the expansion of the educational system. While the colonial state was resented, not even its opponents could deny the dominant role of the European nation states within world politics, nor their economic and scientific success. The freedom movement in India was inspired by the nationalist ideas from Europe, and the mainstream of the INC adopted a form of liberal and territorial nationalism where the nation was defined more or less through its geographical borders, and where all individuals living within these borders were considered as citizens, regardless of faith, race, language, or any other form of primordial criteria. The Hindu nationalists, however, had a different definition based more on religion and culture as the deciding criteria, drawing primarily on ideas found in German and Japanese nationalism (Hansen 1999: 39–44; Srivastava 1973). This form of nationalism emphasizes that it is the right and duty of every Hindu to protect the national Hindu culture and that only within this culture can the individual citizen develop and prosper. This is evident in *Hindutva* and all other major texts of the Hindu nationalist movement, and the term *cultural nationalism* was also applied by the RSS chief Golwalkar when describing the essence of Hindu nationalism (Golwalkar 1980).

In the 1920s and 1930s, the Hindu nationalist movement continued to develop, strengthened by the foundation of the Rashtriya Swayamsevak Sangh (RSS), a cultural organization that has historically been the backbone of the movement (Andersen and Damle 1987; Basu et al. 1993; Noorani 2001). It is a cadre-based organization with thousands of local groups (*shakas*) all over India, working in areas such as education, social work, cultural activities, and sports.

The RSS was formed by Dr. Keshav Baliram Hedgewar largely as a response to what many Hindu nationalists perceived as a Muslim threat, and as a reaction against the growing influence of Mahatma Gandhi. It is a nonpolitical organization, but has throughout the years worked closely with the Hindu Maha Sabha and the BJP and its predecessor the Jana Sangh. Together with a number of other organizations it forms the Sangh Parivar, a family of organizations devoted to *Hindutva*.

The Relation between Politics and Religion in Independent India

The ideology of the RSS under Hedgewar, and under his successor Madhav Sadashiv Golwalkar, was very similar to the Hindu nationalism defined by Savarkar, and his nationalism differed from that of both the Gandhians and secularists in the INC. Mahatma Gandhi argued that both nationalism and politics should be influenced by religion, since humanity would otherwise end up in a moral void, but he strongly rejected the Hindu nationalist solution, which he regarded as chauvinistic and intolerant. The secular camp included both liberals and socialists, which despite their political differences agreed that religion should play little or no role in the politics of a future independent India. The Hindu nationalist movement participated in the broader nationalist movement, and some Hindu nationalists also preferred to stay within the INC, but the tensions between the liberal and the Gandhian factions on the one hand, and the Hindu nationalists on the other, increased and peaked in the years before and after independence. This power struggle was decided to the disadvantage of the Sangh Parivar because of its general lack of public support, but also due to the discrediting of the movement by its alleged involvement in the murder of Mahatma Gandhi (Graham 1993: 83–108). These events also negatively affected the possibilities of the Hindu nationalists to influence the character of the new independent state, and the INC did, after some internal discussions, decide to establish secularism as the guiding principle for postindependence India. Indian secularism has never been officially defined, but the practice of the Indian state suggests that the Indian definition of the concept differs from those adopted in Western Europe and North America, in the sense that it does not include a separation of state and religion, but could rather be defined as "equal treatment of all religions."

A complete separation of state and religion has never been on the agenda in India, and the lack of an ecclesiastical structure within both Hinduism and Islam has required the Indian state to intervene in religious matters (Puri 1990: 153–56). Also the practice to let issues like marriage, divorce, and adoption be decided by the laws and traditions of the various religious communities is an example of the special form of secularism adopted by the Indian state, where the purpose of the state is more to guarantee the well-being of all religions, rather than to secure a separation of state and religion. While a majority of the political forces in India saw secularism as the only solution in a multicultural state with sizable and distinct minorities, the Sangh Parivar has always been critical. The political theory of the Hindu nationalist state is based on the cultural nationalism of Savarkar, which defines Hindu culture as the core of everything Indian. As a consequence the state should be permeated with Hindu values and work for the protection and development of Hindu culture and not for the development of a multicultural state. The issue of minority rights was never thoroughly discussed by either Savarkar or Golwalkar, but it is clear in their writings that Muslims and Christians in India are expected to adapt to the values and traditions of the majority and to recognize Hindu culture as their own, a position that clashes with the established form of Indian secularism. The Sangh Parivar, and especially the BJP, further accuses the INC and the parties on the left of practicing a form of "pseudosecularism" that benefits the minorities at the expense of the Hindu majority, with the purpose of gaining votes from the minorities.

In the late 1980s the Hindu nationalist challenge transformed into a violent campaign against the established practice of Indian secularism in which religion became a weapon in the struggle for political power. After independence the Hindu nationalist movement consolidated its presence in Indian society by continuing its social and cultural work but also by launching a new political party: the Bharatiya Jana Sangh. The party contested both national and state-level elections between 1952 and 1971, but apart from some success in Delhi and parts of northern India, the Jana Sangh failed to develop into a serious alternative to the Congress Party. It contested the 1977 and 1980 elections as a faction of the Janata Party, but regrouped as the BJP in 1980.

The Rise of the BJP

After failing in the 1984 elections, the BJP was reorganized, and for the coming decade the whole of the Hindu nationalist movement was mobilized in a nationwide campaign against the INC and the left. The BJP claimed Hindu nationalism to be the only possible form of nationalism in the country, equated "Hindu" with "Indian," and argued that the kernel of Indian culture had always been Hindu. The INC and the left were accused of appeasing the minorities in order to win electoral support, and the *Hindutva* movement picked out a few key issues on which their campaign focused, drawing special attention to the position of the Muslim minority. This had been a contested issue ever since the partition of British India in 1947, and while Pakistan in practice had developed into a state based on a religious identity, the Indian leaders had opted for a secular state in which no religion had a special relationship to the state. In preindependence India, a multitude of different social and legal practices regulating family relations and disputes existed alongside each other. The British authorities did not introduce uniform legislation, and the law varied depending on the faith of the subject. Amir Ali suggests that the colonial experience included the development of a public sphere, but that the private sphere was left not to the individual citizens, but to the native elites, which may have resulted in the cementing of community-based identities both before and after independence (Ali 2001). Because of this, the formation of a public sphere and the subsequent division between state and civil society did not have the same effects in India as in Western Europe, as the preferences of the individual citizens were to some extent dominated by the strength of presupposed religious identities. This domination came to blur the boundaries between state and civil society, and between the private and the public sphere. The private sphere in India turned out to be outside the immediate reach of the state, but nevertheless not in the hands of the individual citizen.

When India gained independence, the question arose: should a uniform civil code be introduced, or should family law remain within the religious sphere, with different legislation for each community? In the first constitution of independent India, the need for a uniform civil code was clearly established. The 44th article states: "The State shall endeavour to secure for the citizens a uniform civil code throughout the territory of India." Despite this, the legal practice has ever since independence been to have separate civil codes for each community, based on a widespread resistance to the introduction of a uniform civil code, especially among Muslims. The Hindu code was reformed after independence, but with great difficulties. The work began already during British rule and was continued by the Nehru government. A comprehensive revision was started in 1941, and what began as the Hindu Code Bill was later divided into four separate bills: the Hindu Marriage Bill, the Hindu Succession Bill, the Hindu Minority and Guardianship Bill, and the Hindu Adoptions and Maintenance Bill. The resistance came from conservative Hindus and was reinforced by the fact that different types of laws and customs prevailed in the various regions of India (Puri 1990: 211–12.) The bills were finally passed in 1955 and 1956, and while some critics claim that a male bias remained in the new laws, substantial changes were made concerning the rights to divorce and adoption (Agnes 1995). Some saw the Hindu Code Bill as the first step toward the uniform civil code recommended in the constitution, and that the next step would be to suggest reforms of the family laws concerning non-Hindus, but apart from reforms regarding the Parsee community passed in 1988, until today no such steps have been taken.

The introduction of the Hindu Code Bill signified an intention from the INC leadership to also reform other civil codes, but it was also known that there would be widespread resistance. The idea of a common civil code was not seriously discussed in the freedom movement. On the contrary, because of the animosity between Hindus and Muslims, which threatened the effectiveness and legitimacy of the whole freedom movement, separate personal laws came to be seen as evidence that the rights of the minorities would be respected in a future independent India (Banatwalla 1992: 153–54; Engineer 1992: 163). During the work on the constitution, the suggestion to provide for a uniform civil code within the section "Fundamental Rights" was rejected. Instead, it was to be regarded as a "Directive Principle." This solution was criticized at the time, both by those in favor of establishing a uniform civil code and by those rejecting it even as a Directive Principle. The issue has been raised a few times since, but proposals advocating a change have so far not been accepted. This debate was revived in 1985 in connection with the Shah Bano case in which a divorced Muslim woman claimed her right to alimony, which according to the majority of the Muslim clergy contradicted Muslim personal law (Engineer 1987; Hasan 1989). The Supreme Court of India had ruled in favor of Begum Shah Bano, but also expressed its dismay with the practice of separate family laws and expressed its support for the introduction of a uniform civil code. The INC-led government with Rajiv Gandhi as prime minister, however, reversed the verdict by introducing a new law that guaranteed the Muslim-minority separate family laws. Gandhi's decision came after enormous pressure from various Muslim groups, and afterward he was attacked by the BJP, branded as a "pseudosecularist" and accused of pampering the Muslim minority for electoral gains.

The Shah Bano case was the starting point of a Hindu nationalist mobilization, which rapidly turned its attention towards another legal case: the Babri Masjid-Ramjanmabhoommi controversy in Ayodhya, Uttar Pradesh, a conflict over a sixteenth-century mosque that according to the Hindu nationalist movement had been built upon the remnants of a Hindu temple signifying the birth place of the Hindu god Ram (Engineer 1990; Gopal 1991; Nandy et al. 1995). The legal case had been pending for decades but it was not until 1989 that the BJP and the rest of the Sangh Parivar fully engaged in it, demanding that the area surrounding the mosque should be returned to the Hindu community, thereby enabling the construction of a new Ram temple. The Ayodhya movement turned into a national movement, with marches and other activities all over India, often accompanied by Hindu-Muslim riots and resulting in thousand of deaths. Despite the violence, the popularity of the BJP accelerated, and in the elections of 1989 the party increased its number of MPs from only two to eighty six. During the 1990s the Ayodhya movement intensified its pressure on the central government, and the agitation culminated in the storming and subsequent destruction of the mosque in December 1992. The destruction triggered Hindu-Muslim riots in many parts of India, leaving more than two thousand dead, the vast majority Muslims. In the elections of 1991 and 1996, the BJP gained further strength and formed a very short-lived government in 1996. In both the 1998 and 1999 elections, the party emerged victorious and led a stable coalition government 1999–2004. The rapid success of the party was, however, stopped in the 2004 elections when the electorate surprisingly voted out the incumbent BJP-led coalition government, and opened up for a comeback for the INC.

The factors contributing to the sudden rise of the BJP are multiple, and an analysis of these will help us to understand also the recent reverses of the party's fortunes. Although the ideological content of the party has generally been Hindu nationalist, its own interpretation of this ideology has shifted throughout the decades, as have the possibilities to communicate it. Based on the idea of *Hindutva*, formulated by V. D. Savarkar, Hindu nationalism stresses the unity of all Hindus, links the destiny of India to that of Hinduism, warns against influences from foreign creeds and cultures, and emphasizes the right and the duty to protect Hindu culture. In many ways the factors that have contributed to the rise of Hindu nationalism are interrelated and may be seen as both external and internal to Indian politics. The effects of the processes of globalization and liberalization are of special importance and will be analyzed separately.

Muslim Fundamentalism

At an external level, the political development in the neighboring countries of India helped the Hindu nationalist movement in its mobilization. Despite the fact that Hindus in India constitute 83 percent of the population, a main theme in the agitation of the BJP has always been that Hindus are vulnerable and threatened from both within and outside the country. This agitation was facilitated by a rise of Muslim fundamentalism in the Middle East and in Pakistan during the 1980s. The Islamic revolution in Iran and the fundamentalist leanings of the Zia ul-Haque regime in Pakistan were the two most important examples, and especially the latter was portrayed by the BJP as a threat to both India and Hinduism. The economic success of the gulf states also contributed to this perceived threat, as many Indian Muslims benefited from the oil economies as migrant laborers, bringing home huge sums in foreign currency. It was claimed by the Hindu nationalists that they brought home also a more aggressive form of Islam, which together with economic support from the gulf resulted in increased tensions between Hindus and Muslims. In the south of India a number of mass conversions took place in the 1980s, where low-caste Hindus converted to Islam, which the BJP linked to an alleged increase of foreign Muslim influence and used to create the image of "the threatened Hindu" (Matthew 1989). The issue of conversion is especially sensitive since this practice is rejected by most Hindus, both in the form of proselytizing Hinduism to non-Hindus, as well as recognizing the conversion of Hindus to other religions. Support for these sentiments has been given not only from the Hindu nationalist movement, but also from many important leaders of the Hindu reform movement, as well as from Mahatma Gandhi (Nadkarni 2003; Pati 2003).

The Collapse of the Congress

The improved position of the BJP must also be seen in relation to its main adversary on the political arena: the Congress Party (INC). Although it had dominated Indian politics since independence, the INC had met with increased resistance from the mid-1960s. Indira Gandhi was at the helm of the party but faced challenges from other leaders, and these conflicts forced several splits of the party and general unrest. She increasingly relied on personal rule, thereby neglecting the democratic process within the party, but also outside of the party she met with strong opposition from other political parties, trade unions, various popular movements, as well as the judiciary. In 1975, Indira Gandhi was convicted of violating the election law in the Lok Sabha elections of 1971, but instead of accepting the verdict, the prime minister interpreted it as part of a conspiracy and declared the country in the state of emergency. All normal functions of the Indian democracy were curtailed, many of the opposition leaders were jailed, and although the emergency was lifted after eighteen months, it caused enormous damage to Indira Gandhi and the INC (Brass 1990: 40–43). The election of 1977 resulted in a landslide victory for the opposition and, although the INC bounced back in 1980, it never regained its previously dominant position. Instead, it was in the following decades reduced to insignificance in many of the biggest states, forced to rely upon various allies.

The Political Mobilization of Religion

The Hindu nationalist movement has ever since its formation faced stiff resistance from the secular parties, and after independence the reputation of the movement was tarnished by its association to the murder of Mahatma Gandhi (the killer, Nathuram Godse, was an ex-member of the RSS). Although the Jana Sangh was successful in gaining electoral support in some states in India, the party remained at the outskirts of Indian politics, and its inability to challenge the INC to some extent lay in the limits set up for Indian politics. Following the horrors of partition, the dominant political forces had established a largely secular constitution based on the principle of equal treatment of all religions. While contested by some, this secularism was regarded by most Indians as a prerequisite for communal peace, and political mobilization on the basis of religion or ethnicity was more or less not accepted. Although large segments of the INC harbored pro-Hindu sentiments, the political climate of the first decades after independence effectively stopped the Hindu nationalist movement from political mobilization of the Hindu identity. This changed with the demise of the INC, starting in the early 1970s. The power base of the party was eroding, partly because of internal conflicts, but also because of pressure from the political opposition on both left and right. Further unrest was caused by various groups basing their political identities on religion and ethnicity while arguing for extended minority rights. Continuous problems in Kashmir, Punjab, and Assam forced Indira Gandhi to "play the Hindu card," as put by some observers, rallying for support within the majority community (Gupta 1985; Kohli 1990; Kothari 1990). While the INC gained in the short term, the usage of religion for political purposes also opened up the arena for parties like the BJP and the Shiv Sena, which had far-reaching consequences for both the INC and the political climate in general.

New Local Hegemonies and Changing Class Relations

While other changes in the political climate had enabled the BJP to more freely promote its Hindu nationalism, the demise of the INC created a political vacuum that was soon filled by the BJP and other political parties. However, these new political forces did not project themselves as heirs of the old INC, which sought to unite the whole nation and which drew support from both high and low castes, northerners and southerners, Muslims and Hindus alike. Rather, from the 1980s and onward we have seen a polarization of Indian politics, based on caste, religion, ethnicity, and regional identities. For the BJP this meant increased opportunities to mobilize on its Hindu nationalist ideology, but also that its ambition to unite all Hindus received a severe blow. Regional parties exploited the discontent that existed in states like Punjab, Assam, and Jammu and Kashmir, while other states saw the developing or strengthening of regional parties based on caste. In some regions the Hindu nationalist movement was able to combine its general Hindu identity with regional identities, e.g., the Shiva Sena in Maharashtra that combines an aggressive Hindu nationalism with strong appeals to a Marathi identity, favoring "the sons of the soil"—the Marathi-speaking majority—over both Muslims and Hindus from other areas of India. Another example is the BJP in Rajasthan, which has successfully mobilized its supporters on a *rajput* identity, drawing on the specific culture and traditions of the warrior caste in the region.

The electoral success of the BJP was also related to changes in the class relations of Indian society. The ambition of the INC was to unite the whole nation, bridging caste differences and possible ethnic and religious tensions, and to include land owners, capitalists, peasants, and workers in the same fold. Some groups felt uncomfortable with this arrangement and sought other outlets for their political aspirations, and sections of the middle and upper classes grew increasingly dissatisfied with the principles of central economic planning and what was perceived as a strong socialist flavor of INC politics. The deregulation of the economy strengthened these sections and allowed them to formulate new political visions, which included a stronger belief in market solutions and in individual choices rather than a planned economy. The political outlet of these visions was visible in a rightist turn of many of the major parties, but most evidently in the increased support for the BJP. (Corbridge and Harriss 2000: 143–72).

The Increased Caste Polarization of Indian Politics

The prevalence of the caste structure within Hinduism is a social phenomenon that has existed for thousands of years and that still influences everyday life for most Hindus, as well as the political scene on both national and local levels. The caste system is legitimized on religious grounds in the vedas, most explicitly so in *manusmrti* (Manu's law), estimated to have been written in 500 BCE. It contains detailed instructions on how caste relations are to be observed, emphasizes the impurity of the lower castes, and establishes a firm social order based on the dominance of the higher castes. This system has a further legitimization in one of the creational myths of Hinduism (there are several others) where mankind is supposedly created from the body of the god Purusha, and where its head is said to have been used to create the highest caste group, the *Brahmins*, while the feet constituted the lowest group within this hierarchy: the *shudras*. It should be noted that a large section of the Hindu population, the *dalits*, are considered to be outside the system itself, which in daily social practices has rendered them a position below the shudras, and have made them highly vulnerable to all kinds of oppression, even in modern India.

One possible way of escaping this oppression is through conversion to Islam, Christianity, or Buddhism. From the 1950s, sections of the dalit and shudra communities have converted to Budhhism, which has caused some resentment from the Hindu nationalists that, however, regard the Buddhist faith to be a part of Indian (and therefore Hindu) culture. They consider the instances of conversion to Christianity and Islam to be far worse, and the Hindu nationalist movement has during the last decade put great efforts and huge financial resources into a campaign against conversions. This campaign focuses also on groups that have never had a fixed place in the Hindu family: the tribals. Living on the outskirts of society—in both social and geographical terms—the tribal groups have for centuries been the target of Christian missionaries, resulting that millions of tribals today regard themselves as Christians. This development is now challenged by the Hindu nationalists who through work conducted by their cultural and religious branches are now trying to stop the work of the Christian missionaries and also reconvert parts of the tribal population to Hinduism.

Caste discrimination has long been formally abolished and outlawed, but it still remains a reality, especially in rural areas. Also within the reform movement in the eighteenth and nineteenth century many religious leaders spoke out against caste discrimination, and this development to some extent influenced the Hindu nationalist movement. In its theory, Hindu nationalism is incompatible with the caste system, since it argues that in order to fight their external enemies and to defend themselves against developments that threaten the Hindu culture, all Hindus should unite, and that any division in castes would threaten this unity. In practice, however, the BJP has done very little to alleviate caste discrimination when in power, and the party has always had its base among the higher castes, while the lower castes or OBCs (Other Backward Classes) have generally supported the INC or the left parties: Janata Dal and lately the Samajvadi Party (SP). Recently we have also witnessed a strong rise of political activity among the dalits, where the Bahujan Samaj Party (BSP) has made inroads in what has been traditionally a INC stronghold (Jaffrelot 2003). The caste factor became increasingly important in the north of India when the V. P. Singh government in 1990 announced its plans to increase the quotas reserved for the economically and socially disadvantaged groups of the Hindu community within education and government employment. This decision triggered huge resistance from the upper castes, and in the short run it increased the support for the BJP. On the other hand it strengthened the parties supporting groups at the other end of the caste hierarchy, and while the INC was more or less wiped out from the northern states, other parties except the BJP were on the rise, especially the SP and the BSP.

The Ayodhya movement included a number of low-caste volunteers, and the BJP leadership in the most populous state, Uttar Pradesh, was partly non-Brahmin, which enabled them to make inroads into the vote banks of the lower castes. The party was also able to exploit the animosity between the other parties, on some occasions even forming a loose alliance with the dalit party BSP. When the caste polarization increased, the BJP, however, lost much of its already meager support among both OBCs and dalits. The BJP had gained in upper-caste support, largely at the expense of the INC, but the increased caste polarization obstructed its plans to unite Hindus and thereby win political support also from the lower castes.

Organization and Ideology of the BJP

While changes in the political climate contributed to the political success of the Hindu nationalist movement in the 1980s and 1990s, these gains would have been impossible without changes within the party. The BJP started out in 1980 with what has later been described as a highly confused political ideology, promoting "Gandhian socialism," a form of socialism based on self-reliance and nationalism, along with *Hindutva*. Many of the previous Jana Sangh voters did not recognize the party, and the relations with the RSS dipped to a low, contributing to the poor showing in the elections of 1984. The party, however, quickly regrouped and replaced Gandhian socialism with "integral humanism," an ideology partly based on *Hindutva*, which describes the Hindu nation as an integral unit, defines the nation as an organism, and rejects possible cleavages such as class or ethnicity. The BJP took advantage of the changing political climate and aggressively used the Shah Bano case and the Babri Masjid-Ramjanmabhoommi conflict in its agitation. The party also improved its internal organization through reforms initiated by the new president, L. K. Advani (Malik and Singh 1995). The structure and discipline within the party were strengthened, and after mending relations with the RSS, the BJP was also fully backed by a powerful cadre-based organization with millions of members. The support of the RSS and other organizations within the Hindu nationalist movement proved crucial in the Ayodhya campaign but also during elections. The Vishva Hindu Parishad (VHP), a global organization for the protection of Hindu religion and culture, took charge of the Ayodhya campaign but cooperated closely with the BJP, which in 1989 decided to fully back the campaign. The VHP was formed already in 1964 and works on a global level to promote the Hindu nationalist ideology. The organization has been very successful in organizing Hindus in the diaspora and has through its branches in Europe and North America collected large donations for the Hindu nationalist cause. Some of these funds were made available for the Ayodhya campaign, whose modus operandi was to hold marches and manifestations all over the country in support of the construction of a Hindu temple on the disputed site in Ayodhya. Bricks for the construction of the proposed temple, *ram shilas,* were consecrated in special ceremonies and displayed in processions that reached also remote areas. Large numbers of predominantly young, male activists were recruited by the VHP, activists who would later participate in marches to Ayodhya, as well as in the subsequent destruction of the Babri Masjid. The purpose of the marches was to unite all Hindus around one specific goal: the construction of a Ram temple in Ayodhya. It was also arranged as a display of strength, and a warning to the minority communities, especially the Muslims. Serious riots broke out in connection with the processions, starting in Bhagalpur, Bihar, on 24 October 1989. In the following year thousands of people were killed in communal riots, the vast majority of them Muslims.

Clean Image

Another aspect of the demise of the INC was the constant allegations of corruption and mismanagement directed against the party. While these allegations had always been there, the criticism grew in the 1980s. Rajiv Gandhi had after the death of his mother taken over the party and initially had the reputation of being Mr. Clean, but a severe blow to this image was delivered by the Bofors scandal in the late 1980s. Although never finally confirmed, it was suggested that Rajiv Gandhi used his influence to secure a billion-dollar contract for the Swedish company Bofors, and that a large commission had been paid by the company to Indian business agents with close links to the Gandhi family. The BJP exploited this fully and projected itself as the clean and noncorrupt alternative to the INC, driven by nationalism and patriotism rather than personal gain. While the electorate's opinion of the BJP as a party with honest leaders would later change dramatically due to various corruption scandals, especially when the BJP was in power at the national level in 1999–2004, its supposedly clean image was nevertheless a factor that contributed to the rise of the party in the 1990s. Also the ideology of the party was turned to an advantage. Although most Indians were skeptical about Hindu nationalism as such, the ideological crisis of the left and the INC left the field open for the BJP. The party also promoted its religious and cultural identity, recalling the glory of the *Hindu rashtra,* the legendary ancient Hindu kingdom in which justice and righteousness prevailed.

Electoral Alliances

In the early years of the Jana Sangh, a merger with other smaller Hindu nationalist parties was discussed but never executed, and similarly, an alliance with other rightist parties was suggested but discarded in the 1960s (Graham 1993, chapter seven). The Jana Sangh fought all elections alone until they in 1977 merged into the Janata Party: a loose coalition consisting of the main opposition forces against Indira Gandhi and the INC. The Janata Party included both socialists and Hindu nationalists and was united almost solely on the basis of opposition against the INC government. Due to ideological differences, the party split already in 1980 and as the problems encountered were not conducive for further alliances, the BJP was in its early years looking inward within the Sangh Parivar for allies, rather than reaching out to other parties. Despite its impressive performances in the elections of 1989, 1991, and 1996, it was clear to most observers that it could not capture power without electoral alliances. Although it had made some inroads among the lower castes and also in the south of India, it was still basically an upper-caste party of the north, and while the party leadership continued to argue that Hindu nationalism in the long run would prevail as the dominant ideology, it also realized the need for electoral partners. Before the elections of 1998, the party worked hard in arranging various regional alliances and also decided to fight the elections not on a BJP program, but on the platform of the NDA (National Democratic Alliance). This meant that the party had to compromise on a number of issues, and in order to make the alliance function smoothly, the BJP dropped key demands from previous elections: the construction of a Ram temple in Ayodhya, a uniform civil code, and the revocation of article 370 in the constitution (which gives special status to the Muslim-dominated state of Jammu and Kashmir) (Bhatt 2001). While some leaders and grassroots workers of the party regarded this as a sell out, others saw it as an opening toward new allies and the first serious chance to grab power in Delhi. The NDA was successful in both the 1998 and the 1999 elections, when especially the regional allies in Haryana, Andhra Pradesh, and Tamil Nadu did well, drawing votes to the alliance in states where the BJP had previously had a minimal presence. Together with its allies the BJP received 38.4 percent of the votes in the 1999 elections and gained 296 seats in the Lok Sabha, giving them a comfortable majority.

The formation of the NDA was greatly helped by the strong leadership of Prime Minister Atal Behari Vajpayee. His popularity and credibility as a political leader goes far beyond the Hindu nationalist movement and even stretches into groups that are normally very skeptical toward the BJP. His popularity helped forge the alliance, but also provided the NDA with an obvious candidate for the post of prime minister, and while being an old stalwart of the Sangh Parivar, Vajpayee is nevertheless regarded as more liberal and less extreme than most of the other top BJP leaders of his generation. His more pragmatic outlook on politics also helped to forge the necessary alliances, as well as to attract votes.

Globalization

The doctrine of Hindu nationalism emphasizes a national and religious identity that is in many senses difficult to reconcile with the idea of a global identity or a far-reaching globalization. For example, the traditions of the higher castes earlier put severe restrictions on traveling outside of India. As late as in the early and mid-twentieth century, trips overseas could result in the expulsion from the caste community, and in the writings of both Savarkar and Golwalkar it is clear that the Hindus are in many senses bound to the territory of their motherland: the *Bharat*. Reforms and modernization within Hinduism have, however, slowly changed the attitudes toward foreign exposure. To some extent these reforms were an effect of the Hindu reformist movement mentioned previously where organizations such as the Ramakrishna Mission increased the interest for Hinduism in the West, but also opened up the minds of many Hindus to foreign religions and philosophies. A process of modernization was also forced upon Indian society and Hinduism through the colonial rule. New forms of technology, modern forms of education, and the spreading of liberal and socialist ideas influenced also the Hindu practices. The idea of caste separation is one example of a practice that has weakened due to the constraints of modern society. Some of the most influential religious texts of Hinduism, for example *manusmrti* prescribe very strict rules for the interaction between different castes, stating that Brahmins should avoid physical proximity to the lower castes. This kind of separation is very difficult to observe for those engaged in industries and services, or for anybody living in urban areas. Caste separation, and of course caste discrimination, remains in Indian society, especially in the villages, but the practices have been severely weakened due to modernization. This change also included relations with foreigners who according to most Hindu traditions were considered to be outside of the caste system, and therefore impure and preferably avoided. Through trade and the increased presence of foreigners, large sections of the Hindu population have been forced to change their attitudes when participating in an increasingly global economy.

Within the Sangh Parivar there has been an increased awareness of the importance of Hindus outside of India, especially during the last two decades. The Hindu nationalist movement is now global as it has continuously tried to engage in its activities also Hindus in the diaspora, a development strengthened by the formation of the VHP in 1964. Branches of both the VHP and the RSS have been formed in other countries in Asia, as well as in North and South America and in Europe. In the main campaigns of the Sangh Parivar in the 1980s and 1990s, the economic support of the international Hindu community was vital, and the branches of VHP in the United States and in Great Britain were in many cases successful in collecting funds and in influencing the Hindu diaspora communities. The strategy has been to engage in cultural, educational, and social projects, often targeting children or youths, and to combine these activities with ideological and political training (Matthew and Prasad 2000; Bhatt 2000). The VHP has together with RSS also been active in the current conflict regarding conversions and reconversions in India. The 2008 riots in Orissa, which left more than forty dead and more than twenty-five thousand Christian villagers as internal refugees, is one example of how the Sangh Parivar engages itself in an increasingly aggressive manner (Frontline 2009). While these riots may have more to do with power politics on the local level than globalization, the reactions from the Hindu nationalist leaders can be seen as a response to what is perceived as a global threat against Hinduism. The logic of the Sangh Parivar is that numerous atrocities have historically been committed against the Hindu religion, and that Christian missionaries are still today trying to destabilize the Hindu nation through conversions, now under the disguise of globalization. The VHP and its auxiliary groups argue that Hindus have the right to meet this perceived aggression, even if this leads to violence, and have demanded that conversions should be banned by law. This is a rejection of the free flow of ideas that constitutes globalization and a measure taken in order to strengthen the Hindu nation in the global competition.

The social and political conditions in India have also been affected by the international trends of globalization, liberalization, and privatization. After independence India built an economy of considerable strength based on central planning and strict control of import and export, as well as the flows of foreign currencies. The result was a heavily regulated and in many senses protected market, both for agricultural and industrial products. These economic policies were supported by the INC and the left, but changed dramatically in the early 1990s when India encountered serious problems with its public finances and was forced to rely on the IMF for help. As a result, the Indian government under Rajiv Gandhi deregulated the Indian economy, allowing for more of private initiative and foreign investments. The Hindu nationalist movement was divided on the issue of globalization, with a large segment of the movement arguing against it, advocating instead the ideal of *swadeshi* (self-reliance), while the bulk of the leadership welcomed privatization and deregulation of the partly socialist economy of the INC brand. While having its base in the RSS—which was reluctant to see the Indian economy open up for foreign exposure—the party also had a strong support among other sections of the urban middle class that welcomed the new policies. Although the INC initiated the reforms, the BJP was seen among the electorate as the most reform-friendly party, something that contributed to its continued success. More importantly, the liberalization process itself strengthened the position of the urban middle classes and created a new kind of social climate in which private enterprise, economic wealth, and individualism were key elements. This new set of values clashed with the Nehruvian style of Indian socialism, decreasing the popularity of both the INC and the left, and spread a new feeling of individualism within society, rendering the old ideas of central planning, solidarity, and social cohesion less relevant (Corbridge and Harriss 2000). While this new individualism was to some extent in conflict with the ideology of Hindu nationalism, this development suited the BJP, which regardless of its strong emphasis on tradition was able to project itself as the party of the future. The party largely succeeded in depicting the INC and the left as forces in defense of the old regulated and socialist regime, and promoted themselves as the "fresh alternative," emphasizing the importance of free enterprise and new technology. Within the Sangh Parivar different opinions on globalization and liberalization are found and to some extent the BJP has used this to its advantage, adjusting its rhetoric depending on the audience. A section of the Sangh Parivar have continued to promote the ideal of swadeshi, working against the increased influence of foreign capital in India, one example being the Swadeshi Jagaran Manch, an organization with strong links to the Hindu nationalist movement, which have been very active in campaigning against the perceived threats of globalization.

The mainstream of the Hindu nationalist movement has, however, accepted globalization as a fact, and although some resentment can be registered, a major campaign against the inflow of foreign capital now seems very unlikely. It is almost paradoxical that no political party of significance in India has put the negative aspects of globalization on its agenda, despite the historically strong influence of both socialist and Hindu nationalist ideas. The reactions from the BJP leadership against globalization has for the last decade focused almost solely on cultural issues, such as the influence of "Western decadence" in the forms of alleged sexualization of television media and an increase in the popularity of pageant contests such as Miss World and Miss Universe. In the program of the BJP-led coalition, the NDA, for the parliamentary election in 2004, the issue of globalization was hardly discussed, but simply taken for granted and presented as a fact of life, and mentioned in the program almost in passing. However, when the plans for economic development were presented, globalization formed the background. According to the program, the economy should continue to grow 8–10 percent annually, largely through private Indian companies who successfully compete on the global market. India should, according to the election manifesto, achieve this growth rate through becoming, among other things, "the food factory of the world" and "the global manufacturing hub" (NDA 2004). In the very short paragraph that does present the NDA's stand on globalization, nothing is mentioned of possible negative effects on the lives of farmers and workers. In another document, "Vision Document—2004," the BJP discusses the term *swadeshi*, but never acknowledges that the principle of self-reliance in many senses stands in contradiction to globalization. Instead, the party promotes a vision in which swadeshi is implemented when "Indian products, services and entrepreneurs dominate the domestic and global markets." In this statement we see how Hindu nationalism goes global: domination is attained in a global setting, but nevertheless dependent on a nationalist identity, embodied by the idea of swadeshi. The Hindu nationalist movement in this sense uses the globalization process in order to promote its political ideology. In a globalized world, a strong national identity is necessary in order to survive, and it is exactly this identity that the Sangh Parivar offers. Hindu nationalism then becomes a way to adapt to globalization, and to come out as a winner in the global economic race.

Conclusions

The emergence of a strong Hindu nationalist movement, with considerable political influence, has been dependent on a number of factors. Some of them are internal to Indian politics, but it is evident that the BJP has had few problems adapting its politics to the growing wave of globalization. While the demise of the INC is partly related to the processes of globalization and the liberalization of the Indian economy, the restructuring of the BJP and its ability to repackage its Hindu nationalism, to find suitable electoral partners, and to define a few key issues on which to base its campaign can primarily be related to developments within the party. The most important shift is, however, in how the electorate perceived the message of the BJP in a new way, from the mid-1980s and onward. In a new era of capitalism and consumerism, the BJP managed to project itself as a credible alternative to the other parties, both in dealing with the new economy and in protecting India against the alleged threats of both Muslim fundamentalism and Western cultural imperialism. The process of globalization did not stop the Sangh Parivar; rather, it helped it in its campaign for an increased nationalist awareness. A unified India, based on a Hindu culture and traditions, was the Hindu nationalist cure for the ailing Indian nation and the platform on which to build a state strong enough to succeed in global competition.

REFERENCES

Ali, Amir. 2001. "The Evolution of the Public Sphere in India." *Economic and Political Weekly*, 30 June.

Andersen, Walter K., and Shridhar D. Damle. 1987. *The Brotherhood in Saffron*. Boulder, CO: Westview Press.

Banatwalla, G. M. 1992. *Religion & Politics in India*. Bombay: G. M. Banatwalla.

Banerjee, Partha. 1998. *In the Belly of the Beast*. Ajanta: New Delhi.

Basu, Tapan, Pradip Datta, Sumit Sarkar, Tanika Sarkar, and Sambuddha Sen. 1993. *Khaki Shorts Saffron Flags—Tracts for the Times/1*. New Delhi: Orient Longman.

Bhatt, Chetan. 2001. *Hindu Nationalism—Origins, Ideologies and Myths*. Oxford: Berg.

———. 2003. "Dharmo rakshati rakshitah: Hindutva movement in the UK." *Ethnic and Racial Studies* 23 (3): 559–93.

Brass, Paul R. 1990. *The Politics of India since Independence*. Cambridge: Cambridge University Press.

Corbridge, Stuart, and John Harriss. 2000. *Reinventing India: Liberalization, Hindu Nationalism and Popular Democracy*. Cambridge: Polity Press.

Das, Prafulla. 2009, "Chilling Memories." *Frontline*, 14–27 February.

Embree, Ainslie T. 1989. *Imagining India—Essays on Indian History*. Delhi: Oxford University Press.

Engineer, Asgar Ali, ed. 1987. *The Shah Bano Controversy*. Bombay: Orient Longman.

———. 1990. *Babri-Masjid Ramjanambhoomi Controversy*. New Delhi: Ajanta Publications.

———. 1992. *The Rights of Women in Islam*. London: C. Hurst & Co.

Ghosh, Partha S. 1999. *BJP and the Evolution of Hindu Nationalism*. New Delhi: Manohar.

Gold, Daniel. 1991. "Organized Hinduisms: From Vedic Truth to Hindu Nation." In *Fundamentalisms Observed*, ed. M. E. Marty and R. S. Appleby. Chicago: The University of Chicago Press.

Golwalkar, M. S. 1980. *Bunch of Thoughts*, 2nd ed. Bangalore: Jagarana Prakashana.

Gopal, S., ed. 1991. *Anatomy of a Confrontation*. Delhi: Penguin Books India.

Graham, Bruce. 1993. *Hindu Nationalism and Indian Politics*. New Delhi: Foundation Books.

Gupta, Dipankar. 1985. "The Communalising of Punjab." *Economic and Political Weekly*, 13 July: 1185–90.

Hansen, Thomas Blom. 1999. *The Saffron Wave—Democracy and Hindu Nationalism in Modern India*. Delhi: Oxford University Press.

Hansen, Thomas Blom. and Christophe Jaffrelot, eds. 1998. *The BJP and the Compulsions of Politics in India*. Delhi: Oxford University Press.

Hasan, Zoya. 1989. "Minority Identity: Muslim Women Bill Campaign and the Political Process." *Economic and Political Weekly*, 7 January: 44–50.

Hellman, Eva. 1993. *Political Hinduism—The Challenge of the Vishva Hindu Parishad*. Uppsala: Uppsala University.

Huntington, Samuel. 1996. *The Clash of Civilizations*. New York: Simon and Schuster.

Jaffrelot, Christophe. 1996. The *Hindu Nationalist Movement and Indian Politics—1925 to the 1990s*. London: Hurst & Company.

———. 2003. *India's Silent Revolution*. Delhi: Permanent Black.

Klostermaier, K. K. 1989. *A Survey of Hinduism*. Albany: State of New York University Press.

Kohli, Atul. 1990. *Democracy and Discontent*. Cambridge: Cambridge University Press.

Kothari, Rajni. 1990. *State against Democracy—In Search of Humane Government*. London: Aspects Publications.

Lerner, Daniel. 1964. *The Passing of Traditional Society: Modernizing the Middle East*. New York: Free Press.

Llewellyn, J. E. 1993. *The Arya Samaj as a Fundamentalist Movement—A Study in Comparative Fundamentalism*. New Delhi: Manohar.

Luckmann, Thomas. 1967. *The Invisible Religion: The Problem of Religion in Modern Society*. New York: Macmillan.

Madan, T. N. 1997. *Modern Myths, Locked Minds—Secularism and Fundamentalism in India*. Delhi: Oxford University Press.

Malhotra, Anahu. 2004. "Exploding Myths on Conversions." *Economic and Political Weekly*, 18 September: 4244–45.

Malik, Yogendra K., and V. B. Singh. 1995. *Hindu Nationalists in India—The Rise of the Bharatiya Janata Party*. New Delhi: Vistaar Publications.

Matthew, Biju, and Vijay Prashad. 2000. "The Protean Forms of Yankee Hindutva." *Ethnic and Racial Studies* 23 (3): 516–34.

Matthew, George. 1989. "Politicisation of Religion: Conversions to Islam in Tamil Nadu." In *Religion State and Politics in India*, ed. M. Shakir. Delhi: Ajanta Publications.

Nadkarni, M. V. 2003. "Ethics and Relevance of Conversions." *Economic and Political Weekly*, 18 January: 227–35.

Nandy, Ashis, Shikha Trivedy, Shail Mayaram, and Achyut Yagnik. 1995. *Creating a Nationality—The Ramjanmabhumi Movement and Fear of the Self*. Delhi: Oxford University Press.

Nayar, Baldev Raj. 2001. *Globalization and Nationalism.* New Delhi: Sage Publications.

NDA (National Democratic Alliance) 2004. *An Agenda for Development, Good Governance, Peace, and Harmony—Elections to the 14th Lok Sabha.* New Delhi: BJP.

Noorani, A. G. 2001. *The RSS and the BJP: A Division of Labor.* New Delhi: Left Word Books.

Pati, Biswamoy. 2001. "Identity, Hegemony, Resistance—Conversions in Orissa, 1800–2000." *Economic and Political Weekly,* 3 November: 4204–12.

Puri, B. N. 1990. *Secularism in Indian Ethos.* Delhi: Atma Ram & Sons.

Savarkar, V. D. 1942. *Hindutva,* 2nd ed. Poona: S. R. Date.

Shattuck, Cybelle. 1999. *Hinduism.* London: Routledge.

Srivastava, N. M. P. 1973. *Growth of Nationalism in India.* Delhi: Meenakshi Prakashan.

Tambiah, Stanley. 1992. *Levelling Crowds: Ethnonationalist Conflicts and Collective Violence in South Asia.* Berkeley: University of California Press.

Tully, Mark, and Satish Jacobs. 1985. *Amritsar: Mrs Gandhi's Last Battle.* London: Jonathan Cape.

van der Veer, Peter. 1994. *Religious Nationalism—Hindus and Muslims in India.* Berkeley: University of California Press.

Weber, Max. 2002. *The Protestant Ethic and the Spirit of Capitalism,* 3rd ed. Oxford: Blackwell.

II

Open Conflicts Between Religion and Politics

≪ 3 ≫

CHURCH CONFRONTS STATE

The 2005 *Manifestasaun* in Timor-Leste

David Hicks

They came from every district in East Timor. Like peasants from the country-side in medieval Europe, they descended upon the capital en masse with a view to intimidating the secular authorities.

Figure 3.1. Our Lady is carried through the streets of Dili. The Virgin Mary is the central religious icon of the Timorese people and was on prominent display during the demonstration. Courtesy of Maxine Hicks.

Notes for this chapter begin on page 140.

Day after day, from the third week of April 2005, trucks bursting with young people entered the town of Dili, the adventurous or reckless ones hanging from the sides of the vehicles, to deposit their human cargo. There they joined a multitude of other protesters in daily demonstrations that would alter the relationship between religious authority and secular authority in the first nation-state to become a member of the United Nations in the twenty-first century. The *manifestasaun* or "demonstration" was the first time the Catholic Church had summoned up its human resources to challenge the democratically elected government[1] in the three years the country had existed, but its potential as a rival power had been no secret. The issues that had provoked the demonstration brought the two into open confrontation and helped to undermine the standing of the prime minister, Mari Alkatiri, who had provoked the Catholic clergy into marshaling antigovernment sentiments from all corners of the nation. Indeed, the efficiency and thoroughness of their enterprise threw into relief the ineffectuality of the government, a revelation that contributed to Alkatiri's resignation a little over a year later.[2]

In this essay I examine the form this unique event took and argue that it was instrumental in bringing about a radical change in the relations between the church and state in East Timor.[3] Since the country's independence, the Catholic hierarchy, though in no way intimidated by the government and perfectly willing to express the church's view on a range of issues that included abortion and prostitution, had until 2005 been content to push its policies relatively covertly. There were no impediments to the dissemination of ecclesiastical policy. Senior clergy had access to government officials, parish priests were able to promulgate it among the faithful through the forum of the weekly pulpit, and in the schools nuns and lay teachers alike were free to disseminate Catholic doctrine. Given the high esteem in which priests and nuns are generally held and the great respect accorded the church (decidedly higher than politicians command), the capacity of the institution to mold public opinion to complement or oppose governmental policies is formidable. However, the degree of political power the hierarchy could bring to bear on issues it regarded as important had not been put to the test since independence, perhaps because East Timor's first government had determined that caution was the best policy in dealing with the clergy and also because issues that might have put church and state on a collision course were kept carefully under wraps. Ecclesiastical influence, for its part, had been exerted "under the canopy," as it were, and the hierarchy tended to avoid pushing policies that might have the potential for being too politically contentious and therefore provoke strife between secular and religious.[4] This changed in April–May 2005 with what the Timorese called the *manifestasaun*. In playing out this phenomenon, the power of the clergy was made apparent for all to see, and since that time the ecclesiastical authorities have openly challenged the secular powers when they considered it appropriate. Before considering the chain of events that brought on the manifestasaun, however, and assessing its consequences for the future of secular-ecclesiastical relations, some account of the history of the Catholic Church in East Timor and the ethnographic character of its population is necessary.

Ethnography and History

At its nearest point of convergence the island of Timor lies approximately 560 kilometers north of Australia and is divided geopolitically into two halves, each half roughly of the same extent. Western Timor lies in the Republic of Indonesia while the eastern half is East Timor, a new nation that attained independence on 20 May 2002. The majority of the island's population consists of peasant communities that grow a wide range of swidden and irrigation crops, most importantly maize, rice, and greens. For purposes of governance, the country consists of thirteen districts, in one of which lies Dili, whose current population of about 150,000 inhabitants makes it by far the largest town in a country the total population of which stands at about 920,000. Each district is divided into several subdistricts, both administrative units being governed from a small capital town of their own. These subdistricts are comprised of indigenous local communities called *sukus*, each defined by its own distinctive sociocultural personality. Sukus, in their turn, are divided into villages. Villages are organized into patrilineal/patrilocal or matrilineal/uxorilocal hamlets or house-clusters (*knua*) (Hicks 2004). Many of the subdistricts have a church and attendant priest or else are ministered to by priests of neighboring subdistricts.

Until 2002 East Timor had never received international recognition as an independent nation-state and had been subject to the successive external authorities of Portugal, Indonesia, and the United Nations. The coming of Christianity to Timor in the sixteenth century proved of momentous import in the island's history, and in the imaginative editing of the islanders is represented in the form of a legend whose secular basis has been transformed into a sacred epiphany. The legend tells how a European ship with a man in black standing at its prow one day dropped anchor off a beach near where the local inhabitants were performing one of their traditional rituals. The man, who proved to be a missionary, asked the local leader if he and his companions could settle among them and teach them the word of God. When the request was refused, the priest asked if his men might at least be permitted to disembark to collect water before setting sail. Permission was granted, the water collected, and the ship started to weigh anchor. But as the anchor was being hefted an earthquake shook the island frightening the populace. The missionary told the villagers the tremors were caused by the ship's anchor dragging the island with it. The island and the ship were heading back together to the priest's own land where the villagers would have no choice but to learn God's word. By now the people were thoroughly terrified and full of trepidation at being transported to foreign parts, so they agreed to allow their unwanted visitor to proselytize. This proselytization, so the legend would have it, was met with outstanding success among that local population. The factual circumstances of the arrival of the first missionary on the island, Friar Taveira, were doubtless more prosaic than earth shattering, but the advent of Christianity in Timor introduced an agency that from the very first century of European-Timorese contact played at least as much a part in acculturating the local population as successive Portuguese administrations were to do.

The influence of the church before the Indonesian occupation should not be overestimated, however. Although the generations of missionaries that followed Friar Taveira succeeded in winning numerous converts, when the army of the Republic of Indonesia invaded East Timor on 7 December 1975, the country was very far from being what might be regarded as a Catholic country. The conversion of East Timor from a country where most people were animists to a "Catholic country" came about as a result of the Indonesian government forcing the population to declare themselves adherents of one of what the authorities classed as the world religions: Islam, Catholicism, Protestantism, Buddhism, or Hinduism. In practice the choice was between Catholicism and Islam, the overwhelmingly predominant religion of the Indonesian invaders, and this negative fact together with the positive fact that the Catholic Church had become a respected institution in Portuguese colonial times resulted in the populace overwhelmingly choosing Catholicism as their nominal faith. Thus virtually overnight the church gained the formal allegiance of over something in the order of 95 percent of the Timorese.[5] Later, during the twenty-four years of military occupation, the bishop of East Timor,[6] Carlos Filípe Ximenes Belo, and countless priests and nuns earned the gratitude of the majority of the population for interceding on their behalf with the military authorities, and over time this nominal allegiance developed into an unshakeable devotion to the clergy. So by the time the Indonesians were obliged at last to grant independence to East Timor (in late 1999) and the United Nations (which had assumed responsibility for the fledgling nation-state until its independence) gradually departed from the scene, the Catholic Church had emerged as an institution with the potential to challenge the new government for the loyalty of the Timorese.

The Ecclesiastical Challenge

The first notable challenge by the ecclesiastical authorities to the state preceded the manifestasaun by five months. At a press conference on 19 November 2004, the Ministry of Education released a memorandum announcing changes in the teaching of Catholic doctrine in the primary schools run by the government. The secular authorities, it declared, planned to make optional a subject that since independence had been compulsory. Furthermore the teaching of Catholic doctrine would not be given as part of the daily scheduled curriculum. The plan had received the approval of the council of ministers the previous month and was to be put to the test in grades one to six in thirty-two schools from all the districts starting in January 2005 (ETAN 2005a). The staff and parents would be responsible for implementing the teaching of religious doctrine and ensuring that this religious instruction would not "prejudice" the subjects that were mandatory. The lower pedagogical status into which the teaching of religion was being cast was further underscored by the provision that, unlike the compulsory subjects, there would be no "evaluation" of what was learned by pupils. Neither was knowledge of a religious course's contents to be a condition for a pupil being promoted from one grade to another. As though these conditions were not provocative enough, the government required that while teachers had to be sufficiently qualified to provide adequate instruction and so would have to be accredited by appropriate religious institutions, the instruction of religion would have to be made without the state incurring any extra cost.

This was a challenge the hierarchy could not ignore, since imparting its values through the classroom is an imperative for the Catholic Church. The country's two senior prelates, Dom Alberto Ricardo da Silva, bishop of the Dili diocese, and Dom Basílio do Nascimento, bishop of the Baucau diocese, interpreted the document as an onslaught upon the church's capacity to do so. They understood that if implemented, such a radical altering of the pedagogical ground rules would critically undermine the most effective method the clergy had at its disposal for maintaining the influence of their religion in East Timor. Adding insult to injury was the sudden way in which the new plan had been announced, curtly at a press conference and without consultation with the leaders of the church.[7] Threat, in short, was compounded by slight. Furthermore, the clergy could never forget that the man they considered (almost certainly correctly) behind it, Mari Alkatiri, was a Muslim, a denomination very much in a minority in an overwhelmingly Catholic country. Although hardly a dictator, Alkatiri was the strong man of the government, and all directives that carried any weight required his authorization. Outside his own political party, Fretilin, there were elements of the Timorese population that fervently disliked him, an unpopularity evident in December 2002 when antigovernment and pro-Indonesian supporters joined forces in Dili to set fire to his home and houses belonging to two of his brothers.[8] The mayhem that beset the town on that occasion resulted in ten buildings in all being burned or otherwise damaged, two persons killed, and twenty-five persons injured.

The opening retaliatory shot across the bows came on 14 January 2005 when Bishop Nascimento asserted in public that those who legislated against the church were anti-Christian. "Every time when we reach the end of the year, we always hear the anti-Christian reading. Those who introduce such things are the ones who no longer believe in God," said the prelate (ETAN 2005b) He added that whereas the Timorese tend to blame foreigners for bringing modern and anti-Christian forms of behavior into the country, it is they who without realizing it are the "ones who are anti-Christ." In such a country this was a stern denunciation by any standards, but in the third week of February a second and more significant rejoinder followed in the form of a public announcement by both bishops under the title "Pastoral Note from the Catholic Bishops of Timor-Leste about Teaching Religion in Public Schools" (Appendix 1) (ETAN 2005a). The bishops contended that since most Timorese were Catholic, they had the pastoral duty on behalf of the population to speak out in favor of the compulsory teaching of religion in the state schools. They argued for the cultural and personal benefits that accrue from a religious education and remarked on the important place of religion in civil society, adding that the expenditure of public funds is justified if the role of parents in imparting religious values is not to be vitiated. The prelates' response was an artful ploy to insert ecclesiastical interests into what had been until then widely accepted as the secular sphere's exclusive right to control education. The state, the bishops contended, has to make it possible for all citizens to participate (a "just participation," however that might be defined, is how they put it) in "culture." Having insisted that church and state had, as it were, a conjoint mission, the pastoral note ratcheted up the pressure by encouraging parents to enter the lists on its side in "reminding" them of "the important duty they have of using everything or demanding everything, so that their sons and daughters may benefit from that aid and progress harmonically [sic] within Christian and profane education."

Nor was the Fretilin government lacking enemies on the secular side. Six weeks later other political parties exploited the issue. Taking the side of the clergy, Lucia Lobato, secretary-general of the Social Democrat Party (PSD), is reported to have said that its National Council requested the government to include religion as a compulsory subject in the national curriculum to reflect the "reality" that the Catholic population comprised the majority (ETAN 2005c). The party righteously urged the governing party not to look upon the church as an opponent or enemy but instead treat it as a partner. It additionally resorted to reiterating the hackneyed cliché that most Timorese were Catholic and called to the attention of the government the important contribution the church had made to East Timor's development (ETAN 2005d). The Social Democratic Association (ASDT) similarly threw its weight behind the hierarchy. A third political party, the Democratic Party (PD), weighed in a few days later, its president, Fernando Lasama de Araújo, accusing the government of using the planned changes to the national primary education curriculum as a pretext for separating religion from the state.[9] Araújo went on to affirm that the clergy wished to have a dialogue with the government, at the same time as he introduced a new ingredient into the controversy by asserting that such a dialogue should include community representatives as well as members of other organizations (ETAN 2005e).

Nor were other religions to be outdone. The Muslim spokesman, president of the Centre for the Islamic Community of Timor-Leste (CENCITIL) Arif Abdullah Sagran, threw his community's full support behind the pastoral note. He maintained that the bishops' communiqué was relevant for the Islamic community because if Catholicism were taught in schools, then, he reasoned, so would the precepts of the "minority religions" like his own. Like the bishops, Sagran affirmed the importance of providing children with a "religious and moral education" without which "their future would be cloudy and void of meaning" (ETAN 2005f), concluding, illogically, that the government would then have to provide the necessary funds and teachers.

Mari Alkatiri refrained from entering the dispute on the grounds that the church had sent its pastoral note to the public rather than to the government, and he chose to ignore the chorus of rising criticism, which by now included critics from outside the country. At the Palm Sunday Mass on 20 March, the Vatican apostolic nuncio, Monsignor Malcolm Raamjiph, a citizen of Sri Lanka, urged the faithful to resist "those who attempt to destroy the church." His words did provoke a reaction, but not from Alkatiri, and then were not directed at the substance of his speech. The senior minister and minister for foreign affairs and cooperation, José Ramos-Horta, strongly denounced the nuncio for "unwarranted interference" in Timor-Leste's internal affairs by stepping himself into a national debate on the issue of the teaching of religion in the public education institutions. Nor did Ramos-Horta stop there for he reminded the nuncio of the Vatican's failure to protect the people of East Timor during their subjugation by Indonesia or to bolster their quest for self-determination. "Regarding the role of the Vatican in the history of Timor-Leste's struggle for independence," he said, "better we don't talk about the past. The bishops and priests of Timor-Leste know only too well the Vatican's role and in particular that of the various apostolic nuncios who served in Jakarta from 1975. He noted that the nuncio appeared more interested in "fanning … tensions" than in bridging the differences that divided church and state, and pointed out that the state paid several million dollars a year in teachers' salaries in schools run by the state in addition to permitting the church to occupy many state properties in East Timor (ETAN 2005g).[10]

Aware, perhaps, that their pastoral note had by now succeeded in decisively injecting their institution into what they referred to as the "profane" realm, bishops Silva and Nascimento then increased their pressure on the secular government still further by exploiting a second explosive issue. This was the ongoing controversy about securing justice for those Timorese who had been killed, assaulted, or otherwise physically abused by the Indonesians during their twenty-four years of occupation (ETAN 2005h). Discussions between representatives of the two governments, with the involvement of various international agencies, had been going on about this contentious issue for several years by now, and a definitive step was taken in March in the form of a deal that, while including an agreement to support a Truth and Friendship Commission, would in reality render the commission toothless to mandate sanctions against the perpetrators of what the bishops referred to in the statement they submitted to the so-called Commission of Experts appointed by the secretary-general of the United Nations as "crimes against humanity." The prelates for their part demanded "real accountability" and "genuine justice" (Appendix 2). They were far from alone in taking this stance, which was receiving support from powerful constituencies including the United Nations. The latter had withheld its endorsement of the deal in favor of a proposal to the Commission of Experts to determine why a 1999 Security Council resolution to try those accused of war crimes had failed. It was therefore a tactically astute move for bishops Silva and Nascimento to address their remarks to the commission as well as also including the secretary-general in their missive. In their statement dated 9 April 2005, they contrived to imply that the church represented the people of East Timor.[11] They asserted that "the Catholic community," for which they claimed to speak, "will not condone impunity for crimes against humanity." The victims of the crimes, their families, and "the people [the Indonesian military and its surrogates] in whose names" such crimes were committed deserved nothing less, they asserted. But since such "people" included prominent Indonesian leaders, the bishops were demonstrating that now they aspired to be players in the international arena as well as in the domestic. Further, in the course of listing ten recommendations they hoped the commission and the UN secretary-general would "take into consideration," they not only construed themselves as representing the Timorese people (and in so doing redefined their positions as components of a quasi-political organization); they were also at the same time attempting to draw a distinction between the secular politics of "the Alkatiri Government"—as they referred to it—and the church as in effect a custodian of absolute values that transcended the temporal "interests of political leaders." In their tenth recommendation (Appendix 2) they even went so far as to refer to "political interference" as being "a real issue" and "challenge for any national process," and on a note of self-serving gravitas observed that "the political interests of political leaders" may undermine the "due process of law."

It may have been this blatant thrusting of a Timorese issue into the international theater that prompted Alkatiri at long last to issue a response to the two bishops. On Tuesday, 12 April, he accused the leaders of the church of behaving like an "opposition party" in their contesting his plan to end compulsory religious instruction (ETAN 2005i). The pastoral note, he concluded, would go down in the history of East Timor as the "date the Catholic hierarchy transformed into a political party." Despite this, he invited the prelates to join a commission to oversee the pilot scheme in the thirty-two schools. "Without descending to the same level as the bishops' last statement, we limit ourselves to reaffirming that the decision to change religion classes to a non-compulsory subject is an experiment. We will study the results of this trial to decide if it will be applied to the whole country or not." His words were no palliative to what was developing into an unconcealed power struggle between church and state. Clearly, the two highly public avowals of Dom Alberto Ricardo da Silva and Dom Basílio do Nascimento had propelled the church irrevocably into the sphere of politics. The ambition of the ecclesiastics to play a visible role in the politics of East Timor had by this time become apparent to all. Up to now, though, the clergy's hostility to the government of Mari Alkatiri had been expressed only in verbal terms, but the language and dynamics of the confrontation were on the point of changing. Even as Alkatiri made his response, the clergy was in the process of organizing what would prove to be—by a wide margin—the largest and most sustained demonstration of popular dissatisfaction with their political leaders in East Timor's history.

The Manifestasaun

The identity of the core organizers of the manifestasaun remains obscure, but it has been suggested (Personal communication, 4 May 2005) that the two bishops themselves were not the executive overlords. Still, a national demonstration on such a large scale could not have come to pass without the clergy in the districts coordinating their efforts to the maximum; given the authoritarian character of the ecclesiastical hierarchy, it is scarcely plausible either bishop could have been out of touch with what was pending.

The manifestasaun may be said to have commenced on Tuesday, 19 April, when an estimated crowd, reportedly comprising more than five thousand people, staged an initial demonstration near the parliamentary buildings, which are located on Dili's seafront, demanding Mari Alkatiri's resignation (ETAN 2005j). A spokesman for the Dili diocese, Father Benâncio Araújo, said the protesters would continue their rally for the rest of the week, but would stop if the government agreed to hold talks. Father Araújo provoked the mob into chanting "Justice, justice and truth"—references to the content of the bishops' second proclamation—in rhetoric designed to undermine the standing of the premier, "We will remain here tomorrow and the days after. We are fighting the dictatorship regime of Alkatiri." With such placards as "fight against the Alkatiri regime," verbal rhetoric was reinforced visually, and as though sensing the demonstrators required support to achieve this goal, Araújo called upon its

Figure 3.2. Demonstrators from Ermera parish parade in the streets of Dili. The sign reads "Win war with God, Government with God, Develop with God." Courtesy of Maxine Hicks.

members to summon people from outside Dili to "topple the antidemocratic re-gime." As it happens, the demonstration went on for a lot longer than a week.

From the very outset, therefore, the series of crowd displays orchestrated by the ecclesiastics had as its explicit aim the weakening or even overthrow of the incumbent prime minister, a goal consistent with the conspicuous absence from the slogans and verbal rhetoric of any mention of the purported impulse for the manifestasaun, i.e., the government's intention to eliminate the teaching of Catholicism as a mandatory subject. The absence of this issue was evident during the entire period the manifestasaun lasted and suggests that although the bishops were prepared to negotiate with the administration about this is-sue, they were also using it as a tool for removing Alkatiri. My wife and I were present in the capital at the time, and neither of us saw any placards referring to it. When a few days afterward village youths from the districts began entering Dili, some had no idea why they had been trucked in by their local clergy. They saw the manifestasaun as a jamboree providing them with a unique opportu-nity to get together with fellow youths from other parts of the country while indulging in sessions of guitar playing, loud praying, and hymn singing into the early hours. During daylight they would march down the thoroughfares of the capital—which many were seeing for the first time in their lives—and in the evening, out of sight of priests and nuns, take time off from chanting and singing hymns to enjoy the more carnal pleasures of sexual relations on Dili's beach. Images—statues and large portraits—of the Virgin Mary dominated the iconic imagery, and these served as refined counterparts to the gaudy anti-Alkatiri messages daubed onto the placards and strident diatribes.

The air was filled during the first twenty-four hours or so of the manifestasaun by vituperative rhetoric, the most plangent issuing from East Timor's Catholic Radio, which urged Catholics to "protest against Alkatiri—kick him out" (Murdock 2005) and from the minister of the interior, Rogério Lobato, who threatened that if demonstrators attempted to occupy government buildings, the police would "resort to legitimate use of force" (ETAN 2005k). After an extraordinary meeting on Wednesday, (20 April), Fretilin's central committee firmly asserted that Alkatiri's position was "non-negotiable" (Jolliffe 2005). The speaker of the parliament and president of Fretilin, Francisco Guterres (who also goes by his Timorese name of Lu Olo), within hours had issued a proclamation denouncing the protest as a "profoundly political and preinsurrectional demonstration organized by the church hierarchy" in collusion with opposition forces he did not identify. On the streets the rhetoric was just as strident, and among those who addressed the demonstrators none was more conspicuous on account of his omnipresence and dynamism than a media-savvy and articulate priest called Domingos Soares, whose resistance to the Indonesian occupation had elevated him to the status of a nationalist hero.

Figure 3.3. Demonstrators and police before the Virgin Mary on Dili's seafront. State and church confront each other as people pray. Courtesy of Maxine Hicks.

Although Fretilin had been overwhelmingly elected into a majority in parliament and therefore government in May 2002 largely because of its association with the resistance movement and Soares' sympathies might be thought to favor the government of Mari Alkatiri, Soares was uninhibited in denouncing it from the beginning of the demonstration. For the church Alkatiri's left-wing reputation had always served as a serious impediment to an easy acceptance of his leadership. So day after day, from a platform near the parliamentary building (cordoned off by the police), a microphone in his hands, his aggrieved rhetoric made no bones about what those who supported the hierarchy were demanding. "The people and the Catholic Church have joined peacefully for an end to this extremist government," he declared on the twenty-first of the month, "We want the Alkatiri Government to step down and for Fretilin to choose another" (Jolliffe 2005).

By the second day of the demonstration, police had set up road blocks on the roads into Dili, thereby reducing to some extent the number of would-be participants able to join the crowds near the seafront in the town proper, but those unable to get into town simply sat down to pray and sing hymns alongside the road. In Dili itself the atmosphere was expectant and remained so for the entire time the manifestasaun lasted, giving one the feeling that large-scale violence could break out at any moment. But with the passing of the days, a carnival-like quality began to blend in with the fierce anti-Alkatiri denunciations as the sounds of hymns happily sung to the ubiquitous guitars by young men on the capital's waterfront were eventually augmented by those of traditional dances (*tebedai*) accompanied by gongs and performed by males and females of all ages, some by no means young.

On Tuesday the nineteenth, Mari Alkatiri had publicly aligned himself with the assertiveness of Fretilin's central committee and the belligerent rhetoric of Lobato and Guterres. He complained that the demonstration "did not create conditions for dialogue in any manner." He also issued a statement in which he declared his willingness to talk, although he declared he was "unhappy" the church had organized the protest (ETAN 2005k). A spokesman for the prime minister remarked upon the bishops' assertion to the commission and contended that the church demanded a say in the running of the country, while the premier himself accused the church of "behaving like a political party," adding that "[only] his government had the legitimacy to agree on the commission and make the education ruling." The fact that Alkatiri found it necessary to cite East Timor's constitution shows how defensive the prime minister was becoming, and this weakness may account for the fact that he also praised the demonstrators for their "orderly behavior," and even—in defiance of the mood on the streets—that "the calm atmosphere" would help open "channels of dialogue between the government and the Catholic Church" (ETAN 2005k). He had probably realized the demonstrators were determined to remain protesting until he responded in a manner to their satisfaction, and the irenic tone in his own rhetoric indicated this realization. Alkatiri's famous intransigence modified, thereby opening the door for good-faith negotiations. For their part, in private and as the days went by, whatever the strength of their inherent preference for his overthrow, Silva and Nascimento let it be known the senior hierarchy did not require his departure as a condition for an agreement.

Taking the side of the beleaguered premier, President José Alexandre (Xanana) Gusmão, on Thursday (21 April) condemned the church's demonstration against the government and said he would not allow street protests to overthrow the cabinet. Flanked by Alkatiri and Guterres, Gusmão showed he realized that the character of public discourse between church and state had radically altered and that as a consequence of this alteration the relation between the two was changing. Although not explicitly stating that the church was the process of becoming an overt political force in its own right, Gusmão informed a group of journalists that he disapproved of "partisan symbols" being used in a religious demonstration and of religious symbols being used in political protests (ETAN 2005l). The president also realized the hierarchy's earlier and declared grievance had shifted. The clergy had, he said, "somewhat lost the objective" of the demonstrations. The issue of religion in schools seemed to have disappeared from view. "It's a citizen's right to demonstrate, but, if the demonstrations' objective is to bring down the government, I will not permit it." A government could be replaced only by means of an election, he reminded his listeners, and a cabinet reshuffled only by the party in power (ETAN 2005l).

As the week wore on and the demonstrators showed no sign of losing their aggressive vitality or their robust determination to pressure the government, the three parties to the negotiations—Alkatiri, Silva and Nascimento, and Gusmão—were taking quiet, tentative steps toward coming to an agreement. Not that there were no setbacks along the way. The *Catholic News* on 26 April reported that talks had broken down, and the assistant bishop of Dili, Apolinário Guterres, informed reporters that the demonstrators' demands had still not been met. "People do not trust the government," he said, and in adding that "right now the church is only willing to open a dialogue with the parliament and Fretilin," he was with some disdain dismissing the prime minister and his government from the picture (*Catholic News* 2005). For its part, the government, through a spokesman, declared that negotiations had failed because the church's demand that the premier be removed ran contrary to the constitution.

By this time the international community was becoming concerned about the festering dispute, as was revealed on Wednesday (27 April) when the

United Nations Mission of Support in East Timor (UNMISET), under the chairmanship of Dr. Sukehiro Hasegawa, the UN special representative of the secretary-general for Timor-Leste, held a round-table discussion for representatives of the various international agencies in East Timor. The colloquium was designed to inform them about the respective positions of the two parties with regard to the question of the teaching of religion in public schools. The government's arguments were put forward by the minister of education, culture, and youth, Dr. Armindo Maia, while the views of the clergy were argued by Father António Gonçalves, the chancellor of Baucau diocese. "I hope the exchange of views would help the participants of the International Symposium on the UN Peacekeeping Operations in Post-conflict Timor-Leste to appreciate the complexity of the situation in a post conflict country," Hasegawa announced (UNMISET 2005).

Still Domingos Soares continued haranguing the crowds listening to him during the daylight hours, however, and still the noise of singing and chanting unabatedly disrupted the tranquility of the nights. Nuns remained, as ever, conspicuous, even hectoring the police who for their part behaved, as did the demonstrators, in a restrained way. There were few incidents. A United Nations employee caused a scene by driving his vehicle carelessly near some demonstrators, and the internet cafe my wife and I patronized was temporarily shut on 4 May because some young men had skirmished in front of it. But although a certain sense of menace continued to hang over the town, violence remained in abeyance. The two bishops themselves said nothing in public, but negotiations were quietly going on behind the scenes against the raucous background with Gusmão, Alkatiri, and Ramos-Horta continuing to profess hopeful sentiments that an accommodation between the authorities was feasible.

Their optimism proved justified. At long last a deal was struck and a formal agreement was signed on 7 May by Mari Alkatiri, Dom Alberto Ricardo da Silva, and Dom Basílio do Nascimento, in the presence of President Gusmão (Appendix 3). By its terms the governmental plan was in effect abandoned. Catholic instruction would be continued on virtually the same basis as before; a draft penal code was to define abortion as a crime, except in cases where it was "absolutely necessary" to avoid the mother's death; and voluntary prostitution would be classed as a crime, though it should protect "victims," i.e., those "forced" into prostitution. For good measure the "exploitation" of children (which was not defined) was to be classed as yet another crime. The accord was generally interpreted as a victory for the church, but the clergy's success was watered down by a clause that made it possible for parents to refuse to have their children take religious classes. A "Permanent Working Group" was to be established within a month from the date of the signing of the joint declaration to examine its provisions about abortion, prostitution, and exploiting children, but nothing that would bring accustomed mores into line with what the prelates wished was actually carried out. Indeed three weeks later the prime minister made the argument that in respect to prostitution and abortion, the agreement "deals with issues affecting the conscience of each citizen and has the merit of opening debate to all society." Hardly words that suggested that his government planned to accommodate the hierarchy's concerns (Lusa 2005). Still, the agreement reached meant that the clergy no longer required the demonstrators to threaten the secular authorities, and they quietly returned for their homes in the capital or set out for their more distant habitations in the hinterland leaving their garbage littering the streets. With their departure, the manifestasaun came to a quiet end.

Conclusion

Regardless of which party may be adjudged the "winner," the seventeen-day stand-off on the Dili streets that Easter changed the terms of their future relationship. After 7 May, the clergy would not be at all reticent in pressing what its leaders saw as the church's interests. Thus on 5 December the United Nations received another missive from the church in East Timor (Appendix 4). Bishop Alberto Ricardo da Silva wrote to the secretary-general and in no uncertain terms railed against the "political leaders" who by their reluctance to issue the Report of the Commission for Reception, Truth, and Reconciliation (CAVR), whose mandate included establishing the truth of what human rights abuses had taken place in East Timor, had conspired to "bury the truth." Tellingly, the prelate's letter contained little that might be construed as directly pertaining to "religious" matters at all. The document can be read as a straightforward political statement issued by an ecclesiastical politician self-consciously wielding substantial political power in his own right. This, of course, is what he *was* doing and would thereafter continue doing. When the senior clergy had played politics before the manifestasaun seven months previously, their discourse, though insistent, had tended to be discreet rather than tactless and their maneuvers quietly diplomatic. Now that their defiance of the government had garnered them public success, their indulgence as politicians could become explicit. Ecclesiastical authority had emerged from under the canopy.

The constitution of the Republic of East Timor specifies no religion as the state religion. While the state recognizes and respects the different religious denominations, and they may organize and exercise their activities as they wish in due observance of the constitution and the law, and while the state "shall promote the cooperation with the different religious denominations that contribute to the well-being of the people" (Constitution of the Democratic

Republic of East Timor 2005), no single religion is privileged over any other. In other words, there is no state religion, and state and religion are separate. As I noted earlier, however, when the constitution was being worked out the clergy did attempt to make Catholicism the state religion, and it will be recalled that the president of one of the parties, the Democratic Party, accused the government of separating religion from the state. This remark suggests that some quarters in East Timor would be perfectly satisfied were Catholicism to be installed as the state religion. This feeling, I judge, is not universal among the political class, though were the matter put to the people, they might well endorse it. Those running the government and probably the majority of their rivals see their country as aspiring to the status of a modern nation-state which means that they wish to be regarded in the United Nations—at least in formal terms—as sharing the ideals of the Western democracies. Hence, I think it unlikely that any serious attempt by a political party to bring the clergy into the secular governance of the country would be at all likely to meet with success, but at the same time the lesson of the manifestasaun is that the church has tested its strength and not found it wanting. The future will probably witness the ecclesiastical and secular domains continuing to contest their interests but now in the full light of public scrutiny, without inhibition.

For Galina

Since I submitted the final manuscript version of the present article to Galina Lindquist—emended in accordance with the suggestions she made after what was quite clearly a painstaking and close reading—Galina passed away. Regretfully, I only met her once and unlike, I believe, the majority of contributors to this volume cannot be said to have a lengthy acquaintance with her. I met her after I had written to her from Cambridge University in March 2007 regarding a book to which I was contributing an article, and she wrote back to say she was shortly coming to Cambridge to give a seminar and examine a doctoral dissertation. A few days later, around our table at Strada's, I professed in passing (as I had supposed) a new direction in which my research was moving, namely, religion and politics. This avowal incited a quick interest in her eyes and immediately I had finished my rather brief affirmation, she had asked me to consider submitting a contribution to another volume she was in the process of editing. Hence, my presence here. Although I knew Galina for all too short a duration, I learned enough to signal her scrupulous concern for scholarship and remark her graciousness in adversity. I wish our dinner had been many more years ago.

Appendix 1

Pastoral Note from the Catholic Bishops of Timor-Leste
about Teaching Religion in Public Schools

The ministry of education of Timor-Leste issued a memorandum to a press conference which took place on November 19th, 2004, regarding primary school curriculum. The memo says that "the plan of implementation of primary school curriculum was approved by the minister council in October 2004 and the programs related to it were approved to be tested in 32 experimental schools, in 13 districts, ranging 1st to 6th grade, from January 2005 on."

Further on it says: "Religion is an optional subject. Its timetable will be determined individually by each school, without prejudice to mandatory subjects (…) Religion won't be accountable for evaluation nor conditional for grade transition (…) Regarding teaching staff, they must be qualified enough and accordingly credited by suitable religious institutions, with no extra cost to national budget (…)."

Recently, the Minister of Education stated further that "We respect the freedom of belief, bound by the Human Rights [Declaration] which we signed and acknowledged that this is a freedom, we can't force someone to follow any religion he/she doesn't believe in, that's wrong enough, but that doesn't mean it's forbidden, instead it's an option, lots of people think that optional means forbidden. Optional means that we can teach any subject, not as a mandatory one, like in Indonesian time (…)" (Semanário, 11–02–05, p.5). Statements from many government officials have been presented to the public according to STL, 11–02–05, Timor Post, 10–02–05 and 11–02–05. In 12–02–05, Timor Post published a story presenting allegations from the Ministry of Education in favor of an optional [Religion subject]. At the same time, it leaves to schools and parents the responsability [sic] of organizing Religion classes, without specifying any structural mechanisms.

I. THE RELIGIOUS DIMENSION OF LIFE
Considering the fact that most of the population of Timor-Leste being catholic by its option, the catholic bishops have the pastoral duty of addressing christians and presenting to the whole catholic community and to the public opinion which relevant catholic principles apply to this matter. The Concillium [sic] Vaticanus II says that "Amidst every other mean of education, school has a special importance because of its mission which, while attentively cultivating intellectual faculties, develops the capacity of judging rightfully, introduces [us] to the cultural heritage left by past generations, promotes the sense of values, prepares to working life and, creating a friendly relationship between

students with different nature or condition, favours mutual understanding. Besides, school is like a center and families, teachers, groups who promote cultural, civic and religious life, civil society and the whole human community should take part in its functionality and progress (Gravissimum Educationis 5a). In this context the parents' role is extremely important because they are guardians of their sons' and daughters' integral good: "Parents, whose first and inalienable duty and right is to educate their sons and daughters, must have real freedom to choose any school. Therefore the public power, responsible for protecting and defending citizens" freedoms, must assure, following distributive justice, that public money should be granted in a way that parents may be able to choose, by their own conscience, with all freedom, in which schools to put their sons and daughters" (Gravissimum Educationis 6a).

Based on these principles, the role of the State is a service to the community: "Besides, is part of the public power role to provide that every citizen may reach a just participation in culture and be prepared to rightfully exercise their civil rights and duties" (Gravissimum Educationis 6b). So, the Church reminds the parents that "the important duty they have of using everything or demanding everything, so that their sons and daughters may benefit from that aid and progress harmonically within christian and profane education. Therefore, the Church praises those civil authorities and societies which, despite pluralism in modern society and because of fair religious freedom, do help families so that their sons and daughters' education may happen in every school according to those families' moral and religious principles" (Gravissimum Educationis 7b). The Church itself, aware of its most serious duty of taking care of its sons' and daughters' moral and religious education, "knows that it must be present with its affection and help to those who are educated in non-catholic schools: either through the apostolate action of colleagues, or mostly by the ministry of priests and non-priests who teach them the doctrine of salvation, adapted to the age and condition of each one, and help them spiritually according to circumstances" (Gravissimum Educationis 7a). Public school has a role of educating according to some values, including the transcendental values of the religious dimension of life, which children and youngsters are entitled to. Those values are transmitted through culture, history and faith. This happens in many religions and cultures. To most East-Timorese, that faith is the Catholic Faith, which lives peacefully side by side with other religions.

Source: ETAN 2005a.

Appendix 2

Subject: Catholic Church of ET Position on Justice Presented to COE

THE CATHOLIC CHURCH OF EAST TIMOR POSITION ON JUSTICE FOR CRIMES AGAINST HUMANITY

Presented to the Commission of Experts appointed by the Secretary-General

The Catholic Church of East Timor welcomes the initiative of the Secretary General to appoint a Commission of Experts to evaluate the current processes both in East Timor and Indonesia and to recommend future measures.

We hope that the voice of the East Timorese people, who have suffered from impunity, would be heard.

The decision of political leaders to deny the Timorese people the right to justice reflects a disintegration of reason and the principles of the natural moral law that is necessary for the common good.

The Catholic doctrine is clear on the need for justice as the preservation of human dignity is meted in truth and justice. Therefore democracy must be based on the true and solid foundation of non-negotiable ethical principles which underpins life in society.

East Timor is a nation with a Catholic majority that cannot support the Government's policy of impunity. Acceptance of this policy would undermine fundamental ethical requirements and principles of absolute value necessary for the dignity of the human person, democracy and progress of the people of East Timor.

It is the right and duty of Catholics and all citizens to seek the truth and to promote and defend justice. On this basis, the Catholic community will continue to insist on the moral and legal accountability of all individuals that committed human rights violations and crimes against humanity in East Timor from 1975 to 1999.

The Catholic community will not condone impunity for crimes against humanity. The victims who suffered these crimes, their families and the people in whose names such crimes are committed deserve nothing less.

International justice is now a crucial last resort to bring justice for the victims particularly as both the East Timorese and Indonesian Governments have agreed on a Truth and Friendship Commission that will not submit to a process for genuine justice and real accountability.

Recommendations

The Catholic Community requests the continued intervention of the United Nations to achieve justice for the people of East Timor for serious international human rights violations and humanitarian law, amounting to crimes under international law. As the Catholic Bishops of East Timor we recommend the following:

1. The Truth and Friendship Commission should not be treated as a substitute for criminal justice.

2. The United Nations and the International Community continue to pursue real accountability for crimes against humanity, war crimes and genocide committed in East Timor between 1975 and 1999. It is important that the international community recognizes the consequences of failing to address impunity. There will be no progress in the implementation of the rule of law and democracy in East Timor if impunity prevails.

3. The Security Council continues to uphold Resolution 1272 in response to the 1999 violence. The Security Council resolution 1272 condemned and called for the immediate end to all violence, and demanded that all those responsible for such violence be brought to justice.

4. Insist that Timorese political leaders honor the commitments made to the international community to bring the perpetrators to justice for the crimes that they had committed.

5. Insist that the Alkatiri Government respect the commitment made to the people through the Constitution for justice and observe Section 160 of the Constitution of RDTL that provides for criminal proceedings with the national or international courts for crimes considered against humanity or of war.

6. Insist that the RDTL Parliament demands international standards of justice and due process of law occurs to achieve justice and accountability for crimes committed in East Timor.

7. The United Nations promotes and urges the political leadership of East Timor to develop a constructive and values based relationship between East Timor and Indonesia to ensure a lasting reconciliation between the people of Indonesia and East Timor.

8. The United Nations ensure that reconciliation based on the interests of political leaders will not undermine human dignity and the need for justice.

9. The United Nations and the international community recognize the weaknesses of the judiciary system in East Timor. The judiciary lacks independence and has low levels of competence. Trials must comply with international human rights standards to ensure their legitimacy and credibility.

10. The United Nations take into consideration the fact that political interference is now a real issue and challenge for any national process. Due process of law may be undermined because of the political interests of political leaders. This factor intensifies the need for international justice for the East Timorese people.

Conclusion:

Based on the above factors the Catholic Church of East Timor urges the United Nations Secretary General to employ international justice mechanisms to bring perpetrators of crimes against humanity to account.

We hope that the cost factor and slow moving procedures encountered by international criminal tribunals in the past will not deter the Secretary General from recommending to the Security Council the appropriate international justice mechanism as the remedy necessary to ensure the preservation of human rights and to act as the alternative to impunity.

The Catholic Church of East Timor looks forward to hearing the Commission of Experts recommendation to the Secretary General.

The people of East Timor offer our prayers for the real discernment of this issue by the Security Council and for the members' proper execution of the United Nations Charter in the interests of human rights, justice and the common good

D. Alberto Ricardo Bishop of Dili

D. Basilio do Nascimento Bishop of Baucau

East Timor

April 9, 2005

Source: ETAN 2005h.

Appendix 3

Joint Declaration

Taking into consideration that article 42 of the Constitution of the Democratic Republic of Timor-Leste defines that everyone is guaranteed the freedom to assemble and peacefully demonstrate;

Taking into consideration that the Constitution of the DRET defines that the objectives of the State is to defend and guarantee political democracy and participation of the people in the resolution of national problems;

Having observed the peaceful and orderly manner in which sentiments have been manifested that raise fundamental questions of governance worthy of consideration for the political orientation of the country;

Taking into consideration that the Constitution of the DRTL guarantees freedom of conscience, of religion and cult, and establishes separation between religious denominations and the State;

Taking into account that the Constitution of the DRET attributes to the State the duty to promote cooperation with all different religious denominations;

Recognizing the competences the Constitution of the DRET attributes to the Government;

The Government and Bishops of the Catholic Church of East Timor, based on the due respect for the Constitution of the DRET, affirm jointly and solemnly:

1. Recognize the important contribution that religious values have in the construction of the national identity, in the construction of the nation, and in the socio-economic, cultural, and political level;

2. Recognize the fundamental role that moral and religious values play in the formation of the individual;

3. Recognize that these values should be incorporated in the educational mission entrusted to Schools;

4. Recognize that education should adequately correspond to the aspirations of all citizens, without any form of discrimination;

5. Recognize that the teaching of Religion must be included as a regular discipline in the curriculum, and consequently, taught during normal hours, and attendance subject to a decision at the time of enrollment and in accordance with the options freely expressed by their Parents—who are the irreplaceable partners in making concrete options that relate to the education of their children.

6. The Draft Penal Code should address the abortion issue in all its dimensions; abortion must be defined as a crime, except in cases where it is absolutely necessary to avoid the mother's death. The law must equally define the practice of voluntary prostitution as a crime, but should protect victims forced into prostitution. Likewise, as already envisaged in the Draft Penal Code, art. 155 and 156, the exploitation of children is defined as a crime.

7. To guarantee that there will not be threats or retaliation from the authorities against the demonstrators when they return to their place of residence, and to guarantee their physical security and social environment free of intimidation;

To establish a Permanent Working Group within a month from the date of signing this Joint Declaration. This Permanent Working Group will be composed of representatives from the Government, the Catholic Church and other religious denominations, and its mission is to accompany the concretization of the principles here established, to make recommendations that are relevant and opportune in all areas of its intervention and to provide better understanding of the existing problems and prevent future problems.

Dili, 7 May 2005

Dr. Mari Alkatiri D. Alberto Ricardo da Silva D. Basilio do Nascimento Prime Minister Bishop of Dili Bishop of Baucau

In the presence of: Kay Rala Xanana Gusmao President of the Republic

Source: http://pascal.iseg.utl.pt/~cesa/documento%20acordo%20dili.pdf, http://www.etan.org/et2005/may/15/09joint.htm.

Appendix 4

Paqo Episcopal
Avenida dos Direitos Humanos
Lecidere—DILI

5 December 2005
Dr. Kofi Annan
UN Secretary-General
UN Headquarters
1st Ave., 46th St.
New York, NY 10017

Excellency,

Thank you for mandating the Commission of Experts to Review the Prosecution of Serious Violations of Human Rights in East Timor in 1999 and for submitting the Experts Report to the Security Council for its consideration.

We understand that the Secretary General is also in the process of preparing a Report to the Council on this matter. It is to this end that we write to reiterate the importance of justice to the people East Timor and to our nascent and fragile democracy.

The reluctance of political leaders to issue the CAVR Report to the people is confirmation that politicians want to bury the truth to ensure that there is no accountability for those responsible for the atrocities committed in 1975 to 1999.

The people of East Timor want to build this nation on the durable values and principles that other democratic nations around the world uphold. Foregoing justice and consenting to impunity will send the message to the international community that the United Nations Charter on Human Rights and the Security Council Resolution 1272 is of little consequence and not binding to the Member Nations.

We entrusted our right to self determination to the United Nations throughout our struggle for independence. Once again, we entrust to the United Nations, this basic fundamental human right to justice for the people of East Timor.

We therefore urge the Secretary General to recommend that the Security Council adopt a Resolution under Chapter VII of the United Nations Charter to create an international tribunal for East Timor.

We remain in prayers that the outcome puts human rights and the dignity of man above all.

Please accept, Excellency, our highest consideration and esteem.
Yours Sincerely
Dom Alberto Ricardo da Silva, Bishop of Dili
Contactos: Tel./ Fax: (+670) 33.22.308; Cel.: 723.53.83

Source: http://www.etan.org/et2005/december/03/05ricardo.htm.

Appendix Five

Religion in the Constitution of East Timor

Section 12

(State and religious denominations)

1. The State shall recognise and respect the different religious denominations, which are free in their organisation and in the exercise of their own activities, to take place in due observance of the Constitution and the law.

2. The State shall promote the cooperation with the different religious denominations that contribute to the well-being of the people of East Timor.

Section 45

(Freedom of conscience, religion and worship)

1. Every person is guaranteed the freedom of conscience, religion and worship and the religious denominations are separated from the State.

2. No one shall be persecuted or discriminated against on the basis of his or her religious convictions.

3. The right to be a conscientious objector shall be guaranteed in accordance with the law.

4. Freedom to teach any religion in the framework of the respective religious denomination is guaranteed.

Source: http://www.etan.org/etanpdf/pdf2/constfnen.pdf.

NOTES

1. The conventional long form designation for the nation-state that is popularly known as "East Timor" is officially the "Democratic Republic of Timor-Leste" but

      it is also commonly referred to as "Timor Lorosa'e," "Timor-Leste," and formerly "Portuguese Timor," "Timor Timor," and "Timtim."

2. This might be considered an appropriate place for a comment on what perhaps may be characterized as the excessively nonchalant attitude government officials tend to demonstrate toward public affairs, a flaw that could be considered as something approaching indifference. This indifference has contributed to the rift in secular governance apparent between East Timor's capital and its hinterland (Hicks 2007), a perilous disjunction that strikingly contrasts with the success the Church has met with in merging the two domains for the purposes of ecclesiastical administration.

3. This essay results from the accumulated experience of five trips I made to East Timor, the most recent being a stay of seven months in 2005. My original research in 1966–1967 was funded by the London Committee of the London-Cornell Project for East and South East Asian Studies which was supported jointly by the Carnegie Corporation of New York and the Nuffield Foundation. Subsequent field research was funded by the American Philosophical Society and the J. William Fulbright Foreign Scholarship Board. For sources on the events of the period discussed here an excellent resource is the ETAN ("East Timor Action Network") website at http://www.etan.org. The majority of sources cited in this study were originally accessed through that site.

4. Cf. The relatively unobtrusive—and unsuccessful as it happened—lobbying the clergy carried out to make Catholicism the State religion during the time East Timor's constitution was in the process of being formulated.

5. All such estimates need to be treated with caution, however. Many Timorese, perhaps the majority outside the towns in the rural hinterlands, even today remain steadfastly wedded to their animistic traditions and many who appear devotees of the Church combine indigenous beliefs with Catholicism to fashion a syncretic mix. The other denominations, with small representation, are Protestantism and Islam.

6. In those days there was only one bishop in East Timor.

7. Whether or not the prelates had had any forewarning of what was pending has not been reported, though it scarcely conceivable they did not have at least some inkling.

8. The question has been raised regarding the religious affiliation of these two constituencies. i.e., were they Catholic and if so why did they support Muslim Indonesia? The religion of the rioters was never established, though there is no reason to suppose they were anything other than Catholic or at least nominally Catholic. At the core of the pro-Indonesian group were probably malcontents who had never acquiesced in Indonesia's granting East Timor independence three years before. The anti-government protesters disliked Alkatiri because he was associated with the left and was the leader of the Fretilin party, which they also disfavoured. Grievances going as far back as 1974 were further grist for the mills of antagonism. These remain a potent factor in the politics of today.

9. It might be noted that the constitution of Timor-Leste does indeed do exactly that. Church and State are separate.

10. As with certain other statistics issuing from East Timor the numbers of religious teachers said to be teaching in State schools and their costs to the government in 2005 must be regarded circumspectly. One report mentions there were about 1,000 of them and that they cost about US$1,800.000.00 per year in salaries. An average estimated cost of US$2,500,000 covered salaries, text books, and other requirements (ETAN 2005g).

11. "We hope that the voice of the East Timorese people, who have suffered from impunity, would be heard."

REFERENCES

Catholic News. 2005. "East Timor Church-Govt Talks Collapse." 26 April. http://www.cathnews.com/news/504/135.php.

Constitution of the Democratic Republic of East Timor. 2002. http://www.etan.org/etanpdf/pdf2/constfnen.pdf.

ETAN (East Timor Action Network) 2005a. "Pastoral Note from the Catholic Bishops of Timor-Leste about Teaching Religion in Public Schools." http://www.etan.org/et2005/march/13/16pastor.htm.

ETAN 2005b. "Bishop Nascimento: Those Making Laws Against the Church Are Anti-Christian." *UNMISET Daily Media Review.* Friday, 14 January 2005. http://www.etan.org/et2005/march/20/24relig.htm.

ETAN 2005c. "Political Parties Support Church in Curriculum Battle." *UNMISET Daily Media Review.* Monday, 28 February 2005. http://www.etan.org/et2005/march/20/24relig.htm.

ETAN 2005d. "Church Not the Enemy of the State." *UNMISETDaily Media Review.* Monday, 28 February 2005. http://www.etan.org/et2005/march/20/24relig.htm.

ETAN 2005e. "Government Wants to Separate Religion from the State." *UNMISET Daily Media Review.* 8 March. http://www.etan.org/et2005/march/06/dailym08.htm.

ETAN 2005f. "Islamic Leaders Supportive of Church Stance." UNMISET *Daily Media Review.* Tuesday, 15 March. http://www.etan.org/et2005/march/20/24relig.htm.

ETAN 2005g. (1) "Ramos-Horta Blasts Catholic Opposition to School Curriculum Change." *Lusa.* March 24. (2) "Press Release: Foreign Ministry Reacts to Apostolic Nuncio's Statement." Direcção das Relações Publícas do MNEC [Ministry of Foreign Affairs and Cooperation Timor-Leste]. 24 March. http://www.etan.org/et2005/march/20/24relig.htm.

ETAN 2005h. "The Catholic Church of East Timor Position on Justice for Crimes Against Humanity: Presented to the Commission of Experts Appointed by the Secretary-General." 9 April. http://www.etan.org/et2005/july/01/01cathlc.htm.

ETAN 2005i. "RC Church Leaders Behaving Like 'Opposition Party', Says PM." *Lusa.* http://www.etan.org/et2005/april/10/13rc.htm.

ETAN 2005j. "Date: 19 Apr 2005 East Timor's Catholic Church Rallies Thousands in Anti-Government Protest by Rosa Garcia." Agence France-Presse (AFP). http://www.etan.org/et2005/april/17/19etcath.htm.

ETAN 2005k. "East Timor: Catholics, Gov't Lower Their Rhetoric as Church Protests Continue." *Lusa. Notícia SIR-6934206*. Dili. 20 April. www.etan.org/et2005/april/17/20cthlcs.htm.

ETAN 2005l. "East Timor: Gusmão Says He Won't Allow Catholic Protest to Topple Alkatiri Gov't." *Lusa*. Dili. 21 April. http://www.etan.org/et2005/april/17/21gusmao.htm.

Hicks, David. 2004. *Tetum Ghosts and Kin: Fertility and Gender in East Timor*. Prospect Heights, IL: Waveland Press Inc. 2nd ed.

———. 2007. "Community and Nation-State in East Timor: A View from the Periphery." *Anthropology Today* 23 (1): 13–16.

Jolliffe, Jill. 2005. "Activists Call on Timor PM to Resign." *Sydney Morning Herald*. 21 April. http://www.etan.org/et2005/april/17/21actvst.htm.

Lusa (Agência de Notícias de Portugal). 2005. "End of Church Dispute Allows Debate on Abortion, Prostitution—PM." 2 June. http://www.etan.org/et2005/june/01/02debate.htm.

Murdock, Lindsay. 2005. "Dili on Edge after Church Urges Protest." 20 April. http://www.theage.com.au/news/World/Dili-on-edge-after-church-urges-protest/2005/04/19/1113854199053.html#.

UNMISET. 2005. "Unmiset Holds Discussion on Religion in Public Schools in Timor-Leste." 27 April. http://www.unmiset.org/unmisetwebsite.nsf.

RELIGION, SECULARISM, AND POLITICS IN CONTEMPORARY SPAIN

The Case of the Imam of Fuengirola

Eva Evers Rosander

This chapter deals with the case of the imam of Fuengirola, on the south coast of Spain. He published a book concerning women in Islam, was sentenced to prison by a Spanish court for the gender-discriminatory content of the book, and was released from prison a few weeks later, a chain of events that took place between 2000 and 2004. I have chosen this instance since it well illustrates Islam as a theology and practice in present-day Spain and the application by its representatives of rules and regulations that appear to contradict the spirit of the Spanish constitution, as well as various principles established and adopted by Spain in the Convention of Human Rights.

Conflicts arising when different religions clash, and when religion, secular society, and law-governed civil society confront each other, still aroused debate in the Spain of 2007. The key expression is *religious freedom*, in the sense of having the right to freely practice one's religion without it being questioned, constrained, or chastised. For the imam of Fuengirola it concerned the ability to refer to the Koran (his interpretation of the Koran) as a guiding principle in conflicting situations where the husband's right to punish his wife for so-called disobedience was the issue. He did not question the ethical aspect in his publication. It was, according to the imam, the Word of God (which he saw as taking shape in the Koran) that stood over all other moral considerations and conventions.

In Spain the state, separated in theory from the church since 1979, is working toward a general secularization by way of a series of measures with regard

---

to family rights and a tougher penal code for gender-related crimes and offences—laws, in effect, that promote equality between the sexes. The Spanish government hopes, for example, to introduce nonconfessional education in the state school system with an emphasis on civil rights and obligations in a modern society, measures to which representatives of both the Islamic and the Catholic communities are offering resistance.

As regards the conflicting notions concerning the content in state-school religious education, the foremost explanation for the difference of opinion lies in the power struggle that has existed for a long period of time in Spain mainly between two parties. One is represented by the Spanish Catholic Church and its adherents, often exercising a concealed but substantial influence in the affairs of the state. The other party consists of nonconfessional and secular institutions and individuals perceiving the church as an instrument of repression and abuse of power—a point of view with deep roots in Spanish history. Obviously there are devout Catholics among left-wing, liberal, and secular elements in the community who share sympathy with the conservative and nationalist groups in society, but they by no means make up a majority. A government left of center is currently in power. Furthermore, demands have been put forward by Muslims for a religious instruction program of their own in which Islam alone is taught. This demand is in the process of being satisfied in the shape of voluntary religious instruction for both Catholic and Muslim school children, which in turn upsets the church since it wants compulsory and not voluntary instruction in Catholicism. Muslim parents are uncertain as to how Islam can be presented in a secular Spanish school, and have adopted a doubtful and questioning attitude.

Confrontations between, on the one hand, freedom of religion, expression, and publication, and on the other respect for human rights and a safeguard against personal discrimination are burning issues for both religious believers and politicians and for other members of civil society. This is particularly the situation since two important bills were passed aimed at further consolidating gender equality under the socialist government's auspices. One of the new laws, passed in 2004, deals with gender-related violence, and the other, the Law of Equality from 2007, focuses on gender discrimination at the workplace and in society in general. Both laws bring to the fore matters concerning secularization, religion, and power/abuse of power in relation to the nonconfessional nature of the Spanish constitution. Difficulties arise in following the legal guiding principle in parallel with the free practice of religion, and compromises of different kinds are the inevitable result.

The various actors involved in the Mohamed Kamal case include the following: secular women's organizations, Spanish converts to Islam, Spanish groups opposed to Islam, immigrant Muslims representing a number of nationalities and religious persuasions, the mass media, the Spanish court of law, and representatives for the Spanish government in office. All of these made their voices heard in the course of the case, and the complex nature of the issue is hardly understandable unless we lend some attention to the Spanish context in which the different points of view were aired.

It is important to familiarize oneself with, on the one hand, the situation of those Spanish people who represent a conservative policy, often typifying a stance that rejects what they see as exaggerated secularism and disdain for traditional values; and on the other hand their opponents, left-wing adherents of various shades. It is not out of place to recall the existence of two Spains, occupying the same geographical area ever since the time of the Spanish Civil War (1936–1939). According to the historian Raymond Carr, the true victors of the Civil War were the conservative elements: those monarchists who supported Franco and those groups which represented the Catholic Church. The church was an integral part of the political system, and bishops to whom Franco was *homo missu a Deo* sat in the parliament. Two organizations were particularly concerned with the penetration and influencing of the latter, says Carr, namely, the Catholic Association of Propagandists, founded in 1904, and the Opus Dei, founded in 1928 (Carr 1989: 702).

Simply put, these two elements in the political spectrum, right and left of center, are represented by the largest opposition party, the conservative Partido Popular (PP), and the Partido Socialista Obrero Español (PSOE), the Spanish labor party in power under the government of Prime Minister José Luis Rodríguez Zapatero. The gap emerging between the two camps may be said to have widened in recent years as the government's reforms are being seen by the conservative elements as more and more radical, and are being interpreted as a threat to stability, Christian/Spanish traditions, and Christian values. The Catholic Church considers that it has an undeniable right to involve itself in civil affairs where it has no legal standing. It ranks itself as superior to worldly powers, aided and assisted by the Vatican State as the universal Catholic watchtower.

We have referred to the present government's tendency to shape up as a radical party in which the rights of the individual citizen precede religious traditions and traditional moral values when these find themselves on a collision course with each other. Notions regarding religion and politics are thus sharply divided in a society characterized by an individual person's or his or her group's religious beliefs vis-à-vis a secular *Weltanschauung*—a worldly view that takes as its point of departure an attempt to diminish the political importance of religion as well as its social significance in general, while consciously striving as far as possible to make religion a purely private affair.

At the same time that Prime Minister Zapatero urges developments forward in a secular direction, among other measures via a law permitting homosexual marriage (2005), signs of protest appear from the Catholic Church, mainly by way of the bishops. Demonstrations follow one another against most of what Spain's government proposes, with the PP party and representatives of the church making common cause. The Spanish flag is widely exploited at these demonstrations as an ideological weapon against the government in office in a way that takes one back to the days of Francisco Franco's dictatorship (1939–1975). In this connection any sign of tolerance or acceptance of Islam as a religion on equal footing is seen as heresy by most adherents of the Catholic Church.

Islam in Spain

When the Moors invaded the Christian Visigothic Iberia around 711, they were led by Tariq ibn Ziyad, whose forces were joined by his superior Musa bin Nusair. After eight years of campaign, the most part of the Iberian Peninsula was brought under Islamic rule. The long period of Arab-Berber and Islamic dominance in the greater part of what is today called Spain lasted around eight hundred years (to 1492). The territory, under the Arab name of *Al Andalus*, became first an emirate and then an independent Umayyad caliphate, the Caliphate of Córdoba (929–1031).[1] During this caliphate the Arabs in Spain reached their peak of fame for intellectual and artistic prosperity. The setting was multicultural (cf. García Gómez 1976) as many tribes and races coexisted in Al-Andalus, contributing to the intellectual richness. Literacy in Islamic Iberia was more widespread than in any other country in the West. As an example, the city of Córdoba is said to have had seven hundred mosques and seventy libraries, filled with books (Previté-Orton 1971: 376, cf. Fierro 2001).

After the caliphate had dissolved (in 1031), it was split up into smaller administrative units, and the Christian kingdoms, which had already by then started their recapture (*Reconquista*), gradually gained terrain. The Christian kings' warfare went on during the following centuries until at last, in 1492, Granada fell under the so-called Catholic kings. In 1492 a pact was signed between these two monarchs, King Fernando of Castile and Queen Isabel of Aragón. The Spanish Muslims were guaranteed the freedom to practice their cult, a system of religious belief, after the Arab capitulation in Granada. The guarantee turned out to be of no value, because a period of harsh religious violence followed in Spain, still referred to by many Moroccans and other Muslims with ancestor roots in Spain as one of the most tragic periods in history. The Muslims were persecuted and expelled from Spain just like the Jews and the non-Catholic Christians. For many centuries Islam was not allowed to be practiced in Spain. The Catholic Church hegemony was total.

A question that has remained unanswered is how Islamic Al-Andalus actually was. Did the population at large embrace the Muslim faith? According to historians specializing in Medieval Islam such as R. Bulliet (1979), Bernard

Lewis (1992), and Hugh Kennedy (2008), not much is known about this issue with exactitude. Kennedy tells us that the early Muslims brought with them a great cultural self-confidence. They thought that God had spoken to them through his Prophet Muhammad, in Arabic, and that they were the bearers of true religion and God's own language. Arabic became the language of administration and "high" culture at least until the twelfth century, which meant that to make a government or intellectual career, one had to be literate and preferably a Muslim (Kennedy 2008: 375). For the Christian and Jewish people in general, Islam may have seemed approachable. It had a prophet, a holy book, established forms of prayer, dietary and family laws. Abraham and Jesus were also both prophets in the Islamic tradition. These similarities may have aided conversion (cf. Kennedy 2008: 376). Nonetheless, the Catholic Church had been an important power factor in Spanish society ever since the Reconquest began (cf. Saz 2007: 33–57).

After Franco's death in 1975, the Spanish church's grip over society weakened considerably. In the constitution drawn up in 1978, Spain was declared a country in which freedom of religion was an established element. The next step in an even more liberal direction was taken in 1989, when Islam was officially recognized in Spain as a well-established and deeply rooted religion (in Spanish: *de notorio arraigo*). In 1992 an agreement of cooperation was signed between the Spanish state and the Islamic Committee (*La Comisión Islámica*)[2] (Prado 2006).

Abdennur Prado, a converted Spanish Muslim, in his book *El Islam en Democracia* (Islam in Democracy) (2006) underlines the fact that the Catholic monopoly over other religions not only totally dominated the scene in Spain up to 1978 but has continued influencing Spanish policy also in contemporary Spain. Even if some Spanish converts to Islam like Prado himself talk about the current "return of Islam to Spain" (2006: 13f),[3] they nonetheless complain about the negative attitudes toward Islam in contemporary Spain. The Catholic Church still sees diversity and religious pluralism as a danger especially in relation to religious education in schools. It seems to dislike the revival of Islam just as much as it fears the secular state.

The agreements mentioned above, the Spanish constitution and the human rights conventions, all focus on the individual's freedom of opinion, including religious freedom. This notwithstanding, Prado is probably right when he points out the injustices and discrimination to which Islam and its believers are currently exposed in Spain. Not only Muslims like Prado, but also secular people mention with dismay examples of the privileged position of the Catholic Church in Spanish society. One example are the lavish subsidies the church receives from the state[4] and another is the Catholic bishops' right to hire and fire teachers of religion at their discretion, in both private and state schools (Prado 2006; Savater 2007).

Muslim communities face economic difficulties that cause a great dependence on external financial help, and have to confront the problem of finding places to practice their religion. Most Spanish non-Muslims do not want mosques in their neighborhoods. Many Muslim women feel embarrassed because of the negative reactions of the Spaniards to women wearing veils in public. According to a survey carried out by the Global Attitudes Project about the relationship between what is referred to as "Westerners" and "Muslims," Spain was the only country among the thirteen ones selected for the project that had experienced a dramatic reduction in the number of people with a positive attitude to Muslims in general, from 46 percent in 2005 to 29 percent in 2006. According to the same survey, 83 percent of the Spaniards considered Muslims to be "fanatics"; 43 percent of the Spaniards who participated in the survey said many or most Muslims living in Spain supported Islamic extremists. The Spanish respondents were also more critical than the others concerning Muslim men's treatment of women: 83 percent said that Muslim men show little respect for women, and treat them as inferiors. (*El País* 24 June 2000: 11).

Compared to France, the Spanish prejudices are less articulated in the mass media, but in France the discontent with Islam comes mostly from people and state institutions embracing a secular ideology. In Spain, the conservative PP and the Catholic Church unite in criticizing the increasing influence of a non-Christian religion such as Islam in Spanish society. According to another survey made by a Christian magazine, published by the Catholic community called Sacred Hearts Congregation, the Spanish priests qualified Islam as "fanatic, fundamentalist and male-centered" (*El País* 1 November 2006: 36).

Moreover, traditionally there exists a fear of Muslims in Spain, going back to the eight hundred years of Islamic dominance. This ancient scare and the triumph of having defeated the intruders find their expression in the annual poking fun at the *Moros* (Arabs) in Spanish folklore in the form of so-called Moors and Christians Festivals (*fiestas de moros y cristianos*). They are held in various places, predominantly in Andalusia and in the regions of Alicante and Valencia. The performances contain dramatic scenes of battles, expressing many centuries of unfavorable comment (*leyenda negra*) about the Arab-Berbers, ending happily from the Christians' point of view with the Reconquest and the inglorious disappearance of the moros. The stereotypical Spanish ways of performing the figures of the Prophet Muhammad and his believers in these dramas had been put into another, somewhat threatening light after the Muslims' harsh and violent reactions all over the world to the caricatures of Muhammad shown in a Danish newspaper in September 2005.

Advocated by certain Muslim groups in Spain, who saw the celebrations as racial and religious discrimination, quite a number of the organizing committees and the mayors of the villages concerned opted for changing the most bloody and provocative parts of the performances. One of the more drastic elements consists of throwing a rag doll representing the Prophet from a castle into a precipice while fireworks explode, destroying his paper-doll head while the audience applauds what is happening. In one particular case the church took measures to avoid conflicts with what some of them saw as presumptive terrorists among the Muslim immigrants in or around Valencia, where these folkloristic village festivals and plays about the Arabs and the Christians are frequently enacted in Spring (Savater 2007). They insisted that celebrating the victory over the Moors had partly acquired a new meaning in the current situation when some people—converted Spaniards and Moroccan immigrants—dreamt of the "revival of Al Andalus." The terrorist acts in Madrid on 11 March 2004, on the other hand, when almost two hundred persons died and a couple of thousand were injured, strongly contributed to the polarization. The perpetrators declared that they would not stop short at anything to get Spanish soldiers out of Iraq. They were soon revealed to be associated with Al Qaida and smaller Islamist networks.

The secularist trend dominates the younger generation. Young people are generally indifferent to any form of religion, especially to Catholicism, which they see as an old-fashioned institution with too strong an influence on society. In his book, Fernando Savater, a well-known Spanish philosopher and an assiduous defender of secular values, reflects on the prevailing conservative attitude toward Islamists that he finds among people in Spain, especially among members of PP, and in the rest of Europe. The conservatives defend the Enlightenment values vis-à-vis the Islamic value system not so much for these values' universal import, but rather seeing them as "ours" and not "theirs" (Savater 2007: 137). In this connection a certain sociopolitical turnabout has taken place, a phenomenon that Savater finds well explained in Ian Buruma's book *Murder in Amsterdam* about the murder of the Dutchman Theo Van Gogh in 2004. I cite Buruma on The Netherlands, since the same development of attitudes towards Muslims is recognizable in present-day Spain:

> The Left was on the side of universalism, scientific socialism, and the like, while the Right believed in culture, in the sense of "our culture," "our traditions." During the multicultural age of the 1970s and 1980s, this debate began to shift. It was now the Left that stood for culture and tradition, especially "their" cultures and traditions, that is, those of the immigrants, while the Right argued for the universal values of the Enlightenment. The problem in this debate was the fuzzy border between what was in fact universal and what was merely "ours." (Buruma 2006: 30)

Savater emphasizes the relevance of Buruma's observations also in Spain and adds:

> Having said this, in the panorama of Spanish politics, we have had the same uneasy and pathetic change of direction in the ideals of the left with their recent enthusiasm for the nationalist and ethnic separatist movements in the Basque Countries and in Catalonia. (Savater 2007: 137) (The author's translation.)

Here Savater touches upon a theme connected with the Muslims' situation in Spain and with the case of the imam of Fuengirola: the current PSOE
government shows respect for those who represent "different cultures" in Spain
and thereby for multiculturalism, legal pluralism, and religious freedom. But
what about universal values such as gender equality, and what about abiding by
various human rights conventions? Which of these should be given priority?

Muslim Women in Spain

Around one million Muslims live in Spain, including first- and second-gen-
eration immigrants from Morocco, Algeria, Islamic countries in sub-Saharan
Africa, Asia, and the Spanish converts to Islam. The unknown size of the illegal
Muslim group in Spain makes the total number uncertain. Among the immigrants with Islam as their religion, the Moroccans are by far the biggest group in
number, constituting more or less 75 percent of the total number of Muslims in
Spain. Generally more men than women from Islamic countries have migrated
to Spain. Recently one can see that this trend is changing, owing to labor market
conditions. The number of Moroccan female immigrants has increased from 32
percent in 1995 to 45 percent in 2002 of all Moroccans in Spain, mostly owing to the fact that Moroccan women easily get jobs as domestic workers while
many Moroccan men do not find employment (López Garcia 2004: 46).

Among the women who have arrived from Islamic countries to Spain, the
majority do not have Spanish nationality, as their arrival has been fairly recent
and the immigration laws are setting increasingly harsh prerequisites for naturalization. They do not participate in any activities normally associated with
civil society. Instead, the development of an organized Islamic movement led
by women is a fact among the group of Spanish women converted to Islam.
They are devout Muslims, stressing their Muslim identity and claiming that the
true essence of the Koran is very favorable to women. By rereading the scrip-
tures in favor of a modernizing interpretation of the role of women, they offer
a tolerant and plural model of Al Andalus. They are devoted to countering the
bad image of Islam in Spanish society, promoting gender equality in the face of
the imams of some mosques in Spain who, like the imam of Fuengirola, defend
men's right to beat their wives.

"Women in Islam"—A Controversial Book

At the beginning of 2000, Mohamed Kamal Mustafa published his book in
Spanish called *La mujer en el Islam* (Women in Islam). The book had an edition
of 1,668 copies. He was, as already mentioned, an imam (religious leader of the
mosque) in Fuengirola, a seaside resort on the Spanish Costa del Sol. More-

over, he was the director of an Islamic center called the Suhail Islamic Culture Center (Centro Cultural Islámico Suhail) and since 1997 has been advisor to the Spanish Federation of Islamic Unities (Federación Española de Entidades Religiosas Islámicas), where he occupied the role of religious expert. By nationality an Egyptian, with a poor knowledge of Spanish, his ability to communicate orally and in writing with Spanish people was considerably reduced, and he had little contact with non-Muslims. He did not really participate in Spanish society, nor was he interested in or informed about its value system or ideology, as can be understood from his comments to the reactions to his book (see below).

Kamal Mustafa had studied at the Al Azhar University in Cairo, from where he had got his degree, which was equivalent to a PhD in Islamic Studies. The Fuengirola mosque was financed by the Saudis, Saudi Arabia being known for practicing a conservative form of Islam.[5] Kamal represented an orientation of Islam that from a Western perspective was more "fundamentalist" in the sense of being closer to a literal interpretation of the Koran than that of many other Muslims in the West, including those converted Spanish Muslims who had reacted with disgust when reading the book. It was especially the chapter called "Uncertain Questions" (Cuestiones dudosas) that aroused a storm of indignation and anger against the imam. The reason was the author's answer to a question posed by himself in the book about the husband's right to beat his wife. He referred to the much-discussed part of the verse 4:34 in the Koran, which says: "And those you fear may be rebellious admonish; banish them to their couches, and beat them. If they then obey you, look not for any way against them; God is All-high, All-great." (Marín 2003: 5, quoting Arberry 1996).

In the imam's answer, he pointed out that he did think battering of a disobedient wife as a punishment was something one should avoid as much as possible. He explained the three steps to be taken, as indicated in the verse, which meant first asking the husband to try to solve the problem by talking to the wife; then, in case she still behaved badly, by banishing her from his bed as a corrective measure; and finally, as a last resort, by giving her a little smack on her hands and feet with a wooden stick the size of a pen, which used to be employed as a tooth "brush" or tooth cleaner in former times and which is still in use in many places. It is the husband's privilege to "correct" his wife; no woman has the right to "correct" a man who does not obey her. The mere thought of a man obeying a woman is ridiculous and a sign of weakness according to the gender ideology into which the imam was socialized. However, it is the man's duty to see to it that no physical damage is caused to the woman's body or that any signs are left on the woman's body of the wife having been beaten. Kamal Mustafa wrote the following:

> In order to avoid greater harm one should never beat out of blind or extreme rage. One should not hit the sensitive parts of the body. The blows should be applied to specific parts of the body such as the feet and hands, using a rod that is

not too thick, that is to say, it should be thin and light in order to not leave scars or bruises on the body. The blows should not be hard or heavy, because the end sought is to cause psychological suffering rather than to humiliate or physically ill-treat. (Kamal Mustafa 2000: 87, translated by A. Prado)

Ironically enough, with the cited paragraph the imam probably wanted to put a limit to the uncontrolled and blind wife battering of which he must have known and seen examples. He must have been aware of wife beating being a sensitive issue in a country like Spain, where its government lately had made a great affair of the issue, trying by legal reforms to ameliorate the conditions for women—mostly wives—living with or hiding from violent husbands or ex-husbands. Kamal Mustafa might have written the passage with the intention of giving the harsh formulation of verse 4:34 (quoted above) a more liberal interpretation. When reading the controversial chapter in the imam's book, one is struck by the regard the imam actually shows for the well-being of the women in question, considering the strictly fundamentalist and male-centered attitudes of many Muslims with a background such as his. He explicitly says that the husband's punishment of a "rebellious" woman or of a woman who "refuses to fulfil her conjugal duty" (Kamal Mustafa 2000: 85) should not cause more than slight physical pain but rather cause her psychological and moral suffering, as women are expected to feel shame when misbehaving. Kamal Mustafa writes, "And even if the physical punishment is mentioned in one of the verses of the Koran this does not mean that Islam permits it; it exists, rather, on a scale of measures which men can take against their wives in a positive sense, limiting themselves to a symbolic dimension through a series of restrictions" (2000: 86).

In Egypt, where the verses of the Koran are deeply respected and the gender ideology is related to and marked by a patriarchal and hierarchical interpretation of the Koran, Kamal Mustafa's explanations about wife beating would have had a different and more subtle resonance. However, in Spain and other Western countries the chapter evoked strong reactions among both Muslims and non-Muslims.

The national and international secular women's organizations were the first ones to respond. Three Spanish women's organizations sued the imam at the court in Barcelona in July 2000.[6] They found Kamal Mustafa's advice about wife beating both ridiculous and upsetting, because it reflected a denigrating view of women as inferior to men, and they considered it certainly not to be in accordance with the Spanish constitution or the international human rights conventions. The imam's arguments about permitting just a little battering or "only" psychological punishment for women were absurd, they said, in a society where gender equality and respect for women were civil society's and the government's goal, while his interpretations represented just the opposite.

The prosecution charged the imam with an offence against Article 510 of the Criminal Code (*Código Penal*), i.e., for the offence of incitement to violence on the basis of gender. The imam was sentenced to one year and three months in prison and a fine of EUR 2,160. Copies of his book were to be retracted and the technical tools (files with the manuscript on the imam's and others' hard disks, on his and others' diskettes and USB flash drives) had to be destroyed. According to Spanish legal practice, as mentioned above, those sentenced to less than two years and who have no criminal background are generally spared any deprivation of liberty. In his case the imam had to stay in jail for three weeks before he was released on his defense council's plea, which made reference to current legal practice in similar cases. The reason Kamal Mustafa, in spite of his irreproachable former life, was put into jail stemmed from the judge's opinion that Kamal Mustafa constituted a "social danger" to society and should therefore be kept in prison during the period of time stipulated by the verdict. But, as was pointed out later, the damage had already been done by selling the book; the imam himself constituted no danger.

The media presented the imam's instructions as an example of "the discriminatory nature of Islam" (Prado 2005: 2), and described Muslim men as sexist, oppressive, and violent (see Roded 2004: 64). Some Muslim female organizations in Spain issued strongly negative reactions to the text, seeing it as confirming the worst prejudices against Islam and encouraging hostility toward their religion. They asked Kamal Mustafa in a letter to remove the paragraph from the book, in order to avoid Islam being interpreted as if it were recommending physical and psychological ill treatment of women. Such a negative image of Islam was hard to swallow for Spanish Muslim converts, male as well as female, already exposed to non-Muslims' critical attitude toward their choice of religious faith and practice. Also the Spanish Federation of Islamic Religious Organizations (Federación Española de Entidades Religiosas Islámicas/ FEERI) asked the imam to change the text of the chapter. But Kamal Mustafa refused to change or delete anything, and declared that what was written in the Koran was not to be censored. He branded as heretics those Muslims and non-Muslims who disagreed with his interpretation. According to Prado, the imam wrote a correction and an explanation, saying that the Koran had once been revealed to "uncultured Bedouins" and that he had just tried to soften the text. However, the imam of the Marbella mosque, also financed by Saudis, was of another opinion. He considered the book "a provocation, out of place in an advanced, democratic society" (Prado 2005: 4; http://www.feminismeislamic .org/eng/index.htm).

The Spanish Muslims challenged Kamal's conviction that even if the practice of wife battering could be modified the way he had proposed in his book, the Koran still recommended husbands to "correct" wives by beating those who were refractory. The converts interpreted what the imam of Fuengirola had written as if the Koran legitimized a certain kind of patriarchal violence toward women. This was unacceptable for the Spanish Muslims, who said Islam was peace and love towards one another and toward God. They did not, as Kamal did, consider that the imam was in his full right in interpreting the Koran according to his religious knowledge and in demanding acceptance for it. The fact that he was educated at Al Azhar in Cairo, knew Arabic perfectly well, and was born a Muslim did not qualify him to any greater authority in religious interpretations than the Spanish converts possessed. Kamal, on the contrary, saw himself as the one of two imams in Spain with the formal right and competence to interpret the Koran. This had long been a sore point in inter-Muslim relations in Spain, and the Spanish converts refused to accept arguments of the sort.

During the trial, due to the polysemous nature of the Koranic text in Arabic, the manifold interpretations of the noun *idribûhanna* and the verb *daraba* (Arabic: beat, strike) became a key issue for the judges, as well as for the witnesses and for Kamal Mustafa. According to numerous authors, including Kamal Mustafa, the verb *daraba* in the context of the sentence cited above ("And those you fear may be rebellious admonish; banish them to their couches, and beat them") actually means "beat," and the intention of the imam had consequently only been to indicate some limitations when resorting to physical punishment. However, as many as eleven Spanish Muslims bore witness contrary to the imam's explanations and interpretations of the Koranic verse, trying to prove that Islam was not such a violent and misogynist religion as the imam was indicating in his text. They meant that *daraba* should be interpreted metaphorically as something in the way of "to set an example" and drew the judge's attention to the Prophet Muhammad's statements (according to the traditions) about wife battering: "Never beat God's handmaiden!" "He who beats his wife is the worst of all men," and "The best among you men is he who treats best his wife" (Marín 2003). They also pointed out that in the Koran there appear at least ten different meanings out of about thirty of the Arabic verb *daraba*, which means that Kamal Mustafa's interpretation and use of the word do not reflect the true character of Islam. (Prado 2005: 3; http://www.feminismeislamic .org/eng/index.htm).

The Verdict

The judge, Juan Pedro Yllanes Suárez, ruled that the book *Women in Islam* was not an objective statement of the principles of Islam as had been asserted by the author; rather, it should be taken as his personal opinion. The judge said he was dealing with the personal reflections of the imam, and then focused on the offensive character of these reflections or opinions, arguing that they attacked head-on the right to physical and moral well-being protected by Article 15 of the constitution. This article prohibits inhuman and degrading treatment, mirrored in Article 3 of the European Convention of Human Rights and in Article 7 of the International Agreement of Civil and Political Rights, Yllanes wrote in his verdict. The articles state that not only the motivation to humiliate and maltreat physically is criminal but that it is also forbidden to make the victim suffer psychologically, showing deep contempt for the victim's dignity and "creating in one's victims sensations of fear, anguish and inferiority enough to humiliate them, breaking down their moral and mental resistance" (Yllanes Suarez 2003: 7).

The Spanish judge used the various translations from the Koran available in order to assess whether *daraba* might have other meanings than "beat" or "strike." According to Prado, many Muslims were upset that the Koran could be treated by the judge just like any other book, which was read, compared, and evaluated in the hands of a nonbeliever, but it obviously helped the judge to formulate his verdict against Kamal Mustafa. He recognized the existence of a variety of interpretations of the Koran and drew the conclusion that the imam's interpretation was to be considered to be an expression of his private opinion. "And as such, nobody may use the Book of God as a basis for justifying opinions contrary to the laws in force." Furthermore the judge made reference to the conclusions drawn at the Third Conference of Muslim Women held in Córdoba in 2002 about domestic violence, where it was emphasized that physical or moral ill treatment is absolutely prohibited in Islam (Prado 2005: 8).

The verdict on Mohamed Kamal Mustafa passed by the judge accuses the author of the book of the crime of provocation to commit sexist violence. The defense's appeal invoked existing "religious freedom" in Spain. The judge had contended that, in the confrontation between the right to religious freedom in its external dimension and the right to moral well-being for the women whom the imam's discourse concerned, the women's well-being claimed priority, even if this incurred limitations to religious freedom. He had taken his stand based on Article 224.4 of the Penal Law formulated in 1995 after the genocide in former Yugoslavia, and after several manifestations of racism. This law had only once earlier been applied in a case of anti-Semitism.[7]

"Defending ill-treatment is an offence in Spain and should be judged as such. No argument, as religious as it may claim to be, can justify it," Prado adds in a commentary to the verdict (Prado 2005: 7; http://www.feminismeislamic .org/eng/index.htm). He also points out the negative consequences of the affair of the imam in Fuengirola for the reputation of Muslims in Spain and mentions some examples of the journalists' devastating critique of Islam. Below I quote one conservative daily newspaper's comment on the case of Kamal Mustafa and the strong reactions not only toward the religion itself but also toward the Spanish government, who at the time (2004) had proposed Islamic education for Muslim pupils at school as a step toward religious pluralism and a change in the Catholic hold on education:

> In view of these texts that collide with our constitution and in which discrimination on the basis of gender and the right to domestic violence against women is established, one must ask oneself why the socialist government wishes to subsidize the teaching of the Koranic religion in Spanish state schools. (*La Razón*, 12 September 2004)

Another conservative Madrid newspaper with a large daily circulation expresses the matter as follows:

> The Koran is a civil code and contemplates women as one step below men. Little reproductive animals which can be flogged for disobeying a man. The teaching of Islam cannot be encouraged by public powers as it is unconstitutional. (*El Mundo*, 13 November 2004)

The offending paragraph in Kamal Mustafa's book soon became known all over the world. According to Manuela Marín, a Spanish researcher and Arabist, the offending paragraphs in Kamal Mustafa's are hardly original. The main difference between the conservative and what she calls "progressive" exegesis of the Koran is that the latter insists on taking into account its historicity (see Marín 2003: 7). Referring to a number of statements about whether to beat and how to beat wives in Islamic literature, Marín observes that, while the discussion of this issue has a relatively short history in Western societies, it has been on the agenda in Muslim societies for a long time. In Spain, the whole question of beating one's wife, disobedient or not, has become a burning political issue, creating a new awareness and being considered a social and political problem of growing relevance.

Based on Medieval Islamic literature, Marín demonstrates that, historically, the notion of a "rebellious wife" could be applied to a wide range of attitudes. It depended, among other things, on social standing, on whether the woman was a slave or free, on the local custom, and on the subjective criteria legal experts chose to apply. In general, the experts agree that the idea that a husband is superior to his wife and that he can judge and punish her disobedience has deep roots in Islamic law. If a woman openly defied her husband's authority, both the Koran commentators and law experts agreed that the Koran advocates a moderate punishment (Marín 2003: 38). Thus in the Kamal Mustafa case, a literal interpretation of the Koranic verse 4:34 overlooks the historical complexity of the subject (Marín 2003: 39).

The verdict was greeted with satisfaction and relief by all those who found the imam's book offensive. Those who attended "his" mosque in Fuengirola, mostly male immigrants from Egypt and Syria, many of a Wahabist or Salafist orientation, reacted differently, however. Manifestations of sympathy with him and his family were organized both inside Spain and outside, mainly in Egypt.

Conditionally Released

The supporters of Kamal Mustafa amassed the money for his fines and paid them. They collected eight thousand signatures in favor of his release. Some weeks later his lawyer succeeded in getting the imam liberated after he had spent three weeks in jail. The High Court of Barcelona suspended the execution of the verdict, freeing him immediately on condition that he take a course on the Universal Declaration of Human Rights and parts of the Spanish constitution within six months. The high court motivated its standpoint in a decree stating that the book had already been distributed, which was an irreparable fact, and that the imam did not himself constitute a social danger, even if the judge had stated such in his verdict (see above).

As the imam left the prison, feeling bitter and unjustly treated, Mohamed Kamal Mustafa was received with hugs and kisses from his family members and hailed as a hero by his supporters. To the journalists assembled at the entrance to the mosque in Fuengirola, he said that the twenty-one days in jail had been like twenty-one years and that he had spent his time there reading the Bible, the Koran, and the Spanish Human Rights Conventions. The imam said that if the authorities thought that what he had done—to write a book about how to beat a woman without leaving signs—was supposed to be an error, he would have to change it "because every human being has to learn from his errors." To his supporters he stated that he had never changed his opinion about the rightness of his action: in his book, he repeated, he had just "softened" God's words as they were written in the Koran.

Spain's government, through the general secretary for Equality Policies, Soledad Murillo, expressed its "strongest protest" when confronted with the judicial decision to release the imam from jail. "You cannot prescribe a course in human rights as a substitute for imprisonment," she said. "It is true that you could do so as a supplementary measure, but in cases of domestic violence the penalties should be applied without alleviation" (El País 21 December 2004). In her opinion, decisions of this nature unfortunately further confirmed a growing tendency to tolerate gender-related violence at legal institutions. This opinion, issued by the Spanish government, coincided with that of the president of the Themis Association of Women Jurists, Ángela Alemany, who thought that the punishment of the imam of Fuengirola could have been important in setting an example.

The harshest reaction came from the deputy prime minister, María Teresa Fernández de la Vega. She qualified the act of setting the imam of Fuengirola free as "absolutely stupid" and meant that such a decision "did not contribute toward ending the macabre evil of the maltreatment of women" (El País 21 December 2004). The Spanish minister of justice at that time, Juan Fernández López Aguilar, reacted strongly to the deputy prime minister's statement. He said that the reasons for the measure were strictly legal and that the government was not supposed to make public statements about the change in verdict. This statement made Fernández de la Vega later declare in a TV program (Antena 3) that she respected the High Court's decision because Spain is a democratic country. However, she persisted in considering that the release of Kamal Mustafa was contrary to the line chosen by the Spanish government in showing zero tolerance in all cases where the end result might be construed as support of gender violence.

The imam of Fuengirola left jail on the 21 December 2004, one day before the Spanish Law Relating to Gender-discriminatory Violence *(Ley Orgánica de medidas de protección integral contra la violencia de género)* was unanimously accepted by the parliament and was ratified on 28 December 2004.[8] The deputy prime minister reassured the press and other media that once that law was passed and put into function, a similar turn of events as the one experienced in the case of Kamal Mustafa would become impossible. The law permits a certain amount of positive discrimination in the sense that the legal application is stricter for men than for women: male perpetrators get a more severe penalty than women for an offence of gender violence.

When Kamal Mustafa had finished his studies of the Spanish constitution in 2006 to which he had been sentenced on his release, he had reached very good results, according to his instructor. He stated his innocence with the following words in an interview with a journalist: "Among other things, I have learned that I never did anything against the constitution, even if I did not know all the articles" *(Málaga* 16 July 2006). This brings us back to the question raised earlier in this discourse: what are the limits of religious freedom, of religious and legal pluralism, and what do the values expressed in the human rights conventions and the Western European constitutions stand for in real life and in confrontation with other guiding principles?

We have witnessed the fact that the imam of Fuengirola did not change his mind during the trial and its aftermath. He still thinks he was in his full rights in approaching the holy text in the way he did—by advocating acceptance of the gender-related violence implied by this interpretation. The great majority of Spanish people, on the contrary, found the content of the book unacceptable for what they thought characteristic of a civilized society. In the following and last paragraph, this case will be summed up and analyzed in its different aspects in an endeavor to better understand the various opinions and commitments that came to light in connection with the book and its author.

Summing Up the Case of the Imam of Fuengirola

The Italian political scientist Renato Moro points out in one of his articles that differences which manifest themselves between political and religious fields of activity do not necessarily imply that they are independent of each other, or that some form of interaction does not occur between the two. On the contrary, religion and politics continue being united in a complex relation, competing with one another and being mutually influenced by one another. Concerning the diverse metaphoric explanations about the social world, about religions and secular modern ideologies, it is true that they sometimes contradict each other with respect to the autonomy and the relative importance of reason and faith in the conformation of the destiny of our human destiny. Traditional religions insist on the belief that the supernatural possesses a supreme authority over human affairs, while modern political ideologies take for granted human liberty in a physical and social world (Moro 2005: 71–86).

Still, as Moro shows, the ambition of the secular state is to redress the political systems in an era of "mass politics" of an almost sacred character and a transcendent aim, as well as to create a feeling of community between citizens who are separated by class, geographical origin, religion and ethnicity. "Borrowing" or copying symbols, myths, rituals and vocabularies from traditional religions for secular aims, placing the state or the nation on "the altar of communal adoration" has created a kind of "sacralization of politics", (ibid 2005: 71–86). Democracy, human rights and gender equality represent sacred values, especially since the present socialist government defines itself as in opposition to Franscisco Franco's dictatorship and his close collaboration with the Catholic Church. The secular religions give a symbolic legitimization to the public and social order, to civil society and to public life (Boyd 2007:3). But even so, the socialist government in Spain collaborates to a certain degree with the still powerful Church (see above).

The political adversaries of the government in contemporary Spain, the conservatives, are working for the preservation of traditional Catholic values. Both PP and the Catholic bishops fortify their political positions by exploiting each other's resources. The "politicization of religion" of the Catholic Church, which took partly new forms and meanings during the Franco era, is fully visible in the Spain of 2007. The Church is engaged in education policy, medical ethics, family politics and in supporting PP with a view to winning the next general elections in Spain (2012). The politicization of Islamic countries worldwide and the missionary activities in the name of Islam also constitute current examples of the politicization of religion in Spain. The "revival of Al Andalus" may sound a romantic idea or a wishful dream on the part of idealistic Spanish converts to the Islamic religion, but the same plans on a larger scale and by more violent methods have been proposed by Ceuta and Melilla Muslims and Moroccans living in the Spanish enclaves on the Moroccan side of the Straits of Gibraltar.

The case of the imam of Fuengirola has offered us a lesson in religious pluralism, multiculturalism, the sacralization of politics, and the politicization of religion in its own very concrete yet bewildering way. Efforts to understand it can benefit from Gerd Baumann's proposal to analytically divide complex realities of modern multicultural societies into three areas: the relationships between nation-state cultures and "their" minorities, the relationship between and among minorities, and the processes that reach across nation-state borders (Baumann 1999: 146).

Political life in Spain is to a certain extent colored by a PSOE culture benevolently open for religious pluralism but unaware of the deeper content of some religions, which might be termed oppressive by Western standards. The Spanish government takes for granted the religious freedom characteristic of a democratic society, but in practice this freedom collides with other values, such as gender equality and respect for all human beings. The Muslim minority considers God, the Koranic verses, and the Islamic laws interpreted in accordance with the Koran to have a supreme authority over secular ideologies, legal systems, and human rights conventions. The gap between opinions based on religious belief is considerable and will not automatically disappear by studying the Spanish constitution, as we saw in the case of Kamal Mustafa.

Prado, the Spanish convert, saw the trial of Kamal Mustafa as "a landmark in the process of the return of Islam to Al Andalus." He considered it as dealing with the complete acceptance of religious freedom within a democratic society, and as such it affects the way that Muslims live and understand Islam (Prado 2005: 11, http://www.feminismeislamic.org/eng/index.htm). So for Spanish Muslims this case underlines the open nature of revelation as opposed to reified and obsolete interpretation. The trial of the imam of Fuengirola gave the Spanish Muslims an occasion to reflect over which parts of orthodoxy could and could not be tolerated. The eleven witnesses against the interpretation of the imam of verse 4:34 were all Spanish Muslims. According to some internet reports, a few Spanish converts were exposed to threats and harassment by Muslims from other countries who live in Spain, representing more fundamentalist orientations of Islam. The imam himself called his Spanish fellow Muslims "heretics." The relationship between the two minorities constituted by Spanish converts and Arab Muslims and their supporters has become more strained than before.

Internationally the imam case created headlines in the press: most people knew Fuengirola as a typical summer tourist resort in the south of Spain, far from any connection with Muslims and mosques. With very few exceptions journalists did not know that the debate had gone on for centuries in Muslim countries about the Koranic verse 4:34 and its interpretation (see Marín 2003: 38). In that debate, however, the verse in itself was never questioned nor the fact that women were perceived of as inferior. Their inferiority was not in the first place before God, but definitely in relation to men and as members of civil society. Women were thought of as a source of chaos (Arabic: *fitna;* "disorder";

see Mernissi 1975) unless controlled by men, and some of these ideas about women still prevail in Muslim societies.

This gap between Western secular and Islamic discourses has once again been illustrated by the very different reactions in public opinion to the case of the imam of Fuengirola: while in Arab Muslim countries and among many Muslims in Spain, Kamal Mustafa was glorified as a hero, in the Western press the case was often presented as a horrifying example of the religion of the "Other."

The imam of Fuengirola will probably never understand why he was sentenced for incitement to violence on the basis of gender. The deputy prime minister of the Spanish government may not have accepted the imam being freed from imprisonment, but she will be satisfied reflecting over the fact that next time something similar happens she has the Law Relating to Gender-discriminatory Violence to put her trust in. There is also the new Law on Gender Equality, passed in March 2007, which will support even more effectively women's legal rights in society. The converts were pleased that Kamal Mustafa's interpretation of Islam, which was inspired by Wahabism or Salafism, had been condemned in the Spanish court. These Spanish Muslims felt strengthened in their view of their own community as molded by European democratic values and of themselves as Western Muslims (cf. Rosen 2002: 155). Muslim feminists both in Spain and internationally who had a negative opinion of some male Muslim scholars, considering them misogynists, reacted like the Spanish male converts. The women did not question the divine origin of the Koran and the wise and peace-loving mind of the Prophet Muhammad, known to them for his respectful and caring attitude toward women. They claimed gender equality within the framework of Islamic religion as taught by the Prophet (Mir-Hussaini 2006). That is why they unanimously condemned the passage in Kamal Mustafa's book that approved of male punishment of women within marriage. On the other hand, Egyptian, Syrian, and other Muslims in Spain gravitating towards Saudi Arabia, and many Moroccan Muslim migrants, showed solidarity with Kamal Mustafa and probably felt more anchored than before in their mosques and among people of a like mind.

The imam case is still remembered in Spain and often referred to in discussions about religious and legal pluralism. It can be said to serve as an illustration of the divide between religious and secular ideologies in contemporary society concerning the treatment of human beings in accordance with human rights and social justice conventions. According to the Spanish constitution, such rights embrace not only gender relations but also other relations with other groups in society such as the homosexuals. The latter category is not involved in the Kamal Mustafa case, but it is hard not to mention it, as issues related to women and homosexuals are often discussed in Spain by Muslims and Catholics in the same prejudiced way. This is particularly the case in connection with gender equality and legal rights in relation to family law (marriage and divorce, mainly). The new law concerning compulsory education in civics (*Ciudadanía*) in Spanish schools, starting in autumn 2007, has also become a hot issue among religious people, even if a similar school subject already exists in fifteen countries in Europe. Civics includes in Spain "a deepening of the knowledge of human values and human rights, their implication for the organization of social life, and education in personal and collective attitudes and behavior" (*El País* 24 June 2007: 49). (The author's translation.)

At first sight it is hard to understand why the Catholic Church is totally against teaching civics at school. Apparently lessons about the constitution, human rights, and gender equality would not be provocative per se either for Catholics or Muslims, if supplemented with compulsory religious education. What irritates the Catholic bishops and makes Muslim parents with children at school worried are the references to questions concerning homosexuality and the substitution of secular values at school for religious ones. "Religion" has become a voluntary subject at school, and Muslim pupils who do not want to attend religious—read: Catholic—education classes will be able to take classes in Islam instead.[9] Those children whose parents do not want any religious education at school will be excused from it.

So, while teaching civics at school has been compulsory since autumn 2007, Catholic and Muslim education will be voluntary. The church would rather have it the other way around, insisting on placing God and the Catholic doctrine above the state and the secular ideology—just like the imam of Fuengirola with the Islamic doctrine. That is why the church is totally against the government practicing secularism—"excluding religion and its symbols in public life by situating it in the private sphere," as the president of the Episcopal Conference (*La Conferencia Episcopal Española*/CEE), Ricardo Blásquez, expressed it (*El País* 24 April 2007: 37). He reclaimed a concept of secularism, quoting the words of Pope Benedictus XVI, which "recognizes for God and his moral law, for Christ and his Church, the place which corresponds to them in human, individual and social life," accusing the government of making secularism an emblem of postmodernity and modern democracy. At the core of this dissociation from secularism is a fear of a total separation between state and church, considerably reducing the church's scope of power and influence in society (*El País* 24 July 2007: 37).[10] Muslim religious leaders, especially the Syrians and the Egyptians, are afraid of a somewhat similar development in Spain, although formulated in the guise of a fear of influences from the United States and an endeavor to avoid such influences at all costs.

To conclude, we have seen that religion and secularism are closely linked to both right-wing and left-wing politics in Spain. The historical past of the conservatives, the liberals, the socialists, the communists, the anarchists, and other political formations and constellations have all taken up positions with regard to religion—for and against. The Spanish Civil War was as much about religious as political and economic values and beliefs. Before that, Christianity and Islam were conflicting ideologies during eight hundred years on the Spanish peninsula. Reminiscences of religious and political culture are molded into contemporary interpretations of the past, present, and future. The idea of a revival of Al Andalus is such an example. The different interpretations of the Koran, verse 4:34, is another. For these reasons, the historical roots should not be overlooked when analyzing the reactions to a book such as the one written by the imam of Fuengirola on women in Islam, even if it came out as recently as the year 2000 and can be conceived, all things considered, as a product of multiethnic and multireligious contemporary Spain.

For Galina

For some twenty years, Galina and I were close friends. When she died, my everyday life turned poor and gloomy. Our annual celebrations of Christmas Day morning and of the arrival of spring on a particular May morning, ceased forever. And no more parties in Galina's home with that charming tang of "festivitas" that only Galina could provide by her elegant presence, and her somewhat distanced and yet so warm smile.

Twice Galina visited me while I did social anthropological fieldwork in Madrid. Both times she returned from Spain with a wish to go back and see more of that country, above all of Andalusia. She enjoyed thoroughly flamenco dancing and music, and she could make herself understood perfectly well with people she met without great knowledge of the Spanish language. Spain could have made her so happy, had there only been more opportunities. She knew this would not be so, and this saddened her.

One day during Galina's last stay in Madrid (in May 2007), she accompanied me to a Moroccan family living in the outskirts of the city. I was out in the kitchen talking while the wife made food. Galina had disappeared into the only bedroom. I saw her sitting on the matrimonial bed, the television on at top volume, teaching the son of the house, age twelve, the Russian language. The boy, called Ahmed, was a little corpulent and had dedicated more time at home with his books than out in the streets playing football, that's for sure. During the last year he said he had longed for someone to teach him Russian—and there she was, Galina in person as if sent from heaven. An hour later both teacher and pupil were tired and we all had nice Moroccan mint tea together. Whenever I visited the family on later occasions, Galina's visit was brought up. They will never forget Galina, that beautiful lady from Russia, who dedicated time and efforts to their son Ahmed, with such kindness and patience.

The last day of her stay in Madrid, I arranged a lunch party for most of my friends and informants. Around the table one could find Moroccan, Senegalese, Spanish, and Swedish people—and there was Galina. The conversation was lively, but not always pleasant, and burning issues such as racism and religious fundamentalisms came to the fore. One Moroccan Muslim man accused a Senegalese, also Muslim, sitting opposite him, for having married a Spanish woman, who was there as well, to give an example. Galina just listened to everybody without interrupting, and got parts of the conversation translated for her by a guest beside her. Afterward I understood from Galina's comments that not only had she been able to follow what was going on around the table but she also made a rich and insightful analysis of the participants and their interaction, guided by her interest in religion and politics at a micro as well as macro level.

Galina was a great fieldworker, able to analyze field data in an inspiring and gifted way. We shared a passion for the study of religion in the widest sense of the word, though approaching the topic from different angles. Galina enriched my life so much not only privately but also professionally.

NOTES

1. Following the conquest, al-Andalus was divided into five administrative areas roughly corresponding to Andalusia, Galicia and Lusitania, Castile and León, and Catalonia and Septimania. As a political domain or domains, it successively constituted a province of the Umayyad Caliphate, initiated by the Caliph Al-Walid I (711–750); the Emirate of Córdoba (c. 750–929); the Caliphate of Córdoba (929–1031); and the Caliphate of Córdoba's taifa (successor) kingdoms.
2. La Comisión Islámica de España, the Islamic Commission in Spain, a governmental institution acting as intermediary in the development of religious agreements.
3. Abdennur Prado and many other Spanish Muslims want to revitalize Al Andalus and its historical, social, and cultural relationship with the Arabic and Mediterranean world to make the common patrimony known and to contribute to the establishment of links of solidarity between the countries of the Mediterranean.
4. "In an article published in El País 2005, Juan G. Bedoya reported that of the National Budget for 2006, 144 million euros were directed toward the Church in subsidies." (Boyd 2007:1, source El País 21112005). (The author's translation.)
5. *Salafism* is a generic term, depicting a Sunni Islamic school of thought that takes the pious ancestors (*Salaf*) of the patristic period of early Islam as exemplary models. Salafis view the first three generations of Muslims, who are Muhammad's com-

panions, and the two succeeding generations after them as examples of how Islam should be practiced. Salafism seeks to revive a practice of Islam that more closely resembles the religion during the time of Muhammad. Salafism has also been described as a simplified version of Islam, in which adherents follow a few commands and practices. *Wahhabism* is a branch of Islam practiced by those who follow the teachings of Muhammad Ibn Abd-al-Wahhab. This theology is the dominant form found in Saudi Arabia and Qatar as well as some pockets of Somalia, Algeria, Palestine, and Mauritania. The term *Wahhabi* (Wahhābīya) is rarely used by the people it is used to describe. Some use Wahhabism and Salafism interchangeably, though this is speculative and refuted by Salafism. Others understand Wahhabism as ultraconservative Salafism. Wahabism is known to be among the most conservative forms of Islam. Some people have described the doctrine as inspiring violence.

6. The organizations were La Federación de Asociaciones de Mujeres Separadas y Divorciadas (Federation of the Associations for Separated and Divorced Women), El Consejo de la Comunidad de Madrid (Madrid Community Council) and La Asociación de Asistencia a Mujeres Agredidas Sexualmente (Association of Assistance to Sexually Harassed Women).

7. This article could only be applied in cases of "racism, anti-Semitism or other kinds of discrimination in relation to ideology, religion or ideas of the victim, ethnicity, race or nation to which the victim belongs, his/her sex, his/her sexual orientation or illness or physical or psychological handicap." (González-Aurioles 2005: 131) (The author's translation.)

8. The Spanish Integral Law of Gender Violence was ratified in December 2004 (Ley Orgánica 1/2004, 28.12, de medidas de protección integral contra la violencia de género). A number of courts with judges especially trained for the handling of cases of gender violence according to the new law have been established all over Spain. A woman exposed to gender violence (wife battering or other forms of physical or psychological violence by husband, ex-husband, boyfriend, or ex-boyfriend) shall denounce the crime as soon as possible at the nearest police station or a court of law, bringing a medical certificate of the harm she has suffered (within forty-eight hours). The judge assessing a gender violence case will have to treat the case immediately if there is considered to be a real danger to the woman's life; shelter will be offered at a Women's Emergency Center and police protection provided.

   On 15 March 2007 the Spanish Parliament passed a Law of Equality. The law stipulates among other things that fathers are entitled to fifteen days' paid leave to be with small children; that election lists require a minimum of 40% women candidates for posts occupied by both men and women, and that firms with more than 250 employees have to work out a gender equality scheme. Contracts with the Civil Service and the granting of subsidies will favor those firms which have achieved gender balance. Companies listed on the Stock Exchange will endeavor to appoint women to their board of directors. (*El País* 16 March 2007)

9. See http://www.consumer.es/web/es/educacion/es.

10. The Ministry of Education had already during 2006 started education in Islamic values (not practices) in several regions in Spain, for example in Andalusia, Aragón, the Basque Country, and the Canary Isles.

REFERENCES

Álvarez, E. Aranda. 2005. "Objeto y principios rectores de la ley integral." In *Estudios sobre la Ley Integral contra la Violencia de Género,* ed. E. Álvarez. Madrid: Editorial Dykinson.

Arberry, A. 1996. *The Koran Interpreted: A Translation.* New York: Touchstone.

Baumann, G. 1999. *The Multicultural Riddle: Rethinking National, Ethnic and Religious Identities.* London: Routledge.

Boyd, Caroline P., ed. 2007. *Religión y política en España contemporánea.* Madrid: Ministerio de la Presidencia; Centro de Estudios Políticos y Constitucionales.

Bulliet, R. 1979. *Conversion to Islam in the Medieval Period: An Essay in Quantitative History.* Cambridge, MA: Harvard University Press.

Buruma, I. 2006. *Murder in Amsterdam.* London: Penguin.

Carr, R. 1989. *Spain 1808–1975.* Oxford: Oxford University Press.

El Mundo. 13 November 2004.

El País. 21 December 2004.

El País. 11 January 2006.

El País. 24 June 2006.

El País. 24 April 2007.

El País. 24 June 2007.

Fierro, M. 2001. *Al-Andaluz: Saberes e intercambios interculturales.* Madrid: Icaria Editorial.

González-Aurioles, J. "Tutal Penal." In *Estudios sobre la Ley Integral contra la Violencia de Género,* ed. E. Aranda. Madrid: Editorial Dykinson.

Kamal Mustafa, M. 2000. *La mujer en el Islam.* Barcelona: self-published.

Kennedy, H. 2008. *The Great Arab Conquests: How the Spread of Islam Changed the World.* London: Weidenfeld & Nicolson.

La razón. 12 September 2004.

Lewis, B., ed. 1992. *The World of Islam: Faith, People, Culture.* London: Thames & Hudson.

López García, B. 2004. *Atlas de la migración marroquí en España.* In collaboration with Mohamed Berriane, Ediciones UAM and Observatorio Permanente de la Inmigración. Madrid: Ministerio de Trabajo y Asuntos Sociales.

Málaga. 16 July 2006.

Marín, M. 2003. "Disciplining Wives: A Historical Reading of Qur'an 4:34." *Studia Islamica* 97: 5–41.

Mernissi, F. 1975. *Beyond the Veil: Male-Female Dynamics in a Modern Muslim Society.* Cambridge, MA: Schenkman.

Mir-Hussaini, Z. 2006. "Muslim Women's Quest for Equality: Between Islamic Law and Feminism." *Critical Inquiry* 32: 629–43.

Moro, Renato. 2005. "Religion and Politics in the Time of Secularisation: The Sacralisation of Politics and the Politisation of Religion." *Totalitarian Movements and Political Religions,* Vol. 6, No.1, pp. 71–86.

Prado, A. 2005. *The Qur'an in the Spanish Courts: 'The Kamal Case' and freedom of Islam in Spain.* http://www.feminismeislamic.org/eng/index.htm.

————. 2006. *El Islam en Democracia.* Colección Shahada. Córdoba: Editorial Junta Islámica.

Previté-Orton, C. W. 1971. *The Shorter Cambridge Medieval History.* vol. 1. Cambridge: Cambridge University Press.

Roded, R. 2004. "Alternate Images of the Prophet Mohammad's Virility." In *Islamic Masculinities,* ed. O. Lahoucine. London: Zed Books.

Rosen, L. 2002. *The Culture of Islam: Changing Aspects of Contemporary Muslim Life.* Chicago: University of Chicago Press.

Savater, F. 2007. *La vida eterna.* Madrid: Ariel.

Saz, I. 2007. "Religión, política y religión católica en el fascismo español," in *Religión y política en España contemporánea,* ed. C. Boyd. Madrid: Centro de Estudios Constitucionales.

III

THE TIGHT EMBRACE OF RELIGION AND POLITICS

❧ 5 ❧

ACTORS OF HISTORY?

Religion, Politics, and "Reality"
within the Protestant Right in America

Simon Coleman

To a supposedly secular Europe, and even to skeptical anthropologists, the confluence of religion and politics in America remains a source of bemusement. Yet, it shows no sign of disappearing—rather the reverse. In this chapter, I explore the past and present of what has become the Christian, and more specifically the Protestant, Right in the United States.[1] The approach is inevitably broad brush, intended to highlight some general trends and resonances rather than the complex and manifold ideological differences among conservative Protestants. I hope thereby to capture some of the ways in which an over-hasty conflation of secularity with modernity cannot begin to deal with the ambiguities and accommodations involved in the expression of religious commitment within contemporary political, legal, and social arenas in the United States.[2]

I start by juxtaposing the near-present with the distant past, the religious with the political. The following is a quotation that became famous, even notorious in some circles, during the last-but-one presidential election in the United States. It is a description of the remarks of an aide to George Bush to a journalist called Ron Suskind:[3]

> The [Bush] aide said that guys like me were "in what we call the reality-based community," which he defined as people who "believe that solutions emerge from your judicious study of discernible reality. ... That's not the way the world really works anymore. ... We're an empire now, and when we act, we create our own reality. And while you're studying that reality ... we'll act again, creating other new realities, which you can study too, and that's how things will sort

---

Notes for this chapter begin on page 185.

out. We're history's actors ... and you, all of you, will be left to just study what
we do."

Suskind captures the religious character of these remarks by calling his piece
"Without a Doubt." In attempting to read the passage through an evangelical
lens, my eye is caught by a number of things: the repetition of the word "reality" but also the way journalists are seen as caught within a "community" that
is somehow regarded as *limited* by its insistence on being reality based; the intriguing adjective "discernible" when applied here to "reality"; and the distinction between those who merely *study* "discernible reality" and those who are
history's *actors*. But perhaps most striking is the word "empire." It reminds me
of a particular, iconic scene in American and evangelical history, that of John
Winthrop, future first governor of Massachusetts, writing his diary in 1630 on
board the ship that was taking him from "Old Europe" to what would become a
"New England." Winthrop's meditations famously laid out the vision of a "city
on a hill," a Puritan light to the world, extending as far as church and state
"configured in a godly commonwealth" and drawing on the Puritan assumption
that God's covenant to His People now applied to all faithful societies.

Ironically, Winthrop became the first governor of a state that would embody
just the kind of East Coast values that three centuries later the Bush aide would
presumably dismiss as being too "reality based," but the juxtaposition of the two
perspectives is suggestive. Both want be seen as "actors" on a cultural stage that
is visible—as is a city on a hill—to others; but they are also actors in the sense
of being agents legitimately engaged in conflict against a world often perceived
to be secular, weak, and corrupt. Both map America on to a metaphorical landscape where the nation's calling often seems akin—certainly in Puritan and
later evangelical rhetoric—to that of a New Israel.

I mention Winthrop because I shall be arguing that one way of responding to the question of why conservative Protestantism remains popular with
significant sections of the population is to explore recurrences as well as transformations in evangelical Christianity over time. However, I also want to place
that analysis in another frame that I think is implicit in the Bush aide's encounter with a journalist who is taken to represent a world that is not that
of the speaker. I shall be suggesting that we can explore the past but also the
present of what has become the "New" (now rather Middle-aged) Christian
Right by seeing it as wrestling with three creatively paradoxical stances to
the world beyond itself—to the "reality-based community" visible from that
metaphorical hill.

The first involves positions of retreat from the secular world countered by
those of advance and appropriation; I call this an "oscillation" (or "pendulum")
model of perceiving reality.[4] The second entails the simultaneous invocation of
naturalistic and supernaturalistic, secular and religious, approaches to reality;

this I call this a "parallel" model of perception. And the third invokes crucial connections and tensions between self-mastery and mastery of others; drawing on the work of Maurice Bloch (1992), I call this a "rebounding" model.

Each of these models points crucially to the way conservative Protestant-ism in America, of whatever denominational hue, almost invariably implicates others in its conception of itself, with consequences for American action on global, as well as national, stages. But, as noted, they also take us back to a much broader question about the role of Christianity in what we call the mod-ern world. Here, it is worth presenting a very brief comparison with work from a very different cultural context. In her book *Translating the Devil* (1999), Birgit Meyer argues that conversion to Pentecostal Christianity for the people she looks at in Ghana is supposed to involve its own way of viewing the potentially threatening Other: conversion is meant to imply a decisive turn from heathen-dom, a once-and-for all rejection of an old, traditional religion in favor of a new, modern one like Pentecostalism. Yet, it is notable that the Christians she talks to seem always to be caught in a kind of religious limbo, constantly reiter-ating that supposedly decisive moment of separation from satanic powers. How, says Meyer, are we to interpret this? "Pentecostalism, rather than representing a safe haven of modern religion in which people permanently remain, enables people to move back and forth between the way of life they (wish to) have left behind and the one to which they aspire. ... By offering discourse and ritual practices pertaining to demons, believers are enabled to thematise continu-ously the 'old'" (Meyer 1999: 212).

Note that Meyer points to a sense of repeatedly defining the self in relation to a threatening but also alluring Other, a striving to move the self from a past in a way that also *reconstitutes* that past: you have to conjure up an image of the Devil in order to overcome it. Embracing a so-called modern religion is not about leaving the old enchantments, the old temptations, behind; it is about redefining them.

Now Meyer's argument resonates with studies of evangelicalism elsewhere: Diane Austin-Broos has written (1981) of Jamaican Pentecostalists' desire to be "Born Again ... And Again and Again," replaying that vital shift from the unregenerate old person to the new. Joel Carpenter's (1997) book adopts a sim-ilar image in referring not to individual renewal but to the broader reawakening of twentieth-century American fundamentalism involving the plea: "Revive us again." The specific cultural significance will vary in each case, but what is being captured here is a ritual mechanism invoking the repetition of something originally seen as a one-off transition—from unbeliever to believer, from quies-cence to outreach. Crucially, this observation also captures something of what I am describing in these three, creatively paradoxical stances to the world: a constant, restless sense of movement in relation to a world that is sometimes seen as a threat, sometimes an opportunity.

An "Oscillation" Model of Evangelicalism

Historically, American evangelicalism has constituted a broad church.[5] Puritan conceptions of the sacred national calling have coexisted and sometimes competed with Pietist hopes for individual salvation. So one strand of the faith has encouraged a world-rejecting, personalistic strand of religious practice. Another, exemplified by the great religious awakenings of the eighteenth and nineteenth centuries, has encouraged an optimism that has also been translated into a kind of religious nationalism. Or again, some have argued that ultimate salvation and rapture are only attainable after tribulation, a period of severe earthly suffering; others have seen believers working actively toward a Golden Age before Jesus returns. The main point is that these attitudes provide very different visions of agency in relation to the material world: Are political structures and communal, natural resources to be mistrusted because everything is going up in smoke in any case, or are they vital assets, to be appropriated by believers, who are by definition the best stewards of the world?

If we ask how these tensions have played out in recent American history, it is worth remembering that the nineteenth century was in many ways *the* century of the evangelical in America. Scientific strategies of reaching the urban masses ranged from the expansion of the Young Men's Christian Association (YMCA) to the use of secular theaters to reach huge audiences (Coleman 2007). But the beginning of the twentieth century saw evangelicals being challenged by secularist ideas and growing numbers of non-Christian immigrants, and often outraged—especially in a post-Darwinian age—by the attempts of many scholars to see the Bible as unreliable history rather than divine text. One corollary of such self-consciousness, sharpened by educational and racial divisions, was the schismatic creation of numerous theological camps. The liberal, "social" gospel, committed actively to promoting social well-being, was beginning to look distinct from growing "conservative" forms. The term *fundamentalism* emerged at this time and is attributed to Curtis Lee Laws, a pastor well known for his sermon "The Fiery Furnace and Soul Liberty," which included the resonant lines: "We ourselves must pilgrims be,/Launch our Mayflower and steer boldly/ Through the desperate winter sea."[6] If these words replayed a Puritan history of religious dissent, Laws wrote himself into evangelical history in 1920 by rallying those "who still cling to the great fundamentals and who mean to do battle royal" for the true faith.

A key event in the theological and cultural battles that were breaking out was the Scopes Trial of 1925 when, in a Tennessee courtroom, former presidential candidate William Jennings Bryan was pilloried for seeming to embody the intellectual naïveté of an entire antievolutionist worldview (Coleman and Carlin 2004). Scopes was a science teacher who was being prosecuted for supposedly teaching evolutionary theory in a state where it was banned as a topic of education. Bryan—somewhat unjustifiably—became a national emblem of the ignorance and intellectual backwardness of a religion most commonly associated with the South.

That trial acted as one important catalyst for the tactical withdrawal of increasingly self-conscious conservatives from the public sphere, and during the rest of the interwar years conservatives' adversarial attitudes to liberalism were expressed through consolidation of networks that provided institutions— schools, magazines, radio broadcasts—operating parallel to, but distinct from, mainstream society. The very shape of the American polity aided this process of mimesis combined with boundary building. In effect, the "dissenting denomination" has become a widespread religious form (Martin 1978). The separation of church and state, religious pluralism, and relative concentration of power in individual states (at least by European standards) allowed and still allows for a high degree of local autonomy. As one writer has put it (Bruce 1996: 134): "Utah is as Mormon as Spain is Catholic."

But if a principle of "parallel but separate" was evident among many conservatives up until around the 1960s, a key shift in orientation then began to be apparent. Since World War II it had been clear that this was a subculture growing in wealth and economic aspiration, which in the form of people like Billy Graham and Oral Roberts was prepared to reach out into the sports stadium and television studio. Conservative believers were also able to benefit from those who reacted *against* the movements of youth counterculture, gaining the support of those who saw the counterculture as a challenge to morality (Marsden 1982). Debates over prayer in public schools and the teaching of evolution provided powerful evidence of what was at stake in contesting issues relating to public life. Given new wealth and fresh motivation, the relative decentralization of American educational, religious, and political structures actually encouraged political and religious activism because organized evangelicals could try to dominate local elections: for instance, if you wanted creationism to be taught to children, you could start by putting pressure on your local school board.

Mobilization was further prompted by the perceived encroachment of the secular public sphere on to evangelical subculture, most notably proabortion legal judgments such as the famous 1973 Supreme Court *Roe v. Wade* ruling. During the time of the civil rights movement, Jerry Falwell had criticized Martin Luther King, Jr. for politicizing the church. But by the end of the seventies, he had decided to found what became the four-million-strong Moral Majority.[7]

If evangelicals could provide a kind of counter-counterculture built on a rhetoric of reviving us ... *again*, the time was ripe for a rejoining, however ambivalently, of the link between evangelical religion and conservative national politics. Republican political activists were coming to see white conservative Protestants as a potentially significant but untapped block of voters who could be mobilized around moral issues.[8] In support of this strategy, televangelists such as Jerry Falwell and Pat Robertson were important precisely because they had already developed powerful means of communication (mailing lists, fundraising networks, television) in the separate but parallel world of the evangelical subculture.

Yet, significantly, even as conservatives started to enter the mainstream, even as Pat Robertson emphasized his Yale credentials in seeking nomination for the Republican candidacy, the mobilizing work done in the 1980s onward still involved believers frequently defining themselves as *outsiders* monitoring those in power—judges, politicians, teachers. And even among evangelicals some old boundaries proved insurmountable: Robertson attracted the support of Pentecostals and Charismatics for his nomination but did less well with fundamentalists. Furthermore, during the 1980s and 1990s, few New Christian Right supporters gained national office, and President Reagan proved particularly adept at gaining evangelicals' electoral support but not actually supporting their policies. For his first term George W. Bush gained 70 percent of the evangelical vote, but that was still the lowest of any Republican since Reagan.

Four years later, Bush would capture nearly 80 percent of the evangelical constituency after a term in which he had been encouraged to speak openly about his faith.[9] Around one in five voters in the 2004 election could be classed as evangelicals—a record. Quite apart from Karl Rove's skills in getting people who were normally alienated from mainstream politics to vote, Bush seemed to have personal convictions that resonated with many evangelicals, and moreover—as we shall see—he took on the role of national leader engaged in a military drama that touched on key areas of millennial evangelical conviction.

Over the medium to long *durée* of American history, then, conservative Protestantism has been engaged in struggles between stances of separation from and cooperation with mainstream politics. But this redescription of the Christian Right, which presents stances of appropriation and withdrawal as occurring in temporal sequences that bounce off each other in complex ways, does not begin to tell the whole story. So now I want to argue that a rather subtler way of understanding evangelical views on "discernible reality" and political engagement can be explored.

The Hidden (Parallel) Kingdom

A number of years ago I was carrying out fieldwork on the Word of Life (*Livets Ord*) charismatic ministry in Uppsala. The group is one that I have been researching for some twenty years, and it maintains considerable links with politically conservative, "Prosperity-oriented" ministries in the United States (Coleman 2000). I went to a meeting that provided an opportunity for university students to question the head pastor of the ministry, Ulf Ekman, and listened as Ekman responded to the students in terms that I thought were rather calm and witty, even wryly self-knowing. Then, filing out of the meeting, I bumped into a Word of Life supporter and asked how he thought the meeting had gone. To my surprise, he uttered a single word: "*Krig*" (War!).

In retrospect, I realize that what I took to have been a civilized exchange of views could also have been interpreted as a battle. In addressing the meeting, knowing that he had both supporters and opponents in the audience, Ekman was probably engaging in what I later came to term "double talk" (Coleman 2006), using language that could be understood at two levels—indeed, appealing to and even constituting two different levels of reality simultaneously.[10] There was the "discernible," immanent reality detectable by secular observers; but a less visible though more spiritually "real" perspective on the world was being made available to believers. The distinction between the two was sometimes glossed by believers as the gulf between "the natural" and "the supernatural." In due course I saw more explicit examples of how double talk worked when observing Ekman replying to his political, theological, and journalistic critics in the media by deploying a broadly civil discourse, and then providing far more spiritually radical comments in sermons to his congregation. He was in effect reappropriating public language for internal purposes, engaging in a spiritualized deconstruction and translation of his own apparently secular discourse.

A linguistic strategy such as double talk is intriguing within a religious movement so often branded as literalist in its approach to language. However, my argument here is that it provides a means of engagement with the world that does not compromise with it at a deeper level of reality—providing a way to classify the natural as a cultural superstructure overlying a much more profound, more real, sacred realm. The theological underpinnings of such a strategy are exemplified by the way Pat Robertson affirms the primacy of a secret, invisible, but transcendent kingdom in relation to which both religion and civil order are to be judged. Such a double perspective encourages believers to read the world as a manifestation of biblical reality. At times, the connections are made clear, such as when prophecy is applied overtly to America as a new Israel; but more esoteric connections are also drawn. The issues on which Christian Right advocates have often campaigned have been ones for which two levels of struggle can be discerned. Voluntary school prayer is about the rights of citizens to enjoy the protections of the First Amendment, but also about the primacy of divine as opposed to secular authority; abortion is about the conditions under which it is appropriate or not to bring a pregnancy to term, but also about the primacy of divine authority over the giving of life.

Understanding this form of conservative Protestant disposition, this marked double orientation to reality, can provide a further key to appreciating the ways in which believers negotiate relationships between the sacred and secular in ways that seem puzzling to outsiders. For instance, Susan Harding describes how (the now late) Jerry Falwell encouraged followers to send financial support to his ministry—an action that might seem a purely cynical exploitation of the gullible for blatant material gain. But as Harding puts it (2000: 109): "The whole point of giving to a God-led ministry is to vacate the commercial economy and to enter another realm, a Christ-centered gospel, or sacrificial, economy in which material expectations are transformed." The personalized figure of "Jerry" became the figure who mediated between natural and supernatural realms, the key through which secular resources were given divine significance.

Let me take the point closer to political debate by taking us back to Bush's re-election in 2004. Omri Elisha has provided an intriguing analysis of a pre-election email letter from Laura Bush that was sent out on October 26, 2004, to the subscribers of *Crosswalk*, a conservative, "Christ-centered, for-profit corporation" that provides news digests. Elisha notes how Laura Bush begins: "Dear Friend, We've watched as President Bush has led this country through the most historic struggle of our generation." A few lines later, the First Lady writes: "In Ohio, I visited with a woman who summed up our success this way. She said, 'President Bush was born for such a time as this. ... It makes me feel so secure to know that our leader has such a love for our country.'"

Elisha picks up on the apparently insignificant words "for such a time as this."[11] The phrase can be seen simultaneously as a reference to the forthcoming election and as a quotation from the Book of Esther, chapter 4, verse 14. Esther is a Jewish woman who becomes a queen before risking her own life to save the Jewish people from destruction by a wicked enemy, and the story can be read by evangelicals as a sign of the individual's role in faithfully enacting God's sovereign designs for human history. So the biblical narrative can also be applied to a believing president who is wrestling with a so-called axis of evil.

Let us continue this theme of rereading the "discernible" world by considering George W. Bush's words in a famous televised address on Sunday, October 7, 2001, less than a month after September 11 (the speech itself is analyzed in a book by Bruce Lincoln, who juxtaposes Bush's and Bin Laden's rhetoric [Lincoln 2003: 30]). Bush states: "The terrorists may burrow deeper into caves and other entrenched hiding places." This is perhaps an evocation of a particular landscape but also, for those able to read Bush "doubly," a typically glancing but significant gesture toward the book of the Apocalypse, when the Lamb of God (Jesus in his role as avenger at the end of the world) opens the sixth seal on the scroll of doom, a time when "the kings of the earth and the great men and the generals and the rich and the strong, and every one, slave and free, hid in the caves and among the rocks of the mountains, calling to the mountains and rocks" (Revelation of Saint John 6:15–17).

So public speech hints at a biblical narrative that provides a deeply suggestive end-game.[12] This is a coded narrative, appealing both to secular state and sacred nation but without appearing to cross the line that prevents any single religious interest-group from appropriating the public sphere.[13] It is interesting that Bush has apologized for his famous "dead or alive" taunt against terrorists, withdrawing from the cowboy metaphor, but as far as I know he has not had to recant on his religious imagery.

The power of double talk is revealed by those times when evangelical rhetoric becomes openly exposed to the *wrong* kind of interpretative community, such as when Jerry Falwell, talking to Pat Robertson on September 13, 2001, on the *700 Club*, noted the following (Lincoln 2003: 36):

> Throwing God out successfully with the help of the federal court system, throwing God out of the public square, out of the schools. The abortionists have got to bear some burden for this because God will not be mocked. And when we destroy forty million little innocent babies, we make God mad. I really believe that the pagans, and the abortionists, and the feminists, and the gays and the lesbians who are actively trying to make that an alternative lifestyle, the ACLU, People for the American Way, all of them who have tried to secularize America. I point the finger in their face and say: "You helped this happen."

Remember that this passage was initially being produced within the interpretative canopy of religious broadcasting, part of a dialogue between Falwell and Robertson that later led to a call for revival. And note the way Falwell created a form of double-Othering in this passage: Muslim terrorists are to be deplored, but they are mere instruments of a divine wrath directed toward the enemy within—the hodge-podge of liberals who are secularizing the nation.[14] Commenting on the revival of the Christian Right, Capps notes (1990: 182) "a salvation religion is being recommended to guide the affairs of the nation. ... the fundamental axiom is that salvation religion can effectively function as an operational civil religion." This is an important point because it refers to the way the millennial assumptions of such evangelicals can be remapped on to the broader ideals and aspirations of American political piety. By extension, Jerry Falwell and Pat Robertson could interpret 9/11 as prompted by the godlessness of Americans just as much as by the external enemies of the nation, thus proposing a form of "American Jeremiad" (see Bercovitch 1978)

I could say much more about double talk, but here I shall just make two brief points about its apparently concealed nature. First, note how its often apocalyptic implication leads us toward an end-time when the dual nature of reality will actually be resolved: in the rapture of the saints, supernatural will definitively be separated from natural, just as the hidden kingdom will become visible. Second, the anthropologist Peter Pels (2003: 3) has discussed how ideas of magic and the supernatural have supposedly acted as counterpoints to secular, liberal understandings of the "modern world's" transparency and rational progress. But notice here how the interplay between the evangelical and the secular becomes a process of mutual unmasking of the threatening occult, which itself is differently perceived and constituted: if the People for the American Way are concerned to reveal what they see as the political and economic motives behind religious rhetoric, for evangelicals the task is to uncover the supernatural meaning behind all manifestations of mere "discernible reality."

Revival and Rebound

We have been looking at evangelical interpretations of violence as a tool of divine power at a national level. With the idea of revival and rebound I want to reframe these themes of violence and the threatening Other by taking us back to that individualistic lens of "relationalism," that tendency toward advocating internal moral reform *prior* to structural transformation. So we need to look briefly at the key distinction between being "born again" and not, before showing how it can play into a dialogue between the personal and the political in conservative evangelical culture.

Let me begin with a horribly schematic description of conservative evangelical personhood, which draws of course on wider Christian imagery. The spiritual experience attendant upon becoming born again is often seen as a means of regenerating but also bringing mind and flesh under control. But the gaining of a born-again identity also involves the injunction to spread the Good News to others. Avoiding the injunction to missionize can imply to some believers that they are allowing the timid, human part of the person—located in the flesh or the mind—to dictate to the spiritual self.

Scholars often focus on the effects that evangelization has on people *being* missionized. But I have often argued that we also need also to consider its effects on the evangelical self, the way proselytizing can provide an opportunity to relive the narrative of one's own experience of conversion in relaying it to others (e.g., Coleman 2003). So evangelical identity can be reconstituted—revived again if you like—in the missionary act of extending out into the world.

What might be the broader political significance of such a personal orientation? Here, I want to draw selectively on a book by the anthropologist Maurice Bloch called *Prey into Hunter* (1992).[15] Bloch sees himself as attempting to understanding "the politics of religious experience" by looking at how many ritual processes involving initiation involve the symbolically or physically violent conquest of the everyday material world by the transcendental. The first part of many rituals involves participants moving away from the here and now, toward an all-conquering divine realm. In the return, the transcendental continues to be associated with those who made the initial move in its direction, so that the move back to the ordinary world becomes a kind of conquest of that world. "Rebounding" violence occurs because initial co-operation by participants with a transcendental attack on their human vitality is followed by a violent recovery of vitality from an external source. For instance, in the New Guinea Orokaiva initiation (1992: 8ff), participants are transformed from prey into hunters, into a state where—back in the normal world—their spirit ele-ment dominates their mortal element. Bloch argues that such ritual grammars can provide idioms of expansionist violence to people in a range of societies, particularly under circumstances that legitimate military expansionism in the presence of outsiders.

Bloch does occasionally refer to Christianity, talking (1992: 32) of how the lives of Christian saints illustrate the person turning against the bodily aspects of themselves in favor of supernatural invasion. And he argues (1992: 96) that "the aggressive ideology of rebounding conquest ... was particularly evident during the crusades or when religious fervour could be backed by military might, as in the periods of European colonial expansion." Surprisingly, no mention is made of conservative Protestantism, but I am interested in the way Bloch moves from a consideration of personhood to political action, and the way his argument resonates with a conservative evangelical ideology that may devalue mortal flesh in favor of supernaturally derived agency. Original self-abnegation is often accompanied by metaphors of surrender and penetration, followed by the adoption of an identity that is granted divine grace and power. And the idiom of evangelical revival permits, as I have noted, a linguistic replaying of the experi-ence of self-regeneration in the process of missionizing others, ideally converting them to a model of the self, just as my discussion of double agency refers to the ways in which believers can play on two levels of reality and existence, the natu-ral and the supernatural, with the latter ultimately conquering the former.

The extent to which the idiom of evangelical conquest of the self and others leads to physical force will vary, but Jewett and Lawrence's recent discussion of zealous nationalism presents the dilemma well (2003: xiii): "Should America be the 'city set upon a hill' that promises the rule of law even when faced with dif-ficult adversaries? Or should it crusade on the military plane of battle, allowing no law or institution to impede its efforts to destroy evil?" They trace the ways in which George Bush framed his fight against terrorism in world-redemptive terms, but[16] also point to a history of Puritan appropriation of the redemptive violence of the Old Testament as well as the Book of Revelation. Indeed, they note that the Puritans thought of themselves as "standing in the succession of Christian warriors and martyrs that John Foxe had delineated from the Bible down to sixteenth-century England" (2003: 55). Driven by apocalyptic imagery (which, across the Atlantic, permeated the antiroyalist impulses of the English Civil War), American Puritans could see colonists not only as the bearers of Protestant destiny, but also as justified in literally battling against the corrupting influences of Catholic French interlopers in what was a newly Promised Land.

In a further variation on these themes of world- and self-redemption, self-justifying and biblically sanctioned ire could also be directed within, for instance becoming tragically involuted in the destructive passions raised by the infamous Salem witch trials at the end of the seventeenth century.[17] Thus the historians Paul Boyer and Stephen Nissenbaum provide a vivid depiction of Puritan violence aimed—rebounding—against its own community (1974), but they also provide a short but deeply intriguing passage that points precisely to the links with evangelicalism that are being made in this paper. They begin by noting that the accused "witches" in Salem might have taken upon themselves the collective guilt of the community, and if so the cycles of accusation and counteraccusation might have ended then and there. Indeed, "This is very nearly what did happen more than a generation later in the ... Great Awakening of the 1730s and 1740s. For in this massive outbreak of religious revivalism, the ambiguity which underlay the process of accusation in 1692 become open, even ritualized. In the Great Awakening, people accused *themselves* of corruption as passionately as they accused others" (Boyer and Nissenbaum 1975: 215–16).

The link between Salem and the Great Awakening lies partly in the resonances between accusation and confession that are being invoked, as a religious ideology explores possible variations in the conquest of the self leading to attacks on the Other. But it is perhaps not surprising that, in the case of Puritanism and other Protestant forms, such rebounding violence can go on to rebound *within*, as certain unfortunate inhabitants of Salem became the objects of suspicion that power had been converted from the divine to the diabolic, or later evangelicals learned to mistrust their own moral rectitude.[18] So the Salem witch trials and the Great Awakening provide historical examples of a faith using the idiom of violence—both metaphorical and literal—as a means of self-discipline but also as a justification for directing action against others. Indeed, what one might call the obsession with possession that underlies both episodes is concerned precisely with patrolling boundaries of identity; afraid that the other will permeate the self, but absorbed in the mission of penetrating others with one's own agency and ideology.

Both also, of course, illustrate the understanding of political action through personalized, embodied conceptions of morality and threat. And these are themes that we can trace in a much more contemporary debate involving American evangelical expression of rebounding violence: that of direct action against abortion clinics and practitioners. Thus the antiabortionist Randall Terry has talked of being "justified" in breaking the law as part of his Operation Rescue Program (now called Operation Save America). For Terry his personal relationship with God has been crucial since only a righteous individual can accomplish righteous social change, no matter what the secular law may state. Clearly, abortion has become one of the major points of political leverage for conservative evangelicals in justifying their interceptions in the public realms of American society, but note also its parallels with the concerns over exorcism and boundaries evident in Salem and the Great Awakening. Although abortion is about "retaining" a presence within the self, and exorcism is about expelling one, both invoke the boundaries of the body as key points of controversy and debate. And, crucially, in both cases we see the juxtaposition of "justified" with "nonjustified" forms of violence. Salem led to trials and executions of allegedly malicious witches on behalf of a political order that saw itself as divinely instituted; the extreme violence of some antiabortionists has led to action that seems puzzling to secular analysts—the taking of life in the name of a *pro*-life ideology—and yet involves precisely the destruction of a secular humanist form of agency in the name of one legitimated by the discipline of having become born again.[19]

Concluding Remarks

In thinking about what we are to make of these three responses to the world—oscillation, parallelism, and rebound—I have found myself attempting to discern deeper structures in the relations between conservative evangelicalism and politics in America, and ones that exist at more profound levels than those evident in any particular political administration. Implicit throughout has also been an argument about evangelicalism and the modern world, and the suggestion that it is far too simple, as some opponents or scholars have asserted, to see conservative Protestantism as an ideological anachronism. Rather, the movement can be seen as one example of how over-rigid distinctions between religion and modernity rely on forms of what Peter Pels—recalling Latour—calls "modernist purification" that ignore the constant translations and mediations between the two (2003: 32). Such a process—a form of exorcism, if you like—is itself doomed to failure, since purification constantly needs to invoke the presence of the Other against which to rally the forces of modernist transcendence (see also Mitchell 2002).

While my perspective has not been particularly ethnographic, I hope that it has been *anthropological* in its attempt to translate another worldview into terms that we can begin to understand, whatever our personal convictions. This point plays into what one might call a politics of culture. I was intrigued recently to read a newspaper article with the headline "Top scientist gives up on creationists."[20] The evolutionary biologist Steve Jones apparently announced to the Hay-on-Wye book festival that he had given up on debating with creationists and entitled his talk: "Why Creationism is Wrong and Evolution is Right." But the implication of my argument is that figures such as Steve Jones and Richard Dawkins might do well to follow their own inductive principles and find out what debate means to evangelicals before engaging in it with them, thus using social science as well as natural scientific techniques in public debate. We have seen, for instance, that believers negotiate their way through different cultural and epistemological worlds by adopting situational approaches to meaning and expression—forms of double talk reflecting a wider religious ontology where the natural and supernatural worlds are seemingly in parallel but not always in synch with each other. Political or intellectual contests between believers and secularists may thus rely on the latter's naïve notion of consensibility and the referential qualities of language. What is important for many believers is that their message is seen to be projected into public, politically charged space, itself constituting an occupation of that space by Christian personalities and ideas, even if "the world" cannot ever fully understand what they mean.

A further implication of the argument of this chapter relates to the way anthropologists have tended to theorize evangelicals worldwide, and not just in the United States. Much of the current literature talks of the power of missionary forms simultaneously to preserve their distinctiveness from the cultures into which they come into contact *and* to engage those cultures in their own terms. We saw that process in Birgit Meyer's depiction of believers who are caught between heathen spirits and a modern God. This means that there is a wealth of potential here for an anthropology increasingly concerned with understanding the highly complex and often contradictory ways in which ideas, images, texts, people, objects, technologies, and practices are translated and transformed, but are also transformative, in the multiple sites inhabited by a religion that—in Harvey Cox's terms (1995)—seems "made to travel." Nevertheless, the very ubiquity of revivalist forms carries its own irony, because in a sense the conservative evangelical vision that I have been discussing is one that actually denies the unpredictabilities of history as it asserts the recurring salience of biblical or evangelical precedent, or looks toward the end time that will destroy discernible reality, including human temporality. As Jesus tarries, and as revivals are born again elsewhere, spiraling across many other "chosen lands," the evangelical actors of specifically American political history may find it much harder to take their agency for granted. We have already seen how the moral center of Anglicanism is shifting as liberal American Episcopalians are challenged by conservative African bishops (Hassett 2007). In the same way, Pentecostalism and other forms of evangelicalism are rapidly becoming energized and diffused by new infusions from Africa, Latin America, and beyond (e.g., Cox 1995). This century is likely to witness the emergence of many new cities on many hills, each with their own visions of the correct relationships between religion, politics, and the world, and many of which will see the United States itself as a field not only of migration, but also of mission.

For Galina

This piece has multiple origins. It formed part of an inaugural lecture given at the University of Sussex in 2005, and some of the ideas also appeared in a paper for *Anthropological Quarterly* (Coleman 2005). However, it was also given as a piece for a seminar on religion and politics suggested and organized by Galina, and held at the Department of Anthropology, Stockholm University. When I think back to that seminar, what strikes me is that it really formed part of a two-day conversation that I had with Galina all the time that I was in Stockholm, as we wandered round Gamla Stan in search of dinner one night, as we drove from a metro station to her apartment, and as we sat late talking to each other and to another friend and colleague, Mira Amiras. I am writing this a couple of weeks after the anniversary of Galina's death, which occurred on 26 May 2008, but I still feel that I am in conversation with her over many things: the issue of "belief," which we both wrote about in a special issue of *Social Analysis* that we published together in 2008; the powerful aesthetics of religious worship, significant for fieldworkers as well as informants—and part of an exchange that we began in a Japanese restaurant in Washington, DC; and, as we discussed so often, relations with children and how to be a good parent. Galina's honesty, passion, and incisive intelligence permeated all of these conversations, and her anthropology could not easily be separated from her view of life as a whole.

NOTES

1. This chapter was drafted during the penultimate year of the George W. Bush administration, and will be published toward the beginning of the Obama administration. However, I hope that the analysis still holds. Although this paper focuses on religious conservatives, it is not meant to imply that religious affiliation in the United States is an inherently conservative stance in political terms. Sullivan (2004) has noted that more than 60 percent of Democratic voters attend church several times a month and 85 percent say that religion is an important part of their lives. She also points to the rich tradition of liberal political discourse informed by faith involving, for instance, the speeches of Martin Luther King Jr., Robert Kennedy, Mario Cuomo, Barbara Jordan, Jimmy Carter, Bill Clinton, and more recently Barack Obama. Sullivan's argument at least is: "What separates these speeches from those of many political conservatives is that the religious rhetoric is used to supplement arguments that are based on appeals to shared democratic values, not the other way around."
2. See Coleman (2005) for an earlier formulation of the argument of this chapter.
3. The remarks have been much quoted, not least on the Internet. They come from Ron Suskind's article "Without a Doubt" in the *New York Times*, 17 October 2004.
4. These phrases are appropriated with apologies to the anthropologists Edmund Leach (1954) and Ernest Gellner (e.g., 1982).
5. Implicit in my argument in this chapter—and I am hardly alone in this view—is that the relations between religion (and especially Christianity) and the state in

the United States are very different to those evident in Europe. Thus, for instance, the conditions through which conservative Protestants can engage in political action will be different in the two contexts. For an expansion of this argument, see for instance my argument about the articulation of creationist discourse in the public sphere in Coleman and Carlin (2004).

6. Quoted in Freeman 1998: 11.

7. Although the Moral Majority was subsequently wound down, in 2004 Falwell unveiled the Moral Majority Coalition, an organization designed to continue the "evangelical revolution" that swept President Bush back into the White House and saw the election of many pro-life leaders to national office.

8. See Heineman's argument (1998: x) that many Americans often emphasize cultural, rather than class, issues when voting, in contrast to many Europeans.

9. Among Catholic voters, Bush held a slight edge, reversing the previous trend of Catholics to support Democrats.

10. The term comes close in meaning to that of *diglossia,* but the latter tends to refer to the use of two languages or argots, whereas I am describing a process whereby the same language can be taken to have two sets of significance. I should note, however, that the term *double talk* is intended to be analytically neutral, rather than pejorative.

11 Words that, we note, Laura Bush is herself citing from another person.

12. Well after this paper was drafted, and after the George W. Bush administration had ended, the magazine GQ claimed in Spring 2009 to have uncovered regular defense briefings from Donald Rumsfeld to George Bush featuring biblical injunctions on their front pages (http://men.style.com/gq/features/topsecret).

13. Lincoln notes: "For those who have ears to hear, these allusions effect a qualitative transformation, giving Bush's message an entirely different status. This conversion of secular speech into religious discourse invests otherwise merely human events with transcendent significance—by the end, America's adversaries have been redefined as enemies of God, and current events have been constituted as a confirmation of Scripture" (2003: 31–2).

14. People for the American Way subsequently publicized a transcript of the passage and so exposed it to a very different set of readings, leading to something of a national scandal.

15. For a recent overview of the connections between religion and violence (though not one that discusses Bloch), see Faubion 2003. Although I do not explore the issue here, my use of Bloch's work implies that the Christian case I describe should not be seen in isolation, since it permits comparison (although not necessary direct parallels) with other examples of missionizing and militant religion.

16. They note also a longer American tendency to draw on civil religion in this way: "The ideas of holy war have been combined with a distinctively American sense of mission in language that fuses secular and religious images. In major developments of American life—the Civil War, the settling of the western frontier, the World Wars, the Cold War, the Vietnam War, the Gulf War, and the so-called war on terrorism—these ideas have continued to surface" (2003: 5). Even where physical force has not been deployed, the symbolic violence of transformation has been deployed—either "killing" or "converting" the other.

17. The Salem witch trials involved accusation and counteraccusation within both Salem village and town, in Massachusetts. Some twenty people were executed, hun-

dreds of others were accused of witchcraft, and many were imprisoned. The episode started in 1692 when some young girls in the village fell victim to apparent fits, not least when listening to preaching, and others began to exhibit similar symptoms.

18. And, in turn, a further intriguing link with the long durée of American politics is provided by Rebecca Cardozo's (1968) discussion of McCarthyism in the 1950s, where (in common with Arthur Miller's *The Crucible*) she draws out the parallels between the anti-Communist impulses of postwar America and the processes involved in fomenting a "witch craze."

19. While Randall can be seen as an example of civil disobedience, others have been much more violent in their attacks on abortion clinics. Merely one example is provided by the case of Michael Griffin, who murdered the gynecologist and abortion practitioner Dr. David Gunn in Florida in 1993. Griffin is said to have asked his local congregation to pray for Dr. Gunn and to ask that the doctor give his life to Jesus Christ. For a report on this incident, see the Washington Post article at http://www.washingtonpost.com/wp-srv/national/longterm/abortviolence/stories/gunn.htm

20. *The Guardian*, Tuesday, 30 May 2006, 10, by James Randerson—under a piece on Al Gore and Colin Powell.

References

Austin-Broos, Diane. 1997. *Jamaica Genesis: Religion and the Politics of Moral Orders.* Chicago: University of Chicago Press.

Bercovitch, Sacvan. 1975. *The Puritan Origins of the American Self.* New Haven, CT: Yale University Press.

Bloch, Maurice. 1992. *Prey into Hunter: The Politics of Religious Experience.* Cambridge: Cambridge University Press.

Boyer, Paul, and Stephen Nissenbaum. 1974. *Salem Possessed: The Social Origins of Witchcraft.* Cambridge, MA: Harvard University Press.

Bruce, Steve. 1996. *Religion in the Modern World: From Cathedrals to Cults.* Oxford: Oxford University Press.

Capps, Walter H. 1990. *The New Religious Right: Piety, Patriotism, and Politics.* Columbia: University of South Carolina Press.

Cardozo, Rebecca. 1982. "A Modern American Witch Craze." In *Witchcraft and Sorcery,* ed. Max Marwick. Harmondsworth, UK: Penguin.

Carpenter, Joel A. 1997. *Revive Us Again: The Reawakening of American Fundamentalism.* New York: Oxford University Press.

Coleman, Simon. 2000. *The Globalisation of Charismatic Christianity: Spreading the Gospel of Prosperity.* Cambridge: Cambridge University Press.

———. 2003. "Continuous Conversion? The Rhetoric, Practice, and Rhetorical Practice of Charismatic Protestant Conversion." In *The Anthropology of Christian Conversion,* ed. Andrew Buckser and Stephen Glazier. Lanham, MD: Rowman and Littlewood.

————. 2005. "An Empire on a Hill? The Christian Right and the Right to be Christian in America." *Anthropological Quarterly* 78 (3): 653–71.

————. 2006. "When Silence Isn't Golden: Charismatic Speech and the Limits of Literalism." In *The Limits of Meaning: Case Studies in the Anthropology of Christianity*, ed. M. Tomlinson and M. Engelke. Oxford: Berghahn.

————. 2007. "Of Metaphors and Muscles: Protestant 'Play' in the Disciplining of the Self." In *The Discipline of Leisure*, ed. Simon Coleman and Tamara Kohn. Oxford: Berghahn.

Coleman, Simon, and Leslie Carlin, eds. 2004. *The Cultures of Creationism: Anti-Evolutionism in English-Speaking Countries*. Aldershot, UK: Ashgate.

Cox, Harvey. 1995. *Fire from Heaven: The Rise of Pentecostal Spirituality and the Reshaping of Religion in the Twenty-first Century*. Reading, MA: Addison-Wesley.

Elisha, Omri. 2004. "God Save the Queen." *The Revealer*. 15 November.

Faubion, James. 2003. "Religion, Violence and the Vitalistic Economy." *Anthropological Quarterly* 76 (1): 71–85.

Freeman, Curtis W. 1998. "Fundamentalism's Noble Forebear: Curtis Lee Laws." *Christian Ethics Today* 18 (5): 11.

Harding, Susan. 2000. *The Book of Jerry Falwell: Fundamentalist Language and Politics*. Princeton, NJ: Princeton University Press.

Hassett, Miranda K. 2007. *Anglican Communion in Crisis: How Episcopal Dissidents and Their African Allies Are Reshaping Anglicanism*. Princeton, NJ: Princeton University Press.

Heineman, Kenneth J. 1998. *God Is a Conservative: Religion, Politics, and Morality in Contemporary America*. New York: New York University Press.

Jewett, Robert, and John Shelton Lawrence. 2003. *Captain America and the Crusade Against Evil: The Dilemma of Zealous Nationalism*. Grand Rapids, MI: William B. Eerdmans.

Leach, Edmund. 1954. *Political Systems of Highland Burma: A Study of Kachin Social Structure*. London: Bell.

Lincoln, Bruce. 2003. *Holy Terrors: Thinking about Religion after September 11*. Chicago: University of Chicago Press.

Marsden, George. 1982. "Preachers of Paradox: The Religious New Right in Historical Perspective." In *Religion and America: Spirituality in a Secular Age*, ed. Mary Douglas and Stephen Tipton, 150–68. Boston: Beacon.

Martin, David. 1978. *A General Theory of Secularization*. Oxford: Blackwell.

Meyer, Birgit. 1999. *Translating the Devil: Religion and Modernity among the Ewe in Ghana*. Edinburgh: Edinburgh University Press.

Mitchell, Jon P. 2002. "Modernity and the Mediterranean." *Journal of Mediterranean Studies* 12 (1): 1–22.

Pels, Peter. 2003. "Introduction: Magic and Modernity." In *Magic and Modernity: Interfaces of Revelation and Concealment*, ed. Birgit Meyer and Peter Pels, 1–38 Stanford, CA: Stanford University Press.

Sullivan, Amy. 2004. "The Religion Gap: Can Democrats Bridge It?" http://www.washingtonmonthly.com/archives/individual/2004_07/004398.php.

Suskind, Ron. 2004. "Without a Doubt." *New York Times*, Section 6, Page 44, Column 1, 17 October.

≪ 6 ≫

THE AMBIGUITIES OF ISLAMISM AND A CENTURY OF IRANIAN OPPOSITION

David Thurfjell

> What appears in the East under the guise of traditionalism is normally
> an apologetic or radically reformist discourse whose terms of articulation
> and criteria of validation are by no means traditional.
> —Aziz al-Azmeh (1993: 81)

Islamism[1] is often portrayed as an antimodern movement. In 1979, when the Islamist revolution of Khomeyni (1902–1989) took place in Iran, it was often described as "turning back the clock of history."[2] The Islamists were viewed as traditionalists, and their movement was spoken of as a medieval system, an antithesis of Western progress. Following in the footsteps of scholars like Bobby S. Sayyid[3] and Sami Zubaida,[4] this chapter seeks to problematize such an understanding. In doing so I want to focus on one aspect of the Iranian Islamist movement, namely, its ambiguous attitude toward the cluster of ideas and societal solutions that is often referred to as *modernity*. Islamism, not only in Iran, but also all over the world, is caught in a paradox. It is an ideological movement formulated in stark opposition to Western hegemony at the same time as in itself it has many characteristics that are usually associated with the Western societies whose dominating position it seeks to overthrow. It may be said that it contains a tendency toward self-denial and contradiction, an ambiguity that can be found on many different levels. I shall suggest that this situation has its roots in the historical period in which Islamism grew strong, falling back on the anticolonialist political, economic, and cultural processes that created the breeding ground for Islamist ideas.

Notes for this chapter begin on page 204.

The ambiguity that I am discussing here is primarily found on an ideological level, and so my examples will be taken from the words and deeds of political leaders. I do, however, believe that it significantly characterizes the Iranian Islamist community also on its grassroots level. I will therefore begin by giving an example from everyday life in Iran. I will argue that Islamism is partly based on and fueled by an ambiguous relation to "the West." Following this initial illustration, I will touch upon a number of historical instances that may help us understand how the present situation developed.

Everyday Frustration and Islamism

'Ali[5] is an old friend of mine, a twenty-six-year-old student living in Esfahān in central Iran. He comes from the growing social stratum of Iranian society that may be referred to as middle class. His father is a mechanic, and his mother a housewife. They live in a decently big house in one of the suburbs of the city. 'Ali has traveled outside Esfahān a few times in his life, but he has never left Iran. I met him when I was in Esfahān to do research on the Islamist movement there. Over the years we have spent lots of time roaming around the city in his Kian-car, strolling in the parks by the river and watching American films at his house. 'Ali is a fervent supporter of the Iranian Islamist regime. He speaks warmly of Khomeyni and of the Islamic system and looks with great suspicion at the liberalization tendencies among Iranian people. In these circumstances it is important to mention that 'Ali has a girlfriend, Maryam, a woman of his age whom he met in college and whom he is now seeing regularly in secret places.

On several occasions, when 'Ali and I strolled in the parks of Esfahān, we came across young couples taking their refuge there in order to speak with each other undisturbed by the Islamist authorities. These couples must have been of about the same age and life situation as 'Ali. We have seen them talk and sometimes hold hands. On these occasions 'Ali always reacted with a fury that, for me, was surprising. He never said anything to the couples upfront, but I have noticed how his hands trembled with indignation as he impetuously complained about the moral degradation of society and the need for stronger efforts to prevent indecencies among the youth.

'Ali's fury is but one illustration of the frustration that gnaws at the heart of many young Islamists, in Iran and elsewhere. It springs from finding oneself in a situation where one has problems dealing with the simultaneous and contradictory trials of life. The practical everyday challenges that most Iranian families suffer—fear of poverty, unemployment, and economical marginalization—are hard enough to deal with for a young person. But these problems are not only difficult on a materialistic level; they also have an effect on people's self-esteem. Economic problems and marginalization generate feelings of worthlessness, frustration, anger, and self-critique, sometimes even self-contempt. These feelings need to be relieved; someone needs to be blamed. Often that someone is oneself, but external culprits are also sought, in domestic politics as well as on the global arena. Here the fear of marginalization among individual Muslim men and women in their societies is fueled by the feeling of wider marginalization of Muslim countries in the world.

Islamism, arguably, is a cluster of ideas that responds to this feeling of marginalization with a fervent critique of "the West," of its economic, political, and military domination, as well as of the detraditionalized, worldly, and narcissistic lifestyle that it is believed to encourage.

As is the case with most ideologies, the position of Islamism may seem coherent and consistent. But among its adherents, the complete repudiation of the West is not always easy to live up to, and this is where the ambiguity comes in. This is because, even if one is ideologically in agreement with Khomeyni, it is not always easy to remain on a straight path in everyday life. Even active supporters of the Islamist regime in Iran can, so to speak, feel the lure of the West. And also for the most zealous Islamists, it is difficult to completely disregard the vast economic improvements that moving to Europe or America would entail; or, for that matter, to resist the adult television shows made available to those who have a disc antenna installed on their balcony.

'Ali's frustration falls back on exactly this. He is drawn to the West because of the opportunities and freedom that a life there would mean, and to its culture (at least that image of Western culture that is conveyed from certain commercial television channels) because of its light-heartedness and sexual explicitness. 'Ali is drawn to all this but at the same time he is disgusted by it. Being a pious and well-educated Muslim, 'Ali, at least sometimes, views life as a pursuit for spiritual purity and surrender to God. The religious struggle toward this goal is captured in the concept *jihad al-nafs* (struggle of the self), which denotes the religious effort to become virtuous and God-oriented by defeating egoistic tendencies. One side of 'Ali wants to pursue this struggle and feels that the ungodly Western culture and the emotions that it gives rise to within him holds him back. He hates himself for this and he hates the West for what it does to him, for making him weak.

So unfurls the ambiguous emotional situation in which many Islamist young men and women find themselves. Maybe the core of this situation is pinpointed in the concept of *westoxification* (*gharbzādegi*), allegedly coined by Iranian writer Jalal Al Ahmad (1923–1969).[6] Khomeyni used this expression in an attempt to label the situation in his country. As he saw it, foreign commercial and economic interests seek to ruin the souls of Iranian youth in order to seize power. Through popular music, television, and certain philosophical trends that turn people away from God and fill them with narcissistic hubris (*kebr*), young people are made victims of an irresistible, deadly, and even satanic cultural poison, introduced by the West as a part of a cultural invasion (*tahajom-e farhangi*) directed toward Muslims.

The notion of westoxification was coined as a part of an ideological description of the state of affairs in the Iranian society. But, for 'Ali and other Islamists who relate to this notion, it also becomes a part of the conceptual framework through which life is interpreted on a personal level. Hence, as the example of 'Ali illustrates, for individual Islamists a situation may rise when one realizes that it is not only other morally debauched youngsters that are victims of this satanic influence, but that one may be so oneself. In this way the global political struggle that Islamism is a part of becomes internalized into the bodies and minds of its individual adherents. The situation, circumscribed by the notion of westoxification, thus fosters an ambiguous self-understanding on an individual level. People are drawn both to the individualistic and this-worldly lifestyle of the West and to the traditional and God-oriented attitude that is advocated by the Islamic authorities, both at the same time.

This ambiguity can also be seen in concrete societal questions. One big issue that may serve as an example of this, often brought up in the Islamist rhetoric, is the question of marriage age. Although the Iranian Islamic law permits marriage at a very young age (nine for girls and fourteen for boys), the trend in the society for the last twenty years has been that marriage age has gone up considerably (Mehryar and Ahmad-Nia 2004). There are many explanations as to why people wait longer before they marry. The situation on the job market in combination with the fact that Iranian weddings tend to be increasingly costly are often given as important reasons, which contradicts the recommendations of the Islamic authorities who, since they came to power, have promoted early marriages. Although these explanations are valid, the development can also be construed as an example on how Iranian society is going through the same processes of individualization that are taking place in the rest of the industrialized world. Increasing individualization causes people to upgrade the importance of their own life choices, spend more time on education and, therefore, settle down and marry later in life.[7] Since this tendency is strong also among many Islamist supporters, it serves as a good example of the ambiguity of the movement.

Thus, there is inconsistency between ideas and practice in the Iranian Islamist movement, and the emotional life of many of its adherents is ambiguous. Before we go on to look at the historical background to this situation, let me say a few words on the notion of modernity and its relation to the ambiguities of Islamism.

Modernity

Modernity is a vague concept. Scholars in different disciplines have used the term to denote a number of interlinked ideological and societal phenomena that from the French Revolution onward found a dominating position in Europe and North America and from there, through the currents of colonialism, spread throughout the world. Scientific rationalism, individualism, secularism, nationalism, urbanization, colonialism, democracy, capitalism, and gender equality are examples of such phenomena. Of course, there are many instances of these phenomena in history before the European Enlightenment. Indeed, there are examples of what we may call "modern" already in antiquity. Take, for instance, the individual focus in the *Confessions* of Saint Augustine[8] or the materialist worldview of the Epicureans. Definite historical demarcations are, hence, less useful here, and modernity should not be thought of as a static and clearly demarcated set of notions or societal structures. Rather, the term should be seen as an attempt to identify a cluster of partially interdependent processes that have become accentuated during the last centuries of primarily European history and which may be combined in many different ways. In order to emphasize this view, I will here use the term *modernization* instead of *modernity*. Modernization, then, is a cluster of processes that includes rationalization, individualization, and secularization. Islamism, or better, *Islamization*, is an ambiguous form of modernization that has developed in line with certain aspects of European modernization but against other aspects of it. It is, to put it differently, both a result of and a protest against the ideas that colonialism and Western hegemony have brought about.

Needless to say, there is no such thing as a homogeneous European modernization either. The various societal, ideological, and political projects that have emerged in Europe since the mid-nineteenth century instead constitute a number of different European modernizations. In much Islamist rhetoric, however, the hegemonic ideologies of the West are often spoken of as a coherent whole. Many Islamists, it seems, experience and relate to the cluster of certain processes as "European modernization." This attitude defines the Islamist stance toward the West.

One central characteristic of modernization is longing for universality and coherence. In the last two centuries, a number of worldviews have emerged that, despite their differences, share the implicit strive toward universality and coherence. The creation of academic "grand theories" during the nineteenth century is a good example of this. The psychoanalysis of Sigmund Freud (1856–1939), Émile Durkheim's (1858–1917) sociology, and Charles Darwin's (1809–1882) theory of evolution were more than proposed explanations within a limited field of study. They became metanarratives that provided tools for a coherent understanding of our world. Hence, Freudian psychoanalysis, to take but one example, provides an explanation, not just of neurosis and its treatment, but of the human psyche, history, and culture in general. The political ideologies that became important during the nineteenth and twentieth centuries shared this longing for coherence and universality. The prominent examples of communism, liberalism, and democracy are all founded on universalist claims in which the ideology and its way of structuring society are believed to be the superior solution to the problems of all societies regardless of culture, structure, and historical background.

Most expressions of Islamism share this significant feature and therefore belong to this context. It is yet another example of a coherence-oriented ideology that, alongside other similar ideologies, developed in the twentieth century. Islamism cannot be understood as independent of other processes of modernization. Although different from other contemporary ideologies, it developed in the same historical period, many of its notions and solutions are borrowed from the very ideologies it seeks to overthrow.

A Century of Iranian Opposition

I will now go on to show how Iranian Islamism developed through a number of interactions between Shi'ite traditional authorities and various modernization processes in Iran. I will argue that, starting from the late nineteenth century, the Iranian opposition developed as a reaction against these processes. Since it was born within and generated by the modernization processes, we can trace the source of the present ambiguity in this historical background. I will begin by highlighting three examples of Iranian opposition against European imperialism that have had an impact on the development and success of the Islamist alternative.

Struggling with Imperialism: Shirāzi, Nā'ini, and Mosaddeq

The first instance dates back to the late nineteenth century. At this time Iran, a kingdom under the reign of Qajar dynasty, was not totally colonized by any of the great colonial powers of the period, but it was divided into zones of interest between Russia and Great Britain. Qajars were a line of rulers that governed Iran between 1794 and 1925, the years of European colonial expansion. They were known for their appreciation of European culture, expressed, e.g., in their willingness to sell concessions to Europeans. To the discontent of many Iranians, the Qajar government would sell out to foreigners the right to trade within various Iranian markets. One such concession, sold to the British businessman G. F. Talbot, has received much attention among those interested in the history of Iranian Islamism. In 1890 G. F. Talbot bought a concession that granted him the monopoly for tobacco trade in Iran. This caused a venerated Iranian cleric, Ayatollāh Mirzā Shirāzi (1815–1895), to issue a fatwa (Islamic juridical verdict) in which he stated that the use of tobacco is forbidden (*harām*) according to Islamic law. The purpose of the fatwa was, of course, political, and its impact, allegedly, was enormous. Overnight, as the news of the fatwa spread throughout the country, people stopped buying tobacco and hence joined in a large-scale boycott of G. F. Talbot, which resulted in his bankruptcy and the withdrawal of the allowance (Momen 1985: 142).

This example is important since it marks a change of stance among the *'ulamā* (Islamic clergy) in their relation to politics. From this instance onward, Shi'ite 'ulamā in Iran became increasingly activist in their efforts to influence society. This meant a change in the role of the clergy, whose traditional position had been that of passive observers and sometimes critics of the doings of kings. Now, it seems, the clergy started to interfere actively in the political sphere. The example of Shirāzi's fatwa is one of the first clear indications that such a change had taken place. Now, to criticize rulers or to attempt to change society is not particularly new in Islamic history. Indeed, such attempts have been commonplace since the days of Mohammad himself.[9] Among the Shi'ites, especially, criticism against unrighteous rulers has been a major preoccupation throughout history. Still, arguably, the incident with G. F. Talbot in 1890 marks a change. Of course, the fact that it took place in a colonial setting was new and significant. The recently improved level of technology, furthermore, enabled the fatwa to spread faster than it would have ever been possible before. On a more general level, moreover, the incident may be construed as an example of how Islamic opposition became a part of a global struggle against the imperialism of the colonial empires. Internationally, Shirāzi's fatwa did not take place in a political vacuum. It happened in the same historical period in which Mohandas K. Gandhi (1869–1948) began his struggle against discriminatory racial laws in South Africa, a struggle in which Gandhi, like Shirāzi, found ways of using traditional religious institutions as means in a modernized political power struggle. Furthermore, it can be argued that Shirāzi's rebellion indicated a situation in which the Islamic opposition that he represented started to make use of all available political means in order to bring about change. By doing so, they launched a power system that constituted an alternative to the existing one. Islam, as it was presented in the case of Shirāzi, did not only stand for the conservative or religious aspect of the existing societal order; it presented an alternative society altogether, and, hence, made its voice heard in the same field, and by the same means, as kings or politicians. I suggest that this can be seen as the beginning of an Islamist modernization in Iran. Through the active stance taken by Shirāzi, Islam took the first step to becoming a coherent, full-fledged alternative to the existing rule.

If the opposition of Shirāzi was not an obvious example of an Islamic modernization led by Iranian Islamic leaders, the constitutional revolution a few years later certainly was. In 1906, the efforts of many oppositional forces in Iranian society led to the establishment of a parliament, the *majles*. In this event, referred to as the Constitutional revolution, some prominent representatives of 'ulamā played an important role. One of them was Shaykh Mohammad Hoseyn

Nā'ini (1860–1936), a high-ranking scholar and one of the leading Islamic jurisprudents of his time.[10]

It is obvious that by this moment of history, at least some sections of the Iranian Islamic elite had adopted certain recent European political notions, such as the idea of a parliament,[11] and included these in their political agenda. Although the version of parliamentary democracy advocated by Nā'ini was sometimes criticized for being too traditional,[12] it can be said that Iranian Islamism in its early form, which he and his followers represented, drew to a significant extent on European secular democratic ideals. These early Iranian Islamists, it seems, considered democratic political influence to be a natural part of the Islamic struggle against unjust rule and foreign imperialism.

This positive view of European democracy, however, soon came to be challenged. Under the influence and support of the colonial powers, primarily Russia, the king closed down the parliament in 1908. This was a setback for all those who had struggled for increased democracy in the country. For Shaykh Nā'ini, the blow was heavy. It is difficult to know how deep his ideological democratic engagement was. But, arguably, the closing down of the parliament did not only entail a loss of political influence for Shaykh Nā'ini; it also led to disillusionment with the ideals of Western democracy and to questioning the functionality of Western system as a whole. It was something inherently self-undermining in the fact that Europe-oriented Iranian leaders were helped by European states to quench the Europeanization of Iranian politics. Indeed, the whole colonial situation in the world of that time seemed to be built on a contradiction of this kind.

Nā'ini was forced into exile. He ended up in Najaf in Iraq, where he began to sketch the outline of a political system that, he hoped, would not be caught up in a similar self-contradiction. Until his death in 1936 he was engaged in the struggle against the colonial rule. In 1922 Nā'ini issued a fatwa forbidding his followers to participate in the national elections. His political work in the early twentieth century had a great impact on the later development of Iranian Islamism.

My third example of Iranian opposition to imperialism is the Mosaddeq incident of the 1950s. By this time, the Qajars had been replaced by a new royal dynasty, and the influence of Great Britain and Russia had been inherited by interests in the United States, attracted by the rich oil resources of the country.[13] Mohammad Mosaddeq (1882–1967) became the prime minister of Iran in 1951, after the victory of his party in general elections. He was a member of the National Front, a nationalist party that received massive popular support. Immediately after he became prime minister, the decision was made to nationalize the Iranian oil resources then owned by British companies. The reaction from Britain and the United States was strong: this was unacceptable. Mosaddeq was declared a communist, Iranian oil was boycotted, and the dispute was referred to the international court in The Hague. When these measures proved to be insufficient, British intelligence and the CIA arranged a coup in which Mosaddeq was removed from his office. This happened in August 1953, two and a half years after Mosaddeq's controversial decision. As a result of this, the Iranian king, Mohammad Rezā Pahlavi (1919–1980), became more or less autocratic ruler at the same time as the influence of the United States in Iran was significantly strengthened.

There were many in Iran who where critical of Mosaddeq and who supported the measures taken by the king and his foreign allies. But, for people belonging to the political opposition, the coup against Mosaddeq became yet another proof of the self-contradictive nature of the alternative offered by the West. Allegedly, the incident increased the feeling among many Iranians that there was a need to turn to an entirely different system. Something had to change dramatically in the way society worked in Iran. Many people turned to socialist or communist alternatives and fought against the king and his Western allies from these ideological standpoints. Others chose to support the Islamist alternative. It was this option that only a few years after the ousting of Mosaddeq was to become the number one oppositional voice in Iranian politics.

These examples make it clear that Islamism already from the beginning developed as a reaction against the semicolonialism that Iran was subjected to. The colonial-friendly rule of the Iranian kings as well as the influence of Russia and Great Britain over Iranian domestic affairs were opposed. Some early Islamists, hence, were opposed to European economic domination and the global political structure of the colonial times. Their concern was mainly to gain political and economical influence in their country, and the fact that Europe had a hegemonic position in these arenas did not initially stop them from connecting to European ideas and methods in their struggle for justice. They worked for democracy and a constitution based on the European model. The failure of the constitutional revolution and the expulsion of Nā'ini from Iran, however, brought about a change. European ideas could no longer be appreciated as independent of the political agendas of the countries from which they had sprung. The French Revolution's call for freedom, equality, and brotherhood could no longer be separated from the global political oppression and inequality that came in its wake. Although it is difficult to know for certain what went on in the minds of religious leaders like Nā'ini, it can be argued that Islamism here grew out of a felt necessity to treat the different sides of that which Europe had delivered, ideas as well as political systems, as interdependent aspects of a united whole. European modernization needed to be revised in its totality, and the ideals and societal solutions that it gave rise to needed to be rethought. The

Islamists therefore reshaped or abandoned several European key terms, and they criticized the secular ideologies of the Enlightenment for lacking an ab- solute moral authority. But, as we shall see, Iranian Islamism never fully aban- doned its connection to the European modernization.

Fighting European Modernization: The Pahlavi Kings and Khomeyni

Let me now retrace a bit of history in order to pinpoint another aspect of the Iranian Islamism and its relation to European modernization, namely, the Is- lamists' critique of the reforms instigated by the Pahlavi kings.

In 1925 a high-ranking officer of the Qajar military appropriated the royal position in Iran and became Shāh Rezā Pahlavi (1878–1944), the first king of the Pahlavi reign. Initially the new king gained the support of the Islamic leaders, who were fed up with the previous regime and had been promised Is- lamic reforms in society. This support, however, did not last long. Rezā Pahlavi launched a reform program with the clear ambition to modernize Iran. Inspired by his like-minded Turkish associate Mustafa Kemal (1881–1938), Rezā Shāh began a project of transforming Iran into a nation-state of the European model. The power of the central government was strengthened; religious authorities were restricted; nomadic tribes were forced to become resident, and efforts were made to make public space more European in style. Hardly surprising, the re- forms caused protests among Islamic leaders who felt sidestepped and deceived, as their vision of what society should be like became increasingly counteracted.

Rezā Shāh was removed from his office by the allies in the Second World War, but his son, Mohammad Rezā Pahlavi, continued to reform the country along the lines set up by his father. In 1963 this new king launched a reform program that he called the White Revolution. The purpose was, again, to mod- ernize the country according to the European model. Among other things, land properties were confiscated from the 'ulamā, and new laws were passed for the emancipation of women, including a new election law with suffrage for women. A prohibition against women wearing *hejāb* (Islamic veil) in public had existed since 1941 (Keddie 1981: 108–9).

From the Islamist opposition, the staunchest critic of the king's reform pro- gram was a relatively young cleric by the name of Ruhollāh Khomeyni. In 1961 the most high-ranking Islamic scholar in Iran and the foremost spokesman of the 'ulamā, Ayatollāh Borujerdi (1875–1962), passed away. His death created a vacuum of authority among the religious elite, which was cleverly used by Khomeyni. Khomeyni chose a more polemic line than most others and soon became known for his outspoken and ruthless critique of the shāh. In Islamist circles he gained substantial support and quickly became the most prominent leader of Iranian clergy. As such, then, it was only natural that he would be the one to lead the protests against the White Revolution. It is interesting to note that Khomeyni was not always of the opinion that 'ulamā should take an active stance on the political arena. Such a position developed as a reaction to the reforms that he considered so anti-Islamic that active opposition was nec-essary. Among other things, then, Khomeyni criticized the king for having no popular support for his reforms, which therefore were proclaimed illegitimate.[14] Khomeyni was exiled from the country the year after the White Revolution was launched. Interestingly, Khomeyni eventually found his way to Najaf in Iraq, the same city where Shaykh Nā'ini half a century earlier had started to develop a model for Islamic governance that could constitute an alternative to the system of the West. In Najaf, Khomeyni became acquainted with the writings of Nā'ini and was inspired by these in his own endeavor to develop a constitutional model that could replace that of the Pahlavi kings.[15]

What can be said about the Islamist struggle against the reform programs of the Pahlavi kings and its relation to modernization? First of all, the reforms of the Pahlavis were explicitly "modern." Their ambition was to change Iran into the "modern" state that the kings and their advisors had envisioned. In this vision there were many components that are also found in most contemporary European states, such as a strong central government, a high technological level, and efforts to emancipate women in public life. Still, however, there was one significant aspect of the contemporary European states that the reforms of the Pahlavi kings failed to include, namely, that of a democratic political system with popular representation in the processes of governance. After Mosaddeq had been ousted from his position, the king, as I have already mentioned, be-came autocratic. It was from such a position of autocracy that he launched the White Revolution and other far-reaching programs aiming at modernization. Thus, the Europe-oriented position of the king was also ambiguous in its rela-tion to the European modernization that it claimed to reproduce in Iran. Inter-estingly, in the Islamist critique of the king, Khomeyni repeatedly emphasized that his revolutionary movement was not against modernization. In a speech delivered on 15 April 1964, he expressed this view explicitly while commenting on the reputation of his movement in the outside world:

> They introduce us as traditionalists, as reactionists; they regard the 'ulamā of Islam as "black reaction." Those heavily subsided foreign newspapers which have set out to ruin us, introduce us abroad as anti-reformists, as those opposed to modernization. Akhunds [Islamic clergy] are presented as those who travel on donkeys and who argue that they don't want electricity nor do they need airplanes. It is said that they want to return to the Dark ages, that they are reactionaries. … it was the 'ulamā of Islam who, at the dawn of constitutional-ism, fought against the evils of despotism and procured freedom for the nation! (Khomeini 1995: 152–53)

It seems therefore as if both counterparts, although their rhetorics indicate something else, have positions that both rebuke and attach to European modernization, albeit in very different ways.

A Revolutionary Shi'ism: Najaf-Ābādi and Sharia'ti

In 1968 the Iranian cleric and author Salehi Najaf-Ābādi published a book called *Shahid-e Jāvid* (The Eternal Martyr). This publication marks the beginning of a new era in the history of Iranian Shi'ism. It portrays Imām Hoseyn, the grandson of the prophet who was martyred at the battle of Karbalā in 680. He is presented as the righteous leader who stands up against injustice at the cost of his own life. This view of Hoseyn is not new in Shi'ite tradition, but the book still indicates a change of emphasis and a politicization of the role of the Imams (Enayat 1991: 190–94). Hoseyn is no longer primarily a victim of the world's injustice; instead, he becomes a fighting hero. Studies of how the imāms are portrayed in religious sermons from the same period indicate similar transformations there (Ram 1994). This new emphasis has had an impact on the view of what role Shi'ism as a movement should play in society. Unlike the majority of Shi'ite leaders in history, Hoseyn was an activist. He fought and was martyred in an active attempt to seize power and to reinstall a just Islamic rule. From the late 1960s onward, his example, more than ever before, becomes the role model of what Shi'ites should be like today. This happened at the same time as Khomeyni, from his exile, launched his campaign to oust the king from the peacock-throne in Tehrān. Khomeyni, and the 'ulamā that he spoke for, were no longer passive critics of the king but activists with the ambition to seize total control of the political power, just as Hoseyn once had attempted to do. Shirāzi's fatwa had begun such a change of stance. Nā'ini's work had prepared for it. With Najaf-Ābādi and Khomeyni it really happened.

Important in these circumstances is the work of the philosopher and Islamist ideologist 'Ali Sharia'ti (1933–1977). Although he died the year before the revolution, Sharia'ti's importance for its success is hard to overestimate. It was to a large extent his speeches and texts that managed to win support for the revolution among intellectuals and students. Sharia'ti's production was extensive, and it cannot be properly described in a few sentences. Let me just mention some of his many ideas that may help elucidate the reasons for his popularity. Sharia'ti formulated a learned critique of the various ideologies that had appeared in the European thought in the nineteenth and twentieth centuries. Taking his point of departure from existentialist philosophy on the one hand and Shi'ite Islamic tradition on the other, he argued that the worldview that is inherent in the materialistic or sociological explanations of reality fails to deliver humans from their prisons. Humans, Sharia'ti argues, have the ability to transcend the existential confinement that biology and historical circumstances have placed upon them. We can choose to rebel against our biological or social instincts and thereby become free. The in-worldly focus of modernist ideas, however, deprives us of this possibility by denying the existence of an absolute higher truth. These ideas may well help us to understand and control worldly matters but they fail to assist us in reaching a higher goal in our individual lives and in society. This is where Islam comes in. Islam, in Sharia'ti's interpretation, provides a path out of the worst prison of all, namely, that of our own egotism. The core of Islam lies in the teaching of God's unicity and by providing tools by which we may abandon our self-orientation in favor of a God-oriented attitude; this helps us become entirely free. Central to this discussion is the concept of *ithār*, which denotes the self-sacrificing generosity and love that can help humans to be really free. (Shari'ati 1998: 187–95)

In Sharia'ti's teaching, humans can choose to rebel against all the confinements that we are subjected to. This is true on an individual moral and religious level as well as on a societal and political one. Sharia'ti's teaching, hence, is inherently revolutionary. As such it was easy to combine with the more explicit and political revolutionary ideology of Khomeyni and the activist Shi'ite ideal of Najaf-Ābādi's book. The self-sacrificing love of Sharia'ti here merged with the elevation of martyrdom found in the more general Islamist rhetoric and so contributed to the general success of Khomeyni's Islamist revolution.

Important for our purpose here is the way the example of Sharia'ti illustrates the ambiguous relation between European and Islamist processes of modernization. In the conglomeration of ideas that Sharia'ti's teachings constitute, the Islamist struggle for political domination in Iran becomes associated with the existentialist endeavor to choose one's own life path as the readiness to suffer martyrdom develops into a Kierkegaardian leap of faith.[16] Sharia'ti thus provided a sophisticated philosophical superstructure to the struggle that Khomeyni, Najaf-Ābādi, and others motivated on other levels. His striking combination of European philosophy and Islamic traditions is yet another example of an alternative route of modernization. This view is strengthened further by the case of Najaf-Ābādi's book and the changes that followed its publication. When the Islamic opposition in Iran shouldered the role of alternative government, it took the step that marks its transformation from a nonpolitical assessor and critic of the kings to a political party governed by an ideological system alongside other ideologies that modernization has brought about.

The Revolution

When the revolution finally came in the winter of 1978–79, one of its culmination points was a massive popular manifestation of discontent in connection to the *'āshurā*-commemoration festival. 'Āshurā is the tenth day in the month of Moharram. This is the day when Imām Hoseyn, according to Shi'ite tradition, suffered martyrdom while struggling against injustice in Karbalā. On 'āshurā, this event is annually commemorated through public parades and flagellation. Political slogans and other expressions of political discontent are traditional components of these parades. In December 1978 the public parade gathered an unusually large amount of people who used the opportunity to express their disappointment with the regime. This became the culmination of a revolution that had been building up for years. Soon after, the king left the country. Khomeyni returned from his exile on 11 February 1979, and the success of the revolution was a fact.

This is not the place to describe the details of the revolutionary events. There are many such accounts to be found elsewhere.[17] It is, however, important for this discussion to underscore that the Islamic Republic that eventually emerged from the chaos of the revolution was an ideological medley of European democracy and traditional Shi'ite Islam. The constitutional foundation of the Islamic Republic is a unique political construction that combines traditional Islamic law with a European form of government. Essentially, Iran's constitution is based on the French equivalent with an addition of an extensive Islamic amendment. It is significant, maybe almost cynical, that its authors picked the French constitution as their prototype. The French constitution recalls *The Declaration of the Rights of Man and of the Citizen* from the revolutionary year of 1789 when the liberal ideas of individual freedom and equality broke through for real in Europe and brought with them antireligious and secularist sentiments. By Islamizing this symbolically charged legal document, the leaders of the early Islamic republic placed themselves between the dichotomous spheres of religious tradition and secularized society. This cemented the tension that continues to dominate Iranian society on many levels. The second article of the constitution presents the fundamental doctrines upon which the Islamist nation is founded. Among other things, it is here stated that the Islamic Republic of Iran is based upon belief in:

> The exalted dignity and value of man, and his freedom coupled with responsibility before Allah. This system secures equity, justice, political, economic, social, and cultural independence, and national solidarity by recourse to:
>
> a. Continuous ijtihad [interpretation] of the faqihs [Islamic jurisprudents] possessing necessary qualifications, exercised on the basis of the Qur'an and the Sunnah of the Infallibles [Mohammad, Fāteme and the Imāms], upon all of whom be peace.
>
> b. Sciences and arts and the most advanced results of human experience, together with the effort to advance them further. (§2:6)[18]

This paragraph summarizes the main point of this chapter. It clearly illustrates how Iranian Islamism has sought to resuscitate independence and justice by holding on to certain aspects of European modernization, such as science

and technology, while to a certain extent abandoning others, such as a democratic decision-making process, in favor of Islamic authority.

* * *

It is now more than a quarter of a century since the revolution radically
changed the course of Iran's political history. The rule of the jurisprudents does
not seem to waver. After a period of massive popular protests in the late 1990s,
the regime managed to tighten its grip on the situation again, and after the
uncompromising Islamist Mahmud Ahmadinejād was reelected president in
2009, there is little to indicate any dramatic changes coming from within the
system in the next few years to come. The power of the Islamic scholars who
line up behind the regime is increasingly fortified, and in the rhetoric their
ambition is still "just to serve the people" in the way God commands them to.[19]
In order to do this, modern technology is used to as large an extent as possible.
The internationally controversial attempt to develop Iran's nuclear resources
further is but one example of this; President Ahmadinejād's multilingual "blog"
on the Internet is another.[20]

Despite the domination of "hard-liner" Islamists in high offices, the opposition against the Islamist system is more visible today than ever before in the
history of the Islamic Republic. The combination of advanced information
technology, a disproportionately large percentage of youth in the population,
high levels of unemployment, and a politically engaged exile community makes
it difficult even for a totalitarian regime to uphold the image of a united Islamic country. On certain levels, things have changed in Iran since the years
of the revolution and the subsequent war with Iraq. The presidential period of
Mohammad Khātami (1997–2005) did bring about a less strict control of public behavior and, although efforts have been made lately to re-Islamize public
space, the longing for liberalization that is felt among broad layers of the people
cannot be easily concealed.

Iran as a nation is deeply divided. In the three decades that have passed
since the revolution, the authorities have worked hard to strengthen Shi'ite
institutions and infrastructures. Efforts to foster people in the Islamist ideology
of the state have been immense. These exertions have not been entirely futile.
The election of Ahmadinejād, although the fairness of the elections has been
questioned, shows that the radical Islamist line that he represents still has support among certain layers of the people.

In this chapter I have shown how the history of Iranian Islamism displays a
number of ambiguities with respect to various components of European modernization. I have shown how it developed as a reaction to what was seen as a
paradox in the European political project, namely, its combination of Enlightenment ideals on the ideological level, and systematic atrocities and colonial
oppression in politics and in practice. This inconsistency was ascribed to both
the Iranian king and the global superpowers with which he was allied. It fueled

the Iranian Islamist movement and the support for the Islamic Republic that it eventually produced. Furthermore, I have discussed the ambiguous relation between European and Islamist modernization in Iranian recent history. I have argued that it is faulty to describe the various ideologies of Iranian twentieth-century politics as dichotomized into modern and antimodern positions respectively. Modernization is not a static set of beliefs and societal solutions but a cluster of interconnected processes. In Iran royalists as well as Islamists adhered to some of these processes while they rebuked others.

Iranian Islamism, hence, was a reaction against European modernization. But this does not, as is often proposed, entail that it itself was antimodern. Rather, it should be seen as an alternative form of modernization or maybe, to put it slightly differently, as another expression of a universal, albeit immensely varied, modernization process.

Did the Iranian Islamists succeed in creating an Islamic modernization without the inherent paradoxes of its European counterpart? This is not the place for political evaluations, but certainly Iranians who have had to suffer punishment for expressing a divergent political opinion would not agree that the Islamist authorities live up to the ideals of moral righteousness that they themselves have laid down. Rather, the case of Iran seems to suggest that the contradictory combination of high ideals and brutal practice may be inherent in the processes of modernization on a more general level, regardless of whether it is European Western modernization, communism or, as in this case, Iranian Islamist modernization. If this is the case, maybe it can be related to what I earlier pointed out as the most central characteristics of modernization, namely, the longing for universality and coherence. Modernization is, among other things, the process of creating ideology. By this I mean the endeavor to create a coherent description of social and political reality that also suggests solutions to the perceived problems of this reality. When expressed through an ideology, reality is consistent and definable. It is clear what the problems are and what their solutions should be like. Maybe, it is the propensity to seek universal coherence, and not the specific contents, that unites different forms of modernization.

Notes

1. The definition of the term *Islamism* and the characteristics of the movement that is often carelessly referred to by this term are the foci of this article. Scholars have

differed in the way they define Islamism, many have proposed alternative and more precise terminologies and some have argued that the term should be abandoned altogether. Most scholars who do use the term, however, seem to agree that it refers to a politicized version of Islam that has grown in the world since the late nineteenth century as a result of the political and economical discontent felt by many Muslims. Such a basic definition will be sufficient also at the outset of this article.

2. See Sayyid (1997: 88–99) for a discussion about this or Abrahamian (1993: 1–2) for an example of such descriptions.

3. See primarily his book *A Fundamental Fear* (1997).

4. See primarily his book *Islam, the People and the State* (1989).

5. 'Ali is a pseudonym.

6. Al Ahmad (1982).

7. See Berger (1969) for a classic discussion on this development.

8. The *Confessions of Saint Augustine* (1996).

9. Throughout the history of Islam, 'ulamā have debated their role in securing the common good of the people. Much of this debate circles around the Arabic concept of *maslaha 'āmma* (public interest). Muhammad Qasim Zaman has provided an interesting discussion on this matter (Zaman 2004: 129–55).

10. For a thorough presentation of the events of the constitutional revolution, see Said Amir Arjoman's book *The Turban for the Crown* (1989: 34–58).

11. It may be objected that the notion of a council for political decision making (*shurā*) is not new to Islamic tradition; this is of course true. Still, however, I believe it is safe to say that, although the idea of a parliament is not unknown to Islam, the Iranian majles and the constitution of which it is a part is, at least to its form, a loan from other, primarily European modern states.

12. Such criticism was raised by, for instance, the Iranian political scientist 'Abdul-Hādi Hāiri (Enayat 1991: 134).

13. The United States of America was invited by the British to help reorganize Iran's finances in 1922 (Brumberg 1997: 25).

14. Such claims were made on several occasions. See, for instance, Khomeyni's speeches of January 1963 (Khomeini 1995: 39–57).

15. Although Khomeyni considered Nā'ini to have held the same view of the role of 'ulamā in society, this is not necessarily so. Arguably, Nā'ini did not share Khomeyni's view on the active leadership of 'ulamā (Momen 1985: 196).

16. "Leap of faith" is a metaphor used by the Danish philosopher Søren Kierkegaard (1813–1855). It denotes the existential choice to accept and commit oneself to the inescapable uncertainty of human relations to God (Kierkegaard 1992).

17. See for instance the work of Nikki Keddie (1981: 231–73).

18. Acquired from the website of the supreme leader of the Islamic Republic, http://www.leader.ir/langs/EN/index.php?p=leader_law, accessed 11 October 2006.

19. See for instance the speech delivered by Khāmene'i 2 October 2006, retrievable from his website: http://www.leader.ir , accessed 11 October 2006.

20. The address of Ahmadinejād's multilingual "blog" is http://www.ahmadinejad.ir.

References

Abrahamian, Ervand. 1993. *Khomeinism*. London: Tauris.

Al Ahmad, Jamal. 1982. *Plagued by the West (Gharbzadegi)*, trans. P. Sprachman. New York: Center for Iranian Studies, Columbia University.

Al-Azmeh, Aziz. 1993. *Islam and Modernities*. London and New York: Verso.

Arjoman, Said Amir. 1989. *The Turban for the Crown: the Islamic Revolution in Iran*. New York: Oxford University Press.

Augustine. 1996. *The Confessions of Saint Augustine*. New Kensington: Whitaker House.

Berger, Peter. 1969. *The Sacred Canopy: Elements of a Sociological Theory of Religion*. Garden City, NY: Doubleday.

Brumberg, Daniel. 1997. "Khomeini's Legacy: Islamic Rule and Islamic Social Justice." In *Spokesmen for the Despised: Fundamentalist Leaders of the Middle East*, ed. Scott Appleby, 16–82. Chicago: University of Chicago Press.

Enayat, Hamid. 1991. *Modern Islamic Political Thought*. Austin: University of Texas Press.

Keddie, Nikki R. 1981. *Roots of Revolution: An Interpretative History of Modern Iran*. New Haven, CT: Yale University Press.

Khomeini, Ruhollah. 1995. *Kauthar: An Anthology of the Speeches of Imam Khomeini (s.a.) Including an Account of the Events of the Revolution from 1962–1979*, vol 1. Tehran: The Institute for the Compilation and Publication of the Works of Imam Khomeini, International Affairs Division.

Kierkegaard, Soren. 1992. *Concluding Unscientific Postscript to Philosophical Fragments*, trans. Howard V. Hong and Edna H. Hong. Princeton, NJ: Princeton University Press.

Mehryar, Amir H., and Shirin Ahmad-Nia. 2004. "Age-Structural Transition in Iran: Short and Long-term Consequences of Drastic Fertility Swings During the Final Decades of Twentieth Century." Retrieved 16 August 2007 from http://med.sums.ac.ir/icarusplus/export/sites/medical_school/departments/clinical_sciences/community-medicine/educational-programs/download/download.pdf

Momen, Moojan. 1985. *An Introduction to Shi'i Islam*. New Haven, CT: Yale University Press.

The Constitution of the Islamic Republic of Iran. n.d. Tehran: Islamic Propagation Organization.

Ram, Haggay. 1994. *Myth and Mobilisation in Revolutionary Iran*. Washington, DC: American University Press.

Sayyid, Bobby S. 1997. *A Fundamental Fear: Eurocentrism and the Emergence of Islamism*. London: Zed Books.

Shari'ati, 'Ali. 1998. "Humanity and Islam." In *Liberal Islam: A Sourcebook*, ed. Charles Kurzman, 187–95. New York: Oxford University Press.

Zaman, Muhammad Q. 2004. "The Ulama of Contemporary Islam and their Conceptions of the Common Good." In *Public Islam and the Common Good*, ed. Dale Eickelman and Armando Salvarote, 129–55. Leiden and Boston: Brill.

Zubaida, Sami. 1989. *Islam, the People and the State*. London: Tauris.

≪ IV ≫

OPENING NEW SPACE FOR RELIGION

⫷ 7 ⫸

AMAZIGHITÉ, ARAB/ISLAMIC HEGEMONY, AND THE CHRISTIAN EVANGELICAL CHALLENGE

Mira Z. Amiras

> If people do share oppressions, are some more fundamental than others?
> Is it possible to ignore differences in order to form alliances against the
> powers that be? Which differences are to be articulated, and which
> are to be left for a later struggle? Around what points—moments,
> surfaces, events—are people to be mobilized?
> —M. Keith and S. Pile (1993:35)

Introduction

The Amazigh struggle in North Africa has taken the form of a classic nativistic movement. It has consisted of an indigenous people, feeling that their language and identity have reached the brink of extinction, setting out to both "revive and perpetuate selected aspects of their culture" (see Linton 1943: 499). At the same time, both Islam and Arabism have experienced a similar kind of resurgent mobilization—both politically and spiritually—less oriented toward retrieving a lost or disappearing identity than in fulfilling their perceived legacy, the formation of hegemonic scriptural states. Islam and Arabism are inextricably united through Qur'anic revelation in Arabic, the language of God. While not at all nativistic in Linton's terms, resurgent Islamic scripturalism—that is, strict adherence to Qur'anic text and Islamic Shari'at law—and its concomitant global Arabization are both, in Anthony F. C. Wallace's sense, classic revitalization movements with enormous global momentum (see Wallace 1956).

And, more recently, a third strand must be braided into the mix here, the Christian Evangelical movement—in the vein of Yonina Talmon (1962), i.e., a movement in contrast to the above that is millenarian to the core.

Nativistic and millenarian movements may be envisioned as being at polar ends of a revitalization continuum. Nativism seeks to return or preserve aspects of one's own identity, often heavily idealized and filled with nostalgic sentiment—the language of our ancestors, the customs of our people, our ancestral land, homeland, fatherland, mother tongue, tribal religion, sacred clan mythos, drum beats of our spirits, and the like—in the face of hegemonic domination and syncretic or proselytic forces. Here, the preservation of culture is paramount in the face of forced or attempted acculturation. In contrast, millenarianism rejects both the past and the present as equally representative of spiritual corruption—comprised as it is of corporal sinfulness, materialist, covetous attachment to this world; of evil, senility, disease, wickedness wrought of ignorance, isolation, and/or spiritual calamity. The goal, then, is to strive toward an apocalyptic future that will cleanse, purge, or eradicate the corrupted physical world, bring salvation to the chosen few (i.e., believers), and send down hellfire upon those who reject the clear and prophetic vision of the movement. Where nativism idealizes the cultural past, millenarianism glorifies a transcendental future. It preaches and presages the fall of society in its entirety in favor of a postapocalyptic kingdom of God. Both are linear, both may be militant, but they are heading off in opposing directions. Revitalization movements, in contrast to the above, may choose any number of options, past and future, as well as the rectification of the present in a multitude of possible directions, from reform to importation of foreign elements to the creation of something entirely new (Wallace in Lessa and Vogt 1956: 509). They neither seek necessarily to obliterate the past nor to glorify it, but to amend and reconstitute a social system suffering from some kind of diagnosed terminal failure.

Such movements compete, in one way or another, in North Africa and on the global stage, each working hard to win the affiliation, if not the affinity, of the Amazigh people. In sum, these types of movements—nativistic, revitalization, and millenarian—pull at once in opposing philosophical directions. The indigenous people of North Africa are called *Berber* by Europeans, but prefer their own term *Amazigh,* which translates as "Free People." Those Amazigh with nativistic aspirations demand a return to this condition or mythos of "freedom," and the return to and preservation of some semblance of archetypal Amazigh identity in the face of political, social, and cultural domination by the Arabized Islamic regimes of North Africa. This lost Amazigh identity is more rooted in the remembrance of linguistic and territorial autonomy than in less-materialist spiritual or philosophical dogmas. In contrast, millenarian Islam and Christianity preach of a world laden with secular evils and the terrible wrongness of competing religious ideologies. Islam, however, unlike Christian

Evangelical millenarianism, is designed to bring about that more perfect union well within the material, physical, and political world while at the same time awaiting, perhaps, the wrath of God on Judgment Day. Thus, Islam, which entered North Africa as early as the eighth century, was an inherently political religion that attempted to unify competing Amazigh tribal elements and create a more universalist approach to the social order. The classical 'ummah sought to rule not only over its own people, Muslims, but also over the Peoples of the Book, that is, Jews and Christians as well.

As early converts to Islam, in addition to adhering to Islamic prayer and practice, the Imazighen were directed to give priority to the Arabic language not only through their study and recitation of the Qur'an, but also in the naming of their children and changing of their tribal names. While remote Imazighen resisted the translation of tribal names into Arabic, nevertheless Arabic became the language of the courts, administrative offices, legal documents, and education. Tamazight names and Tifinagh, the ancient indigenous writing system of the Imazighen, became proscribed. Tifinagh degenerated into folk art patterns to be found only in women's henna, tattoo, and textile patterns; pottery; and architecture, such as is found in isolated parts of the High Atlas mountains. Later generations of Imazighen outside these resistant mountainous areas came to speak Arabic almost exclusively and to hold thoroughly Arabic first names and Arabicized surnames. They have come to be seen or think of themselves simply as "Arabs." Thus, Amazigh nationalists argue that given this history, the coming of Islam was designed resolutely, consciously, and purposefully to convert the Amazigh population into Arabs by making them Muslims first. Thus, they argue that Islam was the vehicle of a kind of ethnic cleansing: Amazigh identity would cease to exist, and only Arabs would remain. This nativistic point of view was validated when the governments of five North African nations joined together in 1989, officially forming the *Arab Maghreb Union* (AMU), a designation that remains to this day.

The Islamic political order is designed such that the non-Muslim peoples under the hegemony of the state will have relative autonomy and self-administration, even when their own laws conflict with Islamic law. Thus, the classical Islamic State recognizes, accepts, condones, fosters, and defends the rights of peoples practicing divergent religious customs, as long as these practitioners do not attempt to influence or corrupt Muslims. A strictly scriptural approach to Islam in this way recognizes more than one path to salvation as well as more than one religious law within the confines of the state. Once Muslim, however, an individual or a community is under the jurisdiction of Shari'at law. With the collapse of the Ottoman Empire in 1924, Islamic law came to be subsumed under the colonial rule of the French in North Africa. By the 1960s, these same nations became independent, and their national laws integrated Islamic and European legal systems. Deliberations in each nation of North Africa since independence have focused on the degree to which secular law or religious law prevails.

The Genesis of Amazighité in the Face of Perceived Arabization

The Amazigh, or indigenous peoples of North Africa, were called by the Romans "Berber"—Barbarians—and their coast along the southern Mediterranean and eastern Atlantic, the "Barbary Coast." These appellations gave reference to an unruly people, a people, that is, who are unwilling to be ruled. Their own name for themselves, *Amazigh*, means "Free People," and this name too attests to their resistance to and abhorrence of domination. Fourteenth-century Arabic philosopher and jurist Abd er-Rahman Ibn Khaldûn in his classic introduction to history, *Al Muqaddimah* (1377), spoke of these same qualities:

> The Arabs outnumbered and overpowered the Berbers, stripped them of most of their lands, and also obtained a share of those that remained in their possession. ... Their situation approached the point of annihilation and dissolution. (1989: 30)

and

> Whenever one [Berber] tribe is destroyed, another takes its place and is as refractory and rebellious as the former one had been. Therefore, it has taken the Arabs a long time to establish their dynasty in the land of Ifriqiyah [Tunisia] and the Maghrib [Algeria–Morocco]. (1989: 131)

The Amazigh today, like the Amazigh of the past, fluctuate between the poles of compliance and defiance. Both the terms *Berber* and *Amazigh* capture the quality not only of their resistance but of their long-standing resilience as well. From the outside, it might appear that the Amazigh have long ago given up their struggle to remain culturally, ethnically, territorially, and linguistically distinct as a people. The nations comprising North Africa today, after all, are known collectively as the *Arab* Maghreb Union—as if the entire indigenous population of Morocco, Algeria, Tunisia, Libya, and Mauritania had somehow abdicated Amazighité in favor of Arabism and ceased to be Amazigh at all. For some, this is precisely the case. But not for all. Since the coming of the Arabs and Islam in the seventh century CE, Arabic became the legislative language, Islam the prescribed religion. Amazigh proper names and surnames have been increasingly Arabized, and the naming of a child in Tamazight, the language of the Amazigh people, has long been prohibited by the ruling dynasties in North Africa. Nevertheless, the Amazigh as a people remain, remnants of their language do as well, and in the twentieth century they began to perceive themselves as having been too resilient in the past, and a renewed militancy ensued.

The contemporary Amazigh, or Berber, movement ignited in North Africa when the Algerian government prohibited a conference on ancient Tamazight poetry that was to be held at the University of Tizi-Ouzou in the spring of 1980. The conference had been organized by prolific Algerian writer, poet, playwright, and anthropologist Mouloud Mammeri (see Moukhlis 1994: 63–65). This moment—first known as the "Kabyle Spring" or simply as "the events of Tizi Ouzou"—is known today throughout North Africa, and indeed to Imazighen throughout the world, as the "Amazigh Spring"—the moment of Amazigh reawakening—and Mammeri came to be known as the founder of the modern Amazigh movement. While it could be said that North Africa has had more than its fair share of revolutionary movements—from the bitter war of independence in Algeria (see e.g., Fanon 1967; Gibson 1999) to the antimon-archist socialist opposition in Morocco that culminated in the Ben Barka affair (see e.g., Derogy and Ploquin 1999; Guerin 1991)—it could also be said that the movement to preserve Amazigh language and identity is equally critical, uniformly ignored, and increasingly volatile. And like its predecessors, is as well a conflict that easily could have been averted.

The Algerian government's action at the Tizi Ouzou conference on ancient Tamazight poetry kindled the first-ever demonstrations in the history of the independent state. They began as a protest "merely" against the cancellation of a conference on Kabyle poetry. The protests quickly escalated into full-fledged nativism working toward the larger question of the preservation of indigenous language and culture, as well as a demand for constitutional recognition and teaching of indigenous language at least in primary school education (see esp. Chaker 1975).

The call for Tamazight revival in Algeria was met with increasing suppression, violence, demonstrations, arrests, reputed torture, and assassinations. As a result of the growing volatility in North Africa, the movement came to be coordinated by expatriates—increasingly vitriolic Amazigh intellectuals, artists, and exiles living and working abroad, primarily in France—with enough freedom to publicly lift their voices in Europe but not enough to return home to North Africa again without fear of retribution.

The more Amazigh patriots urged legal recognition of indigenous language and culture, the more governments in North Africa steadfastly embraced Arabism. Indeed, Pan-Arabism had been a growing ideology since the late 1940s, especially in Egypt. Moreover, Arabic was not merely the language of political society but the sacred language of Islamic revelation, the Qur'an, for centuries the dominant religion of the region.

It is simplistic to think that these "larger" identities—Islam and Arabism—were promoted by Maghrebi governments in the twentieth century merely for the sake of eradicating tribal and ethnic provincialisms. Instead, it easily could be argued that there was at the time a more current and formidable adversary

pressing its cultural hegemony: French colonialist and postcolonialist dominance in North Africa. Arabism, and especially Pan-Arabism, was a stronger
position from which to defy European influence, whether manifested in the
political, economic, or cultural domain. Arabism and Islam constituted world
civilizations in their own right, known not simply for their conquests but for
significant contributions to natural philosophy, the arts, and the sciences. "Ber-
berism" on the other hand, was associated, in both the Arab and the European
colonial mind, with something like the nineteenth-century social evolutionary
stage, and was, after all, the prototypical Barbary Coast:

> It is easy to find sarcastic Arab references to Berbers such as the story that
> Adam, father of mankind, had declared Eve to be divorced when he was told
> that she was the mother of the Berbers as of the rest of humanity. But in such
> stories the word *Berber* seems to be used to describe a rustic, illiterate person
> rather than a racial or cultural group. (Barbour, quoted in Norris 1982: 3).

Ibn Khaldûn uses the Berbers as the prime example of a population resistant
to the dynastic authority of Muslim Arabs:

> The first [Muslim] victory over them ... was of no avail. The Muslims mas-
> sacred many of them. After the Muslim religion had been established among
> them, they went on revolting and seceding, and they adopted dissident religious
> opinions many times. They remained disobedient and unmanageable. ... When
> the Muslims deprived them of their power, there remained no one capable of
> making a defence or of offering opposition. (Ibn Khaldûn 1989:131)

From the Amazigh perspective, there can be no excuse for the blatant Arab
Muslim suppression of indigenous identity. Ferhat Mehenni, the passionate Algerian singer/poet who was imprisoned for four years in Algeria for his Amazigh
activism, put it this way:

> The Algerian independence had established arabo-islamism at the expense of
> an "Algerian Algeria," nationalist militants [were] excluded from the [indepen-
> dence movement] in 1949 under the pretext of "berberism." What followed
> was a hardening of the official group invaded by pan-arabist ideology ... against
> anything Amazigh. ... Kabylia [i.e., the heart of the Amazigh movement in Al-
> geria], unjustly accused of secession, will have, to this day, a difficult time in rid-
> ding itself of this terrible image of a dangerous specter of constantly threatening
> national unity. In the name of this latter, the Tamazight language is ferociously
> fought by the "Arabization" policy, the citizen recruitment institutes, as well
> as security services such as police, gendarmes, customs and military security.
> History is falsified; it only starts in the 8th century with the advent of Islam.
> (Mehenni 2000)

Mehenni, in his rage, refused to utter a single word of Arabic since his incarceration, retreating to his natal Kabylie dialect of Algerian Tamazight, and

uses the French language quite literally as his lingua franca, given that his own dialect is, for the most part, incomprehensible to other Tamazight speakers of North Africa. The postindependence Moroccan and Algerian governments, in contrast, remind their citizenry that the French had strategically and systematically attempted to divide and conquer its colonial acquisitions in North Africa in part through a century's worth of provocation, if not blatant propaganda, urging Berber discontent, separatism, and revolt.

Eight years after the Amazigh Spring at Tizi Ouzou, a coalition of five North African nations—Libya, Tunisia, Algeria, Morocco, and Mauritania—met in Algeria to discuss the formation of a "Greater Arab Maghreb." One year later, on 17 February 1989, the five signed a treaty declaring the establishment of the "Arab Maghreb Union" (the AMU). Nine days later, Mouloud Mammeri—Dda Lmulud, as he is known affectionately to Imazighen—was killed (or, as Amazigh militants believe, murdered) in a car accident near Aïn Defla, about a hundred kilometers from Algiers. "On a road," claims one expatriate Amazigh activist, "that is quite ordinary—there is no reason for such an 'accident' to have taken place. Of course it was murder." The University of Tizi-Ouzou at Hasnaoua, where the Amazigh movement began, now bears his name.

Curiously, Mammeri's own name is an Arabized Amazigh name, another reminder of the pervasive Arabization of identity in North Africa. "Mammeri" is a *nisba*, an Arabic grammatical form denoting "belonging to" the Mammer tribe or clan—making the name sound as if the family had emerged from Arab rather than Berber tribal origins. In his bilingual Tamazight and French publication of the Kabyle poetry he so loved—published in 1980, the year the Tizi Ouzou conference was to have been held—Mammeri addresses this effacement of his Amazigh ancestry, restoring the Amazigh tribal appellation, Aït Maammer, to honor his father who had taught him most of the poems he had been so intent on preserving (Mammeri 2001:50). The poems themselves, perhaps, can help us understand what made them appear so threatening, provocative, so dangerous. Some take the form of poetic jousting contests: fighting words between competing tribal fractions. Others are resolute affirmations of Amazigh identity, albeit framed by long, high-context introductions, postscripts, and footnotes of explanation. One poem, for example, by Yusef-u-Qasi speaks of warfare, displacement, the disappearance of villages, the transference of populations, and the little that is left of place and identity, all in four short lines:

Abizar ughalen d Iflisen	The Abizar have fused with the Iflisen,
At Yaader d Izerxfawen	The Aït Aader and Izerkhfawen
Igwra-d Berber d Mira	I'm left only the Berber and Mira [2 very small villages]
Ad wtegh agejdur yessen	To lead the procession of my deep mourning (Mammeri 2001: 74–75, my translation)

Folklore, Folklorization, Film, and the Feminine

What Mammeri, Bourdieu, and others were trying to do was to retrieve Amazigh language and culture not only from national political obscurity, but also from out of the hands of well-meaning ethnographers and folklorists—academics who too easily may treat indigenous culture like so many museum artifacts to be catalogued, shelved, and on rare occasion dusted off to be displayed for the curious. The goal was to return the linguistic heritage to the custody of Amazigh conservators of their own identity, as part of their own living tradition. Mammeri, as a Berber academic and anthropologist, endorsed an indigenous anthropology and devoted his life to the preservation of his own people's language and culture. His father had been a bard in the Kabyle, perhaps one of the last of his kind. Mammeri saw fit that the poetry of his lineage was salvaged before it was lost; anthropology was a fitting vehicle for that preservation.

Whether through ethnographic, folkloric, or political objectification, Arabization or Islamification, the end result had been the same: the marginalization and erosion of indigenous identity. Imazighen claim that so stifled had their language become that in many regions Tamazight women had preserved aspects of their forbidden language and symbols not only woven into the fabric of their tapestries or inscribed upon their pots, but tattooed upon their own bodies and the bodies of their daughters. Indeed, the word *Tamazight* denotes both "Berber language" and "Berber woman." Tamazight written text, with the exception of the Tuareg, or Aswara of the Sahara, had been for the most part extinguished. Until quite recently, many, if not most, Imazighen have believed that they have had no written language at all.

Despite the requisite Arab national identity, Amazigh symbols have survived, primarily through the efforts of women. Imazighen remain for the most part matrilineal, in contrast to the surrounding Arab culture and most of the Islamic world. They have an enduring affinity for surrender to the feminine will, if not downright matriarchy. While patriots may honor their mothers and grandmothers for painfully preserving the symbols of Amazigh identity upon their bodies and the bodies of their daughters, Islam condemns tattooing as *haram*, a forbidden act. *Lonely Planet,* one of numerous guidebooks to "exotic" Morocco, however, has no such prohibition; Moroccan tattoo patterns splashed liberally throughout their guidebook no doubt help to sell not just their publication but the country as well. The custom of tattooing, however, is frowned upon as backward and, well, barbaric, in addition to the Islamic sanction against it.

Ironically, there is no question that the rubric of "folklore" has helped to sustain the material culture of Amazigh identity. The forms, however, are increasingly static, frozen in time, commodified. They are, paradoxically, also shifting to adapt to the global marketplace. Tribal textiles, for example, can be ordered over the internet these days, in sizes or colors modified to accommodate the desires of any international buyer.

The survival of the signs and symbols of Amazigh identity through the arts and crafts of women has been well documented. Despite longstanding Islamic condemnation, in the Amazigh territories of Morocco and Algeria where the written language had been lost, women retained a decorative epigraphy of their own, preserving a small portion of the original Tifinagh, or Tamazight script along with magical and healing symbols of their own. These remain in specific arts and crafts: weaving (see Reswick 1985; Khatibi 1994); pottery (see e.g., Gabus 1958; Sijelmassi 1986; Courtney-Clarke and Brooks 1996); body arts such as henna, tattooing, and harkous (e.g., Searight 1984); in addition to ritual and belief (Doutté 1908; Westermarck 1926; Mazel 1971; Akhmisse 1985) and women's exclusive symbols and magical practice (Laoust-Chantreaux 1939; Makilam 1996, 1999). In Tunisia, on the other hand, even the oral language has, for the most part, disappeared. Nevertheless, even Tunisia's renowned Sejnane women potters continue to produce unadorned Amazigh epigraphic angular geometric patterns in their pottery, in sharp contrast to the ornate and colorful swirling flourishes of Arabic and Islamic motifs, colors, and designs.

The works cited above by European authors, with the exception of Doutté, Laoust-Chantreaux, and Westermarck, treat women's epigraphy as entirely decorative, while Maghrebi authors imbue it with cultural, magical, and linguistic meaning—as language. Searight, who wrote the most definitive, although unpublished, three volumes on Moroccan women's tattoo patterns, goes so far as to insist that there is no relation between women's body arts and Tamazight epigraphy. North Africans, both male and female, disagree, claiming that Berber women have preserved language and *meaning* on their bodies and in their crafts, not just decorative patterns, since the Arab conquest and the coming of Islam—some insist it has been since Punic times. Linguistic evidence and Berber ideology equate woman and language: in every Berber dialect, the same word is used to denote both "Berber woman" and "Berber language." The only written work that acknowledges this relationship also dismisses and disparages it in favor of promoting Islamic identification and Arabic calligraphic aesthetics. In a classic dualistic argument separating the sacred from the profane, Khatibi relegates Berber women's tattooing decidedly to the ranks of the crude, unrefined, and provincial, in contrast to the inspired sophistication of Arabic calligraphy. The flowing script carries us closer to the mystical appreciation of the divine, a unique contribution of Islamic civilization's marriage of aesthetics and spirituality (see e.g., Khatibi 1986; Khatibi and Amahan 1995).

The Arab Maghreb Union would be quite pleased to watch Amazigh identity slip back into a rustic, folkloric obscurity, found primarily after a good long trek at higher altitudes. Amazighité is as much a natural resource to be ex-

ploited to attract tourists as the mountains themselves, providing photogenic
backdrops and exotic "scenery." The film industry has long been enamored with
the North African physical and cultural "otherness" of Berber territory. Most
famous is perhaps George Lucas' *Star Wars* series, which not only filmed on
location at the granaries of Ksar Haddad and troglodyte dwellings Matmata in
southern Tunisia, but also adopted Berber clothing as extraterrestrial couture.
Lucas named his "alien planet" *Tatooïne* for the southern Tunisian oasis of Tata-
ouine. Lucas is not even the first to model an extraterrestrial ecosystem and
social order on Berber territory. That honor belongs to Frank Herbert, author
of the *Dune* series. In addition to spicing his fictional vernacular with a smat-
tering of Tamazight dialect, Herbert also named his alien heroes "Fremen"—
free men—a literal translation of the term *Amazigh*—the name Berbers call
themselves. Exotic customs, tribalized crafts, specialized eco-adaptations—the
lure of Berber exoticism has been maximized in Morocco and Tunisia, whose
"other" natural resources pale in comparison to its oil- and natural gas–rich
sister states of Libya and Algeria. Folkorization is a multibillion-dollar industry
and fundamental to Moroccan and Tunisian economic policy.

In Imilchil, one of a number of remote villages in the High Atlas Mountains
of Morocco, the very "Berber"ity of the place is plastered on postcards, posters,
brochures, and covers of *National Geographic Magazine* as the "authentic," primordial Morocco. Its so-called marriage market—where young women are reputed to select their husbands the way they might pick a juicy piece of fruit—is
micromanaged by governmental incentives to encourage participation. In Imilchil and the surrounding villages, women don their distinctive striped henbil
blankets and renowned tribal facial markings only once a year—for the gov-
ernment-subsidized *moussem*, or marriage festival (see e.g., Behri 1994). The
rest of the year Imilchil is indeed an authentic Amazigh village; matrilineal,
yes, seminomadic, yes. But also tuned in to the world through cell phones and
satellite dishes, and men off working abroad. And on the broken, twisted *other*
road to Imilchil, the road that no tourist or photojournalist is likely to see,
spray-painted upon the cliff and rising angrily at least ten feet tall is the symbol
of Amazigh liberation and a hugely scrawled declaration climbing up the cliff
in French, German, and English: "We are Free People Here." *Amazigh* in any
dialect is a proclamation of freedom (although it has at times been translated
as "nobility" [see e.g., Norris 1982]). It is this act of defiance that speaks of
Amazigh authenticity more than the now staged and choreographed, filmed
and photographed charade of painted girls like painted ponies that fill the
glossy pages of coffee table picture books.

"Take some time to learn a few basic Berber words," the *Lonely Planet* guidebook to Morocco urges vacationing trekkers in the High Atlas (Gordon, Talbot, and Simonis 1998: 485). But while the Ministry of Tourism may smile
benignly at this suggestion, the Ministry of Justice is loathe to allow Imazighen

the same privilege. Despite the plea for instruction, Berber dialects are not taught to schoolchildren. Nor may monolingual Imazighen be brought to trial in a language they understand. Tamazight language is not simply unofficial in Morocco and Algeria, it is suppressed, and under some circumstances, illegal. Parents are forbidden, for example, to name their children indigenous Amazigh names; only officially sanctioned Arabic names are permissible.

The Costs and Benefits of Language Affiliation

The earliest studies of Tifinagh, the epigraphic written form of Tamazight dialects, were conducted primarily by Captain Louis Rinn in the 1880s (see e.g., Rinn 1882–1895). There appears to have been little interest in Berber languages until the 1960s, with the exception of Charles de Foucault's four-volume dictionary of Tuareg dialect of the Ahaggar region of the Algerian Sahara (1940), and the linguistic "notes," or brief archaeological descriptions of epigraphic inscriptions (see e.g., Basset 1923; Marcy 1934–37). It is important to point out that Captain Rinn was a French colonial officer and that Père de Foucault's linguistic studies, too, were a means to a very specific end. His primary intention in the Sahara was to convert the Tuareg to Christianity, and thereby, save their souls. For this, and his ultimate "martyrdom" outside of Tamanrasset, he was beatified by the pope on 13 November 2006 and is being considered for canonization. While Père de Foucault's forté may not have been saving souls from hellfire, his legacy from the Amazigh point of view lies in his faithful appreciation for and preservation of Tifinagh, the indigenous Tamazight script. He did not render Tamazight language into Latin script, as Mammeri later did. And, in addition to his French-Tuareg dictionary, Père de Foucault chose to translate not the Bible—but Antoine de Saint-Exupéry's *The Little Prince* into Tifinagh, faithfully reproducing every drawing in the book. Perhaps he thought the Tuareg would identify with de Saint-Exupéry's Saharan fantasy. Three-quarters of a century later, pages of Foucault's Tamazight version of *The Little Prince* is proudly featured in the pages of the *Revue Tifinagh*, the journal of Tamazight language study.

From the 1960s to 1980s—i.e., during the development period following independence from France—the perspective of Tunisians, especially in the countryside, was fairly straightforward: speaking Arabic Arabizes; speaking French Frenchifies, and speaking "Berber" was unthinkable. Each language came with a full set of cultural, religious, and economic expectations. The approach to language usage was based upon constant reevaluation of situational costs and benefits. Each language was considered a powerful indicator of class and/or religiosity, and could be shifted strategically for economic or political gain and survival; language was not seen as a fixed statement of identity as much as a statement of opportunity (Zussman 1992, 2000). If speaking Arabic or French can make one's family more secure, Tunisians have been all for it. In Morocco and Algeria, the attitude has been decidedly less pecuniary. There, Amazigh identity has been guarded more tenaciously, and the advantages of assimilation have been eschewed in favor of reassertion of indigenous identity despite, as we have seen, strong economic and political disincentives.

The language revival movement generated by Mammeri's thwarted conference on Kabylie poetry came to be coordinated by expatriate North Africans in France, with the goal of full cultural revitalization both through promotion of the Tamazight oral tradition (spoken word, poetry, and song) and revival of the written epigraphic orthography. To this end, Mammeri founded the Center for Amazigh Studies and Research and the *AWAL Review* in Paris in 1984. Fellow Amazigh anthropologist Tassadit Yacine and French anthropologist Pierre Bourdieu, who had conducted fieldwork in the Kabyle (1985), supported him in this endeavor. In fact, Mammeri and Bourdieu collaborated on a piece that was published in the first issue of *AWAL* promoting what would now likely be called "advocacy anthropology," befittingly entitled "Du bon usage de l'ethnologie"—"Good Use of Ethnology" (1985). The ensuing scholarship in France continued the linguistic tradition of documenting the varying Berber dialects (e.g., Halevy 1974; Chafik 1980–1982; Chaker 1994).

Regional variation, however, provided a strong barrier to the establishment of an ethnic collective consciousness. How could Amazighité be promoted if each mountain enclave spoke a tenaciously held, distinctive dialect? Studies soon turned to proposals for linguistic standardization (e.g., Mountassir 1999; Oulhaj 2000) and thus, cultural unification (e.g., Aït Amrane 1997; Benyounes 1997, 2000; Chemini 1997; and the *Revue Tifinagh*, 1990s). To this end, the Paris-based Berber Research Center at the Institut National des Langues Orientales and the Center for Amazigh Studies and Research have played a crucial role. The programs provide both undergraduate and graduate degree programs in Amazigh studies, such as linguistics and anthropology, and publish scholarly journals to disseminate the growing body of research. One of the notable contributions coming out of the Center for Amazigh Studies and Research in Paris is the massive international bibliography on Amazighité produced by Lamara Bougchiche (1997) and published by *AWAL*, in collaboration with Ibis Press. Bougchiche thanks her professor of Hamito-Semitic studies, M. Cohen, for the encouragement that "one must never interrupt the chain of knowledge" (Bougchiche 1997: 4). It is a moving acknowledgement, appropriate to a volume so clearly devoted both to knowledge in its more abstract academic sense, and to knowledge that must be passed from generation to generation—knowledge essential to ethnic and cultural survival.

Less scholarly journals, like *Tifinagh*, a journal published in Rabat, Morocco, beginning in 1994, serve a similar role in a more populist setting. Each issue of

Tifinagh (the word denoting Tamazight's own distinctive alphabetic writing) provides a chart of the mid-1990s standardization of the Berber writing system, as well as helpful tips, lessons, and exercises to aid in Tamazight literacy. For some Imazighen, especially in the Middle Atlas Mountains, *Tifinagh* provides not only their first encounter with their own indigenous writing system but also their first knowledge that they had ever had one. The journal has been used judiciously by those so motivated to educate themselves about their language and identity. For some, this has meant teaching themselves to speak, read, and write a language and study a history of which they had no prior knowledge. The first primers, grammars, and dictionaries are only just being produced (e.g., Oulhaj's standardized Tamazight grammar, 2000). Dissemination is problematic.

Pro-Islamicist North Africans, especially those who no longer identify themselves as "Imazighen," argue against indigenous separatist nationalisms, claiming that Islam transcends both ethnicity and national borders. This is certainly not a new Islamic ideology. It was central in the formative period of Islam: tribalism foments dissention, factionalism, territorial disputes, and provides only limited responsibility for the welfare of others, based entirely upon kinship and proximity of relatedness. In contrast, the Qur'an speaks of a community of believers, the 'ummah, which holds responsibility for all Muslims (and even non-Muslims living under an Islamic state) regardless of one's station of birth, tribal affiliation, race, or ethnic identity. Islam, from its inception, rejected religion as the sole property of a particular people, tied to a particular land. Further, Islam hoped to provide the antidote to ethnic religious exclusivism. By being extraterritorial and extragenealogical, Islamic affiliation could unite all peoples through shared faith: unification through truth.

Ibn Khaldûn, the fourteenth-century Islamic philosopher/historian, proposed that Islamic faith could provide a solidarity (*'assabiya*) more powerful and even more enduring than kinship. Ibn Khaldûn actually took this idea much further:

> It is in [this] sense that one must understand Muhammad's remark, 'Learn as much of your pedigrees as is necessary to establish your ties of kindred.' It means that pedigrees are useful only in so far as they imply the close contact that is a consequence of blood ties and that eventually leads to mutual help and affection. Anything beyond that is superfluous. For a pedigree is something imaginary and devoid of reality. (Ibn Khaldûn 1967: 99)

Genealogies can be bought and sold in the marketplace, adoptions are commonplace, and a man might never know his true blood ties. While Ibn Khaldûn is cognizant of the politics and potential abuses of religious propaganda, he firmly believes that the most binding and potent affiliation is that which unifies through a sense of shared spiritual belief, that which is rooted in God. Politics alone (read: politics rooted in shared kinship alone) can never transcend worldly interests (Ibn Khaldûn 1967: 155). Only one's link to the divine is eternal. While this message may be explicit in scripturalist Islamic teachings, it has remained an ideal far from the practice of Muslims in the Middle East and North Africa, where tribe and ethnicity remains a viable ascribed identity.

Nevertheless, the goal of scriptural Islam is the establishment of the 'ummah—a community of believers, regardless of territorial borders, ethnicities, or racial morphologies. Islam can provide spiritual globalism, in addition to insuring a place in the hereafter. The Arabic language, then, from an Islamic perspective, is quite literally the language of Allah. To reject Arabic is to reject Islam, the 'ummah, and one's place in the hereafter—in addition to being an illegal act in the Arab Maghrebi Union.

Amazigh advocates counter this with a query. Why then, they ask, has the sacred Qur'an been translated into almost every language on earth, except their own? The most common Islamic response has been that the Berbers do not have a written language, nor an adequate standardized language suitable for such an endeavor. In effect, the argument comes close to proclaiming that the Berbers, unlike Muslims throughout the rest of the globe, in fact, have no "real" language at all. An attempt at a Tamazight translation of the Qur'an was not begun until the 1990s. The project remains controversial, proscribed, and as yet unfinished (see Naït-Zerrad 1998).

Nationalist assimilationists support Arabism with or without its religious affiliation or promise of everlasting paradise. For the older generation, which still remembers the struggles for independence, Arab identity confers a kind of legitimacy in opposition to the French, Europe, and the colonial enterprise. For the pragmatist, identification with the Arab world is axiomatic. Satellite dishes are ubiquitous in North Africa. There are a plethora of television shows from the Arab world that simply take no effort to watch. Arabic is, after all, the default language throughout the Maghreb. It is in the cities, on the streets, in the courts, and taught at school. No need to struggle deciphering an antiquated, unfamiliar alphabet. No need to seek out a language that almost no one, except one's grandmother, will ever understand. For the assimilationist Arabized Berber, Arabic is the status quo, and the attempt to overthrow it is frivolous, radical, and dangerous.

Enter the Evangelicals

Christianity has had a long and complex history in North Africa, and there was a time—albeit, a very long time ago—when the church flourished from Egypt to Algeria. Saint Augustine, after all, was a Berber, born in Thagaste (today's Souk Ahras) in Algeria's now militantly Amazigh Kabylia. Would not Saint Augustine be a good place to start in the "reconversion" of the Berbers to Christianity? Imazighen rebut the significance of Saint Augustine, noting that he rejected the Amazigh (read: "pagan") ancestry of his father in favor of the Romanized identity of his mother, Monnica. Since traditional Amazigh identity is matrifocal, Saint Augustine's adherence to the Christianity of his mother can be understood both in keeping with the matrifocality of Amazighité and in keeping with rejecting his having Berber identity at all, despite his Thagaste birthplace. He is therefore either a traitorous, Romanized Berber or no Berber at all.

Curiously, and in keeping with the Saint Augustine/Berber debate, John K. Ryan, translator of the *Confessions* of Saint Augustine, does him the injustice (from an Amazigh point of view) of referring to Thagaste today as an "Arab" village, in keeping with the post-Islamic Arabization of the region. Ryan further denigrates the indigenous population (again, from an Amazigh point of view) as having endorsed and practiced "magical rites, human sacrifice, and certain abominable practices" as part of their religious life—further elevating and separating Saint Augustine from his rustic roots (Ryan 1960: 18–20). Saint Augustine, then, from a Christian point of view, is considered to have risen above the base practices of his natal region to spiritual heights at the heart of Roman Christendom. And from the Amazigh point of view, Saint Augustine is a good example of the all-too-common rejection of both the language and culture of Tamazgha. Thus, whether from a Christian or an Amazigh point of view, there is debate over Saint Augustine as a good selling point in the re-Christianization of North Africa:

> If I have to consider St. Augustine as a traitor who adopted a language and culture not his own, I have to first treat as a traitor all those who have proposed a foreign language and culture, starting with the dynasty of Massyssiles of Massinissa up to Ptolemy … then all the Berbers who have used Arabic, and finally, those who use French: Boulifa, Belaid, Aït Ali, Feraoun, Mammeri, Chaker, Sadi, Aït Ahmed, … and even you who use French to write your message, you should be writing in Tamazight, but I doubt you even have the capacity to do so! (Iferman, 7 janvier 2007, Kabyle.com forum; *L'olivier de saint Augustin*—my translation)

Thus, for some contemporary Imazighen, as for Iferman above, Saint Augustine is not significantly different from contemporary Berbers who accept Arabic—or French—as their primary language, including Mouloud Mammeri and Salem Chaker, both key figures in the founding of the Amazigh movement in the twentieth century. Amazigh activist Ferhat Mehenni, too, in this light is not so different from Saint Augustine. He may protest against Arabism, but he has adopted France and French-speaking as Augustine adopted Rome.

Lucien Oulahbib in his consideration of the relationship between Berbers and Christianity in the age of Saint Augustine, argues that Christianity missed a point that Islam, three centuries later, did not in its appeal throughout the Middle East, and particularly in North Africa. This is the preeminent attachment in the region to tribalism (Oulahbib 2004: 22–24). Islam succeeded because it did not threaten tribal structure. In this way, the Amazigh were expected to acculturate well to Arabic customary practice. Further, the form of Islamic law adhered to in North Africa is Maliki Shari'at law—the most supportive of all the Islamic legal traditions of preexisting customary tribal practice. However, while some Amazigh tribes assimilated, linguistically at least, becoming what appeared to be "Arab" tribes, others strenuously resisted.

Evangelical Christians have been exploring the most effective strategies in proselytizing the as-yet unconverted, or "unreached peoples" of the world— particularly in the Islamic world. Out of the current "Top Ten Unreached" peoples of the world of the Joshua Project—a Christian Evangelical Project devoted to converting all non-Christian peoples to Christianity—nine of the ten are Islamic cultures.

The Berbers, or "Moors" as they are called on the Joshua Project Top Ten, are listed as number ten (Joshua Project 2007). Electronic evangelism for un-reached peoples is ubiquitous on the Internet. One advantage of this approach is that in situ evangelism can exact the death penalty in Islamic countries. Not only is proselytism illegal, but conversion from Islam to another religion is illegal as well. Nevertheless, there are militant Imazighen who claim, in the privacy of their own homes, that they are no longer Muslim—or even, that they and their mothers and their mother's mother never have been Muslim. That Islam is as foreign an imposition as French colonialism was. But in public, such Imazighen do not display their non-Islamic (or anti-Islamic) sentiments or identity. But neither does this necessarily draw them to Christianity.

One of the new strategies of Christian Evangelicals targeting the Islamic world advocates a "paradigm shift" for the proselytizing of "shame" cultures. This approach is perhaps a corollary of Mammeri's own spawning of the Amazigh movement, in that it is the use of anthropological methods and/or understand-ing to create conditions of change. The advocate of the "Gospel for Shame Cultures" is Bruce Thomas, an American Evangelical working in Indonesia. "I have discovered," he states, "that one of the most difficult aspects of evangeliz-ing Muslims is getting them to appreciate their need for a Savior. ... Muslims tend to be unaware of their sinfulness" (Thomas 1994: 1).

The classic distinction between "shame" cultures and "guilt" cultures is that the former externalizes culpability while the latter internalizes it. In shame cul-tures, it is the public display of wrongdoings that is central to social control. In guilt cultures, internal retrospection is expected to be sufficient to be aware of one's own sinfulness. Thus, it is easier to proselytize those who have internal-ized their own sinful nature, for they come to their new religion ready to be personally absolved and cleansed of their own wrongdoing. In shame cultures, there is much less emphasis on personal guilt. One shames one's entire family, lineage, village, community, and people. A personal savior cannot readily purify such communicable transgression.

Thus, Thomas comes to the realization that Muslims do not worry as much about lying and cheating ("little sins" in Islam, according to Thomas) as they do about ceremonial purity, such as the abomination of eating pork. He states succinctly, "Thus, because eating pork is the worst possible state of defilement and more attention is given to ceremonial purity than moral purity, the pork eater (George Bush) is worse off than a murderer (Saddam Hussein)" (Thomas 1994: 1–2). Given his epiphany, he proposes proselytizing Muslims through their "deliverance from the tyranny of being in a near constant state of defilement" (1994: 2). He correlates the Islamic "problem" of defilement with the Christian notion of "original sin." The approach then is to demonstrate that man cannot cleanse himself of defilement, but that Christ has done so already. Thomas critiques Christian evangelism as having focused primarily on guilt cultures rather than shame cultures, stating that when Christianity takes into consideration this new cultural frame, Muslims will be more receptive to the Gospel and redemption, and the new approach could revolutionize Christian outreach in the "most resistant parts of the world" (1994: 6).

While Thomas's paradigm shift has yet to demonstrate efficacy in the Middle East and North Africa, another quasi-anthropological approach is proposed by Let Us Reason Ministries, an online Pentecostal mission. Here, a new proselytizing methodology called "redeeming the cultures" has demonstrated if not efficacy then at least relevance to the Amazigh cause. "One can find the purest thing a culture holds and make Christ relatable to them in His holiness" recommends an article on "Culturizing Christianity" (letusreason.org 2007: 1). Here, Christian missions to the indigenous peoples of North Africa have struck gold.

While maintaining a strictly millenarian ideology, Christian Evangelicals have adopted strategic nativistic methodologies. If Islam thrived in North Africa by appealing to the retention of tribal structure (while at the same time attempting to eradicate its Amazigh cultural content), contemporary Evangelicals are appealing directly to Amazighité—promising preservation of language and culture, and the eradication of a culturally hegemonic Islam. While to this day there is no complete Qur'anic translation into Tamazight dialects, the Gospels have been translated into many regional dialects of North Africa. They are available in writing and as MP3 audio files, with instructions online in Tamazight and four European languages—designed perhaps, with expatriate Berbers in mind.

This approach is reminiscent of Père Charles de Foucault, who, in his long sojourn and hermitage in the Hoggar Mountains of the Algerian Sahara, created the very first Tamazight dictionary and translated de Saint Exupéry's *The Little Prince* into the Tuareg dialect, thinking perhaps, the story would resonate with the true inhabitants of the Sahara. While at the time circa 1906–1916) his efforts were little heeded, a century later his efforts adorn numerous issues of the journal *Tifinagh*, which is dedicated to the resurrection of Tamazight written word. Like Père Charles de Foucault, who was beatified in Rome on 13 November 2006 for his sacrifice and martyrdom in the Sahara, contemporary Evangelicals have as yet no record of effective conversions to Christianity. Nevertheless, their embrace of Tamazight as a language worthy of conveying Christian sacred texts has not gone unnoticed by Amazigh patriots.

The translation of the Gospels into Tamazight constitutes an excellent example of the new Evangelical strategy of "culturizing Christianity" and finding "the purest thing a culture holds" as a vehicle for the transmission of their millenarian message.

Conclusions

North Africans today are actively debating competing models for reframing their identity. Perhaps the question to ask is, "Why now?" The Arabo-Islamic venture in North Africa began in the seventh to eighth centuries with the founding of the Great Mosque of Kairouan in Tunisia under the Umayyad Dynasty. Is there anything new in the prevailing dominance of Islamic culture and Arabic language in the Maghreb? And why is ethnic identity at stake here and not, say, in Indonesia or Pakistan, where Arabization is not a threat? Some Berbers answer this by saying that they have been too hospitable in the past, too weak, too adaptable to conquerors—regardless of Arab Muslim perceptions to the contrary—too easily swayed by those claiming to bring them the cultural refinement of a superior civilization. Tamazgha allowed herself to become the Arab Maghreb Union and now, before cultural annihilation is complete, it is time finally to put a stop to it.

Amazigh militants reject both Islam and Arabism, claiming that Islam is nothing more than a mask for Arabism rather than the reverse. They complain that the building of enormous mosques in modest mountain (read: Berber) towns is provocative, coercive Arabism. It is seen not as an expression of governmental devotion to Islam, spirituality, or some generalized form of religiosity, but rather as an attempt to placate Arab states' investment in the Maghreb. Surely, the Arab presence in North Africa is no more or less significant than a hundred years ago, or a thousand?

What makes "now" a juncture in the struggle to maintain identity? Or is it *always* a question of "now"? Always a struggle, always a sense of urgency, always just the moment before that final, impending, imminent cultural demise? What is it about "now"? There are many possible speculations. Is it the threat of global homogenization? It is the cell phone that links the tribal Berber transhumant nomad in Imilchil to his cousin, the intellectual Amazigh activist in Paris. Is it the satellite dish that emits unending transmissions of Islamic sermons, intoxicating Syrian soap operas, worldwide Arab news coverage, and pure entertainment in an Arabic well enough understood—or soon to be understood—by all? French and American programming often appears in North Africa already dubbed into Arabic, while Tamazight programming remains almost unheard of—except in Christian Evangelical broadcasts and downloadable audio files. And in which dialect would that Tamazight program be transmitted? Experiments in radio and television transmission in the newly constructed *fabriqué-en-France* neo-Tamazight have been problematic at best: no one can understand them. The construction of a unified Amazighité speaking a universal neo-Tamazight, written in a Tifinagh script agreed upon by scholars in committee, returning to Tamazgha, the Promised Land, appears a fairy tale, an impossible pipe dream. Yet Christian Evangelicals have not found the plethora of Tamazight dialects an impediment to the spread of their message. They continue their translations into Tamazight, slowly, one dialect at a time.

And as for the Internet, it is primarily in French, or perhaps in a neoglobalized English, in which the debate over ethnic survival takes place. And yet, and yet, against all odds, identities survive. They survive inquisitions and holocausts, discrimination, assimilation, and attempts at ethnic "cleansing." The model is there. It can be done. Is it worth it? This is the debate.

The Amazigh movement continues to grow in North Africa and in the Amazigh diaspora in good part because it is perceived that the preservation of Amazighité culture and language are no threat to the nation-state, no threat to Islam, nor even to Arabism. Instead, it is an opportunity, an exercise in unification that could provide strong historical and cultural raison d'être to the Maghreb Union itself, reinforcing the shared legacy of the past at the same time as it faces the political and economic imperatives of the future.

A curious feature of globalism, however, is that it puts all identities at risk—and at the same time, makes all potentially viable. Nowhere and no one is inaccessible, nowhere is remote. There is today a World Amazigh Congress, not simply a spontaneous, invisible protest of the closure of an isolated ancient poetry conference. Likewise, there is an expanding worldwide Islamic identity. A growing Arabism. An active Evangelical movement. An increased concern with international politics and world markets. Identity, even ethnic identity, increasingly becomes personal "choice" rather than an ascribed identity—at least, in the Amazigh diaspora or in the privacy of one's own North African home, or in the anonymity of one's online persona. One student "chatting" online in an Amazigh forum put it succinctly:

> . . . Globally, I'm berber, moroccan, muslim, and worldcitizen. My home is the whole world. Have a nice day. (quoted in Zussman 2001)

"Globally, I'm berber . ...." In the ongoing (re)construction of identity, it may well be more the process of engagement that matters, rather than the retrieval or manufacture of any "authentic" final product.

This, and more, for Galina, with love

REFERENCES

Aït Amrane, Mohamed Idir. 1997. *Pour la Renaissance et le Développement de Tamazight.* Rabat: Editions Hiwar Com.

Akhmisse, Moustapha. 1985. *Médecine, Magie et Sorcellerie au Maroc—ou L'Art tradition-nel de Guerir.* Casablanca: Imprimerie Eddar El Beida.

Behri, Mohammad. 1994. "Femmes berbères à vendre." *Tifinagh: Revue Mensuelle de Culture et de Civilisation Maghrebine* 1: 70–73.

Benyounes, Arav. 1997. *Imazighen: Idelli Ass-A—Berbères: Hier et Aujourd'hui.* Quebec: Collection: Mémoire/Culture.

———. 2000. *Tamazgha: Amqun!—Sortie de Secours: Une Confédération Maghrebine.* Boucherville, QC: Marc Veilleux Imprimeur.

Bougchiche, Lamara. 1997. *Langues et Littératures Berbères des Origines à Nos Jours: Bibliographie Internationale.* Paris: Awal-Ibis Press.

Bourdieu, Pierre. 1985. *Sociologie de l'Algérie.* Paris: PUF.

Courtney-Clarke, Margaret, and Geraldine Brooks. 1996. *Imazighen: The Vanishing Traditions of Berber Women.* New York: Clarkson Potter Publishers.

Derogy, Jacques and Frederic Ploquin. 1999. *Ils ont Tué Ben Barka: Révélations sur un crime d'États.* Paris: Fayard.

Doutté, Edmond. 1908. *Magie et Réligion dans l'Afrique du Nord.* Paris: J. Maisonneuve.

Foucault, Charles de. 1940. *Dictionnaire Touareg-Français: Dialecte de l'Ahaggar,* 4 vols. Paris: Impremerie Nationale.

Gibson, Nigel, ed. 1999. *Rethinking Fanon: The Continuing Dialogue.* New York: Humanity Books.

Gordon, Frances, Dorinda Talbot, and Damien Simonis. 1998. *Morocco.* Hawthorn, Australia: Lonely Planet Publications.

Guérin, Daniel. 1991. *Ben Barka, Ses Assassins.* Paris: Syllepse & Périscope.

Ibn Khaldûn, Abderrahman. 1989 (1377) *The Muqaddimah: An Introduction to History.* Princeton, NJ: Bollingen Series.

Iferman. 2007. In "L'olivier de saint Augustin." http://www.kabyle.com/L-olivier-de-saint-Augustin.html (last accessed in 2008).

Keith, Michael, and Steven Pile, eds. 1993. *Place and the Politics of Identity.* New York: Routledge.

Khatibi, Abdelkebir. 1986. *La Blessure du Nom Propre.* Paris: Denoël.

Khatibi, Abdelkebir and Ali Amahan. 1995. *From Sign to Image.* Casablanca: Edition Lak International.

Laoust-Chantreaux, Germaine. 1939. *Kabylie Côté Femmes: La Vie Féminine à Ait Hichem 1937–1939.* Paris: Edisud.

Linton, Ralph. 1943. "Nativistic Movements." In *Reader in Comparative Religion, An Anthropological Approach,* 2nd. ed., ed. W. Lessa and E. Vogt, 499–506. New York: Harper and Row.

Makilam (pseudonym). 1996. *La Magie des Femmes Kabyles et l'Unité de la Societé Traditionelle.* Paris: L'Harmattan.

Makilam (pseudonym). 1999. *Signes et Rituels Magiques des Femmes Kabyles.* Paris: Edisud.

Mammeri, Mouloud. 2001. *Poèmes Kabyles Anciens.* Paris: La Découverte.

Mammeri, Mouloud, and Pierrre Bourdieu. 1985. "Du bon usage de l'ethnologie." *AWAL:* 17–29.

Mazel, Jean. 1971. *Enigmes du Maroc.* Paris: Editions Robert Laffont.

Mehenni, Ferhat. 2000. "The Origins of Amazigh Spring." *Le Matin,* April 19. Translated for the World Amazigh Action Coalition website by F. Sadok. http://www.waac .org/amazigh/origins_amazigh_spring.html.

Moukhlis, Mouha. 1994. "Hommage à Mouloud Mammeri." *Tifinagh: Revue Mensuelle de Culture et de Civilization Maghrebine,* no. 2 (Fev./Mars): 63–65.

Naït-Zerrad, Kamal. 1998. *Lexique Religieux Berbère et Néologie: Un Essai de Traduction Partielle du Coran.* Milan: Centro Studi Camito-Semitici di Milano and the Agraw Adelsan n Imazighen deg Telyan (Associazione Culturale Berbera in Italia).

Norris, H. T. 1982. *The Berbers in Arabic Literature.* Beirut: Librairie du Liban.

Oulahbib, Lucien. 2004. *Les Berbères et le Christianisme.* Paris: Editions Berbères.

Oulhaj, Lahcen. 2000. *Grammaire du Tamazight: Eléments pour une Standardisation.* Rabat: Centre Tarik ibn Zyad.

Reswick, Irmtraud. 1985. *Traditional Textiles of Tunisia and Related North African Weavings.* Seattle: University of Washington Press.

Rinn, Louis. 1882–1885. "Essai d'étude linquistiques et ethnologiques sur les origines Berbères." *Revue Africaine—Journal des Travaux de la Société Historique Algérienne,* vols. 26, 28, 29, 37.

Searight, Susan. 1985. *The Use and Function of Tattooing on Moroccan Women,* 3 vols. New Haven, CT: Human Relations Area Files.

Sijelmassi, Mohammed. 1986. *Les Arts Traditionnels au Maroc.* Casablanca: ACR Edition/ Vilo.

Talmon, Yonina. 1962. "Pursuit of the Millennium: The Relation between Religion and Social Change." In *Reader in Comparative Religion, An Anthropological Approach,* 2nd. ed., ed. W. Lessa and E. Vogt, 522–37. New York: Harper and Row.

Thomas, Bruce. 1994. "The Gospel for Shame Cultures: A Paradigm Shift." In *EMO,* July 1994, posted on http://guide.gospelcom.net/resources/shame.php.

Wallace, Anthony F. C. 1956. "Revitalization Movements." In *Reader in Comparative Religion, An Anthropological Approach,* 3rd. ed., ed. W. Lessa and E. Vogt, 503–12. New York: Harper and Row.

Wallace, Anthony F. C. 1970. "Revitalization Movements." In *Magic, Witchcraft and Religion, An Anthropological Study of the Supernatural*, 4th. ed., ed. A. Lehmann and J. Myers, 336–41. Mountain View, CA: Mayfield Publishing.

Westermarck, Edward. 1926. *Ritual and Belief in Morocco*, 2 vols. New Hyde Park, NY: University Books.

Zussman, Mira. 1992. *Development and Disenchantment in Rural Tunisia: The Bourguiba Years*. Boulder, CO: Westview Press.

———. 2000. "Baraka: Grace, Healing and Political Legitimacy in the Middle East and North Africa." In *Mythology, Medicine, and Healing: Transcultural Perspectives*, ed. S. Krippner and H. Kalweit, 87–102. Berlin: Yearbook of Cross-Cultural Medicine and Psychotherapy. (German and English).

———. 2001. "Amazigh Nativism, Islam, and De-Arabization: The Berber Language Revival Movement in Global Perspective." In *Ethnic Identities & Political Action in Post-Cold War Europe*. Xanthi, Greece: International Democritus Foundation, University of Thrace.

Self-Exploders, Self-Sacrifice, and the Rhizomic Organization of Terrorism[1]

Don Handelman

The human bombs of today's terrorism are self-exploders. I do not refer to *self-exploder* lightly. Exploding the self is the self-destruction of one's intimate interior being, one's own journeys of becoming, the existential being-ness through which each of us (in manifoldly different cultural ways) experiences and knows worlds, inside one's self, outside one's self. Since self comes into existence and is formed and forming through relating to otherness, the self is a social being. To self-explode self is then a social act, a social practice, one intended to act on the world through one's own self-destruction. As social practice, self-explosion radiates outwards, into sociality, into its fragmentation, disruption, dismemberment. As social practice, self-exploding leads directly to the potentiality of self-sacrifice in today's world. Self-sacrifice indexes the voluntary giving of one's life for otherness—protecting this, saving this, bringing this into existence through self-destruction. The giving of one's self to otherness no less indexes altruism (Gambetta 2005: 259), the gift of devotion—to a cause, to a belief, to others, and on. Therefore, and I emphasize this connectivity, the social giving of one's self to otherness as self-sacrifice often has *cosmic* implications when selfness and otherness in relation to one another are comprehended as integral to world-making. The creation of worlds through the destruction of worlds. This is the linkage I want to explore through the practice of self-exploding in and from the Middle East by considering, toward the end of this chapter, the self-exploder as a double sacrifice—of the enemy other and of the (purified and consecrated) self, and the implications of this for cosmic destruction and creation.

Notes for this chapter begin on page 253.

Self-exploding and the organization of today's terrorism both have qualities of a nomadic, rhizomic dynamic, in the terms created by Deleuze and Guattari. The rhizomic dynamic of movement has qualities of asymmetry, speed, intensity, laterality, and penetration (Deleuze and Guattari 1983, 1986, 1988). As far as I can tell, self-exploder terrorism adopted these qualities for practical reasons, for putting together (again in Deleuzian terms) assemblages that worked, especially within globalizing, transnational, and urban ecologies. To a high degree, these dynamic, rhizomic qualities potentiate and enable the organization of terrorism to culminate eventfully in self-explosion. Though the rhizomic organization of terrorism and self-explosion have not been brought to conjoin one another in any deliberate, conscious way, they evolved together through practice, coming powerfully to complement one another. The rhizomic organization of terrorism foregrounds self-explosion as sacrifice, and the rhizomic is discussed here prior to addressing the latter.

Following this brief introduction, the chapter continues with a section on "terrorism in modernity," considering thinking on terrorism that situates human bombs as a more "civilian" (though not noncombatant) response to perceived, felt, grievance. I then take up "the rhizome and the self-organization of terrorism," afterward turning to that which I am calling self-exploding, its sacrificial qualities and its implications for cosmic order. I close by thinking on the attacks of 9/11 as ritual sacrifice and cosmic (re)origination. The logic of my argument moves from the phenomenon of terrorism more generally, to the organization of terrorism, to the terrorist act (that itself has rhizomic qualities). I do not discuss any psychology of self-exploders—so far this has been discussed primarily and often only in universal terms of suiciding and suicide. This I regard as of little or no aid in comprehending much of the significance of self-exploders in today's world.[2]

Self-exploders appeared in the Near East in 1983, during the civil war in Lebanon, when attacks by the Sh'ia movement Hezbollah against American and French military peacekeeping forces and against Israeli military targets caused large casualties. The departure of the peacekeepers from Lebanon was linked to these attacks. Major training grounds at the time were in the Sudan, and in Afghanistan during the occupation by and battles against the Soviet armies there. That war in Afghanistan attracted and exported Muslim fighters from and to a broad swath of North Africa, the Balkans, the Caucasus, the Near East, Pakistan, and Southeast Asia. The success of Hezbollah with self-exploders in Lebanon may have influenced their use by the Liberation Tigers of Tamil Eelam (LTTE) beginning in the late 1980s (see Roberts n.d., 2005a, 2005b) and likely had an effect on Al Qaida (Gunaratna 2002: 147).

Human bombs appeared in Israel/Palestine during the 1990s, when Hamas and Palestinian Islamic Jihad (and later, during the Second Intifada, Fatah) adopted the Hezbollah initiative. The first Hamas self-exploders blew themselves up following the massacre in the Cave of the Patriarchs/Ibrahimi Mosque in Hebron, where Abraham is buried in Jewish and Muslim traditions (Beinin 2003: 15). On Purim, 25 February 1994, an annual holiday unusual in Judaism in that it is given over to inversion, license, and the blurring of boundaries between good and bad, a physician, Baruch Goldstein entered the mosque in his army reserve fatigues and shot well over a hundred and fifty Muslim worshipers, of whom twenty-nine died. He was torn to pieces by the survivors. Goldstein undoubtedly perceived himself as a self-sacrifice for the greater Jewish good in the biblical Land of Israel. His remains were buried in Rabbi Meir Kahane Park, and his tomb has become a pilgrimage site for West Bank settlers and their sympathizers. The inscription on his tomb reads: "Here lies the *saint*, Dr. Baruch Kappel Goldstein, blessed be the memory of the *righteous* and *holy* man, may the Lord avenge his blood, who devoted his soul to the Jews, Jewish religion and Jewish land. His hands are innocent and his heart is pure. He was killed as a *martyr of G-d*." (my emphases).

Attackers have detonated themselves or their bombs in numerous locations in the Middle East and Asia and, more recently in European capitals (Madrid, London). Their greatest success has been, of course, 9/11, the 2001 attacks on the Twin Towers and the Pentagon, in which the brilliance of a rhizomic attack and the catastrophe of its aftermath were magnified for all to see, while so too were the severity of the American bureaucratic responses through law, classification, and regulation.[3] Self-exploding terrorism appears as an apparently new means of mass violence (but see too, Dale 1988; Andriolo 2002), joining in the savagery of the twentieth and now the twenty-first centuries, on the edge of the uncomfortably incomprehensible in the religiousness of its self-destructiveness, in its indiscriminate massacring, and in its seemingly tenuous and diffuse social organization.

Responses to terrorism by intellectuals and university academics are commonly moralistic, outraged at the butchering of innocent noncombatants; at the destruction of peaceful, law-abiding civilian sectors; and at the transnational influx into Western states of archaics or primitives in a globalizing world. Scholarly and political thinking join in perceiving terrorism in grandiose terms—a war of civilizations, a war among the so-called universal Abrahamic religions of Islam, Christianity, and Judaism, a theophany of Gog and Magog. With few exceptions there is consensus that suicide bombers are terrorists, though there is no agreement as to what entails terror nor how to define this. Obviously terror can be defined categorically, legalistically, normatively—but whether this can be a substantive rendition of the phenomenal in its social, existential, and eschatological dimensions is quite another matter, one hardly addressed. This affects how liberal scholarship is relating to terrorist phenomena.

The following premises infuse much scholarly thinking about these human precision bombs (as Michael Roberts calls them), about the contexts that shape them, and about the ways in which they organize. First, that the perpetrators are suiciders, often mentally unstable or impressionable, trapped in the unstable flux of modernity, unable to find their footings, alienated and frustrated human detritus (e.g., Moghaddam 2005). In Durkheimian terms, their lives are underintegrated, insufficiently moored in a societal matrix, and they drift into what he called egoistical suicide, killing themselves for their own sake. Or, their lives are overintegrated within an authoritarian religious matrix, and so they are driven to give their lives to the cause in acts that Durkheim called altruistic suicide (Durkheim 1952: 152–240).[4] I return to this theme, briefly, further on.

Secondly, commonsensical and scholarly thinking concur that there is a clear-cut ethical and functional distinction between the civilian and the combatant—combatants are borderers, protecting civilians who live within borders and who are not complicit in the oppressions that are perpetrated by their states, officials, and armies. Therefore attacks on civilians violate this categorical distinction: these attacks treat noncombatants as fully complicit in the oppression and devastation carried through by states of which they are members. Whatever else it is, terrorism is understood as deviant violence against innocent civilians.[5] Today's terrorism, with its colonial and neocolonial legacies, puts this to the question.

Terrorism in Modernity

During the twentieth century, warfare between states turned from battles primarily between armies to violence aimed deliberately at civilian populations. No less, states attacked their own subject populations (the Armenian genocide, the Herero genocide [e.g., Hull 2005: 7–90], the Holocaust). The bulk of casualties during World War I were those of combatants. Poison gas was used by military against military. In World War II this completely turned about: Auschwitz, *einsatzgruppen*, Hiroshima and Nagasaki, Dresden and London, and on and on.[6] States deliberately attacking one another's civilian populations and their own, making them prime targets for mass slaughter. Western states terrorizing Western noncombatants, thereby making them no longer quite that, no longer innocent noncombatants but integral to strategizing the weakening of enemy capacities and capabilities, if not the very extermination of that enemy. If in the more distant past, "The law of nations held that war was a contest between states, waged by official, uniformed, armed forces," in more recent times, "as entire economies and societies have been conscripted to the war effort and military and nonmilitary work have converged, [there has been] a gradual loosening of what constitutes a legitimate military target" (Smith 2002: 361). Civilian targets that also contribute to war use increasingly are treated as unambiguous military targets. "The vogue today is the 'Strategic Ring Theory' of striking critical nodes of infrastructure in order to induce 'strategic paralysis' in one's enemy" (Smith 2002: 362).

The massacring, killing, and brutalizing of subject populations that had flourished during centuries of colonial rule surfaced within the motherlands and fatherlands, internally and in relation to one another. Despite numerous international treaties against the manufacture and proliferation of weapons of mass destruction, against war crimes, and so forth, during the twentieth century it became more and more acceptable to attack civilians and civilian targets. In Edith Wyschogrod's (1985) momentous phrasing, the *logic* of manmade mass death became fully formed during the twentieth century.

Sociologist of law Donald Black argues that "terrorism in its purest form is *self-help* by organized civilians who covertly inflict mass violence on other civilians" (2004: 16, my emphasis).[7] Terrorism, he argues, is highly moralistic, often utopian, and intended to exert social control by responding to grievance with aggression, especially when there is no other redress, or when redress does not work.[8] Religious international terrorists may well resemble millenarian mystical Christian movements of medieval Europe (2004: 18) whose utopian orientation, wrote Karl Mannheim (1936: 220), "tends at every moment to turn into hostility toward the world, its culture, and all its works and earthly achievements" (see also Norman Cohn's [1970] *Pursuit of the Millennium*).

Black (2004: 15) contends, "Violence occurs when a conflict structure is violent"—"Every form of violence," he writes, "has its own structure. ... Structures kill and maim, not individuals or collectivities." The conflict structure of "pure terrorism" (Black uses this as a Weberian ideal type), like some of its organization and strategies, resembles that of the Deleuzian rhizome in relation to the state. Pure terrorism whose aim is the mass killing and maiming of civilians by civilians takes shape on behalf of one collectivity against another that is perceived as culturally and socially foreign, and as superior in military, political, and economic power. Hence the Madrid rush-hour commuter train bombings in 2004, and the London Underground bombings in 2005. Two decades ago, Rapoport (1984: 675) could (perhaps) argue that terrorists tend "to choose methods that minimize the terrorist's risks; the targets, accordingly, are increasingly defenseless victims who have less and less value as symbols and less responsibility for any condition that the terrorists say they want to alter." If this was ever the case, it ceased to be so in the age of the self-exploder, when boundaries between the military and the civilian, between combatant and noncombatant, are blurred and even effaced, and when terrorism extends self-exploding and other opportunities to civilians, both male and female (Gambetta 2005: 283).

In 2003 there were ninety-eight self-exploder attacks around the world (Atran 2004a). Not only are most of the targets of these attacks civilian, but civilians are perceived to be complicit in the oppressive enterprises of the offending states because they do not oppose these states. Of no less significance, implicit in the complicit is the intentional. Complicity is a declaration of intentionality—civilians thereby are intentional accomplices of the oppressive states they are members in and shelter within. The deeper implication is that the distinction between the officially designated armed forces of the state and its civilian citizens no longer holds. Civilians are held responsible for their government and its practices. Civilians, then, should take responsibility for their governments just as Islamist terrorists take responsibility for the well-being of Islam. There no longer are any innocents, only perpetrators and the complicit. This has more than a little prominence in America, for example, in the bombing of the federal office building in Oklahoma City, yet no less in the Columbine high school massacre and in similar mass murders.[9] I will discuss intentionality further, in relation to sacrifice.

However, the brutal converse of all this is that in the name of national security, indeed security even more broadly conceived as Total (and Totalizing) Security, there are no longer civilian innocents also in the eyes of the State (see Bajc 2007).[10] All are at least under suspicion unless cleared for the moment. Thus every stop at a security portal where ID is demanded, every passage through a metal detector, is a form of *interrogation* into whether passage will be permitted, an interrogation into that which is not evident on the surface of being, an interrogation that can be highly condensed in time and act, even left entirely to machines, or stretched out to include questioning, body search, and even incarceration. CCTV systems in civic spaces, and the monitoring of private phone conversations and e-mail no less attest to the fact that all are under suspicion until shown not to be. So too does the current official enthusiasm for simplistic behavior profiling in public spaces: "The authorities at about a dozen U.S. airports now monitor passengers' involuntary actions in hopes of nabbing potential terrorists, and Miami officials are so impressed with such behavior recognition techniques that they plan to have janitors, coffee-shop workers and skycaps trained to detect dangerous fliers."[11] A hostile environment for the unwary traveler who is unaware of his own subtle behavioral habits.

The practice of terrorism is a phenomenon of late modernity, of the last century and this one, as technology has enabled transnational strike trajectories across lengthy distances, separating, for example, a colonial power from those whom it oppresses or oppressed (Atran 2004b). Violent civilians fighting back, attacking the oppressive state through its civilians who are perceived as complicit, rejecting the distinct classification of civilian and military (e.g., Asad 2007: 17, 22).[12] Violent civilians or quasi-civilians (those with limited martial training) in small groups are systematic wild cards, mutating, developing, emerging in their own ways with less of or quite without the external strictures imposed by bureaucratic states, as was the case with terrorism during the Cold War (Ackerman 2006). But the ways in which this is coming to be done, if Al-Qaida is any example, are through rhizomic transformations of state organization.

The Rhizome and the Self-Organization of Terrorism

Much of (pure) terrorism is organized through forms of organization that are antithetical to the modern state. The infrastructure of the modern Western state is highly bureaucratic, its institutions organized around clearly defined offices and tasks, a clear-cut division of labor, hierarchies of officials, and chains of command. This holds no less for the armed forces, the intelligence agencies, and the secret police. The modern state is deeply rooted in clearly bounded territories whose borders are inviolate and within which its sovereignty is supreme. State systems work best when pitted against other states with the same logic of organization or under conditions of colonization when conquering or grabbing territory and economic resources, or controlling these, are often primary goals. So, too, during the Cold War the Soviet Union and the United States sponsored and used terrorist activities as arms of state to further national goals, but also kept the scope and intensity of these activities tempered (Raufer 2003: 392).

The organization of transnational terrorism that has blossomed during the past two decades is different. Consider the following scenario recently posed by a researcher:

> Now, imagine a company, or agency, with global markets, or an international mission, say IBM or the CIA. If their offices have been raided worldwide, or bombarded, tens of millions of dollars confiscated from them, all their known bank accounts blocked, their computers seized, their electronic communication systems destroyed, thousands of their employees and part of their leadership arrested—even killed sometimes—could these organizations still function? No, of course not. (Raufer 2003: 395)

He is referring to Al-Qaida, though whether there is a unified organization (like a corporation, say IBM, or a bureaucracy, say the CIA) that can be called "Al-Qaida" is unlikely. If not this, then what manner of entity is working here? No one seems to know the overall state of affairs— Al-Qaida, and probably other terrorist entities, like the anarchists of the late nineteenth century, constitute an "inscrutable case" (Gambetta 2005), one about which there is no stable truth to find out. This is so not only because terrorist formation may be quite loosely held together, but also because it is in ongoing change. So the forming of terrorist entities varies within a field of potentialities, enabling (indeed, potentiating) the simultaneous emergence of more hierarchical formations, more network-like formations, and more rhizome-like formations, perhaps shifting through these different modalities. I will turn to the rhizome shortly.

In the case of Al-Qaida, the best documented of these organizations, these forms mutate, radically changing their formations. In its early years in Afghanistan, Al-Qaida was a highly structured, more guerilla-like hierarchical formation run from the top by Osama bin Laden, and dedicated to fighting the Soviet occupation there. Bin Laden was reputed to own or control eighty companies around the world (Hoffman 2003: 434). In the Sudan alone he owned construction, manufacturing, currency trading, import-export, and agricultural businesses (Bergen 2001: 47–49), and he had established a set of valuable Islamic charities in Saudi Arabia with international sections. Following the defeat of the Soviets in Afghanistan, bin Laden turned Al-Qaida toward more transnational terror operations (while continuing more of a conventional war against the Northern Alliance). Bin Laden in part reoriented the organization toward more network-like formations that enabled making decisions and carrying out operations to be done locally, without referring to an apex or center. This was the case with the first World Trade Center bombing in 1992; with Ramzi Ahmed Yousef's plan, developed in the Philippines in 1994–95, to simultaneously bomb twelve American commercial airliners in midflight over the Pacific (Hoffman 2003: 436); and with the plan to assassinate the pope in Manila in 1995, using an assassin dressed as a priest who was to explode himself while kissing the papal ring (Hassan 2001; Gunaratna 2002: 175).

More network-like formations strongly contributed to the planning of and putting together the cells for the 9/11 attacks. The terrorists trained in Al-Qaida facilities in Afghanistan, and later received logistical support from sleeper cells in Europe and Southeast Asia in order to enter the United States (Mishal and Rosenthal 2005: 279). The attackers themselves were divided into a number of cells that were unknown to one another, except through operators or cut-outs (in Cold War espionage language)—the pilots met the other attackers only on the morning of 9/11. Moreover, it is likely that not all members of the same cell knew one another. Meetings were held to synchronize distant segments or cells of the network and to discuss progress, but then these ties went dormant.[13] The 9/11 attacks are estimated to have cost under $500,000 (Basile 2004: 172).[14]

An important attribute of this shift in organization is that terrorism becomes more of a bottom-up phenomenon, with local initiatives and local cells whose destruction have limited effects on the viability of larger transnational terrorist networks. Bottom-up formation is highly emergent, spawning a multitude of directions, but also recursiveness and numerous loci of leadership.[15] These are indeed qualities of rhizomic formation. Following the American invasion of Afghanistan and the destruction of Al-Qaida infrastructure—its bases of operation and training camps—Al-Qaida ceased holding to two tenets of conventional organizations: first, attachment to territory—apart from the religious-political imaginary of the first Islamic State shaped by Mohammed after he was driven from Mecca to Medina—and, second, permanent institutional presence (Mishal and Rosenthal 2005: 279).[16]

Thus the networks and cells of Al-Qaida decentralized further, becoming weakly coupled in their connections to one another, though tightly coupled within themselves. Weak coupling allows greater agency, enabling cells to adapt less abstractly and more directly and immediately to their environments, while setting their own agendas. Maksim Tsvetovat and Kathleen Farley (n.d.) who modeled covert (terrorist) networks found that attacking them as one would a hierarchical organization, for example by targeted assassinations of network or cell leaders (a major Israeli weapon)—thereby "beheading" and fragmenting such entities—was not effective. Cells are highly adaptive and heal themselves, either by finding ways to reconnect to the network, by operating on their own, or by becoming dormant and waiting. Al-Qaida's cells have been likened to clusters of grapes, such that a grape plucked does not affect the viability of others of the bunch (Gunaratna 2002: 97). Since cells tend toward the autopoietic in interaction with local ecologies, they also tend not to replicate one another in their organization (Knorr Cetina 2005: 230).

Tight coupling within cells gives them esprit de corps and a sense of fictive kinship.[17] Entities that come into existence in bottom-up ways generate more complex behavior and action than is produced by top-down, deliberate planning according to a hierarchical chain of command (Marion and Uhl-Bien 2003: 70). Bottom-up forming encourages experimentation and learning from experience. Marion and Uhl-Bien (2003: 71) contend that "Al-Qaida leadership provided models of creativity, dropped seeds of innovation, encouraged innovative initiatives, stimulated the growth of supporting resources and largely stayed out of the way of spontaneous growth and innovation." So, Al-Qaida can create or help to create ad hoc cells to carry out local missions of their own choice, specifications, and modes of operation. The March 2004 attack on commuter trains in Madrid is an example. The attack was coordinated by a Tunisian who created an ad hoc cell by connecting to a local group of immigrants called the Moroccan Islamic Combat Group, without direct links to Al-Qaida (Mishal and Rosenthal 2005: 288). The elimination of the Madrid attackers did little or no damage to the nets of Al-Qaida, which probably proceeded to set up other local ad hoc cells elsewhere. The cell that carried out the 2005 London Underground bombings was autopoietic, obtaining most if not all of its bomb-making information from the Internet. Many of these cells "are not durable units but changing implementations of short term projects sequentially replaced by new projects—they are units that their creators plan from the outset to abolish, abandon and recreate as non-identical units at a different location" (Knorr Cetina 2005: 229). A further adaptive or mutating form, emerging from nets of loosely coupled terrorist cells, is what is called *swarming*—terrorists from different groups come together from scattered locations to home in on multiple targets and then disperse, perhaps to form other swarms (Atran 2004a).[18]

The economics of Al-Qaida are especially instructive in relation to the emergent bottom-up forming of cells and nets. Though American bureaucracies have shut down many channels of Al-Qaida monies in the United States, its devolving character makes it extremely difficult to track money sources globally. Al-Qaida seems not to benefit from state funding. Monies raised by Islamic charities, in Saudi Arabia, for example, may be moved through Islamic banks (governed by Shari'at law) that are subjected to little bureaucratic regulation and oversight, and through *Hawala* ("transfer," "exchange," "change") networks, long institutionalized in South Asia and the Middle East. In Hawala, there are no transfers between money traders; instead, one *hawaldar* will fax or phone another, telling him to give a sum of cash to a particular recipient. Particular transactions are not recorded; instead *hawaldara* keep track of the balance of their accounts with one another, the outstanding balance eventually to be settled in various ways (cf. Berkowitz, Woodward, and Woodward 2005). Al-Qaida separates monies for its operational cells from its sources of funding. Until now, every successful operation sponsored by Al-Qaida has used different money sources, the funds for any given operation arriving through multiple routes. According to Al-Qaida's training manual, the commander of a cell is to divide finances into monies to be invested and monies to be saved for operations (Basile 2004: 171–76). Cells are intended to be as financially self-sufficient as possible, in keeping with their loose coupling and agency in choosing targets and organizing attacks.

Transnational terrorism has emerged from the mass killing of civilians characterizing much bloodletting among and within states especially from World War II on, and becoming matter-of-course. These terrorist networks and groupings often are more civilian-terrorists, or at most quasi-military, than they are military. They are, in the main, civilians taking up or turning themselves into weapons against civilians, directly reaching civilian populations whom they hold complicit in the perduring existence of regimes who have or who are oppressing them. Attacks by civilians upon civilians are not only strategic decisions to damage easier "soft" targets—these attacks in their own ways are uprisings that go directly to those held most responsible; those sheltering behind the violent bureaucracies that are the military.

Discussing the history of warfare, Lind et al. (1989) suggest that a fourth generation of forms of war is emerging, and that terrorism is integral to this: terrorism "attempts to bypass the enemy's military entirely and strike directly at his homeland at civilian targets. Ideally, the enemy's military is simply irrelevant to the terrorist." Military culture remains a culture of order even as the battlefields are ones of disorder. Military culture, they point out, "has become contradictory to the battlefield" (but see endnote 18). Both the forming of cells and the trajectories of attack are becoming more rhizomic. The International Institute for Strategic Studies states that the Iraq War is generating "an already decentralized and evasive transnational terrorist network to become more 'virtual' and protean and, therefore, harder to identify and neutralize" (2003). Knorr Cetina (2005: 214) maintains that today's terrorism is not only global, but constitutes "the emergence of global microstructures; of forms of connectivity and coordination that combine global reach with microstructural mechanisms that instantiate self-organizing principles and patterns."

Little by little, terrorist attackers, their cells and nets, are becoming more deterritorialized, more mobile, more *nomadic* in a transnational, globalizing world—they are becoming rhizomic in their forming. In a topological sense, terrorist attackers *are* their movement, and the dynamic of this movement is rhizomic. Deleuze and Guattari (1988) distinguish the rhizomic from the state form, that form of organizing that captures, incorporates, and stabilizes whatever it takes in within its boundaries. Yet as Deleuze and Guattari intend, the state form and the rhizome are metamorphs of one another. Every subversion, uprising, insurrection within the state is a node of the rhizomic, of an unpredictable dynamic that undermines the verticality of the deeply rooted, the beginnings of a line of flight, a trajectory that will destroy distinctions between interior and exterior, erasing borders. No less, every swelling within a rhizome, every shift toward hierarchical self-organization is a node of a potential state form in the making, of the emergence of boundaries, of distinctions between interior and exterior, of verticality, of the deeply rooted. Many transnational terrorists are migrants moving from one state to another, settling in new places yet becoming nomadic, fluid cysts within the weightiness of statist territorial positioning.

What is rhizomic forming, according to Deleuze and Guattari's sense of this vegetal dynamic? The rhizome is not a root, but rather a tuber or bulb that ramifies growth in all directions, on, over, and under the ground, a multiplicity of diversities without clear boundaries, or perhaps whose boundaries are densities of connectedness, with shallow tendrils without any natural points of closure, with multiple entrances and ongoing, spreading movement. Within this dynamic maze of movement any point can be connected to any other, and this making of connection never ceases. Rhizomic organization has no fixed points in its lines of flight (as Deleuze and Guattari call its movements), and therefore has only potentialities to emerge vertically, to grow hierarchy and stratification with differences in status, authority, gatekeepers, and specialized guardians of order sign-posted by the uniform—in other words, to becoming top-down organization, the bureaucratic state in miniature. "A rhizome," they write, "can be cracked and broken at any point; it starts off again following one or another of its lines, or even other lines" (Deleuze and Guattari 1983: 17–18). A crucial dynamic of the rhizomic is *speed*. The bureaucratic state form exists through the stability of its territorialism, the portentousness of its deep-rootedness, the weightiness of its regulations, the density of its institutions. The rhizome turns a point—the potential node of swelling into verticality—into an intense line of flight through the speed with which it moves. Speed vanishes the boundary, its blockage and stoppage disappearing with it.[19]

Deleuze and Guattari (1983: 49) write, "In opposition to centered systems (even multi-centered), with hierarchical communication and pre-established connections, the rhizome is an a-centered system, non-hierarchical and non-signifying, without a General, without an organizing memory or central autonomy." The rhizome cannot answer to a structural or generative model, for there is no grammar through which to generate a rhizome. Therefore the rhizome makes and morphs itself as it moves.[20] Here, in a strange yet powerful way, rhizome and self-exploder join in the same line of flight. In the emergence of its manifold evolution, Al-Qaida has developed qualities of the rhizomic—loosely organized, decentralized, flexible in practice (Gunaratna 2002: 11, 57–58, 95), penetrating fluidly from multiple directions, while encouraging if only by example, the sprouting of autonomous rhizomes, terror cells with potentially these sorts of capacities.[21] Moreover, speed and intensity are the dynamic of the self-exploder, as they are of the rhizome. A founder of Palestinian Islamic Jihad wrote in 1988 on the importance of penetrating the territory of the enemy, in making the case for what he called "exceptional martyrdom," aimed at countering objections by Islamic religious figures to suicide bombing. "We cannot achieve the goal of these operations if our *mujahid* [holy warrior] is not able to create an explosion within seconds and is unable to prevent the enemy from blocking the operation. All these results can be achieved through the explosion" (Hassan 2001). A leader of Hamas commented to Nasra Hassan (2001): "The main thing is to guarantee that a large number of the enemy will be affected. With an explosive belt or bag, the bomber has control over vision, location, and timing." And al-Zawahiri of Al-Qaida, in his post-9/11 book, wrote on "the need to concentrate on the method of martydom operations as the most successful way of inflicting damage against the opponent and the least costly to the *mujahidin* in terms of casualties" (Gunaratna 2002: 224).

It is crucial to recognize here that the individual self-exploder is himself/herself a tiny rhizome in its asymmetric movement and speed, intensity and depth of penetration, a tiny rhizome that is a small piece or segment of a larger rhizome, a cell in self-organization and line of flight, itself perhaps part of a larger rhizomic agglomerate. A recent case in point of the above was the self-exploder Abdullah al-Asiri, who flew from Yemen to Jeddah in Saudi Arabia with half a kilo of explosive secreted in "a bodily orifice" (perhaps in his rectum, since he refrained from eating or drinking for forty hours), and who then succeeded in getting into close proximity to the Saudi interior minister, whereupon the explosives were detonated by a call from his controllers to a cell phone.[22]

Just as some terrorist cells are rhizomic in their dynamics, putting down no permanent roots, deterritorializing their networks, weapons, and finances, combining local conditions and religious-mythic abstraction into practice, so, too, they accomplish the complete synthesis of idea and action, of *perfect praxis*, through the act of self-explosion. Moving in emerging lines of horizontal flight, shifting direction, communicating through cyberspace, cells connect to other cells or to members of these. And so the emerging phenomenon of swarming for a particular operation, gathering together a multiplicity and diversity of persons and resources into what Deleuze and Guattari (1988) call an "assemblage," here a transient proliferation of the dimensions of the phenomenon that also changes its nature. So, too, just as the ruptured rhizome starts up again, cells show adaptability in self-healing after parts of cells or network are destroyed. And, the cell or cells act at speed, refusing to accentuate any point of potential stability, sometimes choosing the objective at the last moment, often angularly penetrating to the target, controlling the line of flight, of access, to a high degree. It is the rhizomic qualities of the terrorist cell and network, the rhizomic qualities of the individual self-exploder, that make them so effective against weighty structures, solidified ponderously in place in the bureaucratic state, making it so difficult for the state to trace the activities of the rhizomic. The terrorist rhizome may become a perduring threat to the promise of the state that total security is the right of civilians and the belief of the latter (who are no less True Believers) in this promise.[23] I return to the response of the state in the conclusion.[24]

Rhizomic terrorism is also complemented powerfully by the character of Islam that is emerging through the jihad declared by Al-Qaida and other Islamist agglomerates. The usual analyses done on the Islamic roots of jihad and their influence on Al-Qaida and others is to classify and pigeonhole according to traditional social movements—Salafi, Wahabi, and so forth (e.g., Sageman 2004)—such that these movements are made to exist historically and currently as the neatly compartmentalized progenitors of today's jihad and as the ideological motivators of Islamic self-exploders. In a much more penetrating analysis, Faisal Devji (2005: 50) argues that, for Al-Qaida and associates, "Islamic history and authority has been completely disaggregated and is no longer clustered within more or less distinct lineages of doctrine or ideology that can be identified with particular groups." Devji (2005: 51) contends, "In effect all traditional forms of intellectual and political grouping or identification have been fragmented, their elements scattered like debris for the picking, to be recycled in ever more temporary constructions." One result of this is what he calls the "democratization of authority in the Muslim world" (2005: 51), and so the "radical individuation of Islam" through which many Muslims become related much more tenuously to traditional modes of collective solidarity "based on some common history of needs, interests or ideas" (Devji 2005: 31; see also Brown 2001: 110). This perspective of global dynamics enables under-standing of how today's Muslim self-exploders and other terrorists constitute such heterogeneous agglomerations, and, so, too, the flexibility, mobility, and tensile strength of their rhizomic self-organization (putting to the question, for example, studies that evaluate the enabling of extremism in jihad in terms of the selective inaccuracy with which Bin Laden and other terrorist leaders and ideologues use the Qur'an and Hadith (e.g., Gwynne 2006). The individuation of the self-exploder, and the self-exploder as a rhizomic segment or piece of a rhizome, are directly relevant to self-exploding sacrifice.

Self-Exploding Sacrifice

The rhizome is a metamorph, transforming itself through its own dynamics of ongoing movement, through its assemblages and lines of flight. In this respect the rhizomic form of terrorism and self-exploder is complemented by the very act of self-explosion and the preparation leading to this, once we understand that the act is one of self-sacrifice, and that sacrifice is a practice of transforma-tion. To get at this, the interior logic of sacrifice needs discussion.

In the most influential work on suicide written in the modern era, Emile Durkheim (1952: 152–240) distinguished between *egoistic suicide,* the intention to kill oneself for oneself, and *altruistic suicide,* the preparedness to kill oneself for others, as in warfare. In either instance, Durkheim abhorred the taking of one's own life. This is the canonical attitude of all three monotheistic universal religions—God gives life and only God has the right to take life. The mod-ern state claims a monopoly on doing violence, primarily through its violent bureaucracies (within which I include military, judiciary, and police). Suicide transgresses both the monotheisms and the states that developed from them.

Though no general theory of sacrifice will satisfy all the phenomena that anthropologists and historians of religion call sacrifice, a few general points are relevant here. Whatever else it is, sacrifice is an act of violence—a violence done to natural form, natural in the sense of form existing in the integrity of its created shape in the cosmos. Kapferer (1997: 189) argues that sacrifice is "a primordial act ... a total act ... [in which] the force of sacrifice [is] constitu-tive both of the being of the person at the center of sacrifice and of the person as himself or herself [as] a being who constitutes. ... The violence of sacrifice underlines sacrifice as the total act: an act that can have immanent within its process the entire potential and process of human being." He (1997: 190) con-tinues: "Violence is quintessentially the form of totalizing action, the explosion of possibility and of possibility exploded. ... The act of killing in sacrifice is a conjunction of the force of life with death, and of the separation of life from death. This conjunctive/disjunctive energy is the vital force of sacrifice. The motion toward killing is the conjunction … of death with life. The moment of killing, the peak of the death-life conjunction, is also the radical separation, the disjunction of life from death."

In sacrifice, natural form is taken apart—cut, rent, torn, split, burnt—so that something else can come into existence.[25] The violence of sacrifice is originary (Kapferer 1997: 190). Put differently, the violence done to form through sacrifice is violence that is done to the boundary, perhaps to the origination of boundary and being that no less is that of cosmos. The violence done to the sacrifice alters, opens, momentarily destroys the boundary between levels, domains, or realms of cosmos. Thus sacrifice, as Kapferer argues, is an act of primordial trans-formation, of radical change. Through this something unseen will take shape or have consequential effects in the world.

Sacrifice is a foundational practice in the three monotheisms (in Judaism, the *akedah*—Abraham's preparedness to sacrifice Isaac, and God's acceptance of an animal substitution; in Islam, Ishmael's *willingness* to be sacrificed by Ibrahim for Allah, the willingness that nears, that perhaps is, self-sacrifice; in Christianity, the self-sacrifice of Christ). In Islam, self-sacrifice must be death in the service of God's plan, but is first and foremost *active* struggle with correct *intention* in the service of God's plan (Lewinstein 2001: 78–81). Self-sacrifice may differ from sacrifice in the degree of its closure and in the totalization of its intensity and dynamic of movement. Its explosion is no less its implosion. The sacrificer is no less the sacrificed—as one dies for an exterior goal or cause, one's self or soul is transformed interiorly, perhaps the purification or release of an authentic self (Verkaaik 2005: 141), perhaps the instantaneous transference of the soul to paradise (Hassan 2001). A Hamas self-exploder whose bomb failed to explode described to Nasra Hassan (2001) how he felt when chosen for martyrdom: "It's as if a very high impenetrable wall separated you from Paradise or Hell. … Allah has promised one or the other to his creatures. So, by pressing the detonator, you can immediately open the door to Paradise—it is the shortest path to Heaven." Another described the immediacy of paradise as: "It is very, very near—right in front of our eyes. It lies beneath the thumb. On the other side of the detonator."

If the victim is made holy or sacred in the act of sacrifice (Hubert and Mauss 1964: 9)—a *sacrificium*—this is because the violence of its destruction momentarily destroys the boundary between cosmic levels, this destruction becoming an originary locus of the reconstitution of cosmos. In Israel/Palestine in the name of jihad, the Islamist self-exploder simultaneously kills himself as a self-sacrifice that transports him to paradise and kills enemies, others, thereby offering them as a sacrifice to Allah to open the way to the creation of the Palestinian nation-state, as part of the 'ummah, the universal Islamic religious polity (Strenski 2003: 4; Hage 2003: 69) that in its making is perforce fragmentary and transnational.[26] I return in a moment to this theme. In the warfare of the modern state, the ethos of heroic death in battle acquires the status of self-sacrifice (Greenhouse 1989; Marvin and Ingle 1999; Handelman 2004; Zerubavel 1995).

Sacrifice is originary; suicide is abhorred. Suicide is a sin, self-sacrifice is not. Sacrifice is transformative; suicide is merely self-destructive. Under what conditions in monotheistic traditions and in modern states does self-destruction become transformative, and so is turned into sacrifice?[27] The question lies at the heart of the emerging conundra of self-exploders. The matter of *intentionality* is crucial here.[28] Intentionality establishes a conscious relationship of consequence between sacrificer and sacrificed, between destroyer and offering (see Kapferer 1997: 192–98). In the case of the self-exploder, much of this relationship is within the self, thereby fusing and totalizing commitment and outcome. Closed into itself—into selfness—the locus of sacrifice becomes absolute. Commitment predicated on the direction of dying, of transformation, exploding exteriorly, transforming interiorly. The idea of "exceptional martyrdom," mentioned above, depends on this embodiment of intentionality. So too, a Muslim cleric making the case for martyrdom argues, "while both suicide and acts of martyrdom require the express act of will of the perpetrator, what matters is not the act, but the intention [*nia*] of the martyr" (Israeli 2002: 35).[29]

Shaping the Ritual Sacrifice

Sacrifice is the perfect praxis—the perfect synthesis—of idea, intention, action. The inner logic of self-exploders—in Israel/Palestine and those of 9/11—configures how this praxis of self-sacrifice is accomplished through the ritual shaping of self. Central to this is an agency different from that of individualism made free for itself, the individual for himself. Devji's argument on the spreading of individuation in today's Islam, mentioned earlier, is especially relevant here. Devji (2005: 34) contends that today's jihad largely rejects "the classical doctrine of holy war as a collective or political obligation [*farz kifaya*]." Instead, holy war becomes "an individual and ethical obligation [*farz ayn*] like prayer. ... [Holy war] becomes spiritualized and finally puts the jihad beyond the pragmatism of political life. ... So, whereas liberals as well as fundamentalist Muslims tried to instrumentalize Islam by attributing social, political or economic functions to its beliefs or practices, the jihad does just the opposite—its task is to de-instrumentalize Islam and make it part of everyday ethics" (2005: 34; see also Gwynne 2006: 14, 16; Brown 2001: 110–11). Today's jihad, like previous movements, develops in the peripheries of the Muslim world, with practices that braid together the charismatic, the heretical, the experiential, the mystical—the Muslim content of which "draws upon the flotsam and jetsam of received wisdoms and remembered histories ... [denying] the existence of distinct orders or genealogies of Islamic authority" (Devji 2005: 41–42). Instead, personal faith, repentance, and the quest for salvation rise to the fore together with the democratization of authority in which prophecy, dream, and messianism are prominent, rather than the traditional, even canonical knowledge of texts (Devji 2005: 42, 48). If this jihad emerged out of oppression of Muslim populations, it has become a metaphysical war, "an effort to define the terms of global social relations outside the language of state and citizenship" (Devji 2005: 76)—and it is through this that self-explosion and sacrifice become sacred practice intended to transform cosmos through individual intentionality and action.[30]

Relevant thinking on individual agency, self-discipline, and ethics in present-day Islam comes, appositely, from a study of putting on the veil by Muslim women. Saba Mahmood discusses how women in Egypt take on veiling through *docility*, though this is not the docility of the passive abandoning of agency—rather, it refers literally to the *malleability* needed to be taught particular skills, and this demands "struggle, effort, exertion, and achievement" (Mahmood 2001: 210). This is an internal struggle within and against one's self, one not distant from the struggle demanded by jihad (see Euben 2002: 12). Putting on the veil is the preparedness to respond positively to shaping oneself, in relation to self and others, as one is being shaped. Thus, "while wearing the veil at first serves as a means to tutor oneself in the attributes of shyness, it is also simultaneously integral to the practice of shyness ... one veils," argue these women, "not to *express* [my emphasis] an identity but as a necessary, if insufficient condition for attaining the goal internal to that practice—namely, the creation of a shy and modest self. The veil in this sense is the means of both *being* and *becoming* a certain kind of person" (original emphases, 2001: 214–15). Putting on the veil is a bidirectional self-declaring practice of ascetic intent—interior and exterior.

Taking on the veil is an exterior practice that develops interior qualities that, in turn, "comes to regulate and govern one's behavior without conscious deliberation" (2001: 216). The practice of shyness, modesty, and patience become inseparable from one's interior intentionality and desire, as both are inseparable from the significance of the theology and eschatology that inspire these. The veil becomes integral to the face, not as covering but as an embodiment of synthesizing interiority and exteriority, of showing one's authentic interior selfness on one's exterior. One's holism, within and without. The distance from face to veil is, at it were, the absence of distance between re-formed self and the practice of self-transcendence, between an ethics of self-accountability and an ethics of self-responsibility, embodied by the veil-face. So, too, when the bomber puts the bomb on himself and becomes a self-exploder, the distance between self and self-transcendence diminishes and then disappears if he self-explodes successfully. Both in the instances of women veiling and in jihad there is the dynamic of making Islam universal. Devji (2005: 94) puts it this way for the forming of the self-exploder: "the forging of a generic Muslim, one who loses all cultural and historical particularity by his or her destruction in an act of martyrdom."

There are three hand-written copies of a four-page document in Arabic that the 9/11 self-exploders left behind. The document can be called a spiritual manual (Kippenberg 2005).[31] If we accept it as a guide to the preparation of the self-exploders (we have no way of knowing whether they followed this), then it gives an inkling of how the self-exploders ritualized and shaped themselves in spirit and body (Mneimneh and Makiya 2002) before attacking and transforming themselves through the total and totalizing act of martyring self-sacrifice.

In Arabic, to be martyred, to have one's martyrdom seen and witnessed, to witness one's own martyrdom, are all highly complementary through the term *shahadat*—"Witnessing means martyrdom. ... there is a close link between seeing and dying in the etymology of martyrdom" (Devji 2005: 94).[32] But the significance of shahadat is much greater than that of the individual martyr's self-experiencing—the term resonates powerfully with medieval and modern understandings of enduring habitus (Nederman 1989; Bourdieu 1977) and too with the Deleuze and Guattari (1988) understanding of dynamic assemblage constituted to momentarily reshape and act on realities. Devji (2005: 94–95) comments that "*shahadat* involves not only the person whose life is voluntarily sacrificed for the cause of God, but *everyone* [my emphasis] annihilated in this cause whether willingly or not. Not only people, but animals, buildings and other inanimate objects as well may participate in the rite, including even those who witness the martyrdom of others without themselves being killed. ... *shahadat* is a fundamentally social and therefore inclusive act, the pity and compassion it excites among witnesses forming part of its classical as much as contemporary definition ... perpetrators, victims, bystanders, other animate and inanimate witnesses, near or far, all of whom constitute by their very seeing the landscape of the jihad as a site of sociability." The total act of self-exploding brings into one another habitus in its more enduring reality and assemblage in its more immediate configuration, through where and when the self explodes. Self-sacrifice in these terms is always an act of *cosmogenesis* that ultimately is social, while the scale and grandeur of the self-sacrifice expands its sociability.

The transitory assemblage that enables the explosion totalizes habitus through the sacrifice, a total act that is intended to be one of cosmic (re)creation. The sacrifice and martyrdom are shaped as their own proof, utterly self-contained (Devji 2005: 102, 104), supremely interior even as they effect the exteriority of habitus. Implicitly or explicitly, this shaping of the 9/11 sacrifice likely speaks to its ritual forming through preparation, even though this aspect of the totality of the act has been quite ignored by scholars and other interpreters.[33]

In the spiritual manual, the attack is called a raid (*ghazwa*) for the sake of God, one whose intention is voluntary and whose preparation is ascetic—in classical Arabic literature, like all wars against infidels, "a kind of worship" (Kippenberg 2005: 36). The term *raid* also referred to each of the groups or cells that came together on the morning of 9/11 to do the attack. The manual orientates the conditions of being of the attackers, toward one another and individually. It opens with "a mutual pledge (*bai'a*) to die and the renewal of intent (*niyya*)" (Kippenberg 2005: 37).[34] Intention and action must braid together, both in worship and in battle and in battle as worship. Intention must be such that the attacker is purified of all personal emotion, such as a desire for personal vengeance, so that the sacrifice is selfless. Selfless, yet self-responsible and the outcome of free choice, the (self-)sacrificial total and totalizing act is turned into the practice of ethics, argues Devji (2005: 102, 120). Only when the action is for the sake of God alone, can violence be turned into sacred act (Kippenberg 2005: 39). In my terms, the sacrificer prepares himself as a vehicle of self-transformation through violence, the pure gift (Kapferer 1997), the self-sacrifice of the selfless self, the sacrifice of other. Through their pledge of mutuality, the self-sacrificers form or re-form themselves as a community. As a microcosm, the entire (male) religious polity goes to a battle of self-sacrifice for the sake of God.[35]

The manual divides the raid into a three-part sequence: the first part, the night before, during which the attacker struggles with his own soul; the second part, the following morning at the airport, when the attacker struggles with the satanic forces all about him, all of the unbelievers and their institutions; and the third part, the battle against the unbelievers inside the airplane. The sequencing of these three parts is significant. First, the purification of deepest interiority within the person, as he takes into himself and embodies the ascetic state of being of the sacrificer for God (Euben 2002: 19). Second, the exteriorization of this condition of being, as the intentionality of the sacrificer's line of flight moves into the world, meeting the first ranks of the enemy face-to-face, yet needing to elude these in order to penetrate the target and close with his victims. Third, the violence of sacrifice.

The manual prescribes fifteen exercises for the night before the attack. These include recitals, prayers, meditations, and purifications.[36] Cook (2002: 25) contends that "during the period of time covered by "The Last Night" the attackers would consider themselves to be dead." Kippenberg (2005: 39) comments that the Arabic word for "recital" (*dhikr*) means "remembering" in a broad sense; and that the manual chooses Suras 8 and 9 from the Qur'an, both originating when Muhammad the persecuted prophet had turned into the warrior and had begun establishing the Islamic State in Medina, breaking off all contact with non-Muslims except that of attack, kill, or convert. Following the recital of the Suras, the manual prescribes Sufi practices of self-forming. The carnal self wants to live, not die. Yet the ascetic, denying the world, must persuade, tame, awaken, and drive the self to action through self-purification. Not unlike the woman who puts on the veil, the self-sacrificer must become patient and modest, with honed will and dedication. Thus Mohamed Atta, thought to be the leader of the four cells, left instructions long before the 9/11 attack that whosoever washed his corpse should wear gloves so that his genitals would not be touched; and asked that pregnant women and unclean persons not be allowed to see his body, attend his funeral, or go to his grave (Gole 2002). There follow instructions on sharpening the sacrificial knife and the wearing of proper clothing for the attack. In the morning, prayers, a ritual washing, the shaving of excess hair from the body and the application of perfume (Mneimneh and Makiya 2002). Cook argues that the attention to preparation of their bodies by the attackers is related to the preparation of a corpse for burial. Thus, "One should note that in Islam, although normally corpses are prepared after death [sic], the body of a *shahid* is deemed to have been purified by the act of martyrdom, and the body is buried in the state in which the person died" (Cook 2002: 25). With all of these purifying acts—spiritual, physical—the first part of the manual ends.

Mneimneh and Makiya (2002) argue that the attackers enter a great sacred drama and the heroic deeds of the Companions of the Prophet of the Seventh Century. Probably so, yet the attackers are preparing themselves both as sacrificers and as sacrificed. For this they ritualize themselves as warriors, re-forming self and body through inner discipline and purification, so that these will awaken with agency, as one. So, too, they prepare themselves as the perfect sacrifice to God, selfless, honed, aimed, totally committed, their intentionality utterly willed and joined to their task. They re-create themselves as the very capacity to deliver both *other* (the infidel) and *self* (the true believer) as the totalizing of sacrificial violence, the entirety of cosmos in the process of transformation.[37]

In the second part of this ritual, the warrior ventures forth from within himself on the way to the airport, advancing his being into a world ruled by satanic powers, yet protected from them, undetected by them. So long as he is in a condition of worship, of living truth, reminding himself repeatedly of God, he can deceive those who live in a world of lies as to his identity (Kippenberg 2005: 42–43). At each point in the journey he silently invokes God's blessing. He wears his purified intentional interiority on his exterior, and this mask or shield cannot be pierced by his enemies, by "Western Civilization," as the manual says, with all its technological might.

In the third part of the ritual, quietly reciting Qur'an and prayers, the attacker enters the plane, and self-sacrifice, martyrdom, dominates, yet as always, this can only be granted by God, by His divinely authorized plan, to which martyrdom is submission (Euben 2002: 26). The manual tells the attackers to

"Clench your teeth as did [your] predecessors ... before engaging in battle. Hit as would heroes who desire not to return to the World" (Mneimneh and Makiya 2002; Kippenberg 2005: 45). If there is resistance to the hijacking, those persons should be killed as a "ritual slaughter" (*dhabaha*, rather than *qatala*, to kill), as an act of grace conferred by God and an offering made to God, through filial devotion on behalf of the attacker's parents. According to Mneimneh and Makiya, dictionaries of classical Arabic give the meaning of *dhabaha* as "to cleave, slit, or rip something open. This is the word used for slitting the two external jugular veins in the throat of an animal. It is quick, direct, and always *physically intimate*: one does not slaughter with a gun, or a bomb, from afar. ... *Dhabaha* is also that which Abraham was prepared to do to his son on God's instructions." And, as the sacrificer enters his own death, the manual says, "When the moment of truth comes near, and zero hour is upon you, open your chest welcoming death on the path of God" (Kippenberg 2005: 46). "Opening his chest," his interior, the sacrificer is himself the perfect sacrifice, selflessly welcoming self-death, self-sacrifice. Devji (2005: 120) argues that this moment of martyrdom is "the purest and therefore the most ethical of acts, because in destroying himself its soldier becomes fully human by assuming complete responsibility for his fate beyond the reach of any need, interest or idea."[38]

I have suggested that the logic of this moment is one of transformation, the totalizing of a microcosmos constituted of self and other in which self dedicates the sacrifice of other and, simultaneously, dedicates his own death by sacrifice, all by the grace of God, in the name of martyrdom and the generation of the transcendent Islamic polity. The entire sequence—which I understand as a ritual sequence (Handelman 2005)—shapes a line of flight through which the self of the sacrificer is first made malleable within itself and shaped through purification and dedication of intent. This self is a self among fellow selves, filiated selves, a band of warrior brothers who selflessly are no longer other to one another among themselves. Self-dedicated, they know one another intimately, indeed a condition of *communitas*. This interior self (and selves) then emerges from within itself, thrusting rhizomically with speed and intensity deep within the world of the alien enemy other, until it penetrates the interior of the selfness of this other (within the aircraft, outside the aircraft). The interior self of the sacrificer kills that of the other, thereby destroying its existence in this microcosmos. The sacrificer, self-witnessing, self-sacrifices, and this microcosmos with its presence of the alien enemy other utterly ceases to exist. In its own way, this is a primordial act of transformation at the very heart of creation; perhaps, as Agamben (1998: 105) puts it, this is the "survival of the state of nature at the very heart of the state."

Sacrifice, as we understand this in traditional moral orders, is an *economy of violence*, of violence calibrated to accomplish transformations necessary for dynamics of survival of person, group, social order, in a self-creating cosmos.[39]

The "state of nature" at the very heart of moral order was calibrated to destroy in ongoing relationship to that which would be created within social orders. The manmade mass death of the twentieth century has exploded through the massive deaths of trench warfare, through the military killings of civilians in World War II, and now through mutations of civilians massacring civilians augmented by rhizomic terrorism. The economy of sacrificial violence inflated in modernity and blew up, as sacrifice already joined to military death and the military slaughter of civilians became joined to civilians slaughtering civilians, and to terrorism. *Sacrifice itself becomes rhizomic,* braided into speed, penetration, and small-scale acts amplified into massive uncertainty by state and global responses. Terrorism and self-sacrificial terrorism target the very complexities upon which modern infrastructures depend, demonstrating the fragility of their jointing, of their coordination and synchronization. Potential targets move toward the infinite in number (Simon and Benjamin 2001–02: 14), certainly a lesson of today's Iraq, and the state mobilizes "to wage infinite war on an indefinite enemy" (Dillon 2002: 77).

The outcome of these amplifications may be what Beck (2002: 41) calls the world risk society, "a world of uncontrollable risk" in which rhizomic terrorism and self-exploders join together with vectors of ecological deterioration, disease, starvation, population movement, mass slaughter, financial crises, all of which overflow the borders of particular states, fill interstices in fuzzy areas among and amidst fuzzy states (Mbembe 2000), and are transnational in differing configurations of presence and effect, amplifying threat, fear, and its administration (e.g., Virilio 2007: 17–18).

State response to rhizomic terrorism is to reify borders; to exact the marking and identification of persons; to slow down, stop, and freeze movement (e.g., Bajc 2007); to increase surveillance in public spaces and private lives—to shape an increasingly gated, exclusionary state. In general to adopt what Virilio (2007: 43) calls the myth of "a precautionary principle," which seems to promise absolute security to everyone selected for inclusion within state bastions manned by fear against exterior threat, demanding what Beck (2002: 41) calls the feigning of control over the uncontrollable. Without doubt, the terrorism I am discussing and state initiatives are intimately complicit and powerfully self-fulfilling (Zulaika 2003). To a serious degree, states contribute to the shaping of terror for their own purposes (American support for Al-Qaida in Afghanistan against the Soviets; Israeli support for the early Hamas as a counterweight to Fatah).

Yet this relationship between terrorism and state cannot be reduced to the methodological rationalism of economistic calculations of the political. Metaphysics stirs just beneath the surface in its world-breaking and world-making capacities. Through rhizomic violence, Muslim self-exploders seek an end to violence in the creation of the goodness of a transcendent polity, even as the destruction they do engenders further violence that denies the realization of this or any other utopia. Americans dote on the badness of rhizomic violence within their borders and elsewhere, even as they erect more and higher walls of the good to imprison this—always failing, always convinced of the utopic righteousness of their cause (see Duclos 1998). Responding to the rhizomic through its transform, the state form, in order to destroy the former just augments and accelerates the rhizome–state form dynamic. Yet in the present day the forming and destroying dynamic of rhizome and state form, each within the other, each growing the other, are increasingly amplified by technological means of control and destruction, threatening life more than any "war of civilizations."

NOTES

1. Though not deliberately, this work has emerged contrapuntally to my *Nationalism and the Israeli State: Bureaucratic Logic in Public Events* (2004). That book thinks on the forming power of the bureaucratic logic of the state. This chapter was given in seminars at the universities of Bergen, Capetown, and Stockholm. My thanks to the participants for their responses. For their comments I am indebted especially to Smadar Lavie, the late Galina Lindquist, Limor Samimian Darash, and Liora Sion.
2. The term *suicide bomber* is an oxymoron. The intention of this bomber is, first and foremost, purposefully to kill other people. (The point is made by Israeli [2002] and others, though I reached this position independently). The formative dynamic of the act is that the bomber dies in killing others; and this conjoining of self and other may index the logic of sacrifice permeating many of these acts. Nasra Hassan (2001) reports that Hamas self-exploders are called "sacred exploders."
3. One should not forget that a terrorist cell on 9/11 also intended the hijacking of a flight from Heathrow to Manchester in order to crash the aircraft into the British Houses of Parliament. By the time the cell members reached Heathrow, the attacks in America already had occurred and the airport was closed to flight traffic (Gunaratna 2002: 119).
4. Durkheim himself was offended by suicide. This may have reflected the deeply rooted monotheism of the modern Western state, and the value given to the individual as an autonomous social unit in France and elsewhere. If the individual is understood as an autonomous microunit, then it a holistic entirety, even if in a limited sense. Then self-killing makes the microunit extinct, the death of no value to social order. However, for the individual to die for group bonds and values is to create death as sacrifice, death that is of value to social order.
5. Thus most scholars and theologians of Islam whom we hear of distinguish between canonical religion that eschews suicide, whatever the cause and intention, and sects that depart deviantly from the canon.

6. See W. G. Sebald's (2004) discussions of the allied bombing of Hamburg, and John Hersey's (1989 [1946]) all but forgotten classic description of Hiroshima nuclearized, as told by survivors.

7. Contrast this with the definition of terrorism given by the US State Department in 1983: "Terrorism is premeditated, politically motivated violence perpetrated against non-combatant targets by sub-national groups or clandestine agents, usually intended to influence an audience" (Kippenberg 2005: 55).

8. Philosophers differ, in their own terms, as to whether terror is a moral act. Cf. Primoratz's (1997) contention that terrorism is morally impermissible, and Held's (1991) claim that terrorism is justified in terms of human rights and distributive justice. See also Devji's (2005: 120) argument that martyrdom entails an ethical act.

9. Pure terrorism seems to be quite absent from conflicts within relatively homogeneous social orders (there, riots, assassinations, and guerilla warfare will be more prominent) (Black 2004: 20).

10. Neocleous (2006: 374–76) charts how, in the United States, the idea of "national security" developed from that of "social security." Social security policies, designed in the main to protect the citizenry against rapacious capitalism, also spawned the idea of national security after World War II. Neocleous (2006: 378–80) argues that the "national security state" was intended first and foremost not for military purposes as such, but to further economic security, in other words to make the world safe for capital expansion and accumulation.

11. *International Herald Tribune*, 9–10 September, 2006. See also, "Judging Evil Intent: It's All in the Body Language—A New Squad at Dulles Airport Is Scrutinizing Travelers for Behavioral Signs of Bad Intentions," *International Herald Tribune*, 18 August 2006.

12. This schematic portrait is much more complex than I have space for here. As Mbembe (2003: 31–33) notes, military operations and the right to killing practices are no longer the monopoly of states—thus mercenaries, child soldiers, citizen soldiers, and privateers abound in different combinations in Africa, in spaces that are "a patchwork of overlapping and incomplete rights to rule … inextricably superimposed and tangled, in which different de facto juridical instances are geographically interwoven and plural allegiances, asymmetrical suzerainties, and enclaves abound" (Mbembe 2003: 31).

13. Krebs, http://www.firstmonday.org/issues/issue7_/krebs/.

14. Before 9/11, Al-Qaida operatives returned over $20,000 in unused funds to leaders in the Middle East (Basile 2004: 172). Hassan (2001) reports that the cost of organizing an armed self-exploder and to enter Israel was about $150. The ingredients are of the order of nails, gunpowder, a light switch and cable, mercury, acetone. The most expensive item is transportation. For that matter, the bombs exploded in London in 2005 cost only a few hundred pounds sterling (*Observer*, 9 April 2006).

15. Researchers of organizations sometimes speak of "autocatalysis"—"a tendency of recursive systems to self-generate catalysts that speed up or enable the emergence and evolution of forms" (Marion and Uhl-Bien 2003: 61).

16. These qualities are why some analysts compare Al-Qaida to a modern corporation whose existence is primarily through the flow of capital, investment, and production, rather than through any permanent physical presence in particular places.

17. According to Scott Atran (2003), Al-Qaida, Hamas, Palestinian Islamic Jihad, and Hezbollah use small cells of three to eight members who are brought to feel the cell as a family of fictive kin "for whom they are as willing to die as a mother for her child or a soldier for his buddies." http://www.interdisciplines.org/terrorism/papers/1. See also Sageman (2004). A rich source of information on self-exploders in Gaza, especially during the First Intifada, is Oliver and Steinberg (2005).

18. Thus Iraq's Ansar al-Islam and Pakistan's Lashkar-e-Jhangvi and Jaish-e-Muhammed may be coordinating operations, following Al-Qaida's example and swarming through their own impetus (Atran 2004b). Swarming in warfare is said to have powerful historical antecedents (Edwards 2005: 13–52), and the language and ideas of swarming are used by strategic planners to describe future warfare built through highly mobile and flexible units that join together for particular operations and then disperse, no longer using fixed weapons platforms as bases from which to launch operations, adapting to continuously changing battlescapes that are related to as ecosystems (Arquilla and Ronfeldt 2000; Dillon 2002: 72). Such imaginaries seem to be rejected by American military brass. See also Dillon (2002: 74). Nonetheless, there is evidence that the initial (and successful) American attacks on Afghanistan and Iraq used swarming tactics. Some Israeli military strategists in low-intensity urban warfare on the West Bank explicitly adapt the rhizome of Deleuze and Guattari to develop strategies of "infestation" in attack (Weizman 2006a) and "necrotactics" (Weizman 2006b). From a military perspective, necrotactics reverse traditional goals of warfare by temporarily entering strategic ground *solely* in order to kill enemies (Weizman 2006b: 81). The last Israeli army offensive into Gaza, called *Operation Cast Lead,* used necrotactics. Asaf Hazani (personal communication) tells me that Israeli Army "infestation strategies" were taken from those used by the French paras in the battle for the Casbah of Algiers. Especially interesting are the rhizomic parallels in movement between self-exploders and some military units. Likely they learn from one another. In response to the Israeli Army's practice of low-density urban warfare, its ethicist, a professor of analytic philosophy, is defining neat moral distinctions (similar to those formulated to cover "ticking bombs") between "preventive killing" and assassination. In other words, as to when murder is moral (see Kasher and Yadlin 2005a, 2005b).

19. Implicit within, though especially germane to the Deleuze and Guattari argument is that the deeply rooted state-form is especially vulnerable where its lines of movement slow down, becoming densely constricted with limited lines of flight. For the self-exploder, such concentrations, approaching stasis in the restricted movement within them, are excellent targets. Perhaps for Al-Qaida the Twin Towers were a lure hard to resist, a gigantic trap of limited, clumsy, machinic, vertical movement, existing (like all skyscrapers) ethereally, seemingly unconnected to their own grounding in the world of human beings, with no ethical responsibility to the earthy struggling "ants" way below. Exploded, the Twin Towers were revealed as ponderous trees deeply rooted in earth masquerading as sky.

20. Consider the implications of the rhizomic dynamic when it is propelled by a universal religion.

21. In differing degrees, Hezbollah (in Lebanon) and now Hamas (in Gaza) are evolving in counterpoint to Al-Qaida, from more rhizomic to more centralized, deeply

rooted organizations. The point is that these are various potentialities actualizing; and so far these organizations have shown high capacities for altering their self-organization in relation to changing circumstance and ecology.

22. *Ha'aretz* (English edition), 13 September 2009.

23. Despite the relevance of rhizomic dynamics to understanding terrorist cells and networks in relation to state structures, I found no such connections in the literature I read, apart from one article by a historian (Griffin 2003). He, however, uses *rhizome* as an ideal type, while Deleuze and Guattari understand the dynamic as entirely relational.

24. *Rhizome* should be differentiated from *network*. The rhizome is its own dynamic, obviating distinctions of the order of "structure" and "process" or "structure" and "content." The rhizomic point is itself dynamic, swelling into verticality, receding into the snaking lateral movement of another rhizome in the making. The conception of network, as this usually is understood, including its application to terrorism (Knorr-Cetina, Sageman), depends on relatively fixed points (the individuals in the net) whose relatedness to one another is analyzed through how the structural properties of these points connect these individuals to one another. Network, then, is first and foremost a structure to which the content of relatedness between points is imputed. This relatedness (through structural properties of points, and through the content of relatedness that connects these points) is confounded with dynamics. On the other hand, network could also be understood as an emergent property of the rhizomic dynamic, one driving toward structuration and verticality.

25. Violence can be done equally well to vegetal form as to animal or human. The ancient Greeks called the "dismemberment" of form *sparagmos*, and the term was used extensively by Victor Turner to denote social order taken apart ritually.

26. From its outset Islam was a political religion, aimed at the creation of an Islamic State, the intention of the Prophet during the last decade of his life, after he left Mecca for Medina. Muhammad can also be cast, in the present era, "as the chief example of both self-sacrificial death and self-sacrifice (*tad'hia'*) that is linked essentially with jihad" (Strenski 2003: 14). Such positions are criticized by Ahmad (2009: 148) who argues that, "it is [only] during the early twentieth century that a fully developed political theory of the Islamic state emerged in the discourse of Islamism."

27. Israeli (2002: 25–26) traces the Hezbollah innovation of what he calls "islamikaze" to the Sh'ia reversal of the tragic mourning of the suffering and martyrdom of Imam Hussein at Karbala into the celebratory attacking martyrdom of the bombers, in which Hussein becomes not someone to be mourned but a heroic model of the battling warrior. Israeli's neologism is based on the similarities he perceives between Islamic human bombers and the Japanese kamikaze of World War II. On kamikaze see Ohnuki-Tierney (2002).

28. As Friedman (2002: 108) comments, intellectuals tend to take intentionality away from the bombers, turning them into representations or embodiments of social problems. Intellectuals thereby miss the workings of praxis that they so often extol.

29. The ultimate decision as to the intentionality of the self-exploder is that of heaven, of Allah.

30. If the appellation of *suicide bomber* is accepted without critique, as Asad (2007) does, this obviates the transformative dynamic of self-sacrifice. Indeed, this is a signal weakness in Asad's analysis. Thus, "Suicide [in the Abrahamic religions] is a sin because it is a unique act of freedom, a right that neither the religious authorities nor the nation-state allows" (Asad 2007: 67). Yet, the self-sacrificer in Islam cannot know beforehand how God will judge his intentionality and whether God will accept his self-sacrifice.

31. Kippenberg (2005: 56–57) notes that *The 9/11 Commission Report* (2004) reconstructs the sequence of events leading to the attack yet utterly ignores the manual. The American "concept of a war against evil portrays the attackers as devoid of religious faith." The faithless cannot have morality in a state that, after all, is one of Christian believers.

32. Lewinstein (2001: 79) comments on early Islam that *shahid* likely acquired its sense as "martyr" as "a reflex of late antique Christian usage."

33. Neria et al. (2005: 7–8) argue that this document presents an "as if" reality, in effect, ritual-as-pretence of ritual that enabled the attackers to dissociate themselves from the real, violent consequences of their action. In my view this demonstrates a complete lack of comprehension of the relationship between sacrifice, violence, and transformation. To date, psychologists have contributed little to comprehending self-exploders (for example, Guss, Tuason, and Teixeira 2007).

34. For Hasan al-Bana, the founder of the Muslim Brotherhood, "death is the very goal of *jihad*, and willingness to die is the key to its success" (Brown 2001: 113).

35. I am not concerned with whether or not such formations accord with "canonical" Islamic traditions. My premise is that in all moral and social orders, religious life, like all other domains of living, goes through innovation and emergence, most of which is disregarded and discarded, though each has its own history, were we able to trace this. This has been a prominent theme of my thinking for the past four decades. As I have discussed this here, the entire phenomenon of terrorism as we are experiencing this is innovative, as is, to a degree, the rhizomic forming this takes, in movement, changing shapes. Must religious forming accord always with Durkheimian genealogical foundationalism? My position here accords in more general substantial terms with that of Faisal Devji (2005).

36. When the practices of the manual are referred to, too often this offers "rational" explanation of the order of, "prayer is ritual designed to block thought, to prevent the spontaneous upsurge of disobedient impulses and inclinations. Prayer is anesthesia" (Holmes 2005: 151–52). For a psychologistic rationalization of the manual, see Neria et al. (2005).

37. Hassan (2001) quotes Palestinian bombers (whose explosives failed to detonate) as saying, "We were in a constant state of worship. ... Those were the happiest days of my life," and "We were floating, swimming, in the feeling that we were about to enter eternity."

38. This argument gives us an idea of just why it is so important on the part of Western media, scholars, publicists, and politicians to demean and denigrate the terrorist self-sacrificer by labeling him or her mentally ill, mentally retarded, lost in despair and hopelessness, brainwashed, and, not least, without true religious belief. Devji (2005: 120) writes that "the Islam of the suicide bomber is an absolutely personal

quality, as distant from the group identity of the traditional cleric as it is from the state ideology of the fundamentalist."

39. This is lost sight of too often by scholars of the logic of "sacrificial violence" in modernity, in which violence and sacrifice are nearly equated. As Martel (2006: 819) puts it, "if everything is sacrifice, then nothing is sacrifice."

REFERENCES

Ackerman, Bruce. 2006. *Before the Next Attack: Preserving Civil Liberties in an Age of Terrorism.* New Haven, CT: Yale University Press.

Agamben, Giorgio. 1998. *Homo Sacer: Sovereign Power and Bare Life.* Stanford, CA: Stanford University Press.

Ahmad, Irfan. 2009. "Genealogy of the Islamic State: Reflections on Maududi's Political Thought and Islam." *Journal of the Royal Anthropological Institute (N.S.):* S145–S162.

Andriolo, Karin. 2002. "Murder by Suicide: Episodes from Muslim History." *American Anthropologist* 104: 736–42.

Arquilla, John, and David Ronfeldt. 2000. *Swarming and the Future of Conflict.* Santa Monica, CA: Rand Corporation.

Asad, Talal. 2007. *On Suicide Bombing.* New York: Columbia University Press.

Atran, Scott. 2003. "Genesis and Future of Suicide Terrorism." *Science* 299: 1534–39.

———. 2004a. "Trends in Suicide Terrorism: Sense and Nonsense." Paper presented to World Federation of Scientists Permanent Monitoring Panel on Terrorism, Erice, Sicily.

———. 2004b. "The Jihadist Mutation." http://www.jamestown.org/publications_details.php?volume_id=400&&issue_id=2929, accessed 21 December 2005.

Bajc, Vida. 2007. "Surveillance in Public Rituals: Security Meta-ritual and the 2005 U.S. Presidential Inauguration." *American Behavioral Scientist* 50 (12): 1648–73.

Basile, Mark. 2004. "Going to the Source: Why Al Qaeda's Financial Network Is Likely to Withstand the Current War on Terrorist Financing." *Studies in Conflict and Terrorism* 27: 169–85.

Beck, Ulrich. 2002. "The Terrorist Threat: World Risk Society Revisited." *Theory, Culture & Society* 19: 39–55.

Beinin, Joel. 2003. "Is Terrorism a Useful Term in Understanding the Middle East and the Palestinian-Israel Conflict?" *Radical History Review* 85: 12–23.

Bergen, Peter. 2001. *Holy Terror, Inc.: Inside the Secret World of Osama bin Laden.* New York: Free Press.

Berkowitz, Steven D., Lloyd H. Woodward, and Caitlin Woodward. 2005. "The Use of Formal Methods to Map, Analyze and Interpret *Hawala* and Terrorist-Related Remittance Systems." *Structure and Dynamics: eJournal of Anthropological and Related Sciences* 1 (2), article 6. http://repositories cdlib.org/imbs/socdyn/sdeas/vol1/iss2/artc, accessed 10 May 2006.

Black, Donald. 2004. "The Geometry of Terrorism." *Sociological Theory* 22: 14–25.

Bourdieu, Pierre. 1977. *Outline of a Theory of Practice.* Cambridge: Cambridge University Press.

Brown, Daniel. 2001. "Martyrdom in Sunni Revivalist Thought." In *Sacrificing the Self: Perspectives on Martyrdom and Religion,* ed Margaret Cormack, 107–17. New York: Oxford University Press.

Cohn, Norman. 1970. *Pursuit of the Millennium: Revolutionary Millenarians and Mystical Anarchists in the Middle Ages.* New York: Oxford University Press.

Cook, David. 2002. "Suicide Attacks or 'Martyrdom Operations' in Contemporary Jihad Literature." *Nova Religio: The Journal of Alternative and Emergent Religions* 6: 7–43.

Dale, Stephen Frederic. 1988. "Religious Suicide in Islamic Asia: Anticolonial Terrorism in India, Indonesia, and the Philippines." *Journal of Conflict Resolution* 32: 37–59.

Deleuze, Gilles, and Felix Guattari. 1983. *On the Line.* New York: Semiotext(e).

———. 1986. *Nomadology: The War Machine.* New York: Semiotext(e).

———. 1988. *A Thousand Plateaus.* London: Athlone Press.

Devji, Faisal. 2005. *Landscapes of the Jihad: Militancy, Morality, Modernity.* London: Hurst.

Dillon, Michael. 2002. "Network Society, Network-centric Warfare and the State of Emergency." *Theory, Culture & Society* 19: 71–79.

Duclos, Denis. 1998. *The Werewolf Complex: America's Fascination with Violence.* Oxford: Berg.

Durkheim, Emile. 1952. *Suicide.* London: Routledge & Kegan Paul.

Edwards, Sean J. A. 2005. *Swarming and the Future of Warfare.* Rand Corporation, Document No.: RGSD-189. http://www.rand.org/pubs/rgs_dissertations/RGSD189, accessed 14 April 2006.

Euben, Roxanne L. 2002. "Killing (for) Politics: *Jihad,* Martyrdom and Political Action." *Political Theory* 30: 4–35.

Friedman, Jonathan. 2002. "From Nine-Eleven to Seven-Eleven: The Poverty of Interpretation." *Social Analysis* 46: 104–109.

Gambetta, Diego. 2005a. "Reason and Terror: Has 9/11 Made It Hard to Think Straight?" *Boston Review.* http://bostonreview.net/BR29.2/gambetta.html, accessed 30 January 2006.

———. 2005b. "Can We Make Sense of Suicide Missions?" In *Making Sense of Suicide Missions,* ed. Diego Gambetta, 259–99. Oxford: Oxford University Press.

Gole, Nilufer. 2002. "Close Encounters: Islam, Modernity and Violence." In *Understanding September 11,* ed. C. Calhoun, P. Price and A. Timmer. New York: New West Press.

Greenhouse, Carol. 1989. "Fighting for Peace." In *Peace and War: Cross-Cultural Perspectives,* ed. M. LeCron Foster and R. A. Rubinstein, 49–60. New Brunswick, NJ: Transaction Books.

Griffin, Roger. 2003. "From Slime Mould to Rhizome: An Introduction to the Groupuscular Right." *Patterns of Prejudice* 37: 27–50.

Gunaratna, Rohan. 2002. *Inside Al Qaeda: Global Network of Terror.* New York: Columbia University Press.

Guss, C. Dominik, Ma. Teresa Tuason, and Vanessa B. Teixeira. 2007. "A Cultural-Psychological Theory of Contemporary Islamic Martyrdom." *Journal for the Theory of Social Behavior* 37: 415–45.

Gwynne, Rosalind W. 2006. "Usama bin Laden, the Qu'ran and Jihad." *Religion* 36: 61–90.

Hage, Ghassan. 2003. "'Comes a time we are all enthusiasm': Understanding Palestinian Suicide Bombers in Times of Exighophobia." *Public Culture* 15: 65–89.

Handelman, Don. 2004. *Nationalism and the Israeli State: Bureaucratic Logic in Public Events.* Oxford: Berg.

Handelman, Don. 2005. "Introduction: Why Ritual in Its Own Right? How So?" In *Ritual in its Own Right: Exploring the Dynamics of Transformation,* ed. Don Handelman and Galina Lindquist, 1–32. New York: Berghahn.

Hassan, Nasra. 2001. "An Arsenal of Believers: Talking to the 'Human Bombs'." *New Yorker,* 11 November.

Held, Virginia. 1991. "Terrorism, Rights, and Political Goals." In *Violence, Terrorism, and Justice,* ed. R. G. Frey and C. W. Morris. Cambridge: Cambridge University Press.

Hersey, John. 1989 [1946]. *Hiroshima.* New York: Vintage.

Hoffman, Bruce. 2003. "Al Qaeda, Trends in Terrorism, and Future Potentialities: An Assessment." *Studies in Conflict and Terrorism* 26: 429–42.

Holmes, Stephen. 2005. "Al-Qaeda, September 11, 2001." In *Making Sense of Suicide Missions,* ed. Diego Gambetta, 131–72. Oxford: Oxford University Press.

Hubert, Henri, and Marcel Mauss. 1964. *Sacrifice: Its Nature and Function.* Chicago: University of Chicago Press.

Hull, Isabel V. 2005. *Absolute Destruction: Military Culture and the Practices of War in Imperial Germany.* Ithaca, NY: Cornell University Press.

International Institute for Strategic Studies. 2003. *The Military Balance 2003–2004.* London: Arundel House.

Israeli, Raphael. 2002. "A Manual of Islamic Fundamentalist Terrorism." *Terrorism and Political Violence* 14: 23–40.

Kapferer, Bruce. 1997. *The Feast of the Sorcerer.* Chicago: University of Chicago Press.

Kasher, Asa, and Amos Yadlin. 2005a. "Assassination and Preventive Killing." *SAIS Review* 25: 41–57.

———. 2005b. "Military Ethics of Fighting Terror: An Israeli Perspective." *Journal of Military Ethics* 4: 3–32.

Kippenberg, Hans G. 2005. "'Consider that it is a raid on the path of God': The Spiritual Manual of the Attackers of 9/11." *Numen* 52: 29–58.

Knorr Cetina, Karin. 2005. "Complex Global Microstructures: The New Terrorist Societies." *Theory, Culture & Society* 22: 213–34.

Krebs, Valdis E. n.d. "Uncloaking Terrorist Networks." http://www.firstmonday.org/issues/issue7_4/krebs/, accessed 11 September, 2005.

Lewinstein, Keith. 2001. "The Revaluation of Martyrdom in Early Islam." In *Sacrificing the Self: Perspectives on Martyrdom and Religion,* ed. Margaret Cormack, 78–91. New York: Oxford University Press.

Lind, William S., Keith Nightengale, John F. Schmitt, Joseph W. Sutton, and Gary I. Wilson. 1989. "The Changing Face of War: Into the Fourth Generation." *Marine Corps Gazette,* October, 22–26. http://www.d-n-i.net/fcs/4th_gen_war_gazette.htm.

Mahmood, Saba. 2001. "Feminist Theory, Embodiment, and the Docile Agent: Some Reflections on the Egyptian Islamic Revival." *Cultural Anthropology* 16: 202–36.

Mannheim, Karl. 1936. *Ideology and Utopia*. London: Routledge & Kegan Paul.

Marion, Russ, and Mary Uhl-Bien. 2003. "Complexity Theory and Al-Qaeda: Examining Complex Leadership." *Emergence* 5: 54–76.

Martel, James R. 2006. "Can We Do Away with Sacrifice?" *Political Theory* 34: 814–20.

Marvin, Carolyn, and David W. Ingle. 1999. *Blood Sacrifice and the Nation: Totem Rituals and the American Flag.* Cambridge: Cambridge University Press.

Mbembe, Achille. 2000. "At the Edge of the World: Boundaries, Territoriality, and Sovereignty in Africa." *Public Culture* 12: 259–84.

———. 2003. "Necropolitics." *Public Culture* 15: 11–40.

Mishal, Shaul, and Maoz Rosenthal. 2005. "Al-Qaeda as a Dune Organization: Toward a Typology of Islamic Terrorist Organizations." *Studies in Conflict and Terrorism* 28: 275–93.

Mneimneh, Hassan, and Kanan Makiya. 2002. "Manual for a 'Raid'." *New York Review of Books* 49, no. 1 (January 17).

Moghaddam, Fathali M. 2005. "The Staircase to Terrorism: A Psychological Exploration." *American Psychologist* 60 (2): 161–69.

Nederman, Cary J. 1989. "Nature, Ethics, and the Doctrine of 'Habitus': Aristotelian Moral Psychology in the Twelfth Century." *Traditio* 45: 87–110.

Neocleous, Mark. 2006. "From Social to National Security: On the Fabrication of Economic Order." *Security Dialogue* 37: 363–84.

Neria, Yuval, David Roe, Benjamin Beit-Hallahmi, Hassan Mneimneh, Alana Balaban, and Randall Marshall. 2005. "The Al Qaeda 9/11 Instructions: A Study in the Construction of Religious Martyrdom." *Religion* 35: 1–11.

Ohnuki-Tierney, Emiko. 2002. *Kamikaze, Cherry Blossoms, and Nationalisms: The Militarization of Aesthetics in Japanese History.* Chicago: University of Chicago Press.

Oliver, Anne Marie, and Paul Steinberg. 2005. *The Road to Martyrs' Square: A Journey into the World of the Suicide Bomber.* New York: Oxford University Press.

Primoratz, Igor. 1997. "The Morality of Terrorism." *Journal of Applied Philosophy* 14: 221–33.

Rapoport, David C. 1984. "Fear and Trembling: Terrorism in Three Religious Traditions." *American Political Science Review* 78: 658–77.

Raufer, Xavier. 2003. "Al Qaeda: A Different Diagnosis." *Studies in Conflict and Terrorism* 26: 391–98.

Roberts, Michael. n.d. "Blunders in Tigerland: Pape's Muddles on 'Suicide Bombers' in Sri Lanka." Unpublished manuscript.

———. 2005a. "Tamil Tiger 'Martyrs': Regenerating Divine Potency?" *Studies in Conflict and Terrorism* 28: 493–514.

———. 2005b. "Saivite Symbolism, Sacrifice and Tamil Tiger Rites." *Social Analysis* 59: 67–93.

Sageman, Marc. 2004. *Understanding Terror Networks*. Philadelphia: University of Pennsylvania Press.

Sebald, W. G. 2004. *On the Natural History of Destruction*. London: Penguin Books.

Simon, Steven, and Daniel Benjamin. 2001–02. "The Terror." *Survival* 43 (4): 5–18.

Smith, Thomas W. 2002. "The New Law of War: Legitimizing Hi-tech and Infrastructural Violence." *International Studies Quarterly* 46: 355–74.

Strenski, Ivan. 2003. "Sacrifice, Gift and the Social Logic of Muslim 'Human Bombers'." *Terrorism and Political Violence* 15: 1–34.

Tsvetovat, Maksim, and Kathleen M. Carley. n.d. "Bouncing Back: Recovery Mechanisms of Covert Networks."

Verkaaik, Oskar. 2005. "Purity and Transgression: Sacred Violence and the Quest for Authenticity." In *MESS—Mediterranean Ethnological Summer School,* vol. 6, ed. B. Kravanja and M. Vranjes, 139–54.

Virilio, Paul. 2007. *The Original Accident.* Cambridge: Polity Press.

Weizman, Eyal. 2006a. "Walking through Walls: Soldiers as Architects in the Israeli-Palestinian Conflict." *Radical Philosophy* no. 136: 8–22.

———. 2006b. "Introduction to Shimon Naveh, Between the Striated and the Smooth." *Cabinet* no. 22: 81–88.

Wyschogrod, Edith. 1985. *Spirit in Ashes: Hegel, Heidegger and Man-Made Mass Death.* New Haven, CT: Yale University Press.

Zerubavel, Yael. 1995. *Recovered Roots: Collective Memory and the Making of Israeli National Tradition.* Chicago: University of Chicago Press.

Zulaika, Joseba. 2003. "The Self-Fulfilling Prophecies of Counterterrorism." *Radical History Review* 85: 191–99.

FIXATION OF BELIEF AND THE DILEMMAS OF FALLIBILITY

Robert E. Innis

The foregoing studies show that the blending, as well as the clashing, of the sacred and the worldly, or the religious and the political, results in a volatile epistemological cocktail, with multiple ingredients in varying proportions. Appeals to the ultimacy of the sacred, specifically with claims to a privileged revelation, whether Christian, Islamic, or Hindu, are fused, at both the micro and the macro level, with opposing claims to procedural or substantive ultimacy both within the realm of the sacred and within the secular domain in its primarily political and economic dimensions—the realm of modernity's great rationalization project. At stake is a contest for establishing not just the locus of authority but the super- and subordination of realms, their relative positionings, whether sacred or secular. The authority that is in question is partially political and partially religious, but the ultimate source of strife is epistemological and symbolic. The weapons are rhetorically sharpened by conceptual tools from incommensurable domains that reflect very different metaphysical commitments or visions of ultimate reality and very differently formed selves. What in the introduction is referred to as the mundane games of power politics, both sacred and secular, really concerns the "right to manage material and symbolic resources." It arises first and foremost out of the quest for certainty or the further quest for power based upon certainty—or, to put it paradoxically, out of the felt, and needed, certainty of being certain and hence having the right to either exercise or wrest power in multiple domains, especially the domains of self-formation and cultural definition.

The quest for certainty, or for the right to be certain, is a kind of epistemological or cognitional quest for purity. It involves, in the first instance, as

---

I see it, a kind of violence toward oneself, and then to others, a forcing of a closure to an inquiry whose inner logic clearly elicits, indeed demands, passionate commitment, but whose inner logic clearly is also eminently fallible. The "great refusal" that lies behind many of the strife-ridden situations discussed in the preceding papers is the refusal of fallibility, or the refusal of others' claim to infallibility or at least exclusive right to determine "what is to be done and thought." The battles, in many ways, revolve around assertions of a kind of "privileged access" and exclusive method of arriving at "the truth" or, once having arrived, at having the right, or rather obligation, to represent it, forcefully if necessary, to oneself as well as to others. The upshot is, as we read in the introduction, a "religious ferment of contrasting epistemologies"—with complex epistemologies of what Peter Berger referred to as the "sacred canopies" of religious orders leaching into the various domains of the political order, with each framework claiming a kind of holistic ultimacy, on both a local and global scale. The quest for certainty, which the American pragmatist philosopher John Dewey subjected to withering criticism in a book of that title, involves what in the introduction is referred to as a quest for "intellectual ontological security." This is the motivating matrix of those mighty struggles charted in this book where politics and religion meet on the rugged terrains of, in the introduction's words, "ideas, bodies, minds and souls."

In a famous essay, "The Fixation of Belief" (Peirce 1877), the American polymath and philosopher Charles S. Peirce explored the epistemological aspects that lie at the core of the conflicts and structures discussed in these studies. The seriously deflating lessons of this essay should be learned by all the striving and contending sides of the debates charted in this book. For Peirce, human life, at the deepest levels, involves the formation and habitualization, that is, stabilization, of beliefs and the further "rationalization" of habits. This is a phenomenologically charted fact about humans, who are not programmed within a closed circuit of action and perceptual powers by their genetic inheritance. The formation of belief, on all levels, affective, actional, conceptual, where we can take on habits, arises through efforts to resolve the "irritation" of real, as opposed to, fictive or merely subjectively motivated doubts, to deal with what John Dewey called "problematic situations." These situations can involve lack of affective attunement, inappropriate or inefficient action, or the failure, or lack, of conceptual means to construe a situation. We must not, Peirce says, pretend to doubt with our minds what we do not really doubt with our hearts. The pressing problems put before us in these studies exemplify the multifarious loci of real, existentially biting, doubts of the heart. They are not "made up," although they are not necessarily just what they present themselves to be. The various "debates" arise out of perplexed "existences," on both the individual and social levels and with varying degrees of scope. The consequent struggles, spanning many spheres of human action and doctrinal systems, are attempts both to arrive at the "truth" and to guarantee its permanency, stability, or power. But it is clear that the participants are utilizing quite different methods and have quite different conceptions of what "truth" is and, metaphysically speaking, of what "ultimately matters." Seeking truth and seeking to defend, institutionalize, or insulate a truth against opposing claims are not the same.

Peirce distinguishes four "ways" for the "fixation of belief" with the goal of, and with severe consequences for, "taking on habits." The problem, from an epistemological point of view, is to determine just which habits, affective, actional, and conceptual, would be "rational" and justified and which "ways" or "methods," or one way or method, are, or is, valid and universally acceptable. Belief, as Peirce uses the term, involves the formation of a multileveled commitment to a "content" or to a system of contents or knowledge claims. These are frameworks of meaning, interpretive schemes that encompass and differentiate not just the conceptual spaces in which one dwells but patterns of affect and courses of pragmatic and material action. The frameworks correspond to Peirce's great semiotic insight that sign systems, the carriers of meaning, engender different kinds of "interpretants," which he called the "proper significate effects" of sign action. These are the "equivalent signs" that "interpret" a previous sign or set of signs in a process of "unlimited semiosis." Looked at rhetorically, that is, from the point of view of the production and interpretation of signs, "the semiotic self" in Peirce's reckoning is structured by "affective" interpretants, "energetic" or actional interpretants, and "logical" or conceptual interpretants. A sign complex elicits and shapes modes of feeling, modes of action, and modes of thought. And the selves engaged are unities, not necessarily wholly integrated, of feelings, actions, and thoughts. In this sense a feeling, say, of isolation or denigration, can be a way in which a self "interprets" the world, just as an action, such as a self-explosion, can be a form of interpretation, or a theory of law with startling nonsecular implications, such as that propounded by the Imam of Fuengirola, can function as an interpretation of the religious frame of legal order within and outside of a purely civil or secular frame.

Now, the complex frameworks under whose protection religious movements operate and in which the secular orders generated by modernity's rationalization project are articulated, following Peirce's schema of sign types, in complex sign configurations: (a) image fields, full of symbolic pregnance, that inform us at the deepest affective levels (Peirce's iconic dimension); (b) patterns of meaningful action that connect us together, or tear us apart, and that elicit and steer, or constrain, other actions (Peirce's indexical dimension); and (c) systems of contesting and contested ideas and conceptual frames at various levels of generality and pertinence (Peirce's symbolic dimension). These configurations circulate in society, through societies, and around the world. These configurations of signs are the matrices for the distinctive consequences, the significate effects, that inform the conflicting and conflicted selves and groups whose diverse contexts and existential and cultural dilemmas are charted in the variety of studies in this book. Peirce offers us a methodological and semiotic way of both explicating and measuring them, a kind of implicitly normative hermeneutical rule, that one should keep in mind when one looks back on the preceding studies. It is contained in his "pragmatic maxim," which runs as follows: "In order to ascertain the meaning of an intellectual conception one should consider what practical consequences might conceivably result by necessity from the truth of that conception; and the sum of these consequences will constitute the entire meaning of the conception" (Peirce 1905: 53).

The foregoing studies display a wide range of "practical consequences" arising from different core conceptions and intellectual frameworks: self-exploders; shamans; protectors and promoters of cultural minorities, political rights and duties of clergy, whether Christian in East Timor, Muslim in Spain, Christian fundamentalist in America, or tolerant anthropologists in worldwide connection. Look at the "sum of consequences" attendant upon the various belief systems charted in this book. It is not a pretty picture—on all sides—and for unfortunately quite intractable reasons, deep seated in the human psyche and in the makeup of the semiotic self.

It should be noted that prior to any conscious attempt to take on, reflect on, act, and feel according to a system of beliefs, we have already been assimilated acritically into one or many. The very spinning of ourselves into language, and the spinning of ourselves out of language, as Handelman has shown, already involves an assimilation, and application, of a whole set of distinctions and weightings of the experiential continuum, and this set becomes a kind of existential tool box for handling the variety of cognitive, actional, and affective tasks, no matter how deadly, we confront or effect at various stages. Following Michael Polanyi's (1958, 1966) lead, we can say that we "pour ourselves" into these articulate systems and come to "dwell in" them. They become "interiorized" on multiple levels—affectively, praxically, and conceptually—and so inform us both "up" and "down" at the thresholds of sense and meaning and "in between" these thresholds. We are assimilated to these frames "acritically" and they become for us "the way the world is." This "epistemic situation" can and does, the foregoing studies show, have deleterious consequences.[1]

There is in humans a deep-seated tendency to hold fast to one's first frame or the frame one has grown comfortable in and to use it as a complete, self-affirming, and self-expanding system of articulation. Peirce (1877) writes that this way of fixating or fixing belief involves a "willful adherence to a belief" (118) primarily on the individual level and the avoidance of any challenge to it—an "occasion of sin," a contamination, an accommodation to infidels—as a giving in to a sort of epistemological temptation. "A man may go through life, systematically keeping out of view all that might cause a change in his opinions, and if he only succeeds—basing his method as he does on two fundamental psychological laws—I do not see what can be said against his doing so" (116). The first law is simply the human inclination to refuse to entertain any challenge to one's present belief system, a kind of intellectual, behavioral, and affective inertia that does not arise from laziness but from our preference for a stable habit. Rather, in accord with the second law, we also have an "instinctive dislike of an undecided state of mind" (116) and hence the reasoning is that if one only held to a belief "without wavering, it will be entirely satisfactory" (116). We could call these laws the *law of confirmed habituation* and the *law of suppressed nucleation*. We seek comfort and a self-confirming expansion, and we exclude, both really and psychologically, any challenges to our psychological well-being. Peirce calls this way of fixing belief "the method of tenacity" (116). It applies both to the aggressive and fearless fanatic, to the sophisticated and principled fundamentalists of high orthodoxy and dominant worldviews, to the timid and afraid seeker after security at all costs confronted with a world of complexity beyond control, and to the resentful and persistent pushback of cultural minorities to overweening majorities. Exemplifications of all of these types are found in the preceding chapters.

But, Peirce notes, no one can be unaware effectively and with impunity of the presence of other belief systems that are equally defended. The social impulse that governs the very matrix of speech and the formation of any articulate system of beliefs and consequent patterns of habits becomes, or *should become*, unstable not because we necessarily discover an unexpected implication of our belief system and therefore tend to modify or repudiate it, but because of the mere presence of other beliefs that we do not have to accept intellectually but at least have to acknowledge in eminently practical or "legal" terms—the confused situation of the Imam of Fuengirola, who still held tenaciously to his position and refused to cede to another locus of authority. The existence of other belief systems not only puts our own system into play but it also induces insecurity and uncertainty because we cannot evade, with impunity, the influence of other's opinions—and the constraints these opinions place upon us.

Now, Peirce observes, "the problem becomes how to fix belief, not in the individual merely, but in the community" (117). This turn to community displaces the locus of authority from the individual to the group. Indeed, the impossibility of the pure method of tenacity derives from the inner social logic of conviviality (see Polanyi 1958: 203–48). Since we are not isolated individuals but mutually dependent upon one another, the principle of *tot capita, quot sententiae* cannot be tolerated in an absolute sense. It would lead to anarchy. Instead of the power of ideas, tenaciously held to as a sovereign, even if individual, right, there arises the idea of power, and it is wielded not individually but socially by the group against its "deviant" members as well as against those "outside," whether locally or globally. Hence, the often "transnational" nature of the conflicts dealt with in this book. For this end we need an "institution" whose object is "to keep correct doctrines before the attention of the people, to reiterate them perpetually, and to teach them to the young; having at the same time power to prevent contrary doctrines from being taught, advocated, or expressed" (117). Worldly and sacred exemplifications come readily to mind. They are clearly instantiated in the cases analyzed in the foregoing studies. The immediate goal of such a way of fixing belief is to terrify, or subtly or not so subtly to manipulate, "unbelievers" or "nonconformists" into silence, or to eradicate them physically, or at least to disenfranchise them from power and from positions of symbolic influence.

Peirce points out that such a method is a "natural product of social feeling," which is often accompanied by cruelties and atrocities wielded by a "most ruthless power" (117). The actual or immediate motivations of this power do not have to be, although they can be, metaphysical or religious in any sense. They can be purely cultural, or economic, or "merely" political. Modern totalitarian regimes as well as the case of the Amazigh illustrate this side of the problem. This "method of authority," Peirce notes, is not without its "majestic results," exemplified in not just "mere structures of stone"—one thinks of the great monuments of civil and religious architecture and of the universal thrust of the fusion of "Arabism," founded in the divine status of Arabic as language of the "ultimate revelation," with "Islam"—but also in the great belief systems of organized faiths, the historical instantiations of maximally differentiated sacred and worldly frameworks within which change is so slow that, until there is a rupture or challenge from without, "individual belief remains sensibly fixed" (118). But, Peirce reminds us, there remains the problem of scale and scope: "no institution can undertake to regulate opinions upon every subject," but only the most important ones. At the same time, just as on the individual level with the method of tenacity one becomes quickly aware of radical and substantive differences, so on the social level the "arbitrary forcing" of a belief on others, just as the "willful adherence to a belief," on the individual level, has to be given up—at least ideally.

But it is clear from these studies that many seemingly irresolvable conflicts arise precisely from a fateful fusion of these two methods, since the points of intersection, as well as the range of relevance, between different psychological commitments and different affinity groups operate within the framework of different ultimate premises and different goals: security within an invulnerable insight or maintenance of social, cultural, and intellectual order. These premises often have to be "ritualized."[2] The problem, as Peirce conceives it, is where to turn to a "more reasonable" method of fixing belief that will not only produce "an impulse to believe" that is rooted in either an individual or a social form of subjectivity, but will be, in some way, "objectively" motivated by allowing a certain "draw" from the subject matter, a pulling of our commitments forward, similar to the way "conceptions of art have been brought to maturity" (118), which often occur without any effort of will but because of a "felt affinity." Such a "felt affinity" has many points of origin, but they, too, as it turns out, are unfortunately "subjective" in a nontrivial way.

Such a method of fixing belief is, on Peirce's reckoning, "agreeable to reason." It accords with premises that have at first glance a kind of intrinsic rationality, such as the preference for regular figures such as the circle over such figures as the ellipse, a preference that Kepler, for example, had to overcome, or the types of preferences for "natural motion" charted by Aristotle that Newton had to overcome. The types of preferences both supported or overcome in favor of other preferences arise from a kind of "taste," which assumes ultimate authority functioning a priori. They are not discovered but rather presupposed. They are what, in another context, Gerald Holton (1973) called "themata." Peirce calls this method the a priori method, but adds, not unsurprisingly, that it does not "differ in a very essential way from that of authority" (119). But the locus of authority has shifted from self-assertion (or self-protection) and coercive action to the accidentality of the sentiments of rationality, which are nevertheless taken as normative—as a kind of protective device for "psychic" and "cultural" identity based on a kind of relativism. But it is precisely recognition of this accidentality, for the ideal observer if not for the engaged participant, that causes, or should cause, a "real doubt" about such a method, based on drift and preferences, no matter how "agreeable" even if contestable. We are accordingly, by a kind of dialectical impetus, pushed in a significantly different direction, a direction toward the fourth method of fixing belief, a direction that is not based on anything human but on "some external permanency" (120). Such an external permanency must not be accessible either to a privileged individual, such as a mystic claims, or to any group that affirms a special revelation or insight with universal rights and privileges, proper to them alone, or to proponents of harmonious orders and irreducible differences.

If we follow Peirce, the need imposed on us by the situations charted in these chapters is to find a method whose goal is "such that the ultimate conclusion of every man shall be the same, or would be the same if inquiry were sufficiently persisted in" (120). This method does not tell us the substantive content of the ultimate conclusion. *Inquiry* here refers to not just the action of reflection but reflective action. The method Peirce is referring to is the method of science, which is "the only one of the four methods which presents any distinction of a right and a wrong way" that is fundamentally "objective" as opposed to "subjective," in the senses defined. The method of science has as its fundamental hypothesis the following:

> There are real things, whose characters are entirely independent of our opinions about them; those realities affect our senses according to regular laws, and, though our sensations are as different as our relations to the objects, yet, by taking advantage of the laws of perception, we can ascertain by reasoning

how things really are, and any man, if he have sufficient experience and reason enough about it, will be led to the one true conclusion. (120)

A critical reader—or committed proponent of contested worldviews—may ask how such a hypothesis exemplifies as well as implies a method different from the foregoing three alternatives, which, in fact, seem also to imply that there *is* a "reality," namely, the one that one is holding to with "subjective certainty." What is really distinctive here? Are not the other three methods also devoted to the central thesis that there are "realities?" What is the real contrast? And, one might ask, the "one true conclusion" *about what?*

The scientific method, or the method of science, as Peirce is construing it, is "the only one of the four methods which presents any distinction of a right and a wrong way" (121). I think it fair to say that for Peirce the other three methods are "subjectively consistent," but "objectively inconsistent," although he does not put it this way. Given their premises, none of the preceding three methods can be "wrong" if they follow faithfully their constitutive rules: be tenacious, put down heresy by any means necessary, follow your inclinations. You cannot be wrong if you follow these rules! The scientific method starts, however, with "known and observed facts to proceed to the unknown; and yet the rules which I follow in doing so may not be such as investigation would approve" (121). Immediate appeal to feeling and purposes is to be replaced by the application of a method—and this method can succeed or fail—to reach the truth, which one does not already possess. In other words, we can be wrong. We can be challenged not just to change our mind, but also to change our lives. The key "formal insight" is into the inevitability of fallibility. It is a "reverse conversion" from dogmatism to open, critical, yet committed, inquiry, informed by heuristic tensions and persuasive passions (see Polanyi 1958: chapter 9 and 10).

At the same time Peirce does not deny that each of the alternative methods can offer "some peculiar convenience of its own" (121), whether comfortable conclusions in the case of the a priori method, the path of peace and social order in the case of the method of authority, or the decisiveness of character exemplified in the strength, simplicity, and directness of those practicing the method of tenacity. But, Peirce notes, there is no reason why the results of the first three methods would enable our opinions to "coincide with the fact" (122). But this is, or at least should be, our deepest desire. Only the method of science, based on abductive inference, resolutely proceeding from the known to the unknown, a process subject to constant criticism, can enable us, within the scope of an always fallible process of inquiry, to do so. It is the only method, Peirce contends, that fully values "integrity of belief" (123) and that looks into the *support of belief* with no avoidance of the possibility that *it may be wrong.* The personal and social burden and consequences can be severe, for "a clear logical conscience does cost something" (123). But one is purchasing not just the truth but the only method of reliably distinguishing it from falsehood. The lover of truth is wedded to this method as to a bride, Peirce floridly opines, "from the blaze of whose splendors he draws his inspiration and his courage" (123).

Peirce's schematization of methods is extraordinarily insightful. It helps us see a host of exemplifications and combinations of the various methods in the preceding studies, to which I have alluded in the course of these reflections. Peirce supplies critical ideas about the semiotic complexity of the selves that are being studied in these papers. In the broadest sense, on Peircean principles, the self is a semiotic phenomenon first and foremost. The conflicted selves displayed in these studies and Peirce's triadic schema of classes of interpretants allows us to see how human meaning-makers push meaning both "up" to an "upper" threshold of articulate socially shared symbol systems, which get wielded as rhetorical weapons, and "down" to the various dimensions of "felt sense" and "action programs" that mark the "lower" threshold of the human drive for significance.[3] Sign systems, as representational devices and embodied access structures, are formative in the strictest sense: of both the "objective" and the "subjective" worlds.

Human semiosis, that is, the production and interpretation of signs, is a complex mix of these various domains of signs that attach us to the world with distinctive weights and powers and in this way inform our subjectivity and shape our selves. We are "informed" or "qualified" on the affective and emotional level, "energized" and physically connected on the actional level, and conceptually "defined" on the "logical" level. On this account the self is a complex and intertwined unity of feeling, action, and conceptual content.[4] Feeling involves complex systems of appraisal and dispraisal, the assignment of positive and negative valences, to the affective tones and quality-defined situations in which we find ourselves. Action involves pragmatic intervention into the situational plenum of perplexity. Conceptual content is the network or lattice of distinctions by which one construes the plenum. The problem is that feelings, actions, and conceptual content do not have to be in accord. In fact, they can be at loggerheads with one another and the result is a deeply conflicted situation and a ferocious struggle within and between individuals and groups.

It is hard to give up an emotional or affective commitment. This side of the play of interpretants certainly fosters tendencies to fix belief by means of both the method of tenacity and the a priori method. The "energetic" side of the play of interpretants, an action or program of actions, likewise is a concomitant of shared "feelings of belonging," a conviviality constitutive of a community, but these actions drive a wedge into the material and social world. The most revolutionary wedge is the combined institutionalization and isolation of self-exploders that Handelman presents. The "logical" or "conceptual" side of the play of interpretants encompasses the world views and mental models that inform and shape feeling and action just as they themselves are informed and shaped by them.

One should, therefore, think of the distinction between interpretants as referring to dimensions of the interpretant domain and hence to dimensions of the significance-seeking self, rather than strictly distinct and autonomous spheres of meaning. It is a matter of "weighting." Certain types of signs, rooted in iconicity, are more oriented toward the informing of sensibility; others, rooted in indexicality, to the eliciting of action; and others, rooted in symbolicity, to the formulation of conceptual content. But all, in one way or the other, have a "content" and are forms of understanding—and hence are matters defined by forms of discursive, communicative, and expressive rationality. Different sign types, to be sure, access the world in different ways. Iconic signs, embodied in the great circulation of affect-laden images, function in the mode of exemplification. Indexical signs, joining us to the world in systems of "real connections," function in the mode of directed steering of perceptual and pragmatic action. Symbolic signs, the domain of our ultimate premises and postulates, function in the mode of conceptual formulation and critical contestation. The method of science leads us to foreground and valorize this fateful union of the discursive and the empirical and to universalize its lessons. It will be dependent first and foremost on fostering conceptual formulation. It is not for nothing that it is the discursive method par excellence. Its "steering function" comes from its orientation toward a reality and not from some desire for power and control that is extratheoretical, for emotional satisfaction or for practical effect. It is after conceptual power, not conceptual stability. And it recognizes the intrinsic fallibility of all belief systems. It is not riven with fear of loss of control over social unity that motivates the method of authority nor with a disruption of a comfortable and harmonious set of habits that motivates the a priori method nor with the refusal to believe that one could possibly be wrong and hence with the resolute refusal to admit the very possibility of conceptual alternative that informs the method of tenacity.

These are some of the thoughts that the clash between the differently motivated and configured frameworks analyzed in this book brought to my mind. Peirce's modeling of "methods" is both descriptive and normative. In one sense it is really a study of psychological attitudes and temperaments. But it is also a study of the various forces and motivations, semiotic factors and processes, that pull and tug us in different directions.[5] When they are activated by such a set of seemingly irreconcilable commitments as are displayed in these case studies, we can see the truth of John Dewey's remark in *The Public and Its Problems* (Dewey 1927), which has a remarkable pertinence to the issues mooted in this book. Dewey writes:

The ties which hold men together in action are numerous, tough, and subtle. They are invisible and intangible. We have before us the tools of communication as never before. … Communication can alone create a great community. Our Babel is not one of tongues but of the signs and symbols without which shared experience is impossible. (142)

He continues:

A community thus presents an order of energies transmuted into one of meanings which are appreciated and mutually referred by each to every other on the part of those engaged in combined action. "Force" is not eliminated but is transformed in use and direction by ideas and sentiments made possible by means of symbols. (153)

Such is our hope, but also clearly our dilemma, as the topics of this book have illustrated. How, in the final analysis, do we handle or answer Ben-Ami Scharfstein's sharp and epistemologically deflating challenge that "the dream of unanimity by means of free intellectual agreement ought to be dismissed" (Scharfstein 1989: 193)?

Whether, then, in the long run philosophy can effectively, as opposed to analytically, intervene in the "situational knots" foregrounded by our authors is a question as weighty as it is currently unanswerable.

For Galina

Sitting in our living room some years ago in Massachusetts, Galina, who had mastered all forms of talk, from high to low, said that she had a fundamental trust that would, and—as it turned out—did, support her, and that, in the deepest ontological sense, she felt that everything was "ok." Not that she was "taken care of," but that there was a fundamental rightness in things, something that one could rely on—or at least that she relied on. Nondogmatic to the core, she did not need to say more. But I knew what she meant, and she knew that I knew. The following day, having lunch in Concord, after visiting the public library named after that great seeker, Ralph Waldo Emerson, we had a long conversation about, among many other things, the tension between religions of revelation and religions of enlightenment and about the implications of a deep religious naturalism—to, I have to admit, the great agitation of someone at a nearby table. But Galina was unfazed. She was, I think, a synthesis of nature and spirit, an "achieved" synthesis with a radiant, even self-ironic, glow about her. Galina's "method," in life and work, was inseparable from her person.

Notes

1. I have explored the philosophical, phenomenological, and semiotic contexts and background of these themes and issues in my 1994 and 2002. Liszka 1996 is a most helpful introduction to the Peircean concepts used in this afterword. My 1985 presents classic semiotic texts with introductions that follow the thread of the intersections of signs and subjectivity in some detail.
2. I have explored the ritualization of ultimate premises, especially ultimate sacred premises, in Innis 2005.
3. I have explored the issue of "upper" and "lower" thresholds and their connection with a "felt sense," especially with respect to language in Innis 2008.
4. See Innis (1994: 16–21).
5. A profound discussion of the biopsychological factors and the cultural consequences of these processes is to be found in Susanne K. Langer's great trilogy (1967, 1972, 1982). I have given an account of this work and the deep social and cultural aspects of it in Innis (2009: chapters 6, 7, 8).

References

Dewey, John. 1927. *The Public and Its Problems*. New York: Holt.

Holton, Gerald. 1973. *Thematic Origins of Scientific Thought*. Cambridge, MA: Harvard University Press.

Innis, Robert E. 1985. *Semiotics: An Introductory Anthology*. Bloomington: Indiana University Press.

———. 1994. *Consciousness and the Play of Signs*. Bloomington: Indiana University Press.

———. 2002. *Pragmatism and the Forms of Sense: Language, Perception, Technics*. University Park: Penn State University Press.

———. 2005. "The Tacit Logic of Ritual Embodiments." In *Ritual in Its Own Right*, ed. Don Handelman and Galina Lindquist. New York: Berghahn Books.

———. 2008. "Language and the Thresholds of Sense: Some Aspects of the Failure of Words." *Journal of Speculative Philosophy* 22 (2): 106–17.

———. 2009. *Susanne Langer in Focus: The Symbolic Mind*. Bloomington: Indiana University Press.

Langer, Susanne K. 1967, 1972, 1982. *Mind: An Essay on Human Feeling*, 3 vols. Baltimore: Johns Hopkins University Press.

Liszka, James Jakób. 1996. *A General Introduction to the Semeiotic of Charles Sanders Peirce*. Bloomington: Indiana University Press.

Peirce, C. S. 1877. "The Fixation of Belief." In *The Essential Peirce: Selected Philosophical Writings*, vol 1, ed. Christian J. Kloesel and Nathan Houser. Bloomington: Indiana University Press, 1992.

―――. 1905 (1982). "The Architectonic Construction of Pragmatism." A fragment from a 1905 manuscript. In *Pragmatism: The Classic Writings,* ed. H. S. Thayer. Indianapolis: Hackett Publishing Co.

Polanyi, Michael. 1958. *Personal Knowledge: Towards a Post-Critical Philosophy.* Chicago: University of Chicago Press.

―――. 1966. *The Tacit Dimension.* Garden City: Doubleday.

Scharfstein, Ben-Ami. 1989. *The Dilemma of Context.* New York: New York University Press.

CONTRIBUTORS

Mira Z. Amiras received her PhD in Anthropology at the University of California, Berkeley, in 1982. Her geographical area of expertise is the Middle East and North Africa. She is Professor of Comparative Religious Studies and Coordinator of the Middle East Studies Program at San Jose State University. Her research has focused primarily on the relationship between the state and the individual in rural North Africa. Mira Amiras has served as president of the Society for the Anthropology of Consciousness, and on the executive boards of the American Anthropological Association and the Association for Transpersonal Psychology.

Henrik Berglund (PhD) is an assistant professor at the Department of Political Science, Stockholm University, Sweden. His research interests include women's organization, religion and nationalism, as well as issues of globalization and its effects on Indian politics. His current research project as analysis of the effects of globalization on Indian civil society.

Simon Coleman is Jackman Professor at the Department and Centre for the Study of Religion, University of Toronto. He works on charismatic Christianity, pilgrimage and religious chaplaincy, and has conducted fieldwork in Sweden, the United Kingdom, the United States, and Nigeria. His books include *The Globalisation of Charismatic Christianity* (2000). Between 2008 and 2010 he was editor of the *Journal of the Royal Anthropological Institute*.

Don Handelman is Shaine Professor Emeritus at the Hebrew University of Jerusalem and a member of the Israel Academy of Sciences and Humanities. He has authored *Models and Mirrors: Towards an Anthropology of Public Events* (1998), *Nationalism and the Israeli State* (2004), and coauthored (with David Shulman) *God Inside Out: Siva's Game of Dice* (1997) and *Siva in the Forest of Pines: An Essay on Sorcery and Self-Knowledge* (2004).

David Hicks is Professor of Anthropology at Stony Brook University and Life Member of Clare College, University of Cambridge. His books include *Tetum Ghosts and Kin; Structural Analysis in Anthropology; A Maternal Religion; Kinship and Religion in Eastern*

Indonesia; Cultural Anthropology (with Margaret A. Gwyn); and *Ritual and Belief* (editor). His papers have appeared in the *American Anthropologist, The Journal of the Royal Anthropological Institute,* and the *Bijdragen tot de Taal-, Land- en Volkenkunde.*

Robert E. Innis is Professor of Philosophy at the University of Massachusetts, Lowell. He is the author of many works, both systematic and historical, dealing with the intersections between philosophy, semiotics, and the human sciences. His book-length publications include *Karl Bühler: Semiotic Foundations of Language Theory* (1981), *Semiotics: An Introductory Anthology* (1985), *Consciousness and the Play of Signs* (1994), *Pragmatism and the Forms of Sense* (2002), and *Susanne Langer in Focus: The Symbolic Mind* (2009). He has been twice Fulbright Professor at the University of Copenhagen and Humboldt Fellow at the University of Cologne.

Michael Jackson has done extensive fieldwork in Sierra Leone and Aboriginal Australia, and is the author of numerous books of anthropology, including the prize-winning *Paths Toward a Clearing* and *At Home in the World.* In a forthcoming book, *Life Within Limits: Wellbeing in a World of Want,* he uses his ongoing fieldwork in Sierra Leone to explore experiences of social injustice and existential dissatisfaction on the margins of the global world. He is now writing on firstness as a fundamental trope in the social imaginaries and political discourse of indigenous peoples in Australia and New Zealand. Michael Jackson is Distinguished Visiting Professor of World Religions at Harvard Divinity School.

Galina Lindquist (1955–2008) was a Senior Lecturer in the Department of Social Anthropology at Stockholm University. She received her PhD in 1998, and did fieldwork among neoshamans in Sweden, among alternative healing practitioners and patients in Moscow, and among shamans and lamas in Tyva, Southern Siberia. She authored *Conjuring Hope: Healing and Magic in Contemporary Russia* (2006), *The Quest for the Authentic Shaman: Multiple Meanings of Shamanism on a Siberian Journey* (2006), co-edited four volumes, and published numerous articles in professional journals.

Eva Evers Rosander is Associate Professor in Social Anthropology, and, since September 2009, Associate Senior Researcher at the Nordic Africa Institute, Uppsala, Sweden. She has published several books and articles in Swedish, English, French, and Spanish on Moroccan and Senegalese women, Islam, and social and economic change. See for example, *Mujeres en la Frontera: Identidad y tradición Musulmanas (2004); African and Black Diaspora, an international journal.* Vol. 3, no. 1, January 2010. Special Issue: Family Dynamics in Transnational African Migration to Europe. Guest Editor together with Marina de Regt and Reinhilde König.

David Thurfjell is Associate Professor and research fellow in religious studies at Södertörn University, Stockholm, Sweden. He has published mainly within the fields of Iranian and Islamic studies, among other things the monograph *Living Shi'ism: Instances of Ritualization among Islamist Men in Contemporary Iran* (2006). He has also published on Pentecostal revivalism among Roma.

INDEX

www.ingramcontent.com/pod-product-compliance
Lightning Source LLC
Chambersburg PA
CBHW060027030426
42334CB00019B/2213